PIAGET
FOR EDUCATORS

Second Edition

RODGER W. BYBEE
BIOLOGICAL SCIENCES
CURRICULUM STUDY

ROBERT B. SUND

D0219048

WAVELAND
PRESS, INC.

Prospect Heights, Illinois

For information about this book, write or call:

Waveland Press, Inc.
P.O. Box 400
Prospect Heights, Illinois 60070
(847) 634-0081

Excerpts on pages 3, 6, 11 and 16 from "Jean Piaget," in A History of Psychology in Autobiography, ed. Edwin G. Boring, Heinz Werner, Herbert Longfeld, and Robert S. Yerkes (Worcester, Mass.: Clark University Press, 1952). Copyright © 1952 by Clark University Press. Reprinted with permission.

Excerpts on pages 192, 194, 197 and 200 from The Origins of Intelligence in Children by Jean Piaget (New York: W. W. Norton & Co., 1963). Copyright © 1963 by International Universities Press. Reprinted with permission.

Material on pages 26 (Figure 2.1), 251–258, and 287 (balloon race exercise) from Teaching Science Through Discovery by Arthur A. Carin and Robert B. Sund (Columbus, Ohio: Charles E. Merrill, 1980). Copyright © 1980 by Charles E. Merrill. Reprinted by permission.

Photo Credits:

© 1982 Yves Debraine from BLACK STAR (18), Celia Drake (27), Contance Brown (28), Tom McGuire (30), Greg Miller (31), Larry Hamill (46), Ronald W. Henderson (48), Rich Mucurel (70), Phillips Photo Illustrators (109), Dan Unkefer (134), Suzette Boulais (136), Paul Conklin (164), Greg Miller (175), Media Vision (199), Strix Pix (202), Dan Birdd (213), Wellington

7 6

For Rodney Croissant

Contents

Contributors of Guest Editorials

Susan Arnold
Lawrence Hall of Science
University of California

Daniel Ball
Department of Science Education
Ball State University

Delbert L. Barber
Director of Reading Academy
Laramie County Community College

Charles R. Barman
Associate Professor of Education
Buena Vista College

Patricia Fahey
Science Teacher
Minneapolis Public Schools

Virginia Ruth Johnson
School of Education
University of Denver

Linda J. Kelsey
Physical Science Program
West Virginia University

Oliver P. Kolstoe
School of Special Education
and Rehabilitation
University of Northern Colorado

Neil Lutsky
Department of Psychology
Carleton College

Alan J. McCormack
Science and Mathematics
Teaching Center
University of Wyoming

Robert A. Pavlik
Department of Reading
Cardinal Stritch College

Darrell G. Phillips
Science Education Center
University of Iowa

William D. Popejoy
Department of Mathematics
University of Northern Colorado

Joe Premo
Consultant in Science
Minneapolis Public Schools

Rex R. Schweers, Jr.
Department of Mathematics
University of Northern Colorado

I. David Welch
Department of Psychology
University of Northern Colorado

Robert Karplus
Lawrence Hall of Science
University of California

David Elkind
Department of Psychology
Tufts University

Preface

Robert Sund began a revision of *Piaget for Educators* in the winter of 1978. The following spring he became increasingly incapacitated due to an illness which lead to his death on July 17, 1979. During that spring, while on leave from Carleton College I was working with Bob on the revision of *Teaching Science by Inquiry in the Secondary School* (retitled *Becoming a Secondary School Science Teacher*). We had many long discussions about Piaget and about *Piaget for Educators*. Bob Sund's enthusiasm for the project is evident in the following statement in which he introduces Piaget's theory to educators.

> The reasons for learning about Piaget's theory may not at first be very apparent. They certainly were not to me when I began to study the theory in 1964. In the beginning, I more or less thought of the theory as an enjoyable intellectual game. Soon, however, I was inspired to look for practical implications that would help me write better learning activities for children. Through the years I have realized how useful the theory can really be in helping one become not only a better teacher and parent, but most of all, a better person. If you really understand the theory and allow it to influence the way you interact with others, you will become a less manipulative person and concomitantly someone who facilitates the development of human potential. I know now that Piaget's theory has tremendous significance for understanding how humans develop, vary, and communicate.
>
> Piaget's theory is relevant to many areas of investigation. A few of these are outlined below. I invite you to consider these possibilities and others as you read the text.
>
> *Mental health.* Discovering that more advanced thought processes enable people to come up with solutions to improve their mental health.
>
> *Developmental psychology.* Learning how the mind develops as a person matures.
>
> *Early childhood education.* Discovering how to help children develop their minds in a way that better prepares them for later educational experiences.
>
> *Preschool education.* Learning how to create an optimal educational environment for children of preschool age.
>
> *Determining cognitive level.* Determining how students from kindergarten through twelfth grade differ in their reasoning abilities.
>
> *Facilitating the development of reasoning.* Learning how to enhance students thinking abililties.
>
> *Assessing educational programs.* Discovering ways to assess how well certain educational experiences or curricula develop thinking abilities; determining procedures to assess texts and tests for reading levels appropriate to the cognitive levels of students.
>
> *Moral reasoning.* Learning how to identify moral development and learning, and how to enhance it.
>
> *Readiness and learning.* Learning how to counsel and guide student learning better and how to determine whether a child is mentally ready to participate in certain educational experiences or classes (for example, algebra).
>
> *Therapy.* Learning how to interpret and respond to a client based on his or her cognitive level.
>
> *Communication.* Learning how to communicate on a level comprehensible to your students or audience and how to diagnose students' reasoning problems.

Discriminating less. Realizing that students vary in their rate, style, and patterns of cognitive development, yet the best grades are often given only to those who are cognitively advanced.

Boosting childrens' self-concepts. Designing educational experiences to fit students' cognitive levels so that they succeed more often and hence have better self-concepts.

Curriculum design. Choosing content appropriate to students' cognitive levels, sequencing concepts, designing teaching approaches relative to the curriculum.

Several research studies have revealed that a significant part of our adult population never attains the highest Piagetian stage of cognitive development. These individuals are seriously handicapped in their ability to think and solve problems. In a sense they are not fully functional human beings. Failure to develop to the highest state severely restricts their educational, professional, and economic opportunities. They are "reasoning-handicapped" people and, as with any handicap, society discriminates against them.

As educators we need to better assess student reasoning abilities and facilitate their development. Research presently indicates that we are not doing a very good job developing these mental processes. The consequences for the individual and for our society are tremendous.

How to rectify this situation is really the central theme of this text. I invite you as educators to enlist in a committed effort to develop the reasoning abilities of our young people so that they will not become cognitively handicapped. By so doing you will help prepare them to improve their lives and to contribute positively to our society in the difficult decades ahead. One warning, however. If you do take up this challenge, you will become disenchanted with many of our present educational practices (such as the overemphasis on memorization). You will also at times become frustrated with your inability to enhance the development of thinking. At the same time, however, you will gain the satisfaction of knowing that what you are doing is exciting and both educationally and humanly significant.

Robert B. Sund
June 1979

Shortly after Bob's death I was invited to complete the revision of *Piaget for Educators.* I gathered Bob's files, notes, outlines, and revised chapters, thinking the task would be a simple one of putting the pieces together. I was wrong. There was everything from pieces of paper with a few words scribbled on them to completely new chapters. My solution of the problem was to approach the project as a coauthor. This allowed me to collect all the bits and pieces Bob had left and then design the book in a manner I thought best. I believe this freedom has resulted in a book that Bob would be proud of. Bob was very practical, while I tend toward the theoretical. The second edition of *Piaget for Educators* represents a happy balance of the theoretical and practical aspects of Piaget's theory.

Piaget for Educators follows a scheme of organization that is carried out in the arrangement of chapters and in the structure of each individual chapter. The design is a modification of the learning cycle developed by Robert Karplus and his colleagues at Lawrence Hall of Science, University of California. The design is explained further in "Note to the Readers."

The first chapter represents an extensive discussion of Piaget's life and an introduction to his work in a biographical context. The second chapter is an exploration of Piaget's theory for educators. The presentation brings to light Piaget's theory through classroom situations and educational problems. Chapters 3 through 6 review the four stages of cognitive development. Each chapter begins with a practical discussion of Piaget's ideas. Then there is an explanation of the stage and associated patterns of reasoning. The chapter continues with interview questions and tasks appropriate to the stage and other means of extending one's understanding of the theory. At the end of each chapter there is a brief evaluation section. Chapters are structured so they begin with the practical, progress to the theoretical, and then return to the practical. This design was intentional, and it is found in chapters 3 through 8. Chapters 9, 10, and 11 present practical discussions of Piaget's theory and its impact on education. The concluding chapter 12 is a summary evaluation of Piaget's theory.

Guest Editorials appear in each chapter. These highlight some aspects of Piaget's theory not covered in the text. The individuals who contributed these essays all knew Bob Sund in some capacity, as professional associates, colleagues, or students, and have been recognized for their contributions to understanding and applying Piaget's theory to education.

Many individuals have contributed to *Piaget for Educators*. I would like to specifically acknowledge some of those who assisted Bob during the first edition and me during the revision: Alan McCormack, James McClurg, Ken Olson, Leslie Trowbridge, George Crockett, Jay Hackett, Don Adams, John Hunt, Bill Tillery, Chet Raun, Don Acheson, David Elkind, Neil Lutsky, Robert Karplus, Brenda Carlson, Laura Mitchell, Janet Carlson, Wendy Gustafson, and Patrick and Michelle Crow. A special note of gratitude is also extended to the doctoral candidates who carried on Piagetian research in association with Bob Sund: Dan Ball, Steve Sayre, Paul Ankney, Lyle Joyce, Bill Gurney, Sandra Bowland, Don Carlson, Tim Cooney, James Fournier, Donald Bird, Gerald Straylor, Ray Anruh, and Linda Kelsey. Many others have given their assistance as this book was being prepared. I thank all who were involved.

Rodger W. Bybee

Note to the reader

This book has a specific plan of organization. The book itself and most chapters within the book are divided into four sections: Exploration, Explanation, Extension, and Evaluation. The first two chapters are an *exploration* of Piaget's life and work and of his theoretical concepts. The next six chapters (chapters 3 through 8) are an *explanation* of Piaget's theory of cognitive growth. Chapters 9 through 11 are an *extension* of the educator's understanding of Piaget's theory through discussions of implications, the disciplines, and activities. The final chapter is a general *evaluation* of Piaget's theory for educators.

Most chapters repeat the four-part pattern of organization. The first section of the chapter presents introductory questions, situations or tasks intended to engage you in the educational ideas discussed in the chapter. The next section is an explanation of Piaget's ideas. Then, if you wish to extend your understanding or apply the ideas, there are references, questions, and interview tasks. Finally, there is a short self-evaluation covering the content of the chapter.

The book's design provides a balance of theory and practice both across chapters and within chapters. The design is also an example of one educational part of Piaget's theory. But, perhaps most importantly, the design allows for an interaction between you and me. For these reasons I encourage you to become actively involved in the questions, classroom situations, interviews, suggested reading, and the ideas offered in the Guest Editorials. I hope you'll see that the book really is *Piaget for Educators*.

Rodger W. Bybee

Obituary: Jean Piaget (1896–1980)

I heard of Jean Piaget's death on my car radio as I was driving home from work on September 16. It was an unusual way to hear of a mentor's death, sandwiched in between other local and national news items. I had known that he was ill, so the news was not unexpected, but it was hearing it on the radio, announced so matter of factly, that left me a little numb. As the memories and images came and a quarter century of association was re-lived, I still could not experience the feelings of loss.

My introduction to Jean Piaget came as a fresh PhD in 1956, when David Rapaport accepted me as his research assistant. I had expected that Rapaport would reveal to me the intricacies of psychoanalytic theory and practice. To my surprise, long before I arrived at Stockbridge, I began receiving boxes of books, not by Freud, but rather by Jean Piaget. Up to that time, my impression of Piaget, gathered from a brief mention in a textbook, was that he was a quaint old man who talked to children on the banks of Lake Geneva.

Once I began reading Piaget (and with the help of Rapaport, who re-vealed the depth and richness of the work), I was, as the French say, "gripped." My training in psychology was in learning theory and clinical psychology. Learning theory satisfied a need for scientific rigor, and clinical work satisfied a need for relevance and applied work. In Piaget I found a nice compromise. His methods were scientific if not experimental, and his concerns with relevant content — the concepts of space, time, causality, mo-rality, and so on — clearly had applied significance. At last I had found a psychology that was right for me.

I then began replicating Piaget's studies to demonstrate that his results could be supported using controlled procedures and statistics. I was skep-tical at first, but when the children I tested behaved as Piaget said they would, I was convinced. This conviction grew as I examined more children and administered more Piagetian tasks.

The first time I saw Piaget was around 1960. Jerome Bruner had invited him to Harvard to give a talk. I sat in the back of the crowded lecture hall and waited for Piaget to enter. At last I was going to see and hear the man whose books I had studied and whose research I had followed to the best of my ability. Piaget walked in from a side door followed closely by a tall blonde woman whom I gathered was Bärbel Inhelder. Piaget looked Euro-pean, wearing a dark, rumpled suit and vest and heavy hiking boots. His hair was long and white and though he was of average height and portly, there was a delicateness about his features and hands that reminded me of Erik Erikson, whom I had met in Stockbridge. After Piaget's talk (which was in French) I wanted to greet him, but I did not have the courage and merely sat and watched until he left.

Seeing Piaget and listening to him furthered my admiration. His presentation was clear, and he was modest and generous in his answers to questions from the audience. He was unpretentious in both manner and appearance, as befit someone who worked well with children. There was a

From *American Psychologist* 36, no. 2 (1981): 911–13. Copyright 1981 by the American Psycho-logical Association, Inc. Reprinted by permission.

rather nice fit between the Piaget I had met on paper and the Piaget I encountered in the lecture hall.

When my replication studies began to appear in the journals, I sent (at Rapaport's suggestion) reprints to Piaget. I did this for several years without ever getting a response. Then one day I got a letter from Piaget inviting me to come to Geneva for a year, so, along with wife, two-year-old son, and miniature dachshund, I flew to Geneva to study with Piaget.

Soon after we arrived, there was an official reception at which I met Piaget for the first time. My French failed me and Piaget chuckled and said that he had little English and that he hardly went beyond "please," "hello," "good bye," and "thank you." It was often said that Piaget really knew English but refused to speak it because of hubris. Some years later, I asked him about this and he explained that he, like most European intellectuals, had intended to spend a year in England to learn English, but that World War I had broken out just at the time he was to go abroad. Piaget never did make the trip and so never acquired fluency in spoken English, although my impression was that he could read it without difficulty.

In Geneva I had the opportunity to view Piaget's research enterprise at first hand. Piaget was located in the Institute of Educational Science, which was committed both to teacher training and to research. Prospective teachers took courses in intellectual development taught by Piaget and others. (At the institute, a student had to hand in a bluebook to the Professor each time he or she attended class, and the Professor had to sign it. Every time Piaget lectured he was simultaneously signing from 200–300 bluebooks!) These students also had to learn to administer the Piagetian semiclinical interview.

As a consequence of this arrangement Piaget had a large pool of research assistants and, since they were teachers in training for the Canton of Geneva, open access to the Genevan schools. Accordingly, and contrary to the erroneous assumption sometimes made on the basis of Piaget's infancy books (for which he did study only his own three children), most of his research was carried out with large samples (hundreds of children) examined by teachers in training who had undergone rigorous preparation for their role in data collection. Piaget thus had, in effect, an institute precisely geared to the conduct of his research without the necessity of soliciting research grants.

The program of ongoing research was discussed weekly at meetings of the interdisciplinary Centre de Epistemology Genetique and at weekly research meetings where the actual conduct of research was reviewed. It was at these meetings that the ingenious method and materials that characterize the Genevan school were suggested and critiqued. At the end of each year Piaget arranged a symposium to go over the year's work. Additional guests were invited to the symposium, and it was a gala event.

Another facet of Piaget's genius became apparent at these meetings. During the presentations of the various participants, Piaget would sit with his eyes closed, apparently dozing, but at the end of a morning's or afternoon's discussion he would become suddenly alert and present a masterful summary and commentary of each of the papers. It was a truly remarkable performance. The meetings were, by the way, not always harmonious. I recall one disgruntled logician stamping out of the room and walking down the halls murmuring "merde, double merde, merde à quatrième puissance (merde to the fourth power)!"

Toward the end of our year in Geneva, Piaget invited my wife and myself to dinner. His home on the Rue du Rang was in a quiet unpretentious suburb of Geneva. The house itself was modest in size, with a small garden where Piaget had plants for his various biological investigations. The house did have a nice view of the Seleve, the crocodile-shaped mountain that is the majestic frame for this ancient city. Piaget was a most gracious host, charming and attentive.

At dinner, a delicious meal starting with a fish course followed by a meat dish in the European way, I for the first (and last) time heard Piaget engage in "small talk." The conversation turned to children, perhaps because we met Piaget's son, who was visiting at the time. Madame Piaget asked my wife a series of questions, "Does your husband ever change the baby? Does he ever feed the baby? Does he ever watch the baby when you go out?" To all of these questions my wife answered, "Yes, sometimes." Then Madame Piaget turned and looked accusingly at Piaget. "Not him," she said with mock indignation and affection. Piaget winked and wickedly proceeded to clean the glass bowl that had contained our chocolate mousse dessert, with his finger!

After dinner Piaget invited me into his study, a small room that overlooked the garden and which had a clear view of the French Alps. The study was jammed full of books, mostly European paperbacks; not only were the bookshelves full but books were also piled on the floor and on Piaget's desk. Piaget, following Bergson, liked to call this "creative disorder" and took pride in knowing where anything he wanted was. The meeting in the study was clearly a chance to ask, on a one-to-one basis, the most burning questions I had about Piagetian psychology.

Following Rapaport, I had become interested in ego psychology, thinking, and particularly concept formation. I was trying to reconcile the Piagetian approach to concept development with the more traditional views of concept attainment such as those proposed by Hull and Heidbreder. Conservation was clearly not a concept in the Hullian sense of a distinctive feature. And yet, if it was a construction, as Piaget insisted, why did he use the term *abstraction*, borrowed from association psychology, which presupposed a fixed reality? Piaget said that abstraction from one's own actions, *reflective abstraction*, avoided that trap because the actions abstracted were themselves created by the subject and were therefore not preexistent. I was not entirely satisfied with the answer then and still have problems with it today. Abstraction just does not seem, to me at any rate, to belong in the Piagetian system.

My next visit to the Rue du Rang was several years later after we had moved back to the United States and I had taken John Flavell's former position at the University of Rochester. After returning to the States I kept in touch with Piaget and managed to see him occasionally on his frequent visits to the United States. On a trip to Europe, I called him and he invited me to take his afternoon walk with him. I had a rented car and we drove to the border kiosk at the foot of the Seleve. As we walked up the mountain

Piaget pointed out various points of interest. For a man in his seventies he had extraordinarily keen eyesight and pointed to wild pigeons at the top of the mountain that I had trouble seeing.

Driving back I told Piaget a story that I thought would amuse him. I reported a remark made by my youngest son, Ricky, when we were driving to the toy store. He said that it was better to go to the toy store in the station wagon than in the sedan because (since it was longer) we would "get there faster." I thought it was a nice anecdotal support for Piaget's finding that for young children speed was essentially "overtaking." But Piaget was amused in an unexpected way. "Oh," he remarked, "you Americans, you always have two cars."

During the 25 years that I have been associated with Piaget's work, its fortunes have waxed and waned. There was the heyday of Piaget's "rediscovery" in the 1960s and the well-intentioned but misdirected application of his work to education. Much of the 1960s were concerned with the assimilation and appreciation of Piaget's work, but by the mid-1970s the criticisms and critiques had begun in earnest. No one challenges the data, which are perhaps the most hardy we have in psychology, but Piaget's stage theory and his logical model of thinking have come under increasing attack.

Piaget himself was always most open to responsible critiques of his work. To me, one of the most moving moments I ever experienced listening to Piaget give a public address occurred at one of the Jean Piaget Society meetings in Philadelphia. Piaget suggested at that meeting (he was then 80 years old) that perhaps some children could attain conservation by strategies other than those he had previously outlined. For a man of his years to change a fundamental tenet of his theory was, I think, a remarkable testament to his extraordinary scientific commitment.

Another dimension of Piaget's integrity was his reluctance to produce disciples. He said, "To the extent that there are Piagetians, to that extent I have failed." It would be a great loss if the critics of Piaget ignored his greater message of scientific courage and integrity, and it would also be a mistake if Piaget's insights were dismissed too summarily. It is unwise to dismiss the intuitions of genius, even if they are wrong in detail, unless overwhelming evidence proves them incorrect.

These and many more ruminations passed through my mind as I drove home. When I arrived I still felt numbed and wandered aimlessly about my study. Then, without really thinking, I put on an old and favorite record, *Toscanini Plays Wagner*. As those majestic sounds filled the room and wave upon wave of sound washed away the numbness, at last I experienced the magnitude of the loss, the feelings came, and I wept.

Jean Piaget was truly a man of heroic, yes of epic, proportions. And yet, as I have tried to suggest here, he was warmly human too.

David Elkind
Tufts University

1 Jean Piaget: An Exploration of His Life and Work

When Jean Piaget died in September of 1980, he left over sixty years of professional work. He was recognized for his contributions to biology, psychology, philosophy, sociology, education, and even literature. His combined work would truly rank him as one of the great intellectuals of our age, if not all times.

We have much to learn from the life and work of Jean Piaget. In order to understand Piaget's theory it is important to know the context within which it was developed. We will look at a man whose work originated in the biological sciences and whose psychological theories subsequently had themes such as adaptation and equilibrium. We will see Piaget as a man whose personal qualities included a simple and natural life, the need for detachment and privacy, a great love of nature and children, a sense of humor and creativity, and finally, a life spent in the pursuit of answers to significant problems and accurate perceptions of reality.

The information in this chapter is based on autobiographies written by Piaget. One work is simply entitled "Jean Piaget" and appears in *A History of Psychology in Autobiography*, vol. 4 (Piaget, 1952a); another source is a chapter entitled "An Account of and an Analysis of a Disenchantment" in *Insights and Illusions of Philosophy* (Piaget, 1971a).

A PERIOD OF EXPLORATION

The Early Years: 1896–1913

Jean Piaget was born in the small town of Neuchatel, Switzerland, on August 9, 1896. His father, a scholar of medieval literature at the local university, had a critical mind and approached matters in a systematic fashion. As we shall see, his father provided a good model for Piaget's later work. His mother was intelligent, energetic, religious, and basically a kind person. She was, however, quite neurotic and her mental health had an important influence on Piaget. As a result of her psychological problems, he always "detested any departure from reality" (Piaget, 1952a). The second influence his mother's poor mental health had was only to be seen later, when at the beginning of his psychological studies Piaget studied psychopathology and psychoanalysis. Though he was always much more interested in normal and healthy development and the intellectual-cognitive side of psychology, his introduction to psychoanalysis did provide the clinical method that was central to later work.

From the age of seven Piaget was interested in nature and expressed his studies in written form. He studied birds, animals, fossils, and seashells. At one time he designed a steam-powered automobile and later completed a small book entitled *Our Birds*. At age ten, Piaget sighted a partly albino sparrow in a park. He wrote up this observation and submitted it to the natural history journal of Neuchatel. The paper was published and Piaget's career began.

Shortly after his first scientific publication, Piaget was invited to assist Paul Godet who was director of the Natural History Museum. Using the Faustian term, Godet referred to Piaget as his "famulus" (an attendant or assistant to a medieval scholar) who helped label collections of mollusks. For four years Piaget worked for and learned malacology from the naturalist, Godet. When Godet died in 1911, Piaget, age fifteen, began publishing articles on mollusks. The results were varied for the young Piaget; he was offered a position as curator of mollusks at the Museum of Natural History in Geneva, foreign "colleagues" wished to meet him, and one editor refused an article because of his age. So, before Piaget completed high school, he was a published scientist.

Piaget recalled that these studies had great value in his scientific development and they acted as a balance for his emerging philosophical interests. With the curiosity of adolescence and troubled family conditions, Piaget entered adolescence with a series of crises (Piaget, 1952a).

When Piaget was about fifteen years old, his mother insisted that he take a six-week course of religious instruction. He studied the fundamentals of Christian doctrine with interest and a free mind. He became concerned about the difficulty of reconciling Christian dogmas with biological principles, and about the rational approach to "proving" the existence of God. In the midst of this struggle Piaget developed a new passion—philosophy.

Piaget's interests, or conflicts, were fueled by his godfather, Samuel Cornut, a Swiss scholar. Sensing that his godson's interests were too narrow, Cornut invited Piaget to spend a vacation with him. During the vacation, Cornut formally introduced Piaget to philosophy, particularly the evo-

lutionary philosophy of Henri Bergson (1859–1941) that claimed there
was *élan vital*, or a life force carried from one generation to the next. Piaget
reported the emotional and intellectual impact of his philosophical study:

> I recall one evening of profound revelation. The identification of God with life
> itself was an idea that stirred me almost to ecstasy because it enabled me to see
> in biology the explanation of all things and of the mind itself.... The problem
> of knowing (properly called the epistemological problem) suddenly appeared to
> me in an entirely new perspective and as an absorbing topic of study. It made me
> decide to consecrate my life to the biological explanation of knowledge. (Piaget,
> 1952a, p. 240)

Piaget turned his thoughts from biology to philosophy—particularly
epistemology, the branch of philosophy concerned with the study of knowledge. We shall see Piaget become concerned with questions basic to epistemology: What is knowledge? How is knowledge acquired? To what degree
is knowledge objective or subjective? But, Piaget did not abandon science.

> Instead of finding science's last work therein . . . I got the impression of an ingen-
> ious construction without an experimental basis: Between biology and the anal-
> ysis of knowledge I needed something other than a philosophy. I believe it was
> at that moment that I discovered a need that could be satisfied only by psychol-
> ogy. (Piaget, 1952a, p. 240)

While Piaget had the insights concerning knowledge and had syn-
thesized his biological and philosophical interests, he was not to pursue his
life work immediately.

Formal Education: 1914–1918

Although he seriously considered philosophical and psychological questions, Piaget studied biology for his undergraduate degree. He received the
baccalaureate degree in biology from the University of Neuchatel in 1915
when he was eighteen. He immediately began graduate study in the Division of Science at the University of Neuchatel. In 1918, at the age of
twenty-one, he submitted a thesis on the mollusks of the Valais region of
Switzerland and received his doctorate in the sciences.

As an undergraduate, Piaget was advised by the philosopher Arnold
Reymond, a man Piaget admired as not only a philosopher, but as a systematic thinker. Reymond, like Piaget's father, approached all problems in a
logical manner. Reymond designed a very taxing program for Piaget: history of philosophy, general philosophy, philosophy of science, psychology
and sociology—all of this while working toward his primary major in biology! (Piaget, 1971a)

While still an undergraduate, Piaget began to write papers on "his" philosophy. Being influenced by the works of William James, Piaget completed
"An Outline of Neo-Pragmatism" in which he tried to show there was a logic
of action, terms that represent a synthesis of his epistemological and biolog-

ical interests, and that were to become central to his psychology. His studies resulted in two ideas that remained:

> The first is that since every organism has a permanent structure, which can be modified under the influence of the environment but is never destroyed as a structured whole, all knowledge is always *assimilation* of a datum external to the subject's structure . . . . The second is that the normative factors of thought correspond biologically to a necessity of *equilibrium* by self-regulation: thus, logic would in the subject correspond to a process of equilibrium. (Piaget, 1971a, p. 8)

With the ideas summarized in this quotation, Piaget had identified concepts important to his theories. But he was also beginning to feel uneasy about Reymond's treating all problems philosophically. Piaget wanted to study experimental psychology so he could confirm his ideas empirically. Reymond tried to advise Piaget away from such activity, informing him that it was a waste of time, and that he should rely on well-directed philosophical reflection. Reflecting on his mentor's studies Piaget found several examples where Reymond's own "well-directed reflection" could well have been improved by a little evidence. Piaget stated, ". . . but where is the boundary between that on which reflection may pronounce with certainty and that which the facts compel us to amend?" (Piaget, 1971a, p. 9)

During this period Piaget seemed to ground himself in the sciences while continuing to pursue philosophical ideas. Shortly after Piaget received his baccalaureate, a bout of physical and mental exhaustion forced him to spend a year in the mountains. This exhaustion was probably brought on by his continuous search for an identity. Was he to be a biologist? Psychologist? Philosopher? While on retreat he "was haunted by the desire to create" so he wrote a philosophical novel entitled *Recherche* (Piaget, 1952a). Piaget also continued to read the works of philosophers such as Henri Bergson, William James, Herbert Spencer, Auguste Comte, Immanuel Kant, and Emil Durkheim.

During this period (circa 1916–1917) Piaget began an inquiry into the relationship of parts to wholes. This too was to have an important bearing on his psychological theories. Piaget found that at all levels of organization one could identify the relationship of parts to wholes. The levels of organization ranged from cells to organisms to societies, but also with reference to psychological states—conscience to concepts and to logical principles. Here was the connection between biology and philosophy for which he had been searching.

This incident is worth further discussion because it was a turning point in Piaget's professional development and because it was preceded by a period of intellectual disequilibrium, a concept that is central to his theory. For some time Piaget had thought about the problem of "species" in zoology. Briefly, Piaget was uncertain about the concept and bothered by the definition and inability to differentiate species of organisms from varieties of organisms. At the same time he was bothered by sociological debates about societies as organized wholes. Then, during a lesson by his mentor, Arnold Reymond, Piaget had a sudden insight. He realized that at all levels one could identify the same problem of relationships between parts of the system and the whole system. Piaget was convinced there were whole systems that were qualitatively distinct from their parts (the whole is greater than the sum of its parts). In turn, the parts were dependent on the structured whole in order to function. Piaget then asked himself about the relationship of the parts to the whole. He postulated the logical conclusions: (1) there could be a predominance of the whole over the parts; (2) there could be a predominance of the parts over the whole; (3) there could be a reciprocal interaction between the parts and the whole. Piaget then concluded that the reciprocal interaction was the only relationship that was stable and beneficial; the other two could become unbalanced by the dominating system or subsystem. This idea is central to Piaget's theory. We will see that his later concern for structures-of-the-whole had their origins with this insight (Piaget, 1952a).

We have seen that during his adolescence and formal education Piaget had two areas of interest: science and philosophy. He became concerned with the reconciliation of two disciplines within these areas, namely biology and epistemology. In his search to find some way to integrate biology and epistemology, he was led to the pursuit of answers to epistemological questions through the application of scientific methods. This, of course, required that he determine how individuals come to know what they know, a determination that could be established best through psychological observation as opposed to philosophical speculation.

Along the way, Piaget had several insights that led him to the conceptual orientation for his theory. In general, his view was one of whole structures, ideas that will later become cognitive or mental structures and cognitive stages. By the time Piaget completed his doctorate in 1918, he was an internationally known malacologist, well grounded in philosophy, and a novelist.

Becoming a Psychologist: 1918–1921

After receiving his doctorate, Piaget left for Zurich with the goal of working in a psychological laboratory. He did gain some experience in two laboratories and further study at Bleuler's psychiatric clinic. In all, Piaget reported that he felt lost during this period. In the spring of 1919, he returned to the Valais region of Switzerland and completed a biometric study showing the variability of land mollusks as a function of altitude (Piaget, 1952a). Still, the experience in psychology, and especially his introduction to psychoanalysis and the clinical techniques used by analysts, were steps toward his eventual work as a psychologist.

In the fall of 1919, Piaget went to Paris where he studied psychology, logic, and the philosophy of science at the Sorbonne University. A course on pathological psychology extended Piaget's clinical techniques through interviews with mental patients at Sainte-Anne (Piaget, 1952a). While in Paris Piaget was recommended to Theodore Simon (1873–1961) who with Alfred Binet (1857–1911) had developed modern intelligence tests. Simon was still director of Binet's laboratory at a grade school in Paris. Simon suggested that Piaget might use the psychological laboratory to standardize reasoning tests developed by the British psychologist, Cyril Burt. The aim of the work was to establish the wording so each subject was presented exactly the same question. Then, any differences in performance could be attributed to the individual's intelligence and not the intelligence test. It was also important to determine how many individuals at each age would respond correctly and incorrectly to the test items.

Piaget started the work of standardizing tests without much enthusiasm. His mood soon changed.

> Now from the very first questionings I noticed that though Burt's tests certainly had their diagnostic merits, based on the number of successes and failures, it was much more interesting to try to find the reasons for the failures. Thus, I engaged my subjects in conversations patterned after psychiatric questioning, with the aim of discovering something about the reasoning process underlying their right, but especially their wrong answers. I noticed with amazement that the simplest reasoning task involving the inclusion in the whole or the coordination of relations or the "multiplication" of classes (finding the part common to two wholes), presented for normal children up to the age of eleven or twelve difficulties unsuspected by the adult. (Piaget, 1952a, p. 244)

Piaget continued his work for two years. During this period he also analyzed the reasoning patterns of children by presenting them with simple tasks involving cause-effect relations. He also worked with abnormal children and investigated their concept of number and conservation. The result of this work was the clarification of Piaget's field of research. It was now clear that he could study psychological processes in an attempt to resolve the problem of relating biology and epistemology. Piaget's work for Dr. Simon marked the end of his exploratory period and the beginning of his empirical work explaining his psychological theory. His work in Paris confirmed several of Piaget's theoretical ideas: first, logic is not inborn, logical patterns of thought emerge in increments over time; second, logical thought is the equilibrium toward which mental structures tend; third, it is possible to study epistemological problems directly; and fourth, the interaction between organism and environment extends into the realm of knowledge. Piaget published his results in the *Journel de Psychologie* and the *Archives de Psychologie*. The latter was edited by the well-known psychologist, Edouard Claparede, who was very impressed with Piaget's work.

The great genius and creativity of Piaget was evident in his work at Binet's laboratory. Standardized tests usually focused on the correct answers and quantitative results. Piaget found the *incorrect* answers and *qualitative* differences between age groups much more interesting. By applying his scientific training, he recognized patterns of wrong answers among children of approximately the same age. By struggling with the problem posed by this finding, he came to realize the qualitative differences in thinking of children of different levels. In order to find an answer to his problem, Piaget applied the clinical methods he had learned earlier to the study of intelligence, an approach that had not been used prior to his time.

Piaget modified the psychiatric interview in two ways. He allowed the child to answer questions and let the child's thoughts determine the course of the interview. The aim was to identify the child's patterns of thought without imposing a preconceived structure on it. Thus, he was able to determine the causes of children's responses. Fortunately, it was not all this simple. During the time when Piaget was studying abnormal children at the Salpetriere Hospital in Paris, he found his method to be inadequate since the abnormal children had deficient verbal abilities. Subsequently, Piaget added a new technique to his clinical method; he provided materials for the children to manipulate and asked questions about the transformed materials. The latter change was to be a major component of his empirical investigations of children's thinking.

In summary, this period marked the point in Piaget's life when he became a psychologist. His psychological theory made use of biological concepts; for example, intelligence was viewed as an adaptation to the environment. He was primarily interested in intellectual development since this was the realm that most closely related to his philosophical interests, and it was his position that one should understand the evolution of intelligence from childhood to adulthood. As Piaget applied his clinical methods he selected content that would allow him insights into the child's perceptions of reality, another long-standing theme in his life. Piaget termed his study genetic epistemology.

EXPLAINING THE DEVELOPMENT OF THOUGHT

The First Period of Studying Children's Thinking: 1921–1929

In 1921, shortly after Piaget published his studies from the Binet laboratories, Edouard Claparede offered him the post of director of research at the Jean-Jacques Rousseau Institute. In the 1920s the Jean-Jacques Rousseau Institute was already internationally known for educational research. The fact that a twenty-five-year-old research assistant was appointed director of research at a prominent educational laboratory demonstrates the respect Piaget had already gained as a child psychologist.

Piaget went to Geneva in 1921. His plan was to study the emergence of intelligence for the first two years of his work at the Jean-Jacques Rousseau Institute, then he would study the problem of thought in general and proceed to construct a psychological and biological epistemology. Piaget started his research on factors peripheral to those of his primary interest—language, concepts of the world, and causality and reasoning processes. At this time Piaget also met and married one of his assistants, Valentine Chatenay.

The work of this period was later published in Piaget's first five books on child psychology. *Language and Thought of the Child* (Piaget, 1926a)[1] was based on naturalistic observations of children's use of language. One of the main findings presented was that young children's speech is more *egocentric* than older children's use of language which Piaget called *socialized*. It

---

1. In this chapter the dates of publications are for English translations, so there may be a discrepancy between the date Piaget completed and published the work and the date of the citation. For example, *The Child's Conception of Physical Causality* was completed in the early 1920s, but an English edition was not available until 1960.

should be noted that Piaget's thesis concerning language has been criticized, especially in light of findings that indicate socialized language is evident at younger age levels. Other books based on Piaget's research during the early 1920s include *Judgement and Reasoning in the Child* (Piaget, 1926b), *The Child's Conception of the World* (Piaget, 1929), *The Child's Conception of Physical Causality* (Piaget, 1960) and *The Moral Judgement of the Child* (Piaget, 1932). The books' titles give a clue to Piaget's research during the period. They also indicate his major themes: changes in reasoning patterns, perceptions of reality, cause-effect, developmental difference between younger and older children.

By his own report (Piaget, 1952a), Piaget published his findings without taking sufficient precautions concerning his conclusions. He really thought the books would not be read, but he was wrong. They were widely read and severely criticized. He was invited to numerous countries to present his ideas to psychologists and educators. Though feeling uneasy about his situation, Piaget still traveled and lectured. He had not worked out many of the underlying principles of his psychology of intelligence. This, combined with his unique "clinical methods" resulted in misunderstandings and criticisms among child psychologists. The result was an early surge of international fame and then an extended period when his writings were largely ignored, particularly in English-speaking countries. In all fairness to Piaget, it must also be noted that during this same period American psychology was being strongly influenced by behaviorism, standardized testing, and to some degree by psychoanalysis. In this context, Piaget's theories were criticized by the behaviorists for lack of tight experimental design, by the psychoanalysts for focusing on normal intellectual growth, and by the standardized testing movement for emphasizing qualitative, not quantitative, differences in development.

During the 1920s Piaget taught at the Jean-Jacques Rousseau Institute at Geneva and also at the University of Neuchatel where he assumed Arnold Reymond's chair of philosophy. Piaget taught courses in psychology, philosophy, history of science, and sociology. Combined with his research, his schedule was indeed full.

During this period, Piaget became a father. His first daughter, Jacqueline, was born in 1925, his second daughter, Lucienne, in 1927 and a son, Laurent, in 1931. With the help of his wife, Piaget spent considerable time observing his children and confronting them with small tasks. The results of these observations provided Piaget with new insights into the origins of intellectual conduct, ideas of conservation and causality, as well as the beginnings of symbolic behavior. He discovered how sensorimotor actions of infants prepared the way for intellectual operations that developed in later years. The results of his studies were published in three volumes: *The Origins of Intelligence in Children* (Piaget, 1952b), *The Construction of Reality in the Child* (Piaget, 1954) and *Play, Dreams and Imitations in Childhood* (Piaget, 1951). The work of this early period has been replicated and criticized on various grounds. Still, the work is an example for all psychologists and educators of naturalistic observations and through both inductive and deductive processes the formulation of general principles. Piaget's training as a naturalist and scientist is clearly evident in this work.

The three books based on the studies of his own children were partly responsible for renewed international interest in his theories. His genius was demonstrated in these studies. Some have criticized his work, stating he should not have completed a study on only three subjects, that twenty-five to thirty subjects provide an adequate sample. Genius is not tricked by a small sample. The observations made by Piaget have been generally confirmed by numerous other researches since his initial observations.

These studies just mentioned had provided new ideas for Piaget's research. They convinced him that his research procedures were too verbal and that it was necessary to involve children in tasks. Prior to this time (the work of the early 1920s), Piaget had relied almost exclusively on verbal reports from children. Along with maturation as a sole factor explaining development, which he rejected during his studies of standardized tests, Piaget now reduced the importance of language and social interaction as sufficient explanations for development. He became convinced that the child's *action* was central to intellectual development. In order to pursue this idea, Piaget recalled his experience with abnormal children at the Salpetriere Hospital in Paris. As a result of these insights, Piaget included the manipulation of materials in his research methodology.

The Second Period of Studying Children's Thinking: 1929–1939

In 1925 Piaget and his wife had moved to Neuchatel while he taught at the University. In 1929 they returned to Geneva where Piaget assumed the position of assistant director of the Jean-Jacques Rousseau Institute and Professor of History of Scientific Thought. In 1932 Piaget became codirector of the Institute. One task of this administrative position was to help reorganize the Institute when it became affiliated with the University of Geneva. In addition, in 1929 he accepted the directorship of the Bureau International Office de l'Education; later this organization was to work in collaboration with UNESCO. Even though this position detracted time and energy from his research, Piaget accepted it for two reasons. First, he felt it would contribute to better teaching through improved understanding of the child's intellectual development, and second, because it was a new venture (Piaget, 1952a).

Three principal events influenced this period of work. First, the course on the History of Scientific Thought provided Piaget the opportunity to study scientific and mathematical concepts that eventually found their way into his research on intellectual development. Secondly, his work at the Jean-Jacques Rousseau Institute was on a scale larger than previous work. The study of children's scientific and mathematical notions was completed in cooperation with Barbel Inhelder and Alina Szemenska. Their work was later published in two volumes: *The Child's Construction of Quantities* (Piaget and Inhelder, 1974) and *The Child's Conception of Numbers* (Piaget and Szemenska, 1952). Thirdly, Piaget finally solved his long-standing problem of parts-wholes or structures-of-the-whole. The work of this period was primarily at a level that differentiated children who could reason logically (concrete operational) and children who could not reason logically (pre-operational). For years Piaget had puzzled over the maintenance and change of total intellectual structures. Research on the formation of the idea of conservation provided the final resolution of Piaget's problem.

At this time in his career, Piaget thought he had evidence for an invariant sequence of stages, each of which was qualitatively different. The sequence approximated more complex levels of thought, the ideal of which was logical thought and formal patterns of reasoning. The sensorimotor stage was from birth to two years, the preoperational stage from two to seven, the concrete operational stage from eight to eleven, and the formal operational stage from twelve through adulthood. Starting with physical activity in the earliest stage, mental structures were developed through motor and mental activity until they reached the level of formal logical thought. Piaget's stage theory did not change in any substantial way for the remaining four decades of research.

The Third Period of Studying Children's Thinking: 1940–1950

When World War II began, Piaget was forty-three years old. His age and the fact of being a citizen of a neutral country left Piaget with a decision about involvement in the war effort. He decided to accept an invitation to give a series of lectures at the College de France. Piaget used the opportunity to present the first general statement of his theory of intellectual development. The lectures were later published under the title, *The Psychology of Intelligence* (Piaget, 1966). Piaget saw this opportunity as important for another reason. He felt that the presentation provided outside support to his French colleagues during the time of German occupation (Piaget, 1952a).

When Edouard Claparede died in 1940, Piaget succeeded him as chairman of Experimental Psychology and director of the Psychological Laboratory at the University of Geneva. He remained in this position until he retired at age seventy-five. Professional duties included coediting the *Archives de Psychologie* and the *Revue Suisse de Psychologie* and presiding over the newly founded Swiss Society of Psychology.

In the early 1940s Piaget's research was in two areas. His interest in the part-whole problem introduced him to the work of Gestalt psychologists. Gestalt psychology emphasized the understanding of phenomena as irreducible wholes. This orientation appealed to Piaget's interest in structures-of-the-whole. Gestalt theory and the continuing work at the Jean-Jacques Rousseau Institute resulted in a long-range study on the development of perceptions in children. Piaget started by replicating some of the experiments of Gestalt psychologists. As one might suspect, in time Piaget undertook studies to show the relation of perception to intelligence. This line of research was published in *The Mechanisms of Perception* (Piaget, 1969).

The second area of research was suggested by Albert Einstein. On different occasions Einstein had suggested to Piaget that he should study the child's understanding of time, velocity, and movement (Piaget, 1971a). In the 1940s Piaget and his colleagues took Einstein's suggestion and applied his clinical methods to the problems. Books on these subjects were published later: *The Child's Conception of Time* (Piaget, 1970a) and *The Child's Conception of Movement and Speed* (Piaget, 1970b).

After the war Piaget's work with the International Office of Education increased. In fact, the agency's work had continued through the war years since it served as a clearinghouse for educational books being sent to prisoners of war. Piaget was designated as president of the Swiss Commission of UNESCO and headed the Swiss delegation at Bayreuth, Paris, and Florence. During his tenure with UNESCO Piaget was briefly assistant director general in charge of the Department of Education. In the late 1940s he became a member of the Executive Council of UNESCO.

In the late 1940s Piaget, Inhelder, and Szemenska extended their earlier work on perceptions to the development of spatial relations. This work was published as *The Child's Conception of Space* (Piaget and Inhelder, 1956) and *The Child's Conception of Geometry* (Piaget, Inhelder, and Szemenska, 1960). Piaget and Inhelder also completed research on the idea of chance and the genesis of probability in children. This work was published as *The Origins of the Idea of Chance in the Child* (Piaget and Inhelder, 1976).

There were two other important works Piaget completed in the late 1940s. Piaget was now in a position to complete the synthesis of biology and epistemology that he had contemplated since his adolescence. Piaget stated his own thoughts on this work:

> Since I had enough experimental data on the psychological processes underlying logico-mathematical and physical operations, it seemed the right time to write the synthesis I had been dreaming about from the beginning of my studies. Instead of devoting five years to child psychology, as I had anticipated in 1921, I had spent about thirty on it; it was exciting work and I do not in the least regret it. (Piaget, 1952a, p. 255)

The result was a three-volume series on genetic epistemology entitled *Introduction a l'Epistemologie Genetique*. The other important work was a book on the basic operations involved in logic, *Traite de Logique*. This was the presentation of Piaget's logical system, which he later applied to the investigation of adolescent thought.

EXTENDING HIS IDEAS

The last thirty years of Piaget's life (1950–1980) were as busy as the first fifty. In general, he continued to develop and apply his ideas in the areas that had long been of interest to him.

A Center for Genetic Epistemology

Piaget founded the international Center for Genetic Epistemology at the University of Geneva in 1956. The purpose of this institute is to encourage distinguished scholars from diverse disciplines and parts of the world to conduct collaborative research on problems related to human knowledge and cognition. Each year a theme or problem is selected for study. Then a group of scholars is invited to attend the institute and participate in the research. While each person conducts his or her own work, the entire effort is coordinated through regular discussions. Each year a symposium is conducted at which findings are discussed. Later the studies are published in monographs entitled *Studies in Genetic Epistemology*.

Adolescent Thinking

Piaget and Inhelder extended their studies of children's thinking to the thinking of adolescents. As we have seen, Piaget's theory postulated four stages of development corresponding to infancy, early childhood, childhood, and adolescence. In his studies of the 1920s, 1930s, and 1940s, Piaget had concentrated on infancy through the childhood years. Now he completed the empirical picture by studying adolescent patterns of reasoning. The resulting book was *The Growth of Logical Thinking from Childhood to Adolescence* (Piaget and Inhelder, 1958)

Other Areas of Psychology

Through most of his career Piaget took a rather narrow view of intelligence. Specifically he directed his studies to logical patterns of reasoning and problem solving. In the 1960s and 1970s Piaget and his colleagues started a new line of research. They investigated the relationship of topics such as memory, imagery, and learning to intelligence. Piaget's position was that generally these capacities are related to the child's stage of development. Books resulting from this research include *Mental Imagery in the Child* (Piaget and Inhelder, 1971) and *Memory and Intelligence* (Piaget and Inhelder, 1973). The latter work presents the intriguing idea that memory may not deteriorate with time, but rather can improve with the development of mental structures.

Still other works in the area of psychological studies should be mentioned. In 1969 Piaget and Inhelder published a short book that attempted to outline their theory for the general public; this book is entitled *The Psychology of the Child*. Other books of the period include *Six Psychological Studies* (Piaget, 1967), *The Child and Reality* (Piaget, 1973a), *Understanding Causality* (Piaget and Garcia, 1974), *The Grasp of Consciousness* (Piaget, 1976) and *Success and Understanding* (Piaget, 1978a).

Before turning to other areas that Piaget addressed in the last years of his life, some mention should be made of his book, *The Development of Thought: Equilibrium of Cognitive Structures* (Piaget, 1977). Here Piaget tried to describe the mechanism for development. It was a return to the part-whole problem that he struggled with during his entire professional career.

Philosophy and Biology

Piaget also returned to his philosophical interests in several of his later works. *Insights and Illusions of Philosophy* (Piaget, 1971a) is a discussion of the

The Nature of Knowledge and the Process of Education: Understanding the Contributions of Jean Piaget

Dr. Neil Lutsky
Department of Psychology
Carleton College

GUEST
EDITORIAL

Jean Piaget dedicated his life to the study of knowledge and how it develops; you are now in the process of becoming a teacher dedicated to the education of your students. What is the nature of the dialogue that the two of you can share?

That the answer to this question should be less than obvious might come as a surprise. After all, Piaget is widely recognized as a preeminent figure in contemporary child psychology who specialized in the analysis of human intelligence. And certainly, scientific knowledge about the development of children's cognitive abilities—how children think and how that thinking systematically matures over time—can be useful in making decisions about teaching strategy, curriculum, and the like. In fact, the purpose of the book you are now reading is to stimulate such a transfer of concrete knowledge. It should be noted, however, that most educational implications of Piaget's theory and findings are derived; Piaget himself wrote very little about the process of education. There is an important reason for this that has to do with the fact that his life's work was guided by an abstract purpose far removed from that of the educator. An understanding of this will help clarify the contributions to psychology and, ultimately, to education that are Piaget's and will also reveal more general (and, perhaps, profound) insights that are of relevance to both.

Piaget was, in the first instance, a scientific epistemologist. What this means is that Piaget was interested in revealing the general nature of knowledge—what it means to know something; how and why knowledge of something develops as it does; what the relationship is between the knower, the known, and reality; and the like—by applying the tools and standards of scientific inquiry. For Piaget, the knowledge that was the object of his attention was evidenced in the child's growing ability to use numbers appropriately or to classify objects systematically, but it was not limited to this type of achievement. Knowledge was also manifested in the evolving structure of biological forms, in the growing coordination and purpose of an infant's movements, as well as in science and formal analysis. In other words, Piaget believed that knowledge development occurred in many forms and that the growth of a child's understanding was but one particular and very salient instance of this.

Piaget's approach to the study of knowledge was developmental or, as he labeled it, genetic. This was an ingenious solution to the very perplexing question, How can one study knowledge scientifically? Certainly, speculatively decomposing some end result, a "piece of knowledge," into its elements and antecedents would not do. Rather, Piaget recognized that knowledge was always in the process of development and that, consequently, a mature ability or understanding could be studied and evaluated from the perspective of the understandings, events, and transitions that had resulted in the achievement of interest. Again, the study of the growth of a child's understanding was particularly well-suited to this kind of treatment. In other words, cognitive developmental psychology for Piaget was not an end in itself but rather a most available and appropriate vehicle for his developmental, or genetic, study of epistemology.

It is within the general context of a study of knowledge, then, that the investigations and contributions of Piaget took form, and these speak to our current concerns in many vital ways. Foremost among them is Piaget's account of knowledge itself. For Piaget, knowledge could not be equated simply with the set of all things learned, represented, or mastered; rather, he used the term to highlight the operations (be they mental or sensorimotor) of an organism that were responsible for intelligent acts or statements. This focus on process rather than outcome reminds us that it is reason more so than idea or understanding more so than fact that is the backbone of intelligence and an object of ultimate educational concern. In other words, it is the organization and coordination of ideas, abstract conceptual qualities, acts, or operations that is the hallmark of Piaget's use of the term "knowledge."

Moreover, the way in which such organization and coordination occurs evolves systematically over time; knowledge is developmental. This is symbolized most strongly in the Piagetian contention that cognitive development takes place in an invariantly ordered sequence of four major stages. Interestingly, this view challenges a conventional static interpretation of truth and falsity, since a child's "error" may be correct within the limits of the system of understanding he employs. Of course, our attention may then shift to the process through which knowledge structures mature ("equilibration" in Piaget's terminology), overcoming the limits of a current stage of reasoning. Here again, Piaget as epistemologist stimulates our thinking. His emphasis on the interactive nature of knowledge, on the intrinsic relationship of knower and known, cautions against a faith that external educational strategies failing to recognize and respect the current ability and readiness of a child, or knower, can affect development. Insofar as what is known can make a difference, it is primarily through actively engaging the operations of the child's intellect in the manipulation and coordination of ideas, observations, and possibilities, and in a confrontation with anomalies, that this is realized. This follows from Piaget's emphasis on the operational character of knowing.

Hopefully, the above observations have helped both to place Piaget's work in a slightly different perspective (that of epistemology) and to suggest that his more abstract study of knowledge is of relevance to an understanding of and to the identification of some of the educational implications of that work. I would be pleased if my comments would also serve to emphasize the importance of your role as a participant in a dialogue with Piaget's ideas. Because Piaget was interested in contributing to a science of knowledge and conceived of knowledge in a certain way—one highlighting the significance of generative intellectual processes—he pursued some topics and employed some perspectives in the study of cognitive development and not others. His purpose, then, and yours are not coincident, and you are left with the responsibility of evaluating just how his insights do fit in with your instructional charge. In addition, Piaget's claims are not necessarily entirely correct and have not been fully verified or, in some cases, even tested. On the other hand, the history of science has shown that key ideas and facts tend to be conserved to a great degree even when supporting conceptual schemes are revised. Just as Piaget conceived of knowledge as a process, his work should be viewed in the context of the process of science to which he contributed and which continues to develop after his contributions. You have now entered into a dialogue with this process and can reap its benefits while at the same time accepting the responsibilities the role of knower always entails.

underlying differences between philosophy and science. The former, according to Piaget, is based on subjective wisdom derived from reflection, and the latter is based on objective knowledge derived from experimentation. Piaget also explained his reason for selecting a life of science over one of philosophy. However, as we have seen, he spent a substantial amount of time dealing with philosophical questions. In *Biology and Knowledge* (Piaget, 1971b) he addressed his early concerns of integrating biological factors with epistemological problems. He later completed another book on biology, *Behavior and Evolution* (Piaget, 1978b). *Structuralism* (Piaget, 1970c) was an application of this philosophy to several different disciplines, including the development of intelligence.

Education

Unfortunately, Piaget had little to say on the topic of education. This is especially true when one considers the importance of his theory for educators. In 1970 he published *The Science of Education and the Psychology of the Child* (Piaget, 1970d) and in 1973 he published *To Understand Is to Invent: The Future of Education*. (Piaget, 1973b)

REFLECTIONS ON A LIFE AND WORK

Jean Piaget's professional career was long, varied, and complete. There is little doubt that scholars will evaluate Piaget's work, finding errors and making revisions. Curiously, this is as Piaget's theories would predict. Still, there is every indication that when the dust of time settles, Piaget, for his psychological contributions, will rank with Sigmund Freud, Carl Jung, Ivan Pavlov, and B.F. Skinner; as a philosopher, he will rank with John Dewey and perhaps Henri Bergson and Immanuel Kant.

Throughout his career Piaget was recognized for his professional achievements. Honorary degrees from Harvard (1936), the Sorbonne (1946), and the University of Brussels (1949) are examples of recognition he received. In 1949 he was also honored with the title of Professor, *honoris causa*, by the University of Brazil. In 1969 the American Psychological Association gave long overdue honor to Piaget for his distinguished scientific contribution to psychology.

Even after Piaget retired as director of the Jean-Jacques Rousseau Institute, he remained active in research at the Center for Genetic Epistemology and continued his prolific writing and publication until his death on September 16, 1980, at the age of eighty-four.

What was Piaget like? Obviously, one gleans some sense of Piaget's personal qualities through discussions of his work, but we can look farther. Piaget was a private person, and this in itself reveals something of his personal life, but it does not provide an abundance of information. Still, there is some information, and we shall use the information available.

When Piaget entered a room, there was an immediate sense of personal and intellectual presence. Though this presence was difficult to describe, anyone who met Piaget, or even heard him give a speech, will confirm that he had an aura that transcended his physical qualities. And even his physical qualities were engaging. He was tall, stout, wore bulky dark suits, had fine, wavy white hair and eyes that sparkled behind horn-rimmed glasses. However, his defining accessories were his meerschaum pipes, blue beret, and bicycle.

Piaget arose each morning, usually before 5:00 A.M., and wrote several publishable pages. Later in the morning he taught classes and attended meetings. In the afternoons he would walk and think about current research. In the evening he read and retired early (Elkind, 1970).

When asked how he accomplished so much, Piaget attributed the quantity of work to two factors: (1) his collaborators who did more than collect information but actually conducted research, and (2) to a personal quality. "Fundamentally I am a worrier whom only work can relieve" (Piaget, 1952a, p. 255).

As Piaget elaborated on his work habits, he revealed some important personal qualities.

> It is true I am sociable and like to teach or to take part in meetings of all kinds, but I feel a compelling need for solitude and contact with nature. After mornings spent with others, I begin each afternoon with a walk during which I quietly collect my thoughts and coordinate them, after which I return to the desk at my home in the country. As soon as vacation time comes, I withdraw to the mountains in the wild regions of the Valais and write for weeks on end on improvised tables and after pleasant walks. It is this disassociation between myself as a social being and as a "man of nature" (in whom Dionysian excitement ends in intellectual activity) which has enabled me to surmount a permanent fund of anxiety and transform it into a need for working. (Piaget, 1952a, p. 255)

Through this chapter, a picture has emerged of what Jean Piaget was like as a person and as a professional. Reviewing these qualities confirms a healthy, self-actualizing life according to the criteria set forth by Abraham Maslow (1970).

Many of the characteristics Maslow described as self-actualizing have already been mentioned. One of the first qualities Piaget demonstrated was a *more efficient perception of reality*. This quality probably originated in Piaget's father's systematic approach to study and his mother's poor mental health, and subsequent poor perceptions of reality. In conversation Piaget was able to detect significance and depth that was not immediately evident to others (Elkind, 1970), and he could detect the dishonest individual (Elkind, 1971; Ripple and Rockcastle, 1964). One characteristic of genius is the ability to find importance and uniqueness in the commonplace. Even at age ten Piaget found one partly albino sparrow among, no doubt, hundreds of sparrows in a park. Later in life his clear perception of reality, his ability to distinguish the unique from the common caused him to examine *incorrect* responses as Simon's assistant and probably contributed in concrete ways to his studies of children's thinking and in abstract ways to his scientific attitudes.

Piaget had the wonderful capacity of acceptance. He was not overly concerned about personal appearance, such as keeping in style. His quality of acceptance was clear in his tremendous understanding and empathy for children. His whole clinical methodology was based on recognizing and accepting the statements of children as truthful and accurate. To say that Piaget accepted nature would be an understatement. He spent his life studying physical and human nature. He even stated "a compelling need for solitude and contact with nature" (Piaget, 1952a, p. 255). Throughout his life he withdrew to his biological studies when he needed to remove himself from the abstract and touch the concrete. This *quality of detachment and need for privacy* is another defining quality of a self-actualizing person.

Piaget's life was one of *simplicity and naturalness*. One could not really say Piaget was unconventional. On the other hand, he lived (and traveled) simply and naturally; there was no straining for effect or assuming of facades. When he was presented a $25,000 prize for his work in psychology in 1973, his response was "I am only a poor psychologist." This was his perception, and somehow one feels that this was really how Piaget perceived himself and the award (*Science News*, 1973).

From adolescence Piaget directed his energies to problems beyond himself. Very clearly Piaget felt he had a mission and a task, which was to establish a link between biology and epistemology. This took the majority of his energy for approximately sixty years.

David Elkind (1970) tells a story of Piaget's nervousness before delivering the Heinz Werner Memorial lecture in 1967. Usually at ease and lively, on this evening Piaget seemed quiet, reserved, and apprehensive. During the dinner two small boys appeared at a window and began tapping and waving. Piaget turned to see what was happening. He smiled and waved to the children. They in turn waved and disappeared. Piaget went on to present his lecture and receive a standing ovation. This small incident demonstrates the *continued appreciation* Piaget had for children. Needless to say, he also continued to appreciate nature throughout his life. One can easily make the connection among our acceptance of others, freshness of appreciation, and ability to relate well to others.

Maslow talked about moments of acute subjective feelings that he called *peak experiences*. Probably Piaget's moments of "ecstatic joy" upon making the connection between biology and philosophy were just such experiences.

When Maslow described *interpersonal relations* of self-actualizing individuals he stated that they "have an especially tender love for children," and this describes exactly what others have said about Piaget's feeling about children. David Elkind has suggested that "Piaget's genius for empathy with children, together with true intellectual genius" (Elkind, 1970, p. 8) were the characteristics underlying his becoming one of the outstanding child psychologists in the world. Piaget also had very close interpersonal relations with several colleagues, in particular Barbel Inhelder. This is also characteristic of self-actualizing persons; they tend to have few, but very close, interpersonal relations. In the last years of his work, Piaget had become internationally known and quite famous. Being in this situation naturally attracted admirers, disciples, and worshippers. Reports by Elkind (1970) and Ripple and Rockcastle (1964) indicate Piaget was not interested in developing such relationships, and he did not. When receiving honorary

Jean Piaget in his later years

degrees and awards or giving lectures, Piaget was kind and pleasant but did little to encourage his followers. In a typical attitude for Piaget, he stated, "Don't build me a church, rather, a forum in which scholars can exchange ideas" (Nodine, Gallagher and Humphreys, 1972).

Maslow also talked about a *democratic character structure* and an *identification for humankind*. The nature of Piaget's work has truly crossed barriers of race and culture. During World War II he physically crossed barriers to support allies in the best manner possible given his abilities. The Center for Genetic Epistemology which he established is also international and intellectually democratic in the true meaning of this word.

Few examples exist of Piaget's humor. It was by accounts *philosophical and unhostile*. This is as Maslow would have predicted. It was a quiet humor, directed at the human situation but not a humor of superiority or dominance. Usually it was the type of humor that brought a smile rather than an outward laugh.

Creativeness is the final personal quality to be discussed. Actually little has to be said about Piaget's tremendous creative abilities. They were and are visible in his theories and the way he went about his work. Evidence for Piaget's creative ability seems abundant enough to support the idea that he was a gifted and talented person, not only a genius but a creative genius.

The personal qualities demonstrated by Jean Piaget are, in their own way, as confirming of human development as his theories of child psychology. Throughout his career, he never failed to find uniqueness in the common, to lose sight of his purpose, and to find new problems to resolve. He lived a full and rich professional life and a personal life of continued actualization of his potentials.

REFERENCES

Elkind, David. *Children and Adolescents.* New York: Oxford University Press, 1970.

Maslow, Abraham H. *Motivation and Personality.* New York: Harper & Row, Publishers, 1970.

Nodine, C. F.; Gallagher, J. M.; and Humphreys, R. D. *Piaget and Inhelder on Equilibration.* Philadelphia: The Jean Piaget Society, 1972.

Piaget, Jean. *Language and Thought of the Child.* London: Rutledge and Kegan Paul, 1926a.

———. *Judgement and Reasoning in the Child.* New York: Harcourt Brace Jovanovich, 1926b.

———. *The Child's Conception of the World.* New York: Harcourt Brace Jovanovich, 1929.

———. *The Moral Judgement of the Child.* New York: Harcourt Brace Jovanovich, 1932.

———. *Play, Dreams and Imitations in Childhood.* New York: W. W. Norton & Co., 1951.

———. "Jean Piaget." In *A History of Psychology in Autobiography,* edited by Edwin G. Boring, Heinz Werner, Herbert Longfeld, and Robert S. Yerkes. Worcester, Massachusetts: Clark University Press, 1952a.

————. *The Origins of Intelligence in Children*. New York: International Universities Press, 1952*b*.

————. *The Construction of Reality in the Child*. New York: Basic Books, 1954.

————. *The Child's Conception of Physical Causality*. Totowa, N. J.: Littleford, Adams, and Co., 1960.

————. *The Psychology of Intelligence*. Totowa, N. J.: Littlefield, Adams and Co., 1966.

————. *Six Psychological Studies*. New York: Random House, 1967.

————. *The Mechanisms of Perception*. London: Rutledge and Kegan Paul, 1969.

————. *The Child's Conception of Time*. New York: Basic Books, 1970*a*.

————. *The Child's Conception of Movement and Speed*. London: Rutledge and Kegan Paul, Ltd., 1970*b*.

————. *Structuralism*. New York: Basic Books, 1970*c*.

————. *The Science of Education and the Psychology of the Child*. New York: Grossman Publishing, 1970*d*.

————. *Insights and Illusions of Philosophy*. New York: The World Publishing Co., 1971*a*.

————. *Biology and Knowledge*. Chicago: University of Chicago Press, 1971*b*.

————. *The Child and Reality*. New York: Grossman Publishing, 1973*a*.

————. *To Understand Is to Invent: The Future of Education*. New York: Grossman Publishing, 1973*b*.

————. *The Grasp of Consciousness*. Cambridge: Harvard University Press, 1976.

————. *The Development of Thought: Equilibrium of Cognitive Structures*. New York: The Viking Press, 1977.

————. *Success and Understanding*. Cambridge: Harvard University Press, 1978*a*.

————. *Behavior and Evolution*. New York: Pantheon Books, 1978*b*.

Piaget, Jean, and Garcia, R. *Understanding Causality*. New York: W. W. Norton & Co., 1974.

Piaget, Jean, and Inhelder, Barbel. *The Child's Conception of Space*. New York: Humanities Press, 1956.

————. *The Growth of Logical Thinking from Childhood to Adolescence*. New York: Basic Books, 1958.

————. *The Psychology of the Child*. New York: Basic Books, 1969.

————. *Mental Imagery in the Child*. London: Rutledge and Kegan Paul, 1971.

————. *Memory and Intelligence*. New York: Basic Books, 1973.

————. *The Child's Construction of Quantities: Conservation and Atomism*. New York: Basic Books, Inc., 1974.

————. *The Origins of the Idea of Chance in the Child*. New York: W. W. Norton, & Co., 1976.

Piaget, Jean; Inhelder, Barbel; and Szemenska, Alena. *The Child's Conception of Geometry*. London: Rutledge and Kegan Paul, 1960.

Piaget, Jean, and Szemenska, Alena. *The Child's Construction of Numbers*. London: Rutledge and Kegan Paul, 1952.

"The Poor Psychologist and His $25,000 Prize." *Science News* 103 (June 9, 1973): 371.

Ripple, Richard, and Rockcastle, Verne, eds. *Piaget Rediscovered: A Report of the Conference on Cognitive Studies and Curriculum Development.* A Monograph. Ithaca: Cornell University, March, 1964.

2 Piaget's Theory: An Exploration

The first portion of this chapter deals with explanations individuals have of their world. Some examples of explanations and the process of changing explanations are introduced in a Piagetian and educational context. The next major section introduces Piaget's theory. The final section briefly outlines applications of Piaget's theory for educators.

I | EXPLORATION
SEEKING EXPLANATIONS FOR CHILDREN'S BEHAVIOR

Consider these observations of infants. A child of six months reaches for an interesting object such as a rattle. When the child obtains the object, he "plays" with it. The object is then removed, and the child immediately behaves as though the object no longer exists. Here is another observation. An infant is holding a small toy and obviously enjoying her interaction with it. Suddenly she drops the toy. But, contrary to what one expects, she does not look down to find the toy. Instead, she continues looking off in other directions, smiling as though she forgot about the toy.

How would you explain these observations?

1. The children have not been taught to look for lost toys.
2. The children simply lost interest in the toys.
3. The children are at an "out-of-sight, out-of-mind" stage.
4. The children probably found other toys that interested them.

Let us look at some observations of preschool children. It is time for juice. The teacher brings a tray of half-pint containers of juice. The glasses used are, however, different sizes; some are short and wide, others are tall and thin. The teacher pours all the juice from one container into a tall glass. Then she proceeds to pour the juice from a second carton into a short glass. Immediately the child with the short glass says that his neighbor has "more to drink." The teacher stops and asks if the juice for both glasses came from the cartons. He replies, "Yes." The teacher places the two cartons next to one another and asks if they are the same. "Yes," the child replies. "So, if each of you had a glass of juice from a carton, you would have the same amount to drink even if the glasses were different." "Oh," replies the boy. "So, is it O. K. now?" asks the teacher. "No, she has more to drink." "Why do you think that?" asks the teacher. "Because her glass is bigger."

How would you explain these observations?

1. The child was trying to get attention.

2. The child has not been taught about "equals."

3. The child really does think the amount of juice is a function of glass size.

4. The child has probably already drunk some of his juice and is therefore correct.

Imagine you are an elementary teacher correcting and grading second grade math problems. The following worksheet emerges from the mountain of papers.

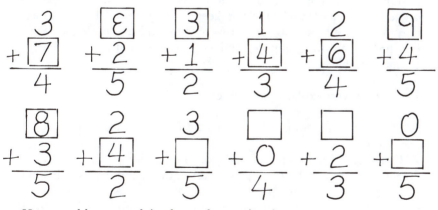

How would you explain these observations?

1. The child does not understand addition.

2. The child does not understand that the reverse operation—subtraction—is required.

3. The child has a learning disability.

A fifth grade teacher is doing a unit on world geography. One day the teacher asks if there are more people or more Americans in the world. To the teacher's surprise eight students reply that there are more Americans! The other students reply that there are more people.

How would you explain these observations?

1. The students did not listen to the question.
2. The students do not understand sets and subsets, or class inclusion.
3. The students are patriotic.
4. The students were probably just playing a joke.

A high school physical science class is presented with a pendulum in the form of a weight suspended from a string that is connected to a stand. The teacher demonstrates ways of varying the length of string, changing the weights and recording the frequency of oscillation. The students are then presented with the problem of finding the factor that determines the frequency of oscillations. As the period progresses the teacher observes the work of various student groups. With time she realizes that students are approaching the problem in widely different ways. Being curious about this she starts observing student problem-solving behaviors. Here are her observations:

Several students seemed unable to understand that their own physical action of pushing the weights influenced the results. Their answers were inconsistent and often contradictory.

A second group was able to test the different lengths, weights, and heights, then record their results. However, they did not systematically separate and control the variables, so they were unable to determine the important variables in the problem.

A third group first isolated all the relevant variables. They then proceeded to test each variable while keeping everything else the same. As they progressed, certain factors were systematically excluded. Finally, the students in the group determined that the length of string was the crucial variable.

How would you explain these observations?

1. The first two groups of students were not mature enough to solve the problem.
2. Only the third group had had experience with pendulums.
3. The students in the third group were gifted, and the students in the first two groups were unmotivated.
4. The groups represent different ways students understand the same problem.

Let us look at a final situation. The setting is a fourth grade class. The teacher enters the room and, without comment, places three containers of liquid on the desk. She holds up an ice cube and asks the class what will happen if the ice cube is placed in the first container. "It will float," is the unanimous response. She places the ice cube in the container and it *sinks*! The students are totally amazed. She holds up another ice cube and asks what will happen when it is placed in the second container. Of course, thinking they are on to her ways, the students respond, "It will sink." She places the ice cube in the container and it *floats*! A third ice cube is shown to the students. "What will happen when I place this ice cube in the third container?" "We don't know." "It will float." "Sink." These are the students' responses to the question. The ice cube is placed in the third container. It remains *suspended*—exactly half way between the top and bottom! Many of the children are obviously surprised and do not know what to think of the counterintuitive results.

The teacher tells the class they can ask questions to try and find out what happened. Immediately six or seven students start asking questions and trying to explain the demonstration. "Are the ice cubes the same?" "Is it the liquid or the ice cube that makes the difference?" The students' enthusiasm is clear. Their eagerness to resolve the problem is evident. Before long the teacher notices that the remainder of the class is not at all interested in the problem. A few students had started working on other things; some watched the students who were asking questions; some simply sat looking as though they already knew the answer; some shrunk down in their seats, as if afraid they would be called upon to ask or answer a question. The teacher began to wonder about the students who were not involved.

How would you explain the behaviors of the noninvolved students?

1. Some already knew the answer and some did not know enough to start searching for an answer.

2. Some were gifted students and some were mildly retarded.

3. All were demonstrating typical behaviors for fourth graders.

4. All had seen the demonstration already, so they were bored.

Explaining Our Observations

Educators have explanations for student behavior. After reading the situations just described, you were probably able to select one of the explanations given or suggest a different account for the described behaviors. In trying to answer the questions explaining students' thinking, you have been involved in the problems that formed the life work of Jean Piaget. How do individuals come to know their world? This is the question Piaget spent a lifetime answering. Piaget's goal was to develop a theory of knowledge—an epistemology—based on actual observations. So, he and his colleagues observed and interviewed children. The child was asked to solve a problem. Often, several variations of the problem would be presented. Always, the children were asked *why* they answered as they did. Piaget listened closely to the different explanations children gave. After years of close observations of problem-solving behaviors, Piaget came to understand children's thinking.

While simple observation confirms that educators have explanations for student behavior, there is an amazing range of explanations. Take, for example, the last situation where some of the students were not involved in trying to resolve the ice cube problem. Here are some explanations one might hear from a group of teachers who knew the students: "They were not motivated." "They were not ready." "They didn't understand the problem." "They did not pay attention." While there may be some evidence supporting such statements, there is often a tendency to answer important questions about individual students, as though there was a substantial body of information supporting the answer. There is the tendency to make generalizations. As we shall see, Piaget's theory provides a body of knowledge concerning the intellectual development of students. Understanding Piaget's theory will help you better explain students' thinking.

Individuals have explanations for their world. All of us—children, adolescents, adults, students, teachers, and professors—can explain objects, events, and situations in our world. This is not to say the explanations are accurate or correct. You can confirm this by asking almost anyone a simple "why" question. The person will usually tell you why. The answer may range from the scientific to the mythologic, but nonetheless it will serve to explain the situation for the particular individual. As educators know, this is especially true of children and adolescents. They can explain virtually everything from the weather to politics. And, while many of their explanations are interesting, they are less than accurate.

The fact that children and adolescents have explanations for their world presents educators with two fundamental questions. First, what explanations do individuals have at various times in their life? Second, how can less adequate explanations be changed to more adequate conceptions of reality? These questions direct us to the primary areas of intellectual development and individual learning.

What Do Children Know and When Do They Know It?

Look at the illustrations in Figure 2.1. What is different about children in each of these groups? Why would you *not* expect children in the first group to do what the last group does?

(0–2 years)

(2–7 years)

(7–11 years)

(11–14 plus years)

Figure 2.1
What do children know and when do they know it?

Since you have chosen to be involved in education, you probably already are sensitive to how children think. You know, therefore, that some questions are inappropriate for some children because they are incapable of reasoning out the answer. You also know, for the same reason, that it would be inappropriate to teach algebra to primary school children. In other words, in some ways you understand what Piaget means when he says: "A child's mind is not an adult's mind." To clarify this statement we shall examine some characteristics of children's thinking at different times in their lives.

During the first two years of infancy, the child mainly interacts with the environment with his senses and muscles and is directed by sensations from the environment. He develops his ability to perceive, touch, and move during this stage. As the child interacts with his surroundings, he slowly learns to coordinate his actions.

The sensorimotor child is "space limited" in the immediate environment in which he acts. Life is a series of disconnected individual pictures without understanding relationships within the whole. Rudimentary concepts about time, space, and causality do not develop until the child approaches the end of this period. This is the *sensorimotor* period, and it lasts from birth to approximately two years of age. *"The active child"* characterizes this period of development.

During the sensorimotor period, the child develops the ability to perceive, touch, and move.

Behavior is preverbal, and the child concerns himself mainly with organizing and coordinating physical actions. Recall the first observations of this chapter. According to Piaget's theory the concept of object permanence has not developed. Thus, the child is limited to definite external stimuli from objects rather than mental pictures of them. In this sense, he is bound by the stimuli about him rather than originating them from his brain. When an object is hidden from the child's immediate view, he does not search for it. For him, an object not directly perceived does not exist. The conception of object permanence only gradually develops through repeated experience.

The next period spans approximately ages two to seven years, thus including most children in kindergarten, first grade, and second grade. Though the child can now form mental images and label them verbally, he has not developed the ability to carry out the mental activities Piaget has termed "operations." Operations include internalized representations of changes on external objects. "Thought" would be a good way to conceptualize this idea. What is a child's "thought" about external objects or events? Though children between two and seven have acquired "thought" in the broadest sense, their thought is often preconceptual and prelogical. In many ways their thought is best described as intuitive. Here is *the intuitive student*. We examined two situations that represented children's thought at this stage. In the first situation the student was confused by the size of the glass containing juice. The child was struck by the height of his neighbor's glass and intuitively thought his neighbor had more juice in spite of the teacher's explanation. The child is unable to think (operate) on the changes that occurred to the juice and to realize that rearranging the juice (via containers) does not affect the amount of juice.

During the preoperational stage, the child often relies on animistic and anthropomorphic explanations of natural events.

The second example of this pattern of thought had to do with the arithmetic problems. The child apparently knows how to add. She adds from the bottom up, the top down, and either end to the middle, always arriving at the correct sum. However, given the actual problem, the child is incorrect. To answer the problems correctly the child must understand and complete the *reverse* of addition—subtraction. Looking over the student's work, one gets a sense of the intuitive, preconceptual approach that students have during this period. This child is able to perform certain functions (i.e., summation) but has not yet reached the level of cognitive development enabling her adequately to conceptualize the series of manipulations necessary to resolve the problems. There are many components of the problem that must be centered on and held simultaneously in the mind; and then operations must be performed on the figures. These mental operations are governed by the symbols. It is possible that the child is unable to complete the operations required by the two symbols, the addition symbol and summation line. Although the symbols tell the child to add, she must, in fact, mentally realize she has to subtract. The child's eventual ability to complete the problem will develop as a result of experience with subtraction in the environment both in and out of school.

During this stage the child is highly egocentric. He finds it difficult to comprehend views other than his own. Understanding of chance and probability is largely absent as he assumes only one truth or one event is possible in any given situation. Animistic and anthropomorphic explanations are commonly expressed for observed natural events. For example, a child might explain a plant's bending toward a window because it "likes light" or it "wants to." "Clouds are smiling at him" would be an explanation for cloud formation. During the latter part of the stage, memory is developed and the child has the ability to think of the past and the future but is limited in how far he goes in either direction. This is the *pre-operational* period.

During the developmental phase between seven and eleven or twelve years of age, the child is able to perform mental operations. Mental processes are incorporated into a coherent system. Thought patterns follow a set of logical rules. The operations are "concrete," because they usually require the presence of actual objects. So, we discuss *the practical student*. If the student is given a piece of clay to roll out, she is aware that the amount of clay has not changed by manipulating it, and she can mentally reverse the action. She can imagine the clay back in its original shape.

Our fourth example concerning the question—Are there more Americans or more people in the world?—was a simple class inclusion problem. Some students were unable to understand the logic of the question probably due to its abstract nature.

Problems involving conservation of quantity, weight, and volume of substances across a series of changes are easily solved by the children at the end of this stage, and they can satisfactorily justify their solutions. They can also consider two dimensions of a problem simultaneously, and changing events can be ordered in a chronological sequence. They observe, judge, and evaluate in less egocentric terms and formulate more objective explanations. But they experience difficulty in expressing hypotheses following a long series of related ideas or if concrete practical referents are not available. While they can form simple groups in classifying objects, it remains difficult or impossible to group classes into more comprehensive groups. This period is termed *concrete operational*.

In the concrete operational period, the child can easily order objects or events in their correct sequence.

Between twelve and fifteen years of age, the student begins to think like an adult. This stage marks the child's emancipation from dependence on direct perception of objects as a mediator of thought. In contrast to the concrete operational child, the adolescent thinker can represent his own thoughts by symbols, consider ideals as opposed to realities, form inferences based on stated sets of assumptions (propositional thought), formulate complex and abstract theories, and reflect upon his thought processes. He can carry out "mental" experiments as well as actual ones. Probability is well understood. He can complete operations on operations. In short, the kind of cognition that is considered adult is now the rule rather than the exception. We have characterized this individual as *the reflective student.*

The high school class presented with the pendulum problem exemplified three levels of thinking that have been described. The first group approached the problem in an intuitive manner. The second group approached the problem logically, but practically and concretely. The final group demonstrated formal thought through their logical and systematic approach to the problem's resolution.

The question—What do children know and when do they know it?—can be answered in very broad terms. At first, during the sensorimotor stage, there is the development of knowledge through physical action. During the second, or preoperational stage, the child's thought emerges but it is pre-

In the formal operational stage, the child can take a logical and systematic approach to problems.

logical and is best described as intuitive. In the next stage—concrete operational—the student's thought is logical but is confined to practical experiences. Finally, in the formal operational stage, the adolescent demonstrates logical patterns of reasoning about abstract ideas and problems. The student demonstrates reflective thought.

How Can Children's Explanations Be Improved?

The basic question of this section is, How do children learn? We shall briefly examine the ways educators have traditionally answered these questions. Start by answering the following questions by selecting the answer that is closest to what you either do or think should be done in teaching the basics.

How should computation be approached in the elementary schools?

1. Wait until the students are old enough to understand the concepts and then teach them.

2. Set up situations where the students will naturally count, add, subtract, and so on; then allow them freedom to explore the situations.

3. Design a program where the concepts are taught in an ordered sequence starting with preconcepts and readiness skills then advancing to complex concepts; teach through the program with ample practice and correction.

4. All of the above.

How should reading be approached in the elementary schools?

1. Delay the introduction of reading until the children indicate they are ready, and then teach them.

2. Provide an ample range of reading materials and allow children free time to pick what they want, read if they want, and be taught if they want.

3. Carefully structure a sequenced program which starts with pre-reading, then advances to basal readers and finally readers; then teach through the sequence with abundant exercise and feedback.

4. All of the above.

How should writing be approached in the elementary schools?

1. Look for signs of muscular coordination and psychomotor skills that indicate the students are physically mature enough to write; then teach them printing and cursive.

2. Make sure there are abundant supplies of paper and pencils and unrestricted time to explore the possibilities of writing; then when the students are interested, teach them to write.

3. Organize a curriculum program that starts with the basics of printing and progresses to the complexities of cursive; then teach the progressive skills allowing for drill and reinforcement to perfect the skills.

4. All of the above.

Educators have several traditional answers to questions concerning learning and the improvement of children's knowledge. For the most part, these answers are assumptions which underlie educational practices and programs. One view is that learning is aligned with physical growth and maturity. In all of the above questions, this was answer number one. The orientation is toward an educational program that takes physical maturity as the primary factor determining educational instruction. Here, the teacher acts as a coordinator between the curriculum and the students' level of physical maturity; when the child is ready, the educator teaches. Children's explanations are primarily improved through maturation and secondarily through education coordinated with their level of growth.

A second view is that learning occurs at the optimum level when children are allowed to explore their environment. This was the orientation of response number two in the questions. Here, the children's freedom and exploration take educational precedence over other factors. The teacher is nondirective but available to aid and explain if the student seeks assistance or advice. How are children's explanations improved? The answer to this question is through their own experiences with the environment; secondary to the child's experience is the teacher's help and support.

The third view is that learning takes place through the direct transmission of knowledge to the student. This is the dominant view of educators, and the orientation of response number three in the questions. While the other two models gave primary attention to children, this model emphasizes formal education as the primary factor in improving children's explanations of the world. The educator's role is to design a program that represents the best possible organization of the subject to be taught. The teacher then presents the material and reinforces the student's correct use of the acquired knowledge or skill.

Piaget's position on learning remains to be explored. As you have probably reasoned, all of the factors discussed thus far contribute to a child's improved knowledge about the world. If you answered "all of the above" for the introductory questions, you were on the right track. But, for Piaget there is more than the three factors described earlier. Children's knowledge of the world is improved through the continuous mental adaptation to physical changes and environmental encounters. Note that the process of physical maturation, natural experiences, and formal education are included in this definition. All of these factors contribute to the way a child perceives her world. But, there must be some process that coordinates and organizes the developing child's various physical systems and environmental encounters.

As individuals interact with their world, whether through design or naturally, they encounter situations, objects, and events. Depending on the individual's level of development and the situation, object or event, one of three things may occur. The individual may well comprehend the situation and thus explain the encounter correctly. If, for example, educators require a response to the situation, the individual gives a correct answer. A second possibility is that the encounter is beyond the individual's immediate comprehension but within the realm of understanding and ability. Here, responses to educators' questions might include the following: "Let me work on this," "Give me a chance to solve it," or some similar comment indicating comprehension but not total understanding. A final possibility is that the encounter is so far beyond the individual's understanding that there is only a sense that nothing is known or understood. If a response is demanded in this case, the individual guesses, makes up an answer, or simply says, "I don't know."

Recall the final situation given at the first of the chapter: the demonstration where ice cubes sank, floated, and remained suspended. After the demonstration the students were allowed to ask questions as they attempted to explain what had happened. Some students were immediately involved; yet, not all were engaged by the problem. Three groups of students could be identified: the bored or uninterested; the involved and interested; and the uninvolved and anxious. For this example, we have tried to show the three responses. For our discussion of Piaget's theory, let us concentrate on the second group since the first group already has answers and the third group doesn't understand the problem. The following discussion would apply to the first and third groups, though the lesson would have to be adjusted up or down so the respective students would respond as those in the second group.

Students in the second group may be described as puzzled, interested, perplexed, absorbed, or engrossed in the situation, object, or event. Their curiosity has been piqued. To resolve the problem, to move from a position of not comprehending to one of understanding, requires a readjustment or slight change in the individual's thinking. That is, the problem is close enough to present thinking that the change is possible. The individual must modify her patterns of thinking. Subsequently this new pattern of thought is incorporated into the individual's intellectual structure.

The alteration of existing patterns of thought is divided into two processes that occur simultaneously when an individual is presented with a puzzling situation. There is the mental modification of the situation, object, or event in an attempt to incorporate it into existing ways of thinking. It is as though the individual says, "Could this be like...?" Thus, there is a slight distorting by the individual. Basically this is an attempt to make reality fit an explanation that already exists. There is also the modification of an existing explanation so it fits reality. Here, existing ways of thinking are changed so that the new experience can be understood and incorporated into the individual's cognitive structure. The dual processes occur simultaneously as the individual tries to adapt to the puzzling situation.

II | EXPLANATION
PIAGET'S THEORY—AN OVERVIEW

This section is intended to be an overview of Piaget's theory. The section reiterates some ideas mentioned earlier, and it anticipates discussions in future chapters.

Piaget's training and experience as a biologist influenced his theoretical formulations and the terminology used to describe various aspects of cognitive development. While Piaget's theory appeals to biological constructs, the ideas are used as metaphors. This point should be very clear. It is even worth repeating—Piaget's theory does not use biological concepts to explain psychological development. He does use biological terms (e.g., organization, adaptation), but they are purely metaphorical.

Central to Piaget's theory are the concepts of cognitive structure, cognitive functions, and cognitive content. The cognitive structure refers, in the most general way, to the stages of development. Cognitive structures are identifiable patterns of physical or mental action that underlie specific acts of intelligence. For example, some patterns of action are more logical than others if one considers a specific act such as separating and controlling variables in the pendulum problem described earlier.

There are four distinct patterns of intelligent action in Piaget's theory: the sensorimotor stage, the preoperational stage, the concrete operational stage, and the formal operational stage.

The sensorimotor period is characterized by the fact that intelligent action is motoric. Internalized thought is largely not evident during the first two years of life. The cognitive structure develops through the overt behavior and action by the infant. This stage is discussed in Chapter 3.

At the preoperational period the child's cognitive structure manifests some internalized thought processes. The thought processes are based on the original sensorimotor processes developed in the prior stage. Though children show signs of "thought," it is not logical. Compared to later stages the thought is intuitive. This stage is described in Chapter 4.

The cognitive structure during the concrete operational period is logical. By operational Piaget means that the individual can establish a mental image of an object or event, change the object or event, and then return the image to its original form. Still, the concrete operational child does not show the most sophisticated level of cognitive structures because she depends on concrete information, objects, events, and so on before thinking is logical. If the situation is too abstract, the child may reason illogically. This stage is the topic of Chapter 5.

The most complete manifestation of the cognitive structure is the period of formal operations. Thinking is abstract, rigorous, and logical. Mental operations, or acts of thought, are completed on situations and information that have not, or may not, ever occur. At this level of development there are logical patterns of thought about ideas that may only exist as thoughts. Conceptual modeling, scenario building, and hypothetical reasoning are examples of thinking at this level. According to Piaget, this is the final and most complete development of cognitive structures. This stage is outlined in Chapter 6.

As students develop they acquire beliefs, values, and attitudes that influence their learning and behavior. Piaget investigated the role of moral development early in his career. Piaget's initial work on moral development and the work of others who followed his lead are discussed in Chapter 7.

Cognitive functioning is the process that accounts for changes in the cognitive structure. The cognitive functions *do not* change during development; they are, to use Piaget's terms, functional invariants.

Here is the problem: How can one simultaneously *maintain* the integrity of the cognitive structure and *change* the cognitive structure? To resolve this problem, Piaget appeals to the biological principles of organization and adaptation. Only here, they are applied as metaphors for cognitive functioning. Organization and adaptation are complementary functions. We shall look at each briefly. Organization can be thought of as a basic inherited tendency of organisms. This is true biologically and for Piaget psychologically. Organization is the tendency to systematize and integrate actions—either motoric or cognitive—into coherent structures of a higher order. So, two experiences that may originate separately (e.g., looking at an object and grasping an object) may be eventually integrated into a higher level action of looking and grasping. This higher level action does not eliminate the original actions. They are still available for use separately. Organization accounts for a continuity of the cognitive structure across time and development. It also accounts for the increasingly higher levels of complexity of the cognitive structure; that is, the patterns of action and thought associated with the major periods of development.

The cognitive structure changes through adaptation. Adaptation is the basic tendency of the organism to adjust to the environment. The central idea here is that experience has an effect on the cognitive structure. Development results from continuous adaptations to the environment. Adaptation is a process with two equally important components: assimilation and accommodation.

Assimilation of motoric or cognitive actions is based on an underlying cognitive structure. The individual "interprets" environmental situations in terms of existing cognitive structures. This is what we meant earlier by the modification of reality to fit existing explanations as individuals attempt to "interpret" reality in ways that presently make sense to them. In other words, the individual attempts to adapt to her environment through assimilation.

Accommodation is the other component of the adaptive process. Here, the cognitive structure is changed to fit incoming information. Earlier this was discussed as a modification of an existing explanation to fit reality. In the process of accommodating to the environment, the cognitive structures are expanded, broadened, or generalized so they incorporate increasingly larger aspects of the world. As we saw in the example of floating, sinking, and suspending ice cubes, there are definite limits on the adaptive process. This point is very important for educators to remember. For Piaget, assimilation and accommodation are two sides of the adaptive coin. They can be separated for discussion, but they are inseparable in development. Cognitive functioning—organization and adaptation—is discussed in Chapter 8.

Cognitive content refers to the motoric or cognitive actions that are termed intelligent. This is what the child says or does that allows one to infer the level of existing cognitive structures or the process of cognitive functioning. Cognitive content is what was most clearly demonstrated in the opening situations where you were asked to explain the behavior. The numerous experiments reported by Piaget are designed to show intelligent behavior in various forms and at different levels. Cognitive contents are clearly and directly observable. Cognitive structures and functions are inferred from the observable actions of infants, children, and adolescents. Cognitive content is discussed through the next six chapters. Some key points of Piaget's theory are summarized graphically in Figures 2.2, 2.3, and 2.4.

Figure 2.2
Concepts of Cognitive Structure, Function, and Stage

Intelligence is the ability to *organize* and *adapt* to the environment.

Cognitive functions of organization and adaptation contribute to the development of the cognitive structure.

Cognitive functions do not vary with development.

Cognitive structures do vary with development.

A set of cognitive structures at relative equilibrium is a stage.

Each stage integrates the cognitive structures from previous stages into a new, higher order structure.

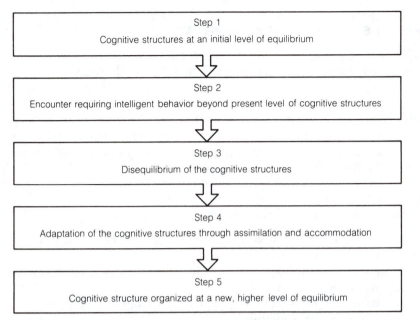

Figure 2.3
Steps in the Process of Adaptation

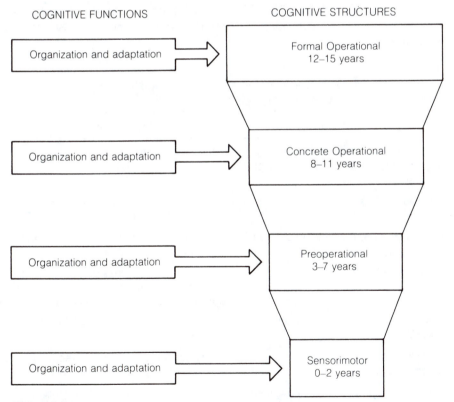

Figure 2.4
The Relationship Between Cognitive Functions, Cognitive Structures, and Developmental Stages

III | EXTENSION
PIAGET'S THEORY—INITIAL APPLICATIONS

The view of cognitive development presented by Piaget is very different from conventional theories that have long influenced education. Figure 2.5 is a comparison of conventional views and Piaget's theories concerning some ideas that are important for educators. As you can see, there is a vast difference between conventional theories and the implications of Piaget's theories for education. Almost all the items important to educators—intelligence, knowledge, learning, development, and teaching—require a restructuring of thought by teachers. Probably one of the first steps in applying Piaget's theory is realizing that there is a different model of education.

Some initial applications of Piaget's theory include

1. Understanding that students will have different explanations of reality at different times in their life.

2. Recognizing the stages of cognitive development in the formulation of lessons, units, and curricula.

3. Attempting to facilitate development through situations that engage learners and require cognitive adaptation.

4. Using methods and materials that require motoric and cognitive activity.

5. Combining activities that allow for difference in physical growth, social experience, and education in the scope and sequence of instruction and curricula.

Figure 2.5
A Comparison Between Conventional Theories and Piaget's Theory on Topics of Interest to Educators

Conventional Theory	Piaget's Theory
Intelligence is mental age divided by chronological age as determined by an IQ test.	Intelligence is the ability to adapt to environmental change.
Knowledge is a copy of reality.	Knowledge is the adaptation of cognitive structures to reality.
Learning is the modification of behavior due to experience.	Learning is the modification of cognitive structures due to activity.
Learning is the process of taking in concepts that represent reality.	Learning is the process of restructuring existing concepts so they are more appropriate explanations of reality.
Learning explains developmental progress.	Developmental progress explains learning.
Development is the accumulation of specific concepts.	Development is a continuous reorganization and restructuring of concepts.
Teaching is the presentation of material in a logical order.	Teaching is engaging the learner with materials that require cognitive adaptation.

The Development of Reasoning

Robert Karplus
Lawrence Hall of Science
University of California

Susan M. Arnold
Lawrence Hall of Science
University of California

GUEST EDITORIAL

Studying the developmental theories of Jean Piaget leads different people to differing conclusions. When we think of Piaget, we think of teaching for the development of reasoning. We suggest that his ideas are tools for teachers to help students reason—for instance, to understand the proper use of conjunctions, the law of supply and demand, commutative properties of numbers under addition, or the classification of small objects according to whether they float or sink in water.

Piaget's work has unique significance for teachers because students' reasoning is exceedingly important and yet has not received much stimulation from widely used school texts and programs. You can verify this claim by looking for activities in which students are really asked to figure things out for themselves—where they are not told what method to use or what set of words to put into the blanks, but are asked instead to justify their answers or conclusions. We have the impression that most children think the key to school success is doing "what you are supposed to do," that each item follows its own rule (to be memorized), that teachers want explanations only when children have made a mistake.

Piaget has made two essential contributions. First, he has pointed out that concept learning and the establishment of new reasoning strategies are active processes for the learner. Teachers should insist on active mental involvement by students in their own learning. To provide learning experiences with students' active involvement but also some guidance, teachers may use the four-phase learning cycle described in Chapter 9 of this book.

Second, Piaget has identified stages of reasoning that are derived from his notions of preoperational, concrete, and formal thought. Since the developmental stages are not rigid, well-defined, and fully age-determined, we prefer to use the phrase "level of reasoning." Teachers should recognize and value their students' reasoning even though it may be at levels different from their own and may lead children to startling or incorrect conclusions.

To deal with students' reasoning, teachers first have to encourage them to explain or justify their conclusions, predictions, and inferences. "Why are you sure of that?" "Could you explain that, please?" "What is your evidence?"and "Why do you think so?" are questions that will get behind the conclusions if asked in a supportive manner. Teachers might invite volunteers or challenge able students at first, because they are more likely to make sound inferences and will be better able to provide justifications. Then other students can be asked to give their ideas. Above all, teachers should avoid creating the impression that they ask for an explanation only after a wrong answer has been given.

The levels of reasoning identified by Piaget will allow teachers to interpret and respond to their students' efforts productively. Students reason at different levels, and a particular student will even reason at different levels in different activities. Trying to classify any student as a "concrete thinker" or "formal thinker" is a mistake—we have found these terms to have little value. Instead, teachers first have to figure out what appropriate or inappropriate reasoning strategy is behind any student's words. Then possibly with the assistance of other students, teachers can make up new situations that allow the same reasoning to be used successfully. Even though specific steps in teaching will not always work out as intended, the notion that reasoning and explanations are important will be communicated to the students.

A good teaching procedure is to provide learning activities in which each student can find a challenge and succeed regardless of her level of reasoning. This approach presupposes activities to which different students can respond in different ways without being wrong. Designing such activities, which can be used for exploration or extension in a learning cycle, is a real challenge for teachers who are concerned about their students' development of reasoning.

Here are some ways to begin by turning around traditional activities: (1) Given a language arts activity with a specified list of nouns to be put into blanks in sentences, students choose their own words or even make a brief list for each of the blanks and explain why their selections are acceptable. (2) Given a mathematics activity on using formulas, students are asked to make up a set of problems in which a given set of formulas is applied, and then to explain how they went about this task. Note how simply students can be involved in a more active, more thought-provoking, more creative fashion. At the same time, their ideas allow the teacher to diagnose misunderstandings rather than merely to identify ignorance of certain facts.

BIBLIOGRAPHY

This bibliography is in keeping with the theme of the chapter; it is only a beginning. The sources listed were selected because they provide an introduction to Piaget's theory.

Boden, Margaret A. *Jean Piaget*. New York: Penguin Books, 1980.
    This little book is one of the best *brief* introductions available. It is highly recommended.
Brainerd, Charles J. *Piaget's Theory of Intelligence*. Englewood Cliffs, N.J.: Prentice-Hall, 1978.
    A good balanced presentation and evaluation of Piaget's theory.
Bringuier, Jean-Claude. *Conversations with Jean Piaget*. Chicago: The University of Chicago Press, 1980.
    Over a period of several years Bringuier interviewed Piaget concerning his life and work. The conversations are reproduced here for a warm introduction to Piaget and a succinct presentation to the theory.
Elkind, David. *Children and Adolescents: Interpretive Essays in Jean Piaget*. New York: Oxford University Press, 1970.
    This book provides an introduction to Piaget—the man and his ideas—in the context of education. It is interesting, readable, and applicable.

Flavell, John H. *The Developmental Psychology of Jean Piaget.* New York: Van Nostrand Reinhold Co., 1963.

This is a classic work on Piaget's theory. It is comprehensive, objective, and critical. It is also graduate level reading.

Gruber, Howard E. and Vonèche, J. Jacques, eds. *The Essential Piaget.* New York: Basic Books, 1977.

An excellent anthology of Piaget's work. The editors have identified the *essential* Piaget. An outstanding reference and interpretation.

Piaget, Jean. "The Stages of the Intellectual Development of the Child," *Bulletin of the Menninger Clinic* 26 (1962). Reprinted in Munsinger, Harry, ed. *Readings in Child Development.* New York: Holt, Rinehart & Winston, 1975.

An excellent introductory article, though slightly abstract.

————. "Cognitive Development in Children: Development and Learning." *Journal of Research in Science Teaching* 2 (1964): 176–86.

A very good discussion of the contrast between Piaget's developmental theory and learning theory. Stages are briefly presented.

————. "The Mental Development of the Child," in *Six Psychological Studies.* New York: Random House, 1967.

This is probably the clearest statement by Piaget of his theory. It includes both cognitive and affective development. An excellent place to start reading Piaget.

————. *Science of Education and the Psychology of the Child.* New York: Grossman Publishers, 1970*a*.

Piaget places his theory in the broader context of education. Historical, philosophical, and psychological foundations of education are incorporated into the discussion.

————. "Piaget's Theory." In *Carmichaels' Manual of Child Psychology,* edited by P. H. Mussen. New York: John Wiley & Sons, 1970*b*. Reprinted in Inhelder, Barbel, and Chipman, Harold. *Piaget and His School.* New York: Springer-Verlag, 1976.

A short treatment of the theoretical concepts underlying Piaget's theory. Important for understanding Piaget's position in relation to other theorists.

Piaget, Jean, and Inhelder, Barbel. *The Psychology of the Child.* New York: Basic Books, 1969.

This is the best introductory book. Though uneven in places, the authors have done a good job of presenting a comprehensive and comparatively easy-to-read introduction to their theory.

IV | EVALUATION

Listed below are some of the main topics covered in Chapters 1 and 2. Read each statement and rate it on the scale TWICE: once according to what you knew about the topic before starting this part of the book and again according to what you've learned after completing it. Circle the appropriate number and mark B for *before* and A for *after* next to the number as indicated below.

Topic	Low		Moderate			High
Example: The distinction among important Piagetian mental operations	①B	2	3	4	5	⑥A
1. Piaget's life and work	1	2	3	4	5	6
2. How Piaget became involved in his life work	1	2	3	4	5	6
3. The names of Piaget's four stages and their age spans	1	2	3	4	5	6
4. The four factors contributing to learning	1	2	3	4	5	6
5. Accomodation	1	2	3	4	5	6
6. Assimilation	1	2	3	4	5	6
7. The role of student explanations	1	2	3	4	5	6
8. How to improve student explanations	1	2	3	4	5	6
9. The process of cognitive functioning	1	2	3	4	5	6
10. How to explain observations of student behavior	1	2	3	4	5	6
11. Basic characteristics of the sensorimotor stage and why we refer to "the active child"	1	2	3	4	5	6
12. Basic characteristics of the preoperational stage and why we refer to "the intuitive student"	1	2	3	4	5	6
13. Basic characteristics of the concrete operational stage and why we refer to "the practical student"	1	2	3	4	5	6
14. Basic characteristics of the formal operational stage and why we refer to "the reflective student"	1	2	3	4	5	6
15. How children's minds vary from those of adults	1	2	3	4	5	6

 # The Sensorimotor Period and the Active Child

This chapter starts with several questions about infants and a general discussion of the first two years of development. Then we shall proceed to a formal introduction to Piagetian concepts and processes of the sensorimotor period. The last section of the chapter provides several opportunities for you to extend and apply your understanding of Piaget's theory.

I | EXPLORATION
THE SENSORIMOTOR PERIOD

Probing the Period

How would you describe the origin and development of different behaviors in infants?

1. They are responses to the environment that are impressed on the infant's mind.

2. They are the result of exercise and expansion of preexisting programs for behaviors.

3. They are imitations of behaviors the infant observes.

4. They result from a series of groping actions that are selectively reinforced.

5. They are the result of continual modification and elaboration of biological reflexes.

44

How do you think infants come to understand different factors about their world (e.g., objects, time, space, causality) during the first two years of life?

1. This occurs through biological maturation of the nervous system.
2. This occurs through experiences they have with their environment.
3. This occurs through trial-and-error learning.
4. This occurs through their need to adapt their physical actions to their environment and their environment to their needs.

What is the role of play in the development of intelligent action?

1. This is one aspect of adapting that occurs primarily through the modification of reality to existing actions.
2. This is one aspect of intelligence that occurs through spontaneous biological development.
3. This is not an aspect of intelligence since infants are not capable of spontaneity, pleasure, disinterested activity, lack of organization, and freedom of conflicts—all of which define play.
4. This is synonymous with imitation, which means behaviors are developed, but they are not intelligent.

What is the role of imitation in the development of intelligent action?

1. This is synonymous with play, which means behaviors are developed, but they are not intelligent.
2. This is one aspect of adapting that occurs primarily through the modification of existing actions to fit reality.
3. This is one aspect of intelligence that occurs through reinforcement of behaviors.
4. This is not an aspect of intelligence since infants are not capable of recognizing behavioral patterns, conceptualizing the patterns, and repeating them through coordinated actions.

An Introductory Discussion

The first stage of mental development, the sensorimotor period, is called this because a child interacts with the environment through her senses and motoric activity: hence, the subtitle—the active child. Humans are born with certain reflexes, such as sucking and grasping. As a baby moves about, she encounters stimuli which activate these reflexes. This behavior, however, tends to be global at first in the sense that, when the infant responds, she may be using several reflexes rather than just isolated ones. These reflex actions are the basis of what will later be intelligent action.

As the child encounters the environment, she slowly begins the assimilation-accommodation process. She increasingly senses stimuli (sensory reaction) and responds to them by moving her muscles (motor reaction). For example, a two-month-old baby girl may see a rattle and become aware of its existence. She tries to reach it. At first, she has difficulty. Her little hand stabs out from her body but misses the target. Her arm moves awkwardly until finally her hand feels the rattle. Slowly, by interacting with objects, the child adapts techniques to better organize muscular actions so that she can eventually hit a target the first time. By having numerous, similar physical experiences, she slowly begins to organize her grasping ability. She is building basic schemata for her mind.

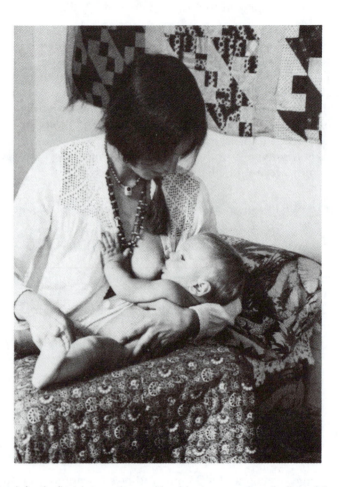

Though the infant's first interactions with objects are primarily linked to physical satisfaction, in these physical activities the infant actively adapts its reflexes to the environment.

Piaget theorizes that physical activity contributes to the development of intelligence. The infant's adapting her reflexes to objects around her enables her to eventually learn to perceive and discriminate. For example, when first born, an infant is incapable of differentiating a woman's nipple from the skin around it. By encountering the breast area through touch and vision, she soon assimilates and accommodates this difference. The more discriminating perceptions a baby makes, the better her chances are later to manifest good concept development. The infant's world is restricted essentially to practical interaction with objects within her immediate environment which are linked to physical satisfaction. Time is now. She neither thinks of the past nor the future. Space involves only that which surrounds her and is limited to the immediate area. She has little understanding of the space included in her home or yard. This gradually changes as she becomes more involved with activities relating to space, time, and causality. The young infant is confused about the difference between herself and the world around her. By twelve months, however, she differentiates between self and other objects.

Increasingly, as the active child experiences herself and her world, she begins to understand that she may control her actions. When an infant, she may cry because of discomfort, or she may be stimulated to cry by hearing another baby. As she gets older, however, she realizes that crying may satisfy some goal. By so doing she has learned to differentiate *means and goals*, demonstrating intention and intelligent behavior. For example, a baby may cry when being restrained by her mother from getting into the pots and pans. She may not be experiencing physical discomfort by such restraint but may realize that by crying needs are satisfied. This does not suggest that she performs a series of complete mental operations, such as "I want to get into the cupboard; mother is holding me back; therefore, I shall cry." Not at all. The child only knows that she cannot get the pans. If she cries, she may get to play with the pots and pans. Often mothers aware of such behavior give the child attention by picking her up or using some distraction to modify her response. How many times have you seen a mother divert the interest of a child from crying or doing something she did not want her to do? She can accomplish this because the sensorimotor child is easily diverted from her original goal because her conception of objects, space, and time is very limited.

Although intelligent behavior is developing, behavior, at this point, is preverbal. Also, in a sense, the infant is *bound by the stimuli* about her rather than being able to originate them from her own thought. However, even in the first months of life, the child does demonstrate some inner stimulation as seen when she originates suckling even though there is nothing present to nurse, when she originates behaviors apparently only for the sake of exercising her newly found capacities.

II | EXPLANATION
THE SENSORIMOTOR PERIOD

Though this period is prior to preschool age, it is not to be overlooked or taken lightly by educators. The very foundation of intelligence is established during the first years of life. The primary task of the period is acquiring and using elementary capacities that will later become intelligent thought. There are several ways of expressing the dominant themes of this period: it is a time of transition from innate reflexes to intellectual representation; it is a time of transition of biological foundations of behavior to psychological foundations of behavior; it is a time of transition from a reality that only is self to a reality that includes others and the environment.

As the infant gets older, crying becomes more than a response to a stimulus, such as discomfort; the child realizes that crying may satisfy some goal.

This section is primarily based on three texts written by Piaget: *The Origins of Intelligence* (1952), *The Construction of Reality in the Child* (1954), and *Play, Dreams and Imitation in Childhood* (1951). Piaget's original observations were based on his own children. Research by others has generally confirmed the stages and behaviors originally described by Piaget.

Stages of the Sensorimotor Period

Piaget spent considerable time observing and investigating the behaviors of his three children as they progressed through this period. He concluded that a child passes through six stages of development in the sensorimotor period. The development progresses in a definite sequence, but the age of attainment of each level may vary considerably from child to child.

Six Developmental Stages of the Sensorimotor Period

Stage One (0–1 month).   Innate reflexes begin to function. Initially an innate reflex, such as sucking, is purely functional. But, before long there is an apparently nonfunctional "exercise" of the reflex. The infant sucks on nothing or sucks on objects other than a nipple. The exercise and extension of innate reflexes provide the infant with environmental experiences that go beyond a strictly biological realm. For example, sucking a nipple, thumb, blanket, and nothing are different experiences. They also strengthen the initial schemes and prepare for their later consolidation.

Stage Two (1–4 months). Primary circular (repetitive) reactions involved with the infant's body develop. Actions are nonpurposeful and repetitive for their own sake (e.g., thumb sucking and fingering blankets). During this stage the reflexive schemes are strengthened through repeated use. While there is formation of habits, there are not complete acts of intelligence since the infant does not establish an end and then pursue the goal through the use of means. The means and ends are to be found in the actions themselves (e.g., sucking for sucking's sake, grasping for grasping's sake, looking for looking's sake). All of this activity is in "preparation" for the next stage when the circular, or repeated, actions extend beyond their innate bounds and coordinate with each other.

Stage Three (4–8 months). Secondary circular (repetitive) actions develop. Now the child manipulates objects (e.g., pulls toys toward him). These are secondary reactions since their origin is not innate. Rather, the actions are acquired through the coordination of schemes. Actions are no longer repeated for their own sake but because of the interesting stimuli they develop. For example, a child hits a hanging toy in his crib several times, demonstrating his ability to apply a scheme—hitting a toy. In this last example, we notice another characteristic of the stage—the infant's use of the same behaviors to try and make something interesting last. Now, there is greater input from the environment; in classical learning theory, there are external contingencies of reinforcement. In contrast, at Stage Two the primary circular reactions were internally reinforcing. In some cases the infant will use the old actions to achieve new ends. While obviously not successful, this behavior does indicate that the infant is on the verge of intelligent behavior.

Stage Four (8–12 months). So far we have seen a continuous sequence of adaptation and coordination leading toward intelligent action. The infant has gone from single reflex actions to habitual actions to coordination of actions. The next step is practical intelligence. In some respects this stage is like the last. Existing schemes are consolidated and expanded as the infant adapts to new situations. Self and world are not differentiated. By practical intelligence Piaget means that new coordinations of schemes are established as the infant tries to achieve a goal. But, the coordination uses only existing schemes. Infants solve problems through the application of existing schemes to new situations.

Stage Five (12–18 months). Tertiary circular reactions develop. These reactions allow the infant to create new behavior patterns in order to resolve new problems. The behavior patterns are best described as "directed groping." The child explores the environment. The child's behavior is intentional; that is to say, it is intelligent by Piaget's criteria. The child is able to systematically adapt schemes of action in order to achieve some purpose. By the end of Stage Five, the infant is progressing toward mental representation.

Stage Six (18–24 months). The transition from overt to covert representations occurs at this stage. The child can reproduce from memory and use symbols to refer to objects not present (e.g., dog, mommy, daddy). He can represent the existence of objects and his actions. If the child is confronted with a problem, he is able to go beyond physical groping (Stage Five) and internalize the problem—think about it—until he has a comprehension and insight into the problem's solution. What might happen at this stage looks like this. A child has been unsuccessful in opening a small box. The child will cease the actions of grasping, pulling, and so on and appear to examine the box, thinking about the problem until there is a new comprehension of the problem and the ability to open the box.

Across the six stages of the sensorimotor period we have seen progress from inherited actions to intelligent actions. We have seen the process of continual reconstruction of basic schemes so they were more adapted to the infant's expanding world. All of this culminated in the capacity for intelligent behavior in response to new situations. These stages set the foundation for further development.

Objects, Space, Time, and Causality

Development through the sensorimotor stages results in representational thought. There is another significant development of the period. The child also constructs broad categories that organize the world—objects, space, time, and causality. At birth these organizational categories are not present. During the next eighteen months to two years, there is continuous realization of a reality beyond.

As the sensorimotor child progresses through this stage of development, he begins to center more on what is happening about him. Slowly, he manifests *object permanence*. That is, he comes to realize that objects continue to exist even when not in his perceptual field.

Six Developmental Stages of Object Permanence

Stage One (0–1 month). The child does not differentiate objects from self. He looks at an object only while it is in his field of vision.

Stage Two (1–4 months). He still does not differentiate between object and self but follows an object and continues to look at the point where it has been even though it has disappeared. A child of this period clearly demonstrates the role of experience in development. For example, he will search for his bottle if the nipple is exposed, but if the bottom of the bottle is slightly shown to him from beneath the covers, the infant will not attempt to uncover it to find the nipple. He has developed some object comprehension about the nipple but not of the entire bottle.

Stage Three (4–8 months). The child briefly searches for objects that have vanished from his grasp. He also anticipates where a moving or falling object will be. The child will search for a partially hidden object but will not search for a completely hidden object.

Stage Four (8–12 months). At this stage the child searches actively for completely hidden objects. If an object is moved from one hiding place to another, the infant looks for it in the first place. So, while the child has a concept of object permanence, he cannot follow successive displacements of an object.

Stage Five (12–18 months). The child realizes an object remains the same even though visibly it appears different because of distance from it. He searches for an object where he last saw it rather than going to the place where it was first hidden. However, if the infant has to infer where an object should be, he may start to look for it in the first place, not the second or third.

Stage Six (18 months). The child achieves the concept of object permanence; he realizes that objects exist separate from self and that they may move in space.

An understanding of the object permanence sequence establishes a relatively good basis for comprehending the child's evolution through this period. It should be further noted that, until and including Stage Three (four to eight months) of the sensorimotor period, the child has only a rudimentary sense of direction and purpose. He cannot move an object without forgetting where he placed it. He may, for example, see his father dangling keys and be stimulated by their glitter and noise. The father slyly places them under the newspaper. The child heads for the father, but once he reaches him, and the keys are no longer present, he may crawl to some other part of the room even though he saw his father place and leave the keys under the newspaper. The child, in a sense, has forgotten the keys while heading toward his father. He has not yet developed the ability to hold in his mind the object. Furthermore, he is unable to remove an obstacle without forgetting where he is going.

By the eighteenth month (Stage Six), however, the sensorimotor child searches for objects hidden in his presence. If you dangle keys before him and place them under a pillow, and then under another and another, he will follow the pattern you used to hide them and go to the last pillow first to obtain the keys. He is now capable of retrieving and retracing a series of actions.

Object permanence is a significant advancement because permanent objects help the child deal with reality. The child no longer just reacts to their presence but begins to understand their properties. Object permanence, Piaget believes, is basic to the development of concepts of identity. First, the child realizes the object is maintained even when out of sight. Later in the child's development, he will come to realize that several actions may be imposed upon an object without its basic identity being altered. For example, the child may fold aluminum foil into many shapes but still realize it is foil. The folding does not alter the identity of the foil. Obviously, the development of conceptualizations of identity is fundamental to the achievement of the various forms of conservation which begin to appear late in the preoperational stage.

Figure 3.1 is a summary of sensorimotor development. Take some time and read over the columns and rows. Doing so is very instructive in gaining an understanding of the interrelationship among many of the ideas of this chapter. Note that at Stage One behavior is reflexive. The infant has no conception of objects (including self), space, time, or causality. There is no conception of reality at this level; there is action. In particular, Piaget posits that there is a spontaneous exercise of the reflexes (called reproductive or functional assimilation) and this exercise has two results important to cognitive development. There are "generalizing" assimilation (i.e., sucking on new objects or no objects) and "recognitive" assimilation (i.e., distinguishing between objects to be sucked and those not to be sucked).

In Stage Two the infant continues to exercise the reflexes and thus further generalizes function and recognition. Still, reality is very much concerned with *me*, *here*, and *now*. This characterization must be understood in context; namely, there is no conception of *other*, *there*, and *later*.

By Stage Three there is the first hint of intelligent behavior and behaviors imply rudimentary concepts of reality. If an infant tries to recover a toy that has dropped from her hand, these behaviors suggest *some* understanding that the toy continues to exist and does so in space and time. Further, her attempt to try and recover the toy indicates a means-end understanding, even though later recovery may be demonstrated by "magical" or inappropriate behaviors such as rhythmic arm waving instead of coordinated reaching.

At Stage Four the child shows the first behaviors indicating a conceptualization of reality. There is a consolidation of actions in an attempt to reach a goal, such as obtaining a toy. The goal has been directly perceived and the means of achieving the goal are already existing actions. This point should be clear as it differentiates this stage from the last. In the last stage, the infant had a rudimentary concept of a goal and only "magical" attempts to use actions to obtain the goal. In this stage, the infant can now apply known behaviors to achieve a new goal, rather than repeating some apparently inappropriate behavior. At the next stage the infant is capable of new means of action, elaborating new sets of behaviors in order to achieve new ends. All of these actions assume an expanded understanding of objects, space, time, and causality.

By Stage Five the child's conception of reality is fairly sophisticated. Objects are conserved and successive displacements of objects across time and space are followed. Likewise, cause and effect are seen in the infant's action as she attempts to recover displaced objects. New actions are devised as the infant seeks new ends. Still, however, the actions are not reflective; children do not make decisions based on abstract intentions. Piaget states it well: "The involvements between schemata are not yet regulated by a system of internal norms: the only verification of which the child is capable is of the type of *success* and not of *truth*" (Piaget, 1952, p. 240). This quotation captures the essence of the period; there is successful action but there is not reflective conceptualization.

Finally, at Stage Six the child shows intelligent action. There is some form of symbolic representation of persons, places, objects, and events. The child has a mental construction of reality, and she is able to adapt these representations to new and unique situations. These patterns of thought are preparatory to the intuitive thinking of children during the next major period of development, the preoperational period. Before going on to the next period, we shall examine the role of play and imitation as they relate to the adaptive process. The next section outlines Piaget's answer to questions of developmental process: How does the development of thought progress?

Play, Imitation, and Adaptation

How does the child's cognitive development progress from reflexive actions to reflective actions? The answer is important for educators. So, through discussions in this section, the process of cognitive adaptation and the twin processes of assimilation and accommodation should be clarified. In large part the discussion is based on Piaget's book, *Play, Dreams and Imitation in Childhood* (1951).

Figure 3.2 shows the relationship between imitation and play as they are related to the development of accommodation and assimilation respectively. Through the early sensorimotor period, activity is primarily assimilatory. The repetition of reflex schemes is used to gradually adapt to the environment through generalization. From the fourth stage on, when intelligent actions first appear, there is the application of known means to new situations (accommodation) and the modification of new situations to known means (assimilation). By the end of the period, the development of thought contributes to deferred imitation and symbolic play. Across the sensorimotor stages, imitative and playful behaviors can be seen as related to the differentiation of the dual processes of accommodation and assimilation. As assimilation and accommodation emerge, there is pronounced movement toward an equilibrium between them as they relate to adaptation (i.e., intelligent behavior).

At the end of the sensorimotor period, children demonstrate they are capable of simple play and imitation. They may act out a role or experiment with symbolic play as in language. For example, they may say "bird, bird." This type of language play further indicates that they are capable of evoking absent objects or events. They can also remember certain actions that can be called upon at will. In other words, they are forming the rudiments of representational thought which will manifest itself more clearly in the preoperational stage. Representational thought occurs when an individual conceptualizes something that is not present. This may be done through symbolic play or deferred imitation. However, this type of thought characterizes more clearly children beyond the sensorimotor period because they are less limited to external stimuli. Even so, children early in the sensorimotor period demonstrate that they are developing representational thought. For example, Piaget noted that his daughter Jacqueline, at the age of one year, four months, and three days, had a small visitor of one year, six months visit her who threw a tantrum. Jacqueline watched with interest, not having seen such activities before. The next day she screamed and stamped her feet in imitation of her friend. Jacqueline evoked the situation she had seen the previous day and closely duplicated it (Piaget, 1951, p. 63).

Figure 3.1 The Child's Developing Conception of the World

SENSORIMOTOR STAGE	OBJECTS Persons, places, and objects continue to exist when they are no longer in perceptual contact.	SPACE Persons, places, objects, and events are located in space.	TIME Persons, places, objects, and events occur with duration and time.	CAUSE/EFFECT Two objects, events, or persons close in time and space can influence one another.
I REFLEXIVE ACTIONS Birth–1 month Behavior is due to innate reflexes.	No concept of object permanence.	No concept of space.	No concept of time.	No concept of cause and effect.
II HABITUAL ACTIONS 1–4 months Behavior shows first acquired adaptations—primary circular (repetitive) reactions.	Objects are real only while visible—"out of sight, out of mind."	"Space" centers on child's own body and reflex actions—visual space, auditory space.	"Time" centers on infant's own body and action.	Cause and effect confused by infant's own feelings and actions.
III COORDINATION OF ACTIONS 4–8 months Behavior shows coordination of actions—secondary circular reactions and attempts to extend interesting sights.	First evidence of object permanence—short attempts to recover interesting objects often through inappropriate "magical" behaviors.	Some spatial coordination in order to extend interesting events and sights.	Rudimentary grasp of duration in prolonging attempts to find objects and to extend interesting sights.	"Magical phenomenalist" conception of causality. Actions are repeated to effect results—even if actions are inappropriate.
IV CONSOLIDATION AND APPLICATION OF ACTIONS 8–12 months Behavior shows coordination of secondary	Objects are conceptualized as permanent. Searching	Space is mostly person-al; there is an emerging concept of space.	Time is beginning to be defined by external referents—the first in-	Infants identify behavioral sequences and consequences.

Figure 3.1 The Child's Developing Conception of the World (continued)

SENSORIMOTOR STAGE	OBJECTS	SPACE	TIME	CAUSE/EFFECT
	Persons, places, and objects continue to exist when they are no longer in perceptual contact.	Persons, places, objects, and events are located in space.	Persons, places, objects, and events occur with duration and time.	Two objects, events, or persons close in time and space can influence one another.
circular reactions and application of actions to new situations.	behaviors continue if the infant is already directed toward the object. The infant has difficulty locating an object in time and space.		dication that displacements of objects are followed across time.	
V ELABORATION AND DIFFERENTIATION OF ACTIONS 12–18 months Behavior shows new actions—tertiary circular reactions and the development of new means to ends via groping.	Objects are conserved and successive displacements are followed to locate objects.	Development of concept of space in order to follow sequential displacements.	Objective time is conceptualized as something beyond personal involvement.	Recognizes causes and effects that result from own actions and actions of others.
VI MENTAL REPRESENTATION OF ACTIONS 18–24 months Behavior shows intelligent action—adaptation through mental representation.	Objects conserved and inferences used to locate objects hidden through complex and extended displacements.	Space is a general concept applying to all persons, places, and objects. Symbolic representation of spatial problems—spatial coordinates are followed or detoured in order to locate an object.	Time is a general concept applying to all persons, places, and events. Anticipation and memory are possible.	Cause and effect as objective concept—understands consequences by observing causes, infers causes by observing effects.

Figure 3.2
The Role of Imitation and Play in the Development of Thought

SENSORIMOTOR PERIOD The emergence of intelligence as an equilibrium between assimilation and accommodation.	IMITATION Transposition of child's activity to actions of others— primarily accommodation.	PLAY Transposition of objects to child's activity— primarily assimilation.
I REFLEXIVE ACTIONS Birth–1 month	No real imitation. Accommodation of innate reflexes to physical reality.	No real play. Assimilation of physical reality to innate reflexes.
II HABITUAL ACTIONS 1–4 months	Echo imitation—occasional repetition of gestures by imitating gestures of another person.	Exercise play—repeats possible actions for the sake of repetition.
III COORDINATION OF ACTION 4–8 months	Systematic imitation— repetition of another's gesture provided the child already can reproduce the gesture.	Exercise play continues. Differentiation between play and intellectual assimilation is advanced through secondary circular (repetitive) reactions.
IV CONSOLIDATION AND APPLICATION OF ACTIONS 8–12 months	Imitation of movements not visible on infant's own body, but the movements are already possible for infant.	Application of new schemes continued for own sake and the formation of new "play" schemes through combination of existing schemes without any effort at
V ELABORATION AND DIFFERENTIATION OF ACTIONS 12–18 months	Systematic imitation of new models, including movements invisible to the infant. Systematic accommodation of schemes to situations beyond limits of adaptation.	Chance combination of unrelated gestures—repetition of gestures in a ritualized motoric game. Assimilation is clearly beyond the limits of adaptation.
VI MENTAL REPRESENTATION OF ACTIONS 18 months–2 years	Deferred imitation—mental representation makes internal accommodation of schemes before external modification of movements. Accommodation dominates over assimilation.	Symbolic play—mental transposition of objects to child's activity. Assimilation dominates over accommodation.

The Active Child

The sensorimotor child spans a tremendous cognitive distance in two years. The infant grows from a reflex dominated creature to a dynamic, reacting, and sometimes exasperating little rascal. The active child has adapted and learned how to obtain satisfaction, thereby demonstrating to some degree intelligent behavior. The active child has advanced from being able to make slight discriminations to identifying objects, places, and people. The sensorimotor child has slowly evolved to some understanding of causality by knowing objects can be removed and replaced. Object permanence has been attained. There has been movement from a gurgling infant to one using verbal means of communicating. The active child has left the crib to become involved and experiment in play by acting out roles and in imitation. Because the infant has developed these and other mental abilities, she is capable of moving intellectually into the preoperational stage.

We shall provide a continuing summary of development across the four stages discussed here and in the next chapters. Figure 3.3 is the first such summary.

Figure 3.3

A Child's Developing Understanding of the World: The Sensorimotor Period

Content	Beginning Characteristics	End Characteristics
Action	Reflexive physical action	Representational thought
Objects	Not permanent	Conceptualizes objects as being permanent
Space	No concept of space	Conceptualizes immediate space
Time	No concept of time	Conceptualizes short sequences and durations between events and persons
Causality	No concept of cause/effect	Conceptualizes simple cause/effect relationships
Play	Repetition of reflexes	First symbolic play
Imitation	Repetition of reflexes	First deferred imitation
Self	No concept of self	First concept of self and others
Language	No language	First language

III | EXTENSION
THE SENSORIMOTOR PERIOD

Observing Infants and Administering Tasks

One of the best ways to extend your understanding of infant development during the sensorimotor period is through observing infants and administering simple tasks to them. In some cases these observations may be made on your own children or those of a neighbor. The following suggestions may help with your observations:

1. *Establish rapport*. Develop a rapport with the infant so he will behave in a normal manner while you are present.

2. *Think about your observations*. Review the six stages of the sensorimotor period. Then, as you observe children, try to formulate hypotheses about their actions.

3. *Allow time for observations*. Schedule enough time to formulate overall patterns of action and behavior.

4. *Have fun*. Most of all, try to have fun while learning more about the origins and development of children's thought.

Observing infants (ages 1 month–2 years).   Actually the task here is to set up a situation where you can observe the behavior of infants. You might volunteer for a round of babysitting for friends who have infants at different ages. Observe your own children or younger brothers, sisters, nephews, or nieces.

The objective is simply to observe and think about infant behaviors and their relationship to the development of intelligence. Depending on the age of infants observed, you might try to identify the following: primary, secondary, or tertiary circular reactions; imitation; and play.

Administering tasks relative to object permanence (5–6 months).   Show the infant an interesting object. Place the object within the infant's reach. When the infant reaches for the object, place a small cover over it. What was the child's response? How long did the infant continue to show interest in the object? Did the infant try to locate the object? Would you classify the behavior as "out of sight, out of mind"?

Administering tasks relative to successive displacements (6–12 months). Place an interesting object in front of the child. When the child has seen the object and shows some interest in it, place the object under a cover to the child's left. Then immediately remove the object and place it under a similar cover on the infant's right. Now allow the child time to recover the object. Did the child look for the object? Which cover did the child look under first? Did the child look under the first and then the second cover? Did the child go directly to the second cover, thus demonstrating object permanence and the ability to follow successive displacements across time and space?

Administering tasks relative to causality (10–12 months).   Show the child an interesting object. Then place the object out of the child's reach but on a blanket that is within reach. Does the infant pull the blanket in order to obtain the object? Next, repeat the procedures but place the object *beside* the blanket. You might also try placing the object on a second blanket that is in front of the child. Does the child pull the first or second blanket?

Does Piaget's Work Explain Animal Intelligence?

I. David Welch
Department of Psychology
University of Northern Colorado

One of the questions that has occupied psychologists since the beginning of experimental psychology is whether or not animals are intelligent. Many thought that the question of animal learning and intelligence had been solved by the early connectionists and behaviorists. Their conclusion was that while animals learned, they did so by a kind of blind fumbling (trial and error) which then built up habits (this represents a crude but essentially fair summary of their conclusions). J. B. Watson's hard-core behaviorism succeeded in extending the same conclusion to people. Early psychology (the beginning of the twentieth century) was fairly smug in the conclusion that animals had no higher reasoning powers. Then, in 1925, W. Kohler published his work, *The Mentality of Apes*, in the United States. Kohler's experiments demonstrated what has come to be called insight learning and seriously challenged the conclusions of the early behaviorists. Although much effort was spent in trying to explain them away, Kohler's research revealed the philosophical shortcoming of early psychology. Unfortunately, many people today still hold to a trial-and-error method of learning that has long been questioned in psychology.

Curiously, while psychologists were hard about proving animals couldn't think, pet owners were equally convinced they could. No matter what the animal psychologists said, people with dogs and cats (not to mention monkeys, chimps, horses, or pigs) watched them solve problems that seemed to them to require thought. What caused this difference of opinion between the scientists and the pet owners? Partly, it was due to the philosophical basis of behaviorism which didn't allow for thinking, as most of us think of it, for any creature. This was the philosophical flaw Kohler's work exposed. On the other hand, it is perfectly possible that common sense is often much more common than it is sensible. People who claimed their animals were solving problems with thought might just have been giving more credit to their animals than they deserved.

How does Piaget fit into all of this? It now appears that the argument lasted so many years because neither the early behaviorists nor the Gestaltists could demonstrate, to the satisfaction of the other, that they were right. We now know why. The problem was that they were both right! Or, rather, they were both partially right. This is where Piaget fits in.

As you have seen in this book, Piaget's first period of cognitive development is called sensorimotor intelligence. This first period is further separated into six stages. It is the last two that concern us here since the rough translation of these is that Substage Five is trial and error and Stage Six is insight. Thus, in Piaget's stage theory, humans go through both of these ways of solving problems and thinking. It seems that the early psychologists, by conducting different kinds of experiments, discovered that animals use these different ways of thinking as well.

To see the remarkable parallel, let's compare an observation of Kohler's apes (actually, chimpanzees) with Piaget's observation of one of his children.

KOHLER'S OBSERVATION
(by a keeper of Sultan, one of the smarter chimps)

Keeper's report: Sultan first of all squats down indifferently on the box, ...then he gets up, picks up the two sticks, sits down again on the box and plays carelessly with them. While doing this, it happens that he finds himself holding one rod in either hand in such a way that they lie in a straight line; he pushes the thinner one a little way into the opening of the thicker; *jumps up and is already on the run towards the railing*, to which he has up to now half turned his back, and begins to draw a banana towards him with the double stick. I call the master: meanwhile, one of the animal's rods has fallen out of the other, as he has pushed one of them only a little way into the other; whereupon he connects them again.[1] (Italics mine)
    1. From George W. Hartman, *Gestalt Psychology* (New York: Ronald Press, 1935), p. 161.

This is an example of what is called insight learning.

PIAGET'S OBSERVATION
(of his son, Laurent)

At 1;4(5) [1 year, 4 months, 5 days] Laurent is seated before a table and I place a bread crust in front of him, out of reach. Also, to the right of the child I place a stick 25cm. long. At first Laurent tries to grasp the bread without paying attention to the instrument, and then he gives up. I then put the stick between him and the bread; it does not touch the object but nevertheless carries with it an undeniable visual suggestion. Laurent again looks at the bread, without moving, looks very briefly at the stick, then *suddenly grasps it and directs it toward the bread ....* He begins by simply touching it, as though contact of the stick with the objective were sufficient to set the latter in motion, but after one or two seconds at most he pushes the crust with real intention. He displaces it gently to the right then draws it to him without difficulty.[2] (Italics mine)
    2. From Jean Piaget, *The Origins of Intelligence in Children* (New York: W.W. Norton & Co., 1952), p. 335.

This is an example of what is called the discovery of new means.

These descriptions seem remarkably parallel to me. Where do these descriptions of learning leave us? First, they provide some tantalizing suggestions for research. The most important is, of course, the question that is the title of this essay: Does Piaget's work provide a model that will help us understand animal intelligence? It becomes an intriguing question of whether Piaget's sensorimotor intelligence represents the upper limits of animal intelligence. Here are three examples of sensorimotor intelligence that may apply to animals: elementary language, problem solving, and memory. These are all within the province of sensorimotor intelligence and may all be within the abilities of animals. A question for research is how far down the evolutionary ladder these abilities extend.

Second, if it is true that Piaget's model explains animal intelligence and represents the upper limits of animal intelligence and that these limits include language, problem solving, and memory as they do in sensorimotor intelligence, then let us ponder how limiting and even dangerous it is to have educators who believe that our children still learn in any major way by trial and error. If you believe, as I do, that trial-and-error learning does not even represent the upper limits for animals, then any such belief for humans is incredibly disabling. It seems clear that language carries the human infant far beyond animals in complexity of thought and problem-solving ability

(Piaget's other, later stages of cognitive development). Further, if it is true that our beliefs have a profound effect on our behavior, then the belief that our children are limited to trial-and-error learning is dangerous indeed.

We are left with two conclusions. In the final analysis, those who believe that animals demonstrated problem-solving reasoning were closer to the mark. Piaget's work may explain all of the remarkable demonstrations of animal learning and training we read of so often in the newspapers (language, mourning, finding their way home over long distances, and so forth). Second, if we are impressed with the achievements of animals, then we can be amazed at the achievements of our own children who move out of sensorimotor intelligence into higher and higher complexities of thought. It is much like comparing a bicycle to a jet. I wonder what sort of schools we would have if we marveled at the abilities of our children rather than demeaned them?

Implications

The implications are few due to the limited capacities of the infant. As you read these suggestions, it is important to understand that there is a basic tendency toward continued development. And, a part of the infant's development is contingent upon action—motoric and/or cognitive.

1. Infants progress through six stages of intellectual development.

2. Infants at the same chronological age may differ in their behavior and understanding.

3. Development results from an interaction between the infants and their environment.

4. Infants should be stimulated through objects and events, for this facilitates the continual transformation of basic structures.

5. Infants should be allowed to explore their world, for their actions contribute to their construction of reality.

BIBLIOGRAPHY

Continued reading of Piaget's theory is a fine way to extend your breadth and depth of understanding.

Boden, Margaret A. *Jean Piaget*. New York: Penguin Books, 1980. See pages 22–42. A clear and concise discussion of the sensorimotor period. Criticisms of theory are included.

Brainerd, Charles J. *Piaget's Theory of Intelligence*. Englewood Cliffs, N.J.: Prentice-Hall, 1978. See pages 46–94.
An excellent discussion of supporting evidence for Piaget's theory of intelligence.

Ginsburg, Herbert, and Opper, Sylvia. *Piaget's Theory of Intellectual Development*. 2d ed. Englewood Cliffs, N.J.: Prentice-Hall, 1979. See pages 26–28.
One of the best introductory presentations of Piaget's theory.

Labinowicz, Ed. *The Piaget Primer*. Menlo Park, Calif.: Addison Wesley Publishing Co., 1980. See pages 60–69.

A practical and graphically illustrated presentation of sensorimotor development.

Piaget, Jean. *Play, Dreams and Imitation in Childhood.* New York: W. W. Norton & Co., 1951.

A discussion of play, imitation, and cognitive representation through the adaptive processes.

————. *The Origins of Intelligence in Children.* New York: W. W. Norton & Co., 1952.

A complete discussion of the six stages of sensorimotor development. Illustrations and analysis are good.

————. *The Construction of Reality in the Child.* New York: Basic Books, 1954.

The development of object permanence, time, space, and casuality are presented. The six stages are described for each of the above-mentioned content areas.

————. "The Child and Modern Physics." *Scientific American* 196: (March 1957): 46–51.

A superb presentation of Piaget's theoretical position as well as practical tasks related to the sensorimotor period.

————. "The Mental Development of the Child." In *Six Psychological Studies*, edited by David Elkind. New York: Random House, 1967.

A very good statement of Piaget's general conception of development.

Piaget, Jean, and Inhelder, Barbel. *The Psychology of the Child.* New York: Basic Books, 1969. See pages 3–27.

An excellent introduction to the theory of intelligence and sensorimotor period. Some discussion of affective development is included. Highly recommended as general introductory reading of primary material.

IV | EVALUATION
THE SENSORIMOTOR PERIOD

Listed below are some of the main topics covered in Chapter 3. Read each statement and rate it on the scale TWICE: once according to what you knew about the topic before starting this chapter and again according to what you have learned after completing the chapter. Circle the appropriate number and mark B for *before* and A for *after* next to the number as indicated below.

Topic	Low		Moderate			High
Example: Important Piagetian mental operations	①B	2	3	4	5	⑥A
1. The role of action in influencing cognition	1	2	3	4	5	6
2. The reason for calling this stage sensorimotor	1	2	3	4	5	6
3. How grasping contributes to cognition	1	2	3	4	5	6
4. The six stages of the sensorimotor period	1	2	3	4	5	6

5. The stages toward object permanence   1   2   3   4   5   6

6. The child's progression toward
   distinguishing ability   1   2   3   4   5   6

7. The development of play   1   2   3   4   5   6

8. The development of concepts of
   time and space   1   2   3   4   5   6

9. The development of naming ability   1   2   3   4   5   6

10. The role of imitation in development   1   2   3   4   5   6

11. The origin and development of
    intelligent behavior   1   2   3   4   5   6

12. The development of causality   1   2   3   4   5   6

13. The role of circular reactions
    in development   1   2   3   4   5   6

14. The reason for characterizing the
    child of this period as the active child   1   2   3   4   5   6

4 The Preoperational Period and the Intuitive Student

Between the ages of two and seven, children break the bonds of infancy. Adults have a difficult time imagining all that a child learns in this short period. In five years the child extends social interactions beyond the immediate family, acquires the formalities of language, increases self-care skills, and starts school.

When children reach the age of two or three, adults change their perceptions of them. Many things that were appropriate during infancy are no longer acceptable. Yet, in many respects children are simply not ready for an adult world. In the adult world the child cannot do many things, especially when it comes to logic and rational thinking. So, while this period may seem grey by comparison with what is to come, it is still one of tremendous growth and development.

I | EXPLORATION
THE PREOPERATIONAL PERIOD

Probing the Period

The following interview was with Michelle who at the time of the interview was two years two months. Michelle was given several Piagetian tasks where materials are presented, then modified in some manner.

Task 1. Michelle was shown two containers of different sizes. The containers had colored water.

Interviewer. Do you see these two containers, Michelle?

Michelle. (Nods affirmatively.)

Interviewer. Do the containers have the same amount of liquid?

Michelle. (Again nods affirmatively.)

Interviewer. (Pours water from one container into a small flat dish.) Now, is this the same water that we had in this container?

Michelle. Yes.

Interviewer. Is there more, less, or the same amount of water as we had in this container?

Michelle. The water doesn't fit.

Interviewer. Do you mean this container has more?

Michelle. Yes.

Interviewer. Why do you think the amount of water is more?

Michelle. Because.

Interviewer. Can you tell me why you think there is more water?

Michelle. The water is red. Cats need water to drink. (Pointing to the empty container.) Why doesn't this have red water now?

Questions

Why do you think Michelle knew the water was the same but the quantity had changed?

How would you explain Michelle's answers?

Task 2. This task involves a pencil falling from a vertical to a horizontal position. The child is then asked to arrange pictures of pencils in a sequence from vertical to horizontal.

Interviewer. Now we'll play another game. For this game I want you to think about how a pencil falls. This is what I mean. (Pencil is placed in a vertical position on the table and allowed to fall to a horizontal position.) Did you see that, Michelle? Watch again. Did you see the pencil fall?

Michelle. (Nods affirmatively.)

Interviewer. Here are some drawings of a pencil falling. Look at these pictures and put them in order, showing how you saw the pencil falling.

Michelle. (Sits, looking confused.)

Interviewer. Which picture comes first? Which one looks like the pencil before it fell? Remember? Do you see a picture here that looks like a pencil before it fell down?

Michelle. (Randomly pointing to a picture with a pencil about forty-five degrees from vertical.) This one.

Interviewer. Did the pencil start like that, Michelle?

Michelle. Do it again.

Interviewer. (Repeats task.) Now can you put these pictures in order? Which one is first? (Shows her the correct picture.) Is it this one?

Michelle. (Shrugging.) I don't know.

Interviewer. You don't know. Can't you remember seeing the pencil fall? (Shows her again.) Now let's really try.

Michelle. (Puts several pictures together, but it seems to be more to please the interviewer than a thoughtful action.)
Interviewer. Why did you place the pictures in this order?
Michelle. Because.
Interviewer. What do you mean by "because"?
Michelle. I want them this way. I like them.

Questions

Why do you think Michelle had so much trouble with the sequence when she had seen the pencil fall several times?
Why do you think Michelle justified her answer as she did?

Task 3.   In this task the child is required to conserve area.

Interviewer. This game is going to be fun. What are these, Michelle?
Michelle. Cows.
Interviewer. That is correct; they are little cows. Let's pretend that these two green sheets of paper are pastures for the cows, and that these red blocks are barns for the cows. (Places two sheets of green construction paper on the table and one cow on each sheet.) Now, do both cows have the same amount of pasture? The same amount of grass to eat?
Michelle. (Nods affirmatively.) Yes.
Interviewer. (Places four barns on each sheet of paper. On one sheet, the barns are grouped together in a corner. On the other sheet, the barns are spread around the sheet.) Now, will each cow have the same amount of grass to eat?
Michelle. Cows eat more grass because they are hungry. Put another barn on.

Interviewer. So, you want to build another barn. O.K., let's put one on this field right here (places it with the group in one corner) and another on this field. Do the cows have the same amount of grass to eat? (Points to the sheet with "barns" clustered in the corner.)

Michelle. This one is eating more grass.

Interviewer. Why do you think that one has more?

Michelle. Because, he's eating more grass. He has more grass to eat. He is very hungry and needs to eat, just like me.

Questions

Why was Michelle "tricked" about the size of the paper?

What factor seemed important in determining the amount of grass to eat? How would you explain Michelle using herself as a justification to the interview question?

Task 4. This is the classic Piagetian task involving the conservation of matter.

Interviewer. Look at the two clay balls, Michelle. Are they the same size?

Michelle. Yes.

Interviewer. I'm going to roll one into a snake.

Michelle. Do this one.

Interviewer. O.K. Do you want to help me roll it into a snake? You go like this. Can you roll the clay like this?

Michelle. Can't.

Interviewer. Here, let me help. (Finishes rolling the clay into a snake.) Does the snake have less, the same, or more clay as the ball?

Michelle. This snake.

Interviewer. This snake has less?

Michelle. More.

Interviewer. (Pointing to the snake.) Is this the same clay that used to be in a ball?

Michelle. Yes.

Interviewer. Why do you think the snake has more clay?

Michelle. Do this. (Imitates rolling the clay.) Do another snake, and you will see. Do this again.

Interviewer. (Repeats the question.) Why do you think the snake has more clay?

Michelle. Snakes are big.

Interviewer. Are all snakes big?

Michelle. Yes.

Interviewer. (Rolls the clay back into a ball for comparison with the second ball.) O.K. Now does this have more clay?

Michelle. Don't we have a snake anymore? The snake went home.

Interviewer. Are they the same?

Michelle. O.K. But what about the snake?

Questions

How would you explain Michelle's answers to this task?
Why could she not understand that the amount of clay stayed the same?
Why do you think she became intrigued with the snake aspect of the problem?
Give a general characterization of Michelle's explanations and thinking on these four tasks.

Reasoning Strategies: Reflexes to Representation

In the preoperational period physical actions become internalized mental representations. This means the child thinks of moving an object (a mental action) before he moves it. For example, a young child wants to pull a small wagon through a doorway. He pulls the wagon almost up to the door. Then he stops, looks at the door, and decides, imagining what will happen if he opens the door, that he needs to push the wagon back a bit before opening the door. He does this; he lays down the wagon handle, goes to the door, opens it wide, and then goes to the wagon and pulls it through the door. By so doing, he is demonstrating that he is capable of representing actions (i.e., opening the door) and that he has the capability of storing such actions in some form to be called upon as he needs them. The sensorimotor child may perform the same act if he sees his sister or brother pull the wagon—he will imitate their actions. However, the preoperational child is capable of imitating these actions in the absence of a model, demonstrating further his representational ability. The child may eventually think of one action and then replace it in his mind. He may combine several actions to produce a new behavior.

Performing these internal (cognitive) actions is fundamental to the development of more complex operational abilities. In other words, the path to logical thought progresses as follows:

Reflex Actions	Representation of Actions
Sensorimotor Strategies ⟶	and Intuitive Strategies
Ages 0-2	Ages 2–7

As we saw with Michelle, the preoperational child's thinking tends to be more static than dynamic. For example, if you drop a pencil from a vertical to horizontal position, then show the child a series of pictures of a pencil falling and ask the child to place the cards in order, showing how the pencil falls, she can't do it. She may, however, show the first pencil and the last one in the series. But sometimes she cannot even do this. A child such as Michelle focuses her attention on individual states, either of the pencil or pictures, and thus is not able to conceptualize the sequence of events. She cannot mentally represent a series of transformations. This level of thinking is further demonstrated by the child not conserving the amount of water or clay across transformations in simple tasks such as those described earlier. While the child has progressed from reflex action to varying degrees of representational thought, she is not capable of reversing her thought.

Preoperational children are animistic; they attribute living qualities to both animate and inanimate things

The Right to Read at the Right Time

GUEST
EDITORIAL

Virginia Ruth Johnson
School of Education
University of Denver

Of all the educational theories today, those of Jean Piaget are perhaps the most widely recognized and discussed. They may also be the most misunderstood and misapplied. Piaget has suggested that everyone talks about "hands on," experiential education but no one does anything about it. Unfortunately, I feel that his indictment of educators continues to be true. A brief visit to almost any public school at any grade level will produce ample evidence of this charge—you will see students filling out workbooks, filling in the blanks on dittoed worksheets, or reading textbooks. We are so avidly engaged in quantifying "right" answers and computing norms that schools frequently resemble an assembly line factory where "two-legged" computers are being programmed with the basic skills. But who is going to "punch" their keys? When are these children going to learn to think and to develop reasoning and problem-solving abilities?

Many obstacles face proponents of experiential learning. One of the problems which has a cumulative effect on students' learning begins in the primary grades. This is the national preoccupation with reading. Before I am misunderstood, let me state here that I believe, with very few exceptions, all children can and should learn to read. However, in our pursuit of reading competence for all, we have forgotten several very important facts: (1) Not all children are ready to read at the same age. (2) Not all children are ready to read by the first grade. (3) Not all children learn in the same manner. (4) Reading is a great deal more than decoding printed symbols on a page and mouthing words. Many poor educational practices stem from giving reading precedence over all other considerations in the primary grades. Unfortunately, much of this is in direct response to pressure from well-intentioned parents who wrongly equate early reading with intelligence. Acquiescence to this pressure is creating serious learning problems for many students.

Piaget's theories were developed empirically; however, support and confirmation of these theories come from understanding the physiological organization and development of the brain and nervous system. The entire brain grows and matures significantly after birth. This growth occurs postnatally because the maturation of these neurons requires specific stimuli for proper maturation and development. All of the brain's potential neurons are present at birth; however, they do not become functional until they are stimulated and used at the appropriate time.

Brain growth occurs in spurts, with each area requiring time to mature before the onset of the next set of neurons to be stimulated. These growth spurts correspond to the sequential emerging of abilities described by Piaget. Hurrying a child through a stage will not speed up brain growth. It will only deprive the child of the proper experience needed for stimulation.

Chronological age is not an accurate means of determining a child's development. It can measure neither the brain development nor the experience of the child. The child's responses to a Piagetian task will provide a much more accurate indication of the reasoning abilities, which do reflect true development. With this information we can match the instruction to the individual child's needs. Present methods, expecting all children to do the same things at the same time, force many children to struggle with abstract materials which they are not yet capable of mastering or understanding. On the other hand, this system causes some students to be held back when they are ready for more advanced and challenging work.

Knowledge of developmental stages will also help the teacher to reassure the parents of a first or second grader who is not ready for formal reading instruction. We must convince them that the time spent now developing language will enhance reading when the child is ready. The child will read more, learn faster, and have a better attitude toward learning.

Success in formal reading instruction requires understanding concepts such as class inclusion, conservation of number, and reversible thinking. Preoperational children do not meet these criteria, yet they are expected to learn phonics and to read. These competencies require neural brain connections not yet developed by the preoperational child. One of the greatest misconceptions today in education is that all children must learn to read by the end of the first grade, or they are retarded, emotionally disturbed, or learning disabled. A wide range of variability in development among children is normal. There is no magic age for brain development. The child matures when his genetic inheritance signals "time," not when the school mandates it because of chronological age.

Today's education students are trained to recognize individual differences and to use a Piagetian approach. Most teachers recognize the need for a child to learn at his own rate, but they all have to work within the present educational system—a system that is resistant to change. But change it must, because children think with their brains. They can only think with the neural connections that they have developed at any particular time. This, I believe, is the message from Piaget.

Mental Operations

As you have no doubt noted, this stage is called preoperational because the child is not yet capable of completing mental operations. We shall examine this idea since it is a characteristic that differentiates this stage from the next.

Central to Piaget's theory of intellectual development is his idea of mental action. This single idea is unique to Piaget's theory. Different theories of cognitive development have maintained different capacities to be the essential qualities of intelligence. For some theorists it is language, for some it is purposeful groping, and for others it is sudden comprehension and insight. But for Piaget, activity through the sensorimotor and preoperational periods is preparatory for mental operations and intelligence.

There are several defining characteristics of mental operations. First of all, mental operations occur in the mind; they are internal actions completed by the person. But there is more. If a child says that 3 plus 1 equals 4, he may or may not have completed a mental operation. A second characteristic of mental operations is that they must be reversible. Can the child in the last example also explain that 4 minus 1 equals 3 and 4 minus 3 equals 1? The latter are examples of reversibility through inversion or negation. Reversibility is also characterized by reciprocity or compensation. Reciprocal operations are very different from inverse operations. The same operation is reversed in inverse operations. Addition and subtraction serve as examples for inverse operations. A different operation is performed in reciprocal operations. Multiplication and division are reciprocal operations. Multiplying 2 times 4 is 8. Reciprocal operations include dividing 8 by 2 to get 4 or 8 by 4 to get 2.

Two other characteristics of mental operations should be mentioned. They are organized, and they occur in whole structures. The organization of mental operations has already been described. The reversibility of thought in mental operations is organized by the logic of inversion or reciprocal processes. Mental operations are organized into complete systems. Piaget calls these systems *structured ensembles*. These structures-of-the-whole or complete systems are best thought of as subsystems within a total system—the intellectual structure. Each subsystem can in turn be thought of as a complete system. Three distinct systems can be identified: (1) the total intellectual structure (i. e., stage); (2) middle level substructures that are identified by categories of action (i. e., time, space, matter, or classification); and (3) basic structures called schemes, which are the smallest system. All three levels of systems are organized and integrated, thus forming a whole system with entities that themselves can be discussed as a whole system. It may be useful to imagine the intellectual system as analogous to the human biological system with a total person who has subsystems such as digestive, skeletal, reproductive, or circulatory. These systems can be thought of as whole; yet they in turn have smaller systems such as organs and cells. The last point of the biological analogy is that all of these systems are organized, coordinated, and integrated as they function to maintain and improve a person's health. This analogy is a close approximation of Piaget's intellectual structure. Though discussed at different levels such as stages and schemes, the entire system operates as a whole, is coordinated, and functions to maintain and improve intellectual abilities. The cornerstone of this process is the person's ability to complete mental operations.

II | EXPLANATION
THE PREOPERATIONAL PERIOD

Several books written by Piaget are concerned with the preoperational period of intellectual development. Educators would be particularly interested in *The Language and Thought of the Child* (Piaget, 1955), and *The Child's Conception of Physical Causality* (Piaget, 1930). In addition, portions of other books are very helpful in understanding this period: *Play, Dreams and Imitation in Childhood* (Piaget, 1951), *The Construction of Reality in the Child* (Piaget, 1954), *On the Development of Memory and Identity* (Piaget, 1968), *Psychology of Intelligence* (Piaget, 1966), and *The Psychology of the Child* (Piaget and Inhelder, 1969).

Two Stages

The period of preoperational thought is divided into two stages: preconceptual thought, which occurs at approximately two to four years of age, and intuitive thought, which appears about age four and lasts until the concrete operational period. In the preconceptual stage the child's actions are mediated by representational thought (i. e., signs, symbols, and mental images). During this stage the child's concerns are associated with the development of language. While Piaget's theory attributes the development of language to the existing intellectual structure, there is no doubt about the role of language in the facilitation of development. The world can be symbolized, imagined; recalled actions can be imitated, deferred, and explained. Still, however, the child is at a preconceptual stage.

During the intuitive stage, the child explains problems (such as those given Michelle at the beginning of the chapter) in a prelogical manner. This is a step above the illogical, preconceptual explanations of younger children. Centering is often the problem at this stage. In order to resolve problems, children must center on the transformation of two or more variables simultaneously (e. g., changes in length and width of the clay balls, and height and width of the water displacement). For younger children the whole transformation is like magic; they comprehend little and give explanations based on one aspect of the problem, and often, something that sounds like magic. At the intuitive stage the child is able to center on different aspects of the problem (e.g., either height *or* width), and gives a better explanation, albeit incorrect, than the younger child. The child's intuitive answers indicate a partial coordination of actions or patterns of thought that are incomplete mental operations, but a preview of the logical explanations that can be expected in the future.

Reasoning Patterns

Two basic reasoning processes used by adults are inductive and deductive thinking. These processes are characterized as follows:

Inductive thinking—Reasoning from the specific to the general
Deductive thinking—Reasoning from the general to the specific

Example of inductive thinking:
   A. This apple has a stem.   Specific apple
   B. Another apple has a stem.   Specific apple
      Therefore:
   C. All apples have stems.   General conclusion

Example of deductive thinking:

   A. All apples have stems.   Generalization
   B. This is an apple.
      Therefore:
   C. It has a stem.   Specific conclusion

Preoperational children are incapable of reasoning inductively or deductively. They can, however, reason *transductively*. This means they reason from *particular to particular*. For example, the mother may prepare pancakes by heating the frying pan. To the child, preparing pancakes means the pan will be heated. If he comes into the kitchen another day and sees the frying pan being heated, he then thinks that pancakes are being prepared. His thinking processes are as follows:

A causes B

B causes A

His thought really is not based on logical processes, but on contiguity of phenomena he sees. He believes if some things occur together, there must be a causal relationship. He relates frying pan to pancakes because they are contiguous, and he may do this even though it is the wrong time of day to eat pancakes in his family.

Other examples of transductive reasoning are as follows:

Mother's cooking means dinner.

A ⎯⎯⎯⎯⎯⎯⎯⎯→ B

Dinner means mother cooked.

B ⎯⎯⎯⎯⎯⎯⎯⎯→ A

Santa Claus comes down a chimney.

Our house has no chimney.

No chimney ⎯⎯⎯⎯⎯⎯⎯→ No Santa Claus

Objects that occur together, he believes, must be causally related. The juxtaposition of Santa Claus and chimneys in his mind means to the child that a chimney is required for Santa Claus to visit a home. The child, in this case, centers on one salient element of Santa's visit—his coming down the chimney—and draws a faulty conclusion from it.

Sometimes, the child using transductive reasoning does come up with a correct answer. However, Piaget cautions that this does not indicate the reasoning pattern the child followed was anything other than transductive. The preoperational child as yet has neither developed the idea of logical necessity nor physical causality. Piaget believes that transductive reasoning occurs before and serves as a basis for the more sophisticated thinking processes following in the later stages of mental development.

A preoperational child is not capable of reversible thought. If you ask him "What is a duck?", he will say, "It's a bird." If you then ask "What would happen to the ducks if all the birds were killed? Would there be any ducks left?", he will probably say "Yes." To an adult this is clearly a logical inconsistency. The interviewer would then undoubtedly ask, "Why?" The child confronted with this demand would probably respond by giving an irrational answer such as, "They go swimming or fly away." The child gives these answers because he is not yet capable of performing mental operations. Even if the child is given instructions in what the answer should be, he will neither retain nor understand them. The reason for this is that the child is not yet capable of reversing his thoughts in the manner shown below:

REVERSIBLE THOUGHT

Ducks (a subclass) belong to the class birds.

If birds (the class) are destroyed, then the subclass, ducks, is also destroyed.

Mathematically, this is the same as saying that the child should be able to do the following:

$$1 + 2 = 3$$
$$3 - 2 = 1$$

This is way above the ability of a child of this stage because he is incapable of performing the reversible thought sequences or the mental operations required in *adding* or *subtracting*.

The preoperational child can't reason about his thinking. He is incapable of analyzing, synthesizing, and evaluating thoughts. We will now examine some other characteristics of children at the preoperational period.

Egocentrism

The word *egocentrism* often connotes selfishness or some other equally negative term. This is not the case with Piaget's use of the term. Until about eighteen to twenty-four months of age, children are not able to define self from the rest of the world, or simply stated, they do not differentiate "self" from "not self." With this "psychological birth" of the infant, there is increasing differentiation of self from the rest of the world. There is a steady process of decentering during childhood. Egocentrism is the degree to which a child views himself as the center of reality. Preoperational children are quite egocentric. It is not uncommon for them to think that all persons view the world as they do. Nor is it uncommon for them to explain phenomena in their world as personally oriented (e.g., the sun apparently moves across the sky from east to west, so it can follow them).

Piaget thinks that egocentrism permeates the majority of what children say and do during the preoperational period. Here is a comment by Piaget on egocentrism:

> However dependent he may be on surrounding intellectual influences, the young child assimilates them in his own way. He reduces them to his point of view and therefore distorts them without realizing it, simply because he cannot yet distinguish his point of view from that of others through failure to co-ordinate or "group" the points of view. Thus, both on the social and on the physical plane, he is egocentric through ignorance of his own subjectivity. (Piaget, 1950, p. 160)

As you can see in this quotation, egocentrism by a young child is not a conscious behavior. The child simply assumes all others see the world as he does. This characteristic should be noted by nursery school and kinder-garten educators. It may be worth the effort to realize that the child may simply be *cognitively* wrong. The remedy is time, social interaction, and experience. Educators are in an ideal position to provide experiences where children are required to take the perspective of the other.

Objects, Time, Space, and Causality

The child's conception of the world continues to expand during the pre-operational period. Objects exist and they are permanent even when not in sight. As we saw with Michelle, however, changing objects can confuse the child.

The preoperational child's concept of time has broadened since the sensorimotor stage. She now thinks not only of the present but the past and future as well. Her extension of time, however, is limited to short periods not too distant from the present, and her ability to predict durations or to arrive somewhere on time is very limited. The child's concept of space has also broadened from the immediate area in which she acts to the house, yard, and the neighborhood. However, the understanding of larger geo-graphic space such as state, country, and world is still very limited.

The child's conception of causality may be of particular concern for educators. Children at this level often seek a *final* explanation for the simplest event, yet give animistic and artificial explanations when asked to explain some phenomenon.

The preoperational child is animistic in his view of the world. He is animistic because he views all objects and events as if they were made or caused by humans. He thinks the sun, moon, mountains, lakes, and so on were made by humans. He is animistic because he also views phenomena and objects such as rocks, wind, buttons, and dishes as though they were alive and had psychological and logical attributes. For example, in his de-scriptions of motion, he might say: "Rocks fall because they want to, because they are mean." Of course, rocks do not have the human qualities of want-ing or meanness. He may also attribute human characteristics to plants and animals. For example, plants lose their leaves in the fall because they wish to change how they look.

Piaget tells the story of how he attempted to teach his young son more scientific explanations. One day as he was walking with him in Switzerland, they passed a lake. He asked his son, "How was the lake formed?" His young son replied, "A giant threw a rock and made it." Piaget replied that this was not so and described how the lake had been formed by a glacier. He then asked his son to repeat his explanation to ensure the boy understood, and the child did so.

Several months later, Piaget and his son again passed the same lake and he asked him how it was formed. The boy replied, "A giant threw a rock and made it." This explanation was maintained in spite of the efforts of the father. The child was not cognitively ready to incorporate a nonartificial explanation into his mind and didn't, as his responses demonstrate. He furthermore continued to believe that the lake was made through artificial and animistic means.

The above episode illustrates artificial thinking and problems with reality. It also shows that parents and teachers can be fooled about what a child is learning. In the lake episode, Piaget believed his son had learned the scientific explanation of its origin. The child initially gave his father satisfaction by telling him what he wanted to know about the lake's history. Unfortunately, this scientific explanation was not assimilated. Piaget would say that the child's parroting his explanation without a real change of mental awareness was an example of pseudolearning.

Parents and teachers should not be concerned about artificialistic explanations. They are natural. As preoperational children experience life, their minds increasingly progress in development. They naturally correct these misconceptions. By the end of the concrete operational period, most of these types of explanations will have been replaced by more adultlike explanations, without the cost of pseudolearning. A part of the educator's role is to improve the explanations so they are aligned with reality.

Number

The child of this period does not truly understand the significance of number. He may know how to count, but he doesn't comprehend the cardinal and ordinal meaning of numbers. For example, you may ask a six-year-old child if he can count. He may reply, "Yes." If you place your fingers in front of him and have him count, he will probably count up to ten. This counting, however, doesn't indicate he knows what he is doing. All he has done is demonstrate that he knows the names of numbers. He doesn't know their significant properties.

Before the child can comprehend the meaning of number, he must first develop mental operations. He has to know the names of the numbers and then place objects in a series. In ordering, he must realize that each of the members of a series are ordered according to some characteristic, and that they are not all equal. The development of the understanding of number by a child, therefore, occurs fairly much in the following way:

1. Learns the name of numbers
2. Learns to place objects in series
3. Orders objects by size or other characteristics
4. Cardinates—assigns the number name to the total members of a series or set (i.e., the fifth finger is number 5 because it is the fifth in order).

Language

During the preoperational period, the child's language is egocentric. Children often engage in monologs, repetitive statements, and dialogues (they should actually be thought of as monologs since they often do not actually include the second party). All of this is to say that while there is language, there is not much communication. For Piaget a prerequisite to language is mental representation, and as we discussed earlier, this aspect of cognitive development is just emerging at the preoperational period. As the child's cognitive structures develop, egocentrism decreases and the use of symbols and language increases. The egocentric language of the preoperational child is like the circular reactions of the sensorimotor period. It is an exercising of a capacity, and through the use of language, the child enhances the capacity and its function. Through natural processes language develops from an egocentric orientation to a public or socialized orientation.

Play and Imitation

Because of their egocentricity, preoperational children are incapable of playing cooperative types of games. They may appear to be playing a game, but what really is happening is that each child is playing a game independently of the others, with little or no concern about the actions of the others. This process of two or more children playing games independently is called *parallel play*, and it may persist into the preoperational period, but in diminishing degrees. The preoperational child also has difficulty in playing games because she confuses the fact that play and reality may operate under different rules. Furthermore, children before age four will not even follow rules. They do not realize that it is by mutual agreement that rules are determined.

Preoperational children often become fascinated with imitative, or make-believe play. They like to play house, store, etc. They will spend long periods of time playing with blocks and building things with wood or certain types of toys. Piaget believes this play fascination, in part, manifests itself because children are now capable of more representational thought. He further thinks that this type of representation is transferred to word symbols and contributes to the development of language.

Identity

The concept of object identity is an extension of object permanence and an important precursor to object conservation and mental operations which are evident at the next period. Piaget has discussed identity in his little book, *On the Development of Memory and Identity* (1968). While the conservation of matter deals with quantitative factors (e.g., weight and volume), the conservation of identity deals with qualitative characteristics. In the interview with Michelle, she *correctly* stated that both the water and the clay were the same after they had been changed, thus conserving their identity or qualitative characteristics. She did not, however, conserve the quantitative characteristics of the materials.

For Piaget identity is an important step toward full logical operations. In his book on this topic, Piaget states:

> However, well before it becomes operational, identity is already a logical instrument. I have often maintained the pre-operational structures were pre-logical, but drawing attention all the while to what I have called "articulated intuitions,"

that is, partial coordinations which sketch out future operations. Now we have found that there is indeed a sort of pre-operational logic, much broader than the notion of identity, which makes up in a way the first half of operational logic, that is, an oriented system which is sufficient as long as it is oriented in the right direction, but which lacks the inverse orientation, or in other words, reversibility. (Piaget, 1968, p. 24)

You can see the important connection among the nonlogic of the sensorimotor period, the prelogic of the preoperational period, and the logic of the concrete operational period. Being aware of the changing properties of materials is an important step toward understanding that materials are conserved across different changes.

The Intuitive Student

As indicated earlier in this chapter, preoperational children widen their perceptions of the environment and demonstrate the gradual evolution of structures, providing the base for operational thinking that emerges in the next stage of cognitive development. Due to the absence of logical reasoning patterns, students often resolve problems intuitively. Representational thought has increased, contributing to the acceleration of language development. They now speak using fairly complex sentence structures but still seldom use connectives in their language. Although preoperational children are still relatively egocentric, they are losing this egocentricity, as indicated by their increasing ability to play games and follow rules. They still, however, have difficulty differentiating among truth, fantasy, and realism in their explanations. Semilogic, using logical patterns of thinking but only in one direction, and transductive thinking have developed. Toward the end of the period these children begin developing the various types of conservation, starting with conserving substance. Their conceptualizations of space and time have broadened considerably from those of the sensorimotor period.

The intuitive student is unable to demonstrate many patterns of thought required in elementary education programs. Students often give intuitive answers when asked questions that require patterns of thought such as the following:

Adding: Combining objects, numbers, etc., to obtain a total.

Subtracting: Taking away objects, numbers, etc., to obtain a total.

Multiplying: Repeating addition.

Dividing: Repeating subtraction.

Corresponding: Aligning one row of objects with another of objects.

Placing in Order: Comparing size, weight, age, color, etc., in an increasing or decreasing order.

Substituting: Replacing something similar with another entity.

Reversibility: Realizing that subclasses belong to a class and that a class has subclasses.

Figure 4.1

The Child's Developing Understanding of the World:
Sensorimotor and Preoperational Periods

	Sensorimotor	Preoperational	
Content	Beginning Characteristics	End/Beginning Characteristics	End Characteristics
Action	Reflexive physical actions	Representational thought	Prelogical—Can reason in one direction
Objects	Not permanent	Permanent objects	Identity conserved
Space	No concept of space	Conceptualizes immediate space	Broadens concept of space
Time	No concept of time	Conceptualizes short sequences and durations of time	Aware of past, present, and future
Causality	No concept of cause/effect	Conceptualizes simple cause/effect relationships	Animistic explanations of cause/effect relationships
Play	Repetition of reflexes	First symbolic play	Representative play
Imitation	Repetition of reflexes	First deferred imitation	Representative imitation
Self	No concept of self	First concept of self/ not self	Egocentrism
Language	No language	First language	Egocentric language

Educators should be aware of the developmental levels of students and structure the learning sequence in such ways as to facilitate the development of logical operations by the students. Educators are encouraged to engage the intuitive student in problems that establish the cognitive structures that are fundamental to more developed patterns of thought. Suggestions include such things as the following:

Observation: Looking at objects and events critically.

Measurement: Establishing the length, height, width, volume of objects using a standard unit.

Quantity: Identifying how much there is of something.

Time: Describing events as present, past, or future.

Seriation: Putting objects in order by following a pattern or property to construct the series.

Classification: Grouping according to similarities, partitioning a group into subgroups based on some property, and arranging these in a hierarchy.

Space: Describing relationships among room, home, community, country, continent, world, universe.

Interpersonal Reactions: Getting along with others, noting the effects of one's behavior on others.

Counting of Objects: Realizing the meaning of cardinal numbers (e.g., 1, 2, 3) and ordinal numbers (e.g., first, second, third), setting up one-to-one correspondence and ordering objects according to number.

Educators should use concrete experiences whenever possible. Still, you should realize that questions about objects, events, or actions can result in illogical explanations, for this is the period of the intuitive student.

III | EXTENSION
THE PREOPERATIONAL PERIOD

Analyzing an Interview

This interview is with Patrick who was four years old at the time of the interview. The Piagetian tasks given in this interview are the same as those given to Michelle at the beginning of the chapter. Now that you understand more about children's explanations at the preoperational period, try to use your knowledge to explain Patrick's answers.

Task 1. Patrick was shown two containers of different sizes. A large slender container had colored water. A short, wide container was empty.
Interviewer. Now I'm going to pour the water from one container into the other. (The water is poured.) Is it the same water as before?
Patrick. Yes.
Interviewer. Is there less, more, or the same amount of water?

Patrick. More.

Interviewer. Why do you think the water is the same, but the amount is more?

Patrick. Because.

Interviewer. What do you mean by because?

Patrick. Because this dish is supposed to have more. I want it to have more.

Based on this explanation by Patrick, what can you say about his concept of identity? Conservation of water?

Task 2.   This is the "falling pencil" task. Actually the task concerns ordering events.

Interviewer. O.K. Patrick. For this problem you should think about a pencil falling. This is what I mean. (A pencil is placed in a vertical position on the table and allowed to fall to a horizontal position.) Did you see the pencil fall?

Patrick. Yes.

Interviewer. Here are some drawings of the pencil falling. Would you put them in order, showing how the pencil would look as it falls?

Patrick. (Doesn't say anything but starts arranging the pictures. He arranges the first picture and the last correctly. All the others are not in order. During the ordering, he seems distracted and confused. He keeps trying to change the subject.)

Interviewer. Why did you place the pictures in the order you did?

Patrick. Because it wanted to fall that way.

What is your analysis of this justification?

Task 3.   This is the conservation of area task. Two identical pieces of green construction paper were placed in front of Patrick. He was told that the

papers represented fields. One toy cow was then placed on each piece of paper. He was asked to compare the papers and establish their equivalence. He was then told that the blocks represent barns that two farmers were going to build on their fields. Four barns were placed on each paper. On one paper the barns were spread out, on the other they were grouped in one corner.

Interviewer. Now, will each animal have the same amount of grass to eat?
Patrick. (Shaking his head) No.
Interviewer. Which cow will have more grass to eat?
Patrick. (Points to one paper) This one.
Interviewer. Why do you think that cow has more to eat?
Patrick. 'Cause this cow is hungry. See—moo, moo.
Interviewer. How could that cow have more?
Patrick. I like them like that. See, he's still eating.

What is your explanation of Patrick's response on this task?

Task 4. In this task the child is asked about the conservation of clay as it is changed from a ball to a "snake" or "hot dog." Patrick was shown two clay balls.

Interviewer. Are these two balls of clay the same, Patrick?
Patrick. Yup.
Interviewer. O.K., now roll one of them into a snake.
Patrick. (Vigorously rolls out clay.) Look, a long snake.
Interviewer. Now tell me, Pat, is the snake still the same clay as it was before?
Patrick. Yup.
Interviewer. Is the amount of clay more, the same, or less than before?
Patrick. The snake is more.
Interviewer. Why do you think the snake has more clay?
Patrick. 'Cause, see, it's a snake and snakes are big.
Interviewer. Is there any other reason for the snake having more clay than before?
Patrick. 'Cause.
Interviewer. Is that a good reason?
Patrick. No, it's a boring reason.

What aspects of the preoperational period are demonstrated in this interview?

Interviewing Students: Tasks for the Preoperational Period

In this section the tasks are designed to probe children's thinking at the preoperational period. Each of the tasks to be administered outlines a basic structure for the interview. Certain specific suggestions for giving the tasks should be followed:

1. *Establish rapport.* It is important that the person giving the interview establish good rapport with the child before administering the tasks (i.e., ask her name, age, etc., as suggested on the interview form which follows). Tell her you have some games to play, and all answers are acceptable.

Try to make the tasks fun to do, smile while the child does them, and do what you can to lessen the child's feeling that the interviews are a threatening experience.

2. *Do not give answers.* Do not tell the child she is wrong or right, just accept her answer and either you or an assistant record them on the interview form.

3. *Ask for justification.* Always ask for the justification of an answer. In the interview we are interested in determining how the child thinks (i.e., Is she really conserving or is she just giving a correct answer?).

4. *Hypothesize about the child's thinking.* Formulate in your mind certain hypotheses about how the child is thinking. Ask the child questions to test your hypotheses to determine whether or not they are correct.

5. *Use the "another child told me" approach.* In asking the child to justify an answer, you may ask her why she thinks it is correct. Experience shows that some children will not respond to why questions. Generally, however, if you restructure your questions giving an episode like the following, they will respond: "The other day a boy told me that the rolled out clay in the form of a hot dog weighed just as much as the clay before it was changed. What would you say to him?"

6. *Allow for wait-time.* Remember that most tasks require some form of logical-mathematical reasoning. Thinking takes time. Therefore, do not rush the child in your interview. Allow her time to think; five or more seconds time allowance is not too much.

7. *Have fun.* Most of all, have fun giving the tasks and try to see that children have similar experiences.

The interview form on page 86 can be copied and used to note the task achievement of the child. It will probably be best for you to record the responses on this form after the interview, or have another person assist you by recording the responses while you interview.

The interview form needs some clarification. In each session you should *plan on giving several tasks*, seven or more to preoperational children. The time for administering these will vary from twenty to forty minutes, depending on the age and cognitive level of the child.

Place a description of each task in the left-hand column. Check in the appropriate column whether the child achieved or did not achieve the task. In the third column, write the stage the child attained. For example, if a child of four achieved multiple classification, you would write "preoperational."

With many children, you will not get a clear demarcation of stage. They might perform preoperationally on six tasks and concrete operationally on two. If this is the case, you probably would mark transitional on the basis of your limited interviewing measures.

We should add an additional note. All of these tasks can be used by educators as activities, games, problems, or puzzles to challenge children's thinking. As such they can provide the same information as tasks but obviously in a less direct and insightful manner. While the tasks can be used in this manner, we caution against evaluating or grading in terms of achievement. The point of the tasks is often the child's inability to resolve the problem. Evaluation and criticism of such answers are neither appropriate nor fair!

Piagetian Interview Form: Preoperational Period

Name of Child _____ Interviewer's Name _____ Location _____

Age ____ Grade ____ Sex ____

Activity description (e.g., conservation of substance, class inclusion)	Achievement: + Task achieved − Task not achieved	Indication of cognitive level (e.g., preoperational). Note: If child doesn't achieve level of task, it is assumed he is at a lower level.	Justification (child's reason for responding as he did)
1.			
2.			
3.			
4.			
5.			
6.			
7.			
8.			
9.			
10.			

How many tasks were achieved?

How would you classify this child's level of development? Preoperational? Transitional?

How would you justify this classification?

How could you confirm this level?

What are the educational implications of your interview?

The answers which are not acceptable as justifications for the tasks in this section are

1. No answer.
2. Wrong answer or no correct justification.
3. Magical type of response.
4. Reliance on authority (e.g., "My brother told me so").
5. Description of procedure.

As you listen to children explain their answers, you should try to identify

1. Animistic justifications.
2. Conservation of qualitative properties of materials and objects.
3. Egocentric justifications.
4. Prelogical (one-direction) responses.
5. Transductive (particular-to-particular) reasoning patterns.

Piagetian Interview Activities

Class inclusion.   Place several wooden beads in a dish. All of the beads except two should be the same color (e.g., two yellow, the rest red). Ask a child, "Are there more red beads or wooden beads?" What do you think the child will say? Why?

Next ask, "If I were to string the beads to make a necklace, would the necklace be longer if I used all the wooden beads or all the red beads? Why?" What will the child say? Why? What responses do you think a preoperational child will make?

Discussion. This is a class inclusion task in classification. Some children have difficulty realizing that what is said about the class is true of all of its members. They are overcome by perceptions—the number of red beads strikes them more than the fact that all the beads are made of wood. They may say, therefore, that there are more red beads than wooden beads. Piaget has found that the nature of the objects used in this task influences the results. For example, if you ask children even up to age seven or eight who are looking at several pictures of the cat family, with more pictures of tigers than other cats, whether there are more tigers than cats, they may not conceptualize the content of the problem correctly.

Conservation of substance.   Obtain some clay; make two round balls of equal size. Ask, "Are these two balls the same size?" If the child agrees, continue with the activity. If he does not agree, alter the putty until he thinks the balls are equal. Roll one of the balls into a hot dog shape. Ask, "Do I have more, less, or the same amount of material now as when I started? Why?" Then continue, "The other day a boy told me that there was more in the rolled out clay. How would you prove that he was right or wrong?"

Discussion. Children who think the flattened shape has more clay do not conserve substance. You can even weigh the clay before and after you roll it out. They still will believe, if they are preoperational, that the rolled hot dog has more clay.

Young children think if you do something with an object (e.g., change its shape), then its other properties (such as weight) also change. To conserve, children must realize that rolling out the clay only changes its form. If a child does not achieve this task, modify it slightly. Pick up the elongated piece of clay. Take some clay from one end. Ask, "What have I done to the clay?" Then, add this pinched off portion to the middle of the elongated clay. Ask, "What have I done to the clay now? Do I have as much, more, or less clay in the hot dog as when I first showed it to you?" Some children who do not conserve might do so with this modification. Piaget says some children indicate conserving in this manner around age 5½, whereas conserving without the interviewer's intervention usually does not occur until age 6 or 7. The achievement with the help of the interviewer would indicate the child is in transition to conserving substance.

To correctly indicate that they have achieved conservation, children should give in the justification of their answers one of the following:

1. *Invariant quantity*—state that nothing has been added or taken away from the material being conserved.

2. *Compensation*—indicate that something done to one part of the material is compensated for in another dimension. For example, in pouring water from a tall, narrow glass to a short, wide glass, the difference in the decrease in height is compensated for by an increase in the diameter or width of the glass.

3. *Reversibility*—state that if the substance were returned to the way it was originally, it would be the same.

One-to-one correspondence.   Obtain several objects that may be used as counters, such as coins, bottle caps, straws, toothpicks, etc. You may want to prepare one group of figures for the counters to make the activity more interesting. Line the counters up as indicated in Figure A and show them to the child. Ask, "What can you say about the two rows? Are there more stickmen than straws or are they the same?"

Take one of the counters out as indicated in Figure B. Ask, "What can you say about the length of the two rows now? Is there the same number of figures as straws, or does one row have more or less than the other?" Add a counter and rearrange them as shown in Figure C. Ask, "What can you say about the two lines? Are they the same, or does one have more or less than the other?" Have the children count each of the lines and ask, "What can you tell me about the lines? Is there more, less, or the same number of objects in each?"

Discussion. This task requires the student to do one-to-one correspondence. This means that he must note that for every counter there is in one row, there is one in the other row. Preoperational children in transition to the concrete stage usually center on the length of the rows. If the two lengths of the lines are the same, the children are perceptually impressed by this and say they are equal. Having them count the objects in each of the lines and then answer the question about the equal number in each line does not seem to help. Preoperational children think from situation to situation (i. e., count the counters in each of the lines) without relating them. As a consequence, they can count five counters in one line and four in another and still say the lines are the same because they are the same length.

One-to-one Correspondence. Obtain eight match sticks. Line them up as shown below. Ask, "Is each of these lines the same? Why?" Alter the

matches as follows. Ask, "Are the two lines the same? Why? Is there more, less, or the same number of matches in each line? Why?"

Discussion. See previous task for discussion.

Successive states vs. transformations. Obtain a straw. Hold it erect and have a child watch it fall. Ask the child to make a series of pictures to show how the straw fell. After doing this, show the child several cards as illustrated below and ask him to place the cards in order.

Discussion. Preoperational children usually center on beginning and end states of changes rather than on the transformations made in changing. As a consequence, they usually will get the first and the last picture in the series correct but mix up the others. To accurately place the pictures in order, they would have to conceptualize their observation and apply this to ordering the cards.

Relating Change. Show the child the diagram below or the apparatus and ask, "What will happen to the length of string A when weight is put on it? What will happen to the B length of string? Will the change in the B length be more, less, or the same as the change in A? Why?"

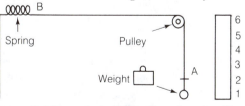

Discussion. Children of this period will realize that A will get longer and B will get shorter. However, since the child cannot think in quantitative terms, he usually thinks the gain in A is more than the loss in B.

Conservation of weight. Obtain some clay. Roll it into a ball, then in front of a child divide it into several small pieces. Ask, "Do all these pieces weigh more, less, or the same as the original ball? Why? How would you know for sure? What would you do to find out?"

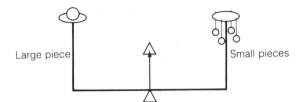

Discussion. Preoperational children do not conserve weight. They may think the little bits of clay press more on a balance and, therefore, weigh more. This activity may be altered and further tested by forming two clay balls of equal size and weight. Weigh them in front of the child, so she sees that they are equal. Take one ball and make it into several small pieces. Ask, "What do you think will happen to the balance if the little clay pieces are hung from the balance in various ways?" (See art above.) Perform this activity and ask, "What happened? Why?"

Space-distance. Place two dolls or other objects at opposite ends of a board about eighteen inches long. Place a brick about halfway between them. Ask, "Are the dolls the same distance, farther, or closer from each other, now that I have placed the brick between them? Why? If I take the brick away, will the dolls be closer, farther, or the same distance from each other?"

Discussion. Children not having a good understanding of distance will say that the dolls are closer because the brick takes up space. When working with linear measurement, primary teachers must realize that the child's concept of distance is different from that of the adult.

Perception of liquid level. Obtain a bottle and tip it in several positions. Then prepare the diagram shown below. (Note: If you are going to evaluate several children, duplicate your drawings.) Ask the children to draw in each of the bottles how the water would look if the bottle were half-filled.

Discussion. The children will respond something like the following:

   1. The early preoperational stage child scribbles all over the bottle.

   2. A child in the next development level will draw the liquid parallel to the bottom of the bottle.

   3. A child in the next stage will draw the liquid obliquely toward the opening.

4. Children ages nine through ten draw the water levels correctly.

Artificialism.   Ask a child, "Who made the sun? Who made the stars? Who made the moon? Who made the mountains? Who made a waterfall, lake, ocean waves?"

Discussion. Preoperational children believe in artificialism. They think all phenomena are made by humans or God. (God to them, however, is just a big powerful person.)

Animism.   Collect several objects, such as buttons, broken buttons, flowers, coins, rocks, straws, toys, pencils, chipped dishes, and pictures of waves, clouds, animals, trees, crystals, grass, and so on. Place these in front of the child. Ask, "What does it mean to be alive? Is a dog alive? How do you know?" Then point to each of the objects and ask the child if it is alive or not. Break some of the objects and ask the child if it is still alive and why or why not.

Discussion.   Preoperational children are characterized by animism. This means they attribute living qualities to all kinds of things. They believe that most things are alive and have a purpose similar to other organisms.

Time, duration, length of time intervals.   Obtain a watch with a second hand. Rap on a desk rapidly for a minute, watching the watch, but not giving the impression that you are noting time. Rap again on the desk, but at a much slower pace for a minute. Ask, "Which took more time, the first or second series of raps I made on the table?"

Discussion.   Children up to age seven believe quick activities take longer. They relate more raps on the table as taking more time because there are more of them. Piaget reports that children do not understand how a clock works in measuring time until age seven or eight. In order to do this, they must understand that each second on a clock is equidistant and that ten seconds of time means the clock's second hand moved ten spaces.

Construction of two-dimensional space.   Obtain two pieces of regular-sized typing paper. Place a dot on one piece of paper about halfway from the top and halfway from the center of the sheet. Place rulers, pencils, string, and scissors next to the papers. Ask, "How will you place a dot on the blank sheet so that it is in the same location as the one on the other sheet?"

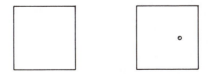

Discussion. The young preoperational child will guess at where the dot should be placed and will not use the rulers. More advanced preoperational children will take a ruler but use it to make only one measurement (i.e., from the top, bottom, or side). They are usually surprised that this does not give them the correct location. Usually by age nine, children make two measurements and coordinate these to locate the placement of the dot exactly. By so doing, they indicate they grasp the concept of the axis of coordinates.

Speed, distance, and time.   Obtain two hollow cardboard tubes such as those that come with sandwich wrap. Cut one tube a few inches shorter than the other. Obtain two small figures or markers of different colors that can pass through the tunnels. Line the tunnels up evenly at one end. Place the markers at the entrance of each of the tunnels where they are lined up evenly. Ask, "If each of these markers were to enter the tunnels at the same time and come out the tunnels together, would they both be moving at the same speed?" Ask, "What do you notice about the tunnels? Are they the same length?" Move the markers through the tunnels to come out the other ends at the same time. Ask, "Did the markers move at the same speed?"

Discussion. Ordering is basic to understanding speed. Young children believe if something moves past another object, it must be going faster. They do not take into consideration the differences in distance traveled. Objects that end together must be going at the same speed even though they covered different distances. Children eventually develop the concept of speed as being related to distance traveled per unit of time.

Memory and seriation.   Obtain several sticks. Make a series of ten sticks, starting with a stick one centimeter long and increasing their length as shown below. Have the child look at the sticks and tell him to remember how they are arranged. After the child has had sufficient time, take the sticks away and ask him to draw what he saw.

Repeat the activity a week later. If you have time and the opportunity, repeat the activity six months later. Be sure to keep the drawings completed by the children. The comparison over time is very informative.

Discussion.   Children will vary in how well they can recall the information, as indicated by the results below:

Age	General Results	Arrangement of Sticks
3–4	Draws several sticks more or less all equal in length.	||||
4–5	May include sticks paired small then large. Draws sticks arranged small large, small large, small large ... or small, small, small, large large, large ...	||||| |||||
5	Draws correct seriation but not enough sticks.	|||||
6–7	Draws correct seriation and number.	|||||||||

There is a high correlation between children's being able to perceive seriation and to note that the objects they see are also heavier, longer, shorter, wider, thinner, darker, etc. The ability to seriate is also dependent upon the kinds of materials used and the type of seriation. Seriation of length, for example, occurs about two years earlier than seriation of weight.

BIBLIOGRAPHY

Boden, Margaret A. *Jean Piaget*. New York: Penguin Books, 1980.
  Chapter 3 is an excellent presentation of the preoperational period. Criticism of the theory and some implications for educators are included.
Brainerd, Charles J. *Piaget's Theory of Intelligence*. Englewood Cliffs, N.J.: Prentice-Hall, 1978.
  Chapter 4 is on the preoperational period. The discussion is clear, and terms are defined with examples. The author does an excellent job of outlining Piaget's theory and then presenting research studies that support, refute, or modify Piaget's original findings.
Ginsburg, Herbert, and Opper, Sylvia. *Piaget's Theory of Intellectual Development*. 2 ed. Englewood Cliffs, N.J.: Prentice-Hall, 1979.
  The authors discuss aspects of the preoperational period in various parts of Chapter 3 and 4. These chapters provide good summaries of Piaget's early (before 1940) and later (1940 and after) work.
Labinowicz, Ed. *The Piaget Primer*. Menlo Park, Calif.: Addison Wesley Publishing Co., 1980.
  The preoperational period is discussed throughout. The author develops Piaget's theory in the context of tasks, explorations and content areas (e.g., number, conservation). The graphics provide an interesting and comprehensive view of understanding at different stages.
Piaget, Jean. *The Child's Conception of Physical Causality*. Totowa, N.J.: Littlefield, Adams and Co., 1930.
  Numerous statements by children are used as the basis for development and clarification of theory. Elementary science teachers should find the different chapters (e.g., nature of air, wind, clouds, movements, floating, steam engines and bicycles) very interesting.
————. *Play, Dreams and Imitation in Childhood*. New York: W.W. Norton & Co., 1951.
  Chapters 3, 7, and all of Part 3—Cognitive Representation—are appropriate reading for those interested in preoperational thought.
————. *The Construction of Reality in the Child*. New York: Basic Books, 1954.
  Primarily concerned with the sensorimotor period, but recommended as basic reading because of the breadth and clarity. Discussion and examples provide a good basis for understanding the preoperational period.
————. *The Language and Thought of the Child*. New York: Meridian Books, 1955.
  Explanations children give of their world form the core of this book. Around the core Piaget develops his theory as it relates to the use of language.

————. *Psychology of Intelligence*. Totowa, N.J.: Littlefield, Adams & Co., 1966.

Though mostly dealing with the theory of intelligence and the sensorimotor level, educators will find Part 3 of interest. The entire book is recommended for educators interested in the psychology of intelligence.

————. *On the Development of Memory and Identity*. Barre, Mass.: Clark University Press, 1968.

This small volume is based on the Heinz Werner lectures given by Piaget in 1967; contains short and clear discussions of Piaget's findings on memory and the relationship of identity in the development of mental operations.

Piaget, Jean and Inhelder, Barbel. *The Psychology of the Child*. New York: Basic Books, 1969.

This is probably the best introductory work to Piaget's theories. Though a bit uneven, pages 28–91 are recommended reading for the preoperational period.

Wadsworth, Barry J. *Piaget for the Classroom Teacher*. New York: Longman, 1978.

Read Parts I and II for an introduction to the theory. The third part discusses teaching principles and practices. Discussion throughout is oriented toward teachers.

IV | EVALUATION
THE PREOPERATIONAL PERIOD

Listed below are some of the main topics covered in Chapter 4. Read each statement and rate it on the scale TWICE: once according to what you knew about the topic before starting this chapter and again according to what you have learned after completing the chapter. Circle the appropriate number and mark B for *before* and A for *after* next to the number as indicated below.

Topic	Low		Moderate			High
Example: Important Piagetian mental operations	①B	2	3	4	5	⑥A
1. The influence of perceptions in the resolution of problems	1	2	3	4	5	6
2. Egocentric language and its influence on thought	1	2	3	4	5	6
3. Counting versus the understanding of number	1	2	3	4	5	6
4. Animistic explorations of events	1	2	3	4	5	6
5. Artificialistic explanations of events	1	2	3	4	5	6
6. Awareness of time	1	2	3	4	5	6
7. Awareness of space	1	2	3	4	5	6

8. Awareness of causality   1   2   3   4   5   6

9. Ability to conserve substance   1   2   3   4   5   6

10. Reasoning strategies of students   1   2   3   4   5   6

11. Mental operations   1   2   3   4   5   6

12. Characteristics of play and imitation   1   2   3   4   5   6

13. Identity of materials   1   2   3   4   5   6

14. Ability to identify "the intuitive student"   1   2   3   4   5   6

5 The Concrete Operational Period and the Practical Student

The sometimes frustrating thinking of the intuitive student starts to disappear at about the third grade, or at age seven to eight. Students start demonstrating patterns of thought that are logical. In Piaget's terminology children start demonstrating operational intelligence. This emerging form of thinking is characterized by the ability to reverse thinking and to demonstrate logical patterns of thought. During later elementary school years, grades 3–6 (ages seven to eleven), operational thought is tied to practical, concrete problems, hence the term, *concrete operational* period, and our characterization of the practical student.

I | EXPLORATION
THE CONCRETE OPERATIONAL PERIOD

Probing the Period

Elementary school children are commonly asked to place objects in order, according to increasing or decreasing length, weight, height, or age. On page 97 are the observations from five different students who were asked to arrange six sticks from smallest to largest.

How would you characterize the arrangements of the five students? Look carefully at the errors. How could you explain the errors? We shall use this problem as an example later in the chapter.

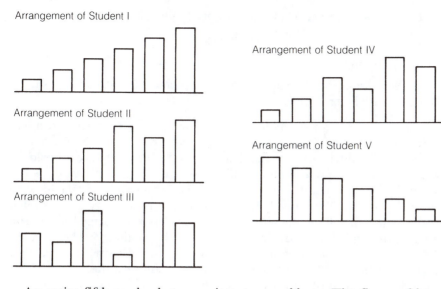

Arrangement of Student I

Arrangement of Student II

Arrangement of Student III

Arrangement of Student IV

Arrangement of Student V

An entire fifth grade class was given two problems. The first problem consisted of giving each student two strips of colored paper. The strips were slightly different lengths. By comparing the papers the students determined that the yellow strip was longer than the red strip. The red strips were collected. The children were then given blue strips and told to compare them to the yellow strips. The blue strips were longer than the yellow strips. The students were then asked to deduce the *relative* lengths of the red and blue strips. They were asked, "Is the blue strip longer, the same, or shorter than the red strip?" The results for the class are presented in percentages: longer — 92 percent, same — 3 percent, shorter — 5 percent.

The second day the same students were presented a second problem. This time the problem was presented orally. "If Joan is shorter than Janet and Janet is shorter than Jane, then who is the tallest?" The results for the class were as follows: Joan—15 percent, Janet—61 percent, Jane—24 percent.

You will note that these are essentially the same seriation problems. Yet, the majority of students solved one problem correctly and the other incorrectly. What is the important difference between the two problems? What is required of the students in the second problem that is not required in the first? How would you account for the different responses to the seriation problems?

Reasoning Strategies: Representation to Reversibility

The concrete operational period begins for most children around age seven and terminates at age eleven. It is called *concrete* because children's thought is restricted to what they encounter through direct experience. They think about existing objects and their properties (e.g. weight, color, and texture), and they think about the actions they can do with these objects. Moreover, during these years, children slowly develop reasoning strategies such as

1. Classifying in various ways, grouping things into a class or subclass.

2. Doing one-to-one correspondence.

3. Reversing thought processes: A→B and A←B.

4. Performing mathematical operations: adding, subtracting, substituting, multiplying, dividing, ordering in space and time.

Concrete operational children are not as easily fooled by perceptual differences as their preoperational counterparts. For example, a preoperational child, shown a wide, shallow glass with a few ounces of colored water that is then poured into a tall, narrow glass, thinks the tall glass has more liquid in it than the wide one. The child makes this mistake because her judgement is determined mainly by perception. A concrete operational child, however, will say the amount in either glass is the same because she *reasons*, she understands the logical necessity, that nothing has been added or taken away from the containers. This child is, therefore, less *perception bound*, but her thinking is limited because she still relies heavily on direct experience instead of abstract reasoning.

As the concrete operational child interacts with the environment, she increasingly calls upon her experiences and her developing mental abilities for direction. The development of reasoning strategies enables the individual to make great mental advancements. Piaget says, "Intelligence is born of action. Any act of intelligence—whether it be on the part of a man involved in scientific research, or the child of seven or eight—consists of operations, carrying out operations, and coordinating them among themselves" (Piaget, 1967, p.38).

Sometime around age seven the first actual reasoning strategies become evident. Until this time any "strategy" has been reflexive or intuitive and, as such, would not really qualify as a strategy or plan of action. For Piaget the major advancement in thought is due to the child's capacity to do mental operations. Operational thought is a quantum leap forward in the child's continuing construction of knowledge.

Mental operations are the internalized (mental) representation and action that are applied to situations confronted by the individual. Mental operations are reversible, and reversibility occurs in two ways. A direct inversion or negation of the process is possible (e.g. $+2$ is reversed by a -2). A compensation or reciprocal change is also possible (e.g., 2×3 is compensation for $6 \div 3$ or $6 \div 2$). Another characteristic of mental operations is that they are organized into complete systems or subsystems within stages. Piaget refers to these systems as whole structures of action. For the educator, all of this means that students are capable of logical thought and can apply reasoning strategies to practical, concrete problems.

We can add one more dimension to our construction of the path to logical thought.

Reflex Actions	Representation of Actions	Reversibility of Actions
Sensorimotor Strategies⟶	Intuitive Strategies ⟶	Practical Strategies
ages 0–2	ages 2–7	ages 8–11

Students in Transition

Discussions of Piaget's theory tend to stress ages and stages. Educators have thus tended to try and identify the characteristic products of development aligned with particular stages. In reality most children are in transition. Even if you can absolutely identify a student's thought as concrete operational, what then is your educational task? Certainly your task must be more than announcing the student's level—"She is beyond the pre-operational period and cannot yet complete formal operational problems." It is still important to encourage further development, to get the student to continue along the developmental path. Thinking of development as a process leads the educator to ask about transitions from one major period to another.

There are three identifiable levels of transition in the development of operational thought. The first level is one of direct physical action on objects without mental representation of the actions. Reasoning strategies (if they could be called this) are overt handling without conceptualization of the problem or an organized approach to solving the problem. Given a seriation problem such as the one presented earlier the child would be unable to establish any order. The task would be completed by placing the blocks in an arbitrary order. Such an arrangement was completed by student III, who was three years old. Slightly older children may place two or three blocks in sequence, but are unable to construct a complete sequence. The arrangement of student IV, age four, characterizes this level.

At the second level (ages five to six) children are able to mentally represent aspects of the problem but cannot conceptualize the entire problem; they are not able to work with a definite approach. Rather, students are greatly influenced by perceptually dominating aspects of the problem and they use an intuitive, trial-and-success (or error) approach to the problem. Results such as those demonstrated by student II and student IV on the seriation problem are common. Once the student starts a sequence or makes a mistake in the sequence, she has difficulty correcting the problem. This is true even if only one block (student II) is out of place. Student V is a case where the sequence is correct albeit reversed. However, the student probably had an intuitive sense of the problem and started with the longest block just because it was perceptually dominant. From this point she completed the ordering problem. Upon examination one would find it very difficult to get the child to change her arrangement, and she may even make a mistake such as that made by student II upon the readministration of the task. This is because the child cannot yet conceptualize the problem and the process of solving the problem.

At the third level, by about age seven or eight, the student is able to conceptualize the entire problem and demonstrates a reasoning strategy as long as she actually has the materials or objects of the problem. Such was the case of student I in the seriation problem and the entire class in the transitive inference problem (determining the length of the blue strip relative to the red). However, as we saw, students could not complete a similar problem when it was presented orally and required completion without the use of concrete aids. Likewise, if students are given long and detailed problems, they may make mistakes such as those of students II, IV, or V in the seriation problems. That is, they may have the basic arrangement but make minor errors in sequence. The lack of correct response is explained by the child's inability to conceptualize all the relevant components and remember the components as the reasoning strategies are applied; thus, partially correct responses to complex problems.

Finally, students are able to conceptualize problems and apply reasoning strategies that are logical. This was probably the approach used by the 24 percent of students who reasoned that Jane was the tallest. The contrast between this problem and the one with colored strips of paper points out the concrete operational and formal operational approaches to problems. The transition levels apply to the conceptual structures discussed in the next section of this chapter—conservation, seriation, classification, number, space, and time.

II | EXPLANATION
THE CONCRETE OPERATIONAL PERIOD

Piaget has written extensively on the concrete operational period. A sample of his works that may be of interest for educators includes *The Child's Conception of Movement and Speed* (Piaget, 1970a), *The Child's Conception of Number* (Piaget, 1953), *Memory and Intelligence* (Piaget and Inhelder, 1973), *The Psychology of the Child* (Piaget and Inhelder, 1969). This is only a sampling of the numerous books Piaget and his colleagues have published on this period. If one includes research on this period completed by individuals outside of Geneva, the total body of knowledge about this period is overwhelming. Great selectivity had to be exercised in the presentation of this chapter.

Conservation

The concept of conservation refers to an individual's understanding that quantitative relationships between materials remain the same even though the material has undergone perceptual alterations. Conservation tasks were used in the interviews with Michelle and Patrick in the last chapter. Typically, the child is shown two materials that are quantitatively and perceptually equivalent. The interviewer and/or the child then changes one material. The change maintains the quantitative properties but changes the perceptual qualities of the material. After the changes are completed, the interviewer asks the child if the quantitative aspects of the material have been changed. Evaluation of the child's response is based on two facets of her response. First, has the child answered the questions about quantitative changes correctly? That is, the materials are the same. Second, when asked to justify the answer, the child demonstrates operational thought; that is, she mentally reverses the action completed on the materials as a part of the justification.

During the concrete operational period, children develop the ability to conserve. They realize that altering the shape of material does not modify the amount present. This use of the mind to check the reasonableness of something rather than just relying on perception fundamentally demarks the practical from the intuitive student. Because this is so, concrete students when presented with a problem are more likely to think about it before answering. Their answers and explanations also appear more rational. In this period they begin to use their minds rather than their intuitions in response to teachers' questions.

A major achievement of the concrete period is the continued construction and refining of concepts plus the discovery of how concepts are interrelated. For example, children through their interaction with materials in the environment gradually develop a conceptual understanding of conservation. First they realize conservation of matter. They understand, for example, that if a ball of clay is rolled into a hot dog shape, it has no more clay than before. Preoperational children, on the other hand, think the longer rolled clay is larger (has more mass) even though nothing has been added nor taken away. Although it is reasonable to expect a child conserving substance to generalize this concept to conservation of length, weight, or volume, such is not the case. Refer to Figure 5.1 for the types of conservation and the approximate age level of attainment.

A CONSERVATION TASK

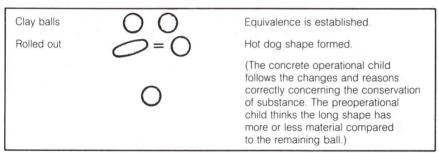

Clay balls	Equivalence is established.
Rolled out	Hot dog shape formed.
	(The concrete operational child follows the changes and reasons correctly concerning the conservation of substance. The preoperational child thinks the long shape has more or less material compared to the remaining ball.)

There is evidence, however, that students in junior and senior high school still have difficulty with conservation. Dr. David Elkind (1961) in replicating some of Piaget's work tested 469 students in junior and senior high school. Elkind found that 87 percent of the students grasped conservation of mass (amount of substance) and weight, while only 47 percent understood conservation of volume by age fifteen. Copeland (1970) reports that many academically disadvantaged children don't conserve number by the fourth grade.

Elkind further found significant differences between boys and girls in the attainment of conservation. Boys generally demonstrated the ability to conserve earlier than girls. This he attributed largely to masculine role socialization. His research also indicated the longer students remained in school, the better they became at conserving.

The constructive process of interrelating perceptual experiences with conservation evolves relatively slowly. The child first demonstrates no con-

Figure 5.1
Approximate Age Levels at Which Conservation Is Attained

Type of Conservation	Age	Characteristic Response of Child
Substance	6–7	Realizes amount of substance doesn't change by dividing it.
Length	6–7	Realizes bending a wire doesn't change its length.
Number	6½–7	Realizes rearranging objects doesn't change their number.
Continuous Quantity	6–7	Realizes pouring liquid from one container to another doesn't change the quantity.
Area	7	Realizes the area of a paper split in half covers just as much area as if it were whole.
Weight	9–12	Realizes a mashed piece of clay weighs the same as when it was a sphere.
Volume	11–12 and beyond	Realizes that a mashed piece of clay immersed in a liquid will occupy as much volume as when it was a sphere.

serving, then conserves in some cases but not others, and finally the child can conserve. The student becomes *certain logically* that materials are conserved across various changes. Having opportunities to manipulate substances involving conservation undoubtedly contributes to a better understanding of these principles and facilitates the learning of higher level understanding at a later time in the development of the child.

Seriation

Seriation is concerned with the student's ability to order a group of objects using a property common to all objects. The relation among objects is most often asymmetrical. Asymmetrical relations can be established between any two objects by identifying a common property that varies between the objects. If A and B have the properties of length, width, height, and color, but B is longer; then this property can be used to differentiate the objects.

The relations we have thus far used are quantitative and transitive. The blue paper was *longer* than the red paper, and a relation was established *between* paper strips (the red and the blue) without direct comparison. Qualitative relations are based on natural properties of objects, people, and so on. One can also establish qualitative relations that are asymmetrical but not transitive. For example, in a problem parallel to that concerning the paper strips, it makes no sense to ask if A is related to C if A is mother of B and B is mother of C. Is A mother of C? No. In fact, A is grandmother of C. During the elementary school years educators involve students in many problems requiring students to establish qualitative and quantitative relations. From a Piagetian view there are three types of relations that are important for educators: simple seriation, multiple seriation, and transitive inference.

In simple seriation problems students are presented with five to ten objects that differ relative to an identifiable property such as length, width, height, or weight. They are then asked to order the objects according to the property. Younger children will often have to complete a series of comparisons between objects before they establish the relation among the entire set of objects. Older children can conceptualize the relations and proceed directly with the task.

Multiple seriation is a variation of the simple seriation problem. In this case the individual must simultaneously use two properties to order the objects. Suppose we give students four small balls with the following properties:

Ball	Width in Cm.	Weight in Grams
1	5	10
2	8	10
3	5	15
4	8	15

We then ask the students to establish an order for the balls according to *both* width and weight. Resolution of the problem would be initiated by first outlining a 2 × 2 matrix and using one axis for increasing width and another for increasing weight. The result (seen below) is a doubly seriated order in which width increases from left to right and weight increases from the top down. Activities such as this are excellent experience for elementary students.

The third type of ordering is transitive inference. In the first two types of problems, students are allowed to make direct comparisons of objects and thus establish an order through concrete experience. Transitive inference tasks require ordering objects without direct comparison of all objects. The student is allowed to compare some objects, but final relations among objects must be established mentally. Let us say a student is given three metal cubes. The cubes are similar except for weight. The student is asked to lift the first two cubes and determine which is heavier. A relation is established; the first cube is heavier than the second. Then the second and third cubes are compared. The second cube is heavier than the third. Then, the student is asked to deduce the weight relation of the first and third cubes and to justify her response. The student would be capable of transitive inference if she responded that the first cube was heavier than the third because the second cube was lighter than the first, and the second was heavier than the third. Transitive inference problems were used at the beginning of the chapter. These activities and other types of problems such as diameter of balls, length of paper strips, and height of containers can be used by educators with elementary students.

Classification

With time individuals develop the capacity to categorize objects and events that belong together—to classify. Classification is the ability to identify symmetrical relations among objects, persons, or events. It would be difficult to imagine what life would be like without the capacity to classify.

Children develop the ability to categorize objects during the elementary school years. Somewhat paralleling the development of seriation, there are three different aspects of classification: simple classification, multiple classification, and class inclusion. Each category represents a different, more complex expression of the ability to categorize objects, persons, or situations.

Simple classification refers to the ability to establish one-dimensional categories. But this capacity is not always available. The early pre-operational child's first step in classificatory development is grouping objects by one characteristic. It is important to realize that this grouping is almost entirely a perceptual activity. The child sees the red blocks and pushes them around into one group. In this first stage a mental representation, such as "There are red and white blocks. I shall separate these into groups," does not occur. This occurs in the next developmental step. Here, children actually mentally represent the properties to be used in the classification. A task at this level would involve the presentation of ten or twelve objects that belong to at least two mutually exclusive categories and the request to sort the objects into the categories. Very simply, students can "put things together that go together" and they can explain how they have "put things together."

Multiple classification is a more complex version of simple classification problems. Like the multiple seriation tasks, individuals are required to classify objects simultaneously using two mutually exclusive dimensions. With time and experience children usually realize that objects may be classified in more than one way. For example, if you give them several pieces of different colored paper cut in various shapes, they realize that the papers can be grouped by color and shape. This insight is represented in a 2×2 matrix as we saw in the multiple seriation tasks. The students may respond to the task with the following scheme:

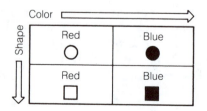

The resulting classification results in a double classification where color changes from left to right and shape changes from top to bottom.

Class inclusion is an understanding that a class can exist within another, more comprehensive class. During the concrete operational period, children usually realize that a major class, paper for example, may be composed of subclasses such as shapes of paper, and that these in turn may belong to other groups such as colors of paper. For example, if you ask a child what material all the objects are made of, she will probably say paper. If there are far more red paper shapes than white and you ask if there are more red shapes than paper, she may be confused. If she has not yet developed an understanding of class inclusion, she will be overcome by the perceptual impact of the red and will say there are more red objects than paper objects. Later the student may change her judgement and reply, "No, there is more paper than red shapes." This is so because as the child makes the transition, she becomes less perception bound and uses her mental abilities to check what she sees.

A CLASS INCLUSION TASK

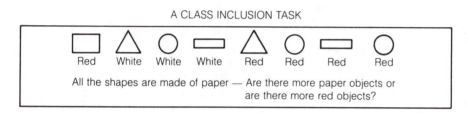

Red   White   White   White   Red   Red   Red   Red

All the shapes are made of paper — Are there more paper objects or are there more red objects?

During the concrete operational period, children construct ascending and descending hierarchies as a part of class inclusion. Children come to realize that subgroups may belong to major groups and that anything that is true for the subgroup is also true of the major group. The child realizes ducks are birds: ducks have feathers and so do birds.

Ascending Hierarchy

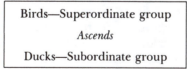

Birds—Superordinate group

Ascends

Ducks—Subordinate group

Although a child can ascend the hierarchy, she may not necessarily be able to descend it. For example, if you ask some children, "What are robins?" they will probably say, "birds." Then ask, "If all the birds are destroyed, will there be any robins?" If the children cannot reverse their thinking and descend the hierarchy they will probably say, "yes."

The ability to descend does not manifest itself until the child develops one of the main operational abilities of the concrete stage—*reversibility*. When a child can reverse her thinking, she may give the correct answer and appear more logical as a result. Some children, however, who can reverse may still not be able to descend the hierarchy. They haven't generalized the reversible operation.

Ascending and Descending Hierarchy

Ascending
Robins belong to Birds
Descending
if all birds are killed — no robins

Educators can see that these problems represent common situations that students must solve through the elementary years.

Number

Development and conservation of the number concept is interconnected with seriation and classification. Piaget has summarized this relationship in his book, *Genetic Epistemology*:

> When we study the development of the notion of number in children's thinking, we find that it is not based on classification operations alone but that it is a synthesis of two different structures. We find that along with the classifying structures... number is based on ordering structures, that is, a synthesis of two different types of structures. It is certainly true that classification is involved in the notion of number. Class inclusion is involved in the sense that two is included in three, three is included in four, etc. But we also need order relationships, for this reason: If we consider the elements of the classes to be equivalent (and this of course is the basis of the notion of number), then by this very fact it is impossible to distinguish one element from another—it is impossible to tell the elements apart. We get the tautology $A + A = A$; we have a logical tautology instead of a numerical series. (Piaget, 1970b, p. 38)

Piaget goes on to suggest that the only way to distinguish among the elements is to introduce order, to arrange the elements one after another in time or space, or to *count* them. So, there is the synthesis of class inclusion and seriation in the development of number. Educators, it would seem, have realized the importance of this synthesis because of the activities in which children are required to order and classify objects as well as do arithmetic.

Natural numbers ($- 1, 2, 3 \ldots$) have two properties that are closely related to seriation and classification. When numbers are used in connection with serial order they are *ordinal* numbers. Ordinal numbers define collections of objects that have been sequenced according to an asymmetrical property. Problems used in earlier sections exemplify this idea. If an asymmetrical property, such as length, is used to order a group of pencils, then there is a first, second, third,... pencil. When the ordinal property of numbers is used, the number 1 refers to the first object in ordered sequence, 2 refers to the second object, and so on. Natural numbers can also be used for their property or classification. These are referred to as cardinal numbers.

Cardinal numbers denote how many objects are contained in different classes. In this case 1, 2, 3 refer to sets of objects, persons, events, etc., taken one, two, or three at a time. The number 1 refers to all classes of single objects, 2 to all classes of pairs, 3 to all classes of trios, and so on. Educators should note that extensive research on students' development of number (Brainard, 1978) indicates that children understand ordinal numbers, simple computation (addition, subtraction), and then cardinal numbers.

Piaget means more than counting and computing, though he obviously includes these when he refers to number. Piaget is also concerned with the conservation of number. He asks questions such as, under what conditions do children understand that two sets of objects are the same or different depending on the number of objects in the set? The traditional task is to present students with two parallel rows of objects such as checkers or coins, and establish a one-to-one equivalence between the objects. Then one row is lengthened or shortened. The interviewer then asks if the quantity of objects in the two rows is the same or different. (See diagrams A, B, C below.)

A TASK FOR CONSERVATION OF NUMBER

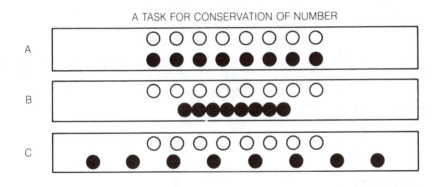

In a task such as that just described, students in the preoperational period will form a numerical judgement based on the relative lengths of the two rows of objects. Next, numerical judgements alternate between relative length and density. Finally, students understand the numerical properties of the objects and respond accordingly. According to Piaget, this understanding is based on a coordination of seriation and classification concepts by the child.

One of the first indications that the dawn of operational thought is taking place occurs when the child shows an understanding of number. Piaget believes this comprehension manifests itself only after an individual has developed certain prior logical attributes. Preoperational children often can count "wum," "two," "tree," but "two" is only a sound that follows "wum." For a child to truly understand number, he must first be able to represent mentally how many objects are involved, order, and classify them. For example, the child may look at his feet and say "shoes" and then ask himself, "How many do I have?" and come up with the statement: "I have two shoes." He first classified the shoes and then determined how many there were before he finally arrived at the answer. A parent or teacher seeking to determine whether a child understood number in the above example would ask: "How do you know you have only two shoes?" In other words, they would ask the child to give some justification for his answer. If the child gives a rational explanation, they know he really comprehends number and has not, by trial and error, just happened on the correct response.

Children cannot count with understanding unless they know the meaning of numbers. In order to do this, they must realize that all objects included in one group are treated as though they were alike and belonged to the group being counted. In other words, the child understands the property of a cardinal number. They have to disregard object differences in classifying them in a set in order to arrive at their number, while still realizing that they are separate entities. For example, apples may differ in appearance, but they are still apples. They must further understand that the number of something is dependent upon its belonging in a set. He must count things in some sequence, demonstrating the property of ordinal numbers. He must realize further that the number of objects in a group remains the same regardless of how they are arranged (conservation of number).

The concrete operational student begins to unfold in his ability to perform mathematical operations. This does not mean that at the dawn of this period he immediately begins to add, subtract, or act in other ways operationally. Nor does it mean that all of the types of operational thinking develop simultaneously. Mathematical operations do not occur in isolation. They are connected to other mental operations. By the end of the concrete period, the child is able to add ($+$), subtract ($-$), multiply ($\times$), divide ($\div$), place in order ($<>$), substitute ($=$), and reverse ($\rightleftarrows$).

Space and Time

Discussions on conservation, seriation, classification, and number were concerned with similarities, differences, or equivalences *between* objects. It is also possible to consider relations *within* objects. Such is the case with spatial operations and the concepts fundamental to the domain of geometry. Geometry deals with spatial relations and the measurement of these relations. There are three domains of geometry: Euclidean geometry deals with the relation of distances in space; projective geometry is concerned with relations of order in space; and topology identifies the qualitative, or categorical, nature of order in space. The differences among the domains of geometry are important to understanding Piaget's conception of spatial development.

During the preoperational period, children understand qualitative, or topological, relations within sets of objects. They understand neither projective nor Euclidean relations. Later, during the concrete period, children can locate the relative positions—distance and order—of objects in space. Piaget and Inhelder summarize their views on this understanding by children:

Historically, scientific geometry began with Euclidean metric geometry; then came projective geometry, and finally topology. Theoretically, however, topology constitutes a general foundation from which both projective space and the general metrics from which Euclidean metrics proceeds can be derived in a parallel manner. What is remarkable is that the line of development from the pre-operatory intuitions through the spatial operations in the child is much closer to theoretical order than to the historical genealogy. The topological structures of ordinal partition (proximities, separations, envelopment, openness and closedness, coordination of proximities in linear bidimensional or tridimensional order, etc.) precede the others in a rather clear-cut manner. These basic structures then give rise simultaneously and in parallel fashion to the projective structures (rectilinearity, coordination of view points, etc.) and the metrical structures (displacements, measurements, coordinates or systems of reference, as an extension of measurements to two or three dimensions). (Piaget and Inhelder, 1969, p. 107)

In a typical seriation task, a student arranges in order five to ten objects that vary in some property, such as length.

Review the interviews with Michelle and Patrick in Chapter 4. In their interviews we saw that their concepts of Euclidean space were at the pre-operational level. Their response to the problem of placing objects (barns) in perceptually different arrangements on identical pieces of paper (pastures) resulted in different qualitative estimates of the space. Another common task for spatial relations has to do with the horizontality of water in a closed container. The child is shown a colored container with a water level indicated and a horizontal surface for reference. Then the jar is tilted in several different ways. The child is asked, "If the jar is tipped as you see in the pictures, how would the water look? Make a line showing how the water would look." Finally, a justification is requested: "Why do you think the water will look like that?" Young children do not respond by maintaining a horizontality of the water level regardless of the bottle's orientation. They orient the water to the jar and not to space. Concrete operational children are able to correctly conceptualize the changes in water level.

A SPATIAL RELATIONS TASK

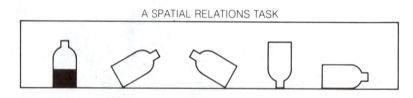

Students come to understand time as they develop these kinds of mental operations. First, there is the seriation of experiences, placing events in temporal order. Second, there is calculation of the duration between events; and finally, the measurement of time which requires a coordination of order and duration. If young children are given a task concerning velocity which includes movement across space in time, they initially use a topological and ordinal view to explain the results. For example, a child is presented with two cars moving along tracks of different lengths. Both cars start and arrive at the end simultaneously, so the car on the longer track must have had a greater velocity (it moved across space faster in the same time). Young children reason the cars moved at the same velocity since they arrived at the end point at the same time. Later in the concrete operational period children include all relations of time and space as they reason correctly about this problem.

The Practical Student

The concrete operational period begins for most students around age seven and terminates at age eleven. It is called concrete because students' thought is mainly restricted to what they encounter in direct experience. So you have practical students. They think about the properties of existing objects. They also think of the actions or the things they actually can do with them. The period is operational because children during the span of these years slowly develop mental operations which appear as logical reasoning patterns and the ability to mentally reverse a series of changes.

The practical student increasingly uses mental representation for physical action. With time mental representation takes the place of physical

Reasoning about Space

Linda J. Kelsey
Physical Science Program
West Virginia University

Have you ever struggled in trying to understand the phases of the moon or seasons, or in deciphering a geologic map, or a diagram of a complex molecule or geometric solid? All of these topics require reasoning about the relationships among objects in space.

What does spatial reasoning involve? Piaget and Inhelder assert that the structuring of space requires much more than simple perception. In fact, the mental structures used in interpreting what we see often dictate our "perception" of a situation. Three groupings of concrete level operations dealing with three specific aspects of space are topological, projective, and Euclidean. The mental structures for topological space start to develop early in the concrete operational stage and concern proximities, separation, order, continuity, and enclosure. They describe the internal relationships between neighboring parts of an object or system of objects. A young child, manipulating objects that he cannot see, will not be able to distinguish between topologically equivalent (continuous) objects such as solid squares, triangles, or discs. Notions of order do not develop until the early school years, and a younger child cannot duplicate the simple order of different colored beads on a string. The relationships of surrounding or enclosure develop at a somewhat later time, while one of the last notions to develop is that of the conceptualization of a continuous figure as consisting of a connected series of points.

Projective relations develop by imposing a "point of view" to the relations of topology, and culminate in the ability to coordinate different perspectives. Many children are unable to look at a set of three objects to determine how they would appear from behind. A young child will insist that his view is the only one possible—an excellent example of egocentrism. Some high school and college students still have trouble in determining the relative positions of the objects as seen from the side.

Projective space also concerns the idea of perspective where parallel lines appear to converge in the distance. One of the last projective groupings of operations to develop is that dealing with the appearance of a single object as seen from different points of view. Many high school and college students are unable to describe the appearance of a stick or ring if it is viewed at an angle or from the side.

Euclidean spatial reasoning allows the formation of an overall reference frame or coordinate system, where distances, angles, and parallels are conserved. Lengths, areas, and volumes are conserved in this space independent of the observer's viewpoint or the orientation of the object. Euclidean spatial reasoning is required for locating an object in two or three dimensions: notions necessary for graphing or using coordinate systems. Reasoning about horizontals and verticals is difficult for children, resulting in drawings of houses and chimneys parallel to a hillside (or roof) rather than horizontal.

The development of reasoning about spatial relationships continues into the formal operational stage of development. It is only with formal reasoning that volume and displacement volume are conserved and two frames of reference can be coordinated.

Many high school and college students are unable to use the upper level mental structures for projective and Euclidean space. The implications for teaching are many, especially for mathematics and the sciences. These data may provide insights into why our students have trouble with topics such as geometry, contour mapping, seasons, orbits, and structural arrangements of molecules or geologic strata. Many courses require the use of formal operational abilities of students who have not fully developed the concrete spatial structures.

What can we do in the classroom? Piaget and Inhelder point out repeatedly that spatial representations are developed through the organization of *actions* on objects in space. The first step must be to provide activities at all levels where students interact on an individual basis with objects—we must give them a chance to create their own mental structures. Two-dimensional drawings are no substitute for real models of three-dimensional objects or systems, and these models must be available for students to handle rather than view as a "demonstration" at the front of the room. Repeated presentations of similar drawings at different grade levels will not result in an understanding of a concept when the necessary mental structures are not there. Nor is there any evidence that continued exposure to the same type of presentation helps to build the necessary structures.

Do we continue to cover the content in the usual way, or do we sacrifice some time to doing activities that could help in developing the basic mental structures? The decision is even more critical when we remember that the concrete level spatial structures are an essential part of intellectual development in general, and are important in laying the foundation for the development of formal thought.

action. Through the elementary school years this representation and action are tied to experience. For example, the concrete operational student knows that, when water is poured from a wide, flat jar to a slender one, the amount of liquid has not changed. He will probably explain, "If you return the water to the wide jar, you will have the same volume as before." He mentally performs the action of refilling the wide jar with water, thus exhibiting reversibility. In this period, then, semilogic, thinking in only one direction, turns into logic. The practical student thinks about objects, their properties, and the possible actions that can be performed on them. Using the mind to perform such operations characterizes students in this period and provides the foundation for more sophisticated patterns of thought.

Conservation, classification, and seriation are all possible for the practical student. The student realizes that the quantity of a substance remains the same if nothing is added or subtracted from it. And this is so even if the substance undergoes a complex series of changes. The student can classify objects based on observable properties. The student can order objects according to an observable property. Knowing these patterns of thought are possible and, as we have seen, related to other educational components such as number and, clearly, language, is an important step in the application of Piaget's theory.

The practical student's conceptual understanding of space and time has broadened to include some notions of geographical space and historical time. She can think of the area of city, state, and she has some notions of different cities and places. She can become fascinated with some historical episodes and has some ideas of their place in time.

Based on the review of this period, it seems we can summarize a few important educational achievements for the practical student.

1. Uses logical patterns of reasoning on concrete problems
2. Understands part-whole relationships
3. Demonstrates conservation of mass, weight, and volume
4. Recognizes the properties of numbers
5. Organizes events, objects, and situations in space and time
6. Reverses thinking to justify changes of objects and events
7. Completes mathematical operations requiring reversibility
8. Establishes an order among objects, events, situations, using a common, but asymmetrical, property

Figure 5.2
The Students' Developing Understanding of the World:
Sensorimotor, Preoperational, Concrete Operational Periods

Content	Sensorimotor Period Beginning Characteristics	Preoperational Period End/Beginning Characteristics	Concrete Operational Period End/Beginning Characteristics	End Characteristics
Action	Reflexive physical actions	Representational thought	Prelogical thought — Can reason in one direction	Logical reversible thinking, but reasoning is related to concrete situations
Objects	Not permanent	Permanent objects	Conservation of identity	Conservation of quantity seriation, classification, and number
Space	No concept of space	Conceptualizes immediate space	Broadens concept of space	Understands relations within objects— elementary geometry
Time	No concept of time	Conceptualizes short sequences and durations of time	Aware of past, present, and future	Coordination of temporal order and duration
Causality	No concept of cause/effect	Conceptualizes simple cause/effect relationships	Animistic	Understands cause/ effect in concrete problems
Play	Repetition of reflexes	First symbolic play	Representative play	Practical play
Imitation	Repetition of reflexes	First deferred imitation	Representative imitation	Practical imitation
Self	No concept of self	First concept of self/ not self	Egocentrism	Reduced egocentrism
Language	No language	First language	Egocentric language	Practical language

In closing, we can make several recommendations for working with the practical student:

1. Use concrete experiences as the bases for educational strategies.
2. Make reference to objects, events, or situations familiar to students who are having difficulty.
3. Recognize that students can be unaware of inconsistencies in their reasoning patterns.

III | EXTENSION
THE CONCRETE OPERATIONAL PERIOD

Analyzing a Task

A displacement of volume task was given to a class of sixth grade students. The teacher used a tall cylinder three-quarters full of colored water and two metal blocks of the same size (volume) *but* different weights for the task (see Figure 5.3). The students were told to compare the weights of the two metal blocks. Each student lifted the blocks and was asked, "Which is heavier?" One student was then asked, "If I take the lightweight block and lower it into the water, what will happen to the level of the water?" The student was then told to place a rubber band around the cylinder at the level she thought the water would rise. The lighter block was lowered into the cylinder. If necessary, the rubber band was moved to the level of the water at this point. The block was removed. The entire class was then asked, "Where do you think the level of the water will be when the heavier block is lowered into the cylinder? Will the water level for the heavier block be lower, the same, or higher than the water level for the lighter block?" After their responses, the students were asked for a justification: "Why do you think this

Figure 5.3
Materials for Displacement of Volume Task

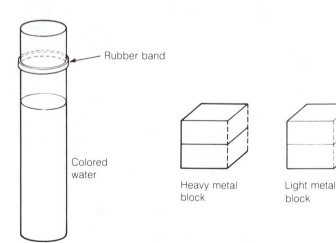

will happen?" The heavier block was lowered into the cylinder. The students' reactions and comments about the results were recorded. About half the class (47 percent) responded to the questions by indicating the heavier block would displace more water than the light block.

Using your understanding of preoperational and concrete operational thought patterns, how would you explain these results?

Listening to Student Explanations

Students' language is the primary way educators determine levels of thought. Explanations students give for problems often contain phrases that reveal logical thought, reversible thinking, and the ability to conserve, seriate, and classify. Here are some typical phrases used by students:

If you order the things....
This shows....
If you changed it back, it would be the same.
It looks like....
If you put it back, it will have....
See what happens.
Except that....
If you added....
If you took away....
While....
Find out....
This is the sequence because....
These are different from those....

Interviewing Students:
Tasks for the Concrete Operational Period

Teachers realize the need for assessing students' understanding of concepts. The administration of the tasks outlined in the following sections should provide you with better insight into cognitive abilities. These tasks have been tested with hundreds of teachers. Educators generally experience little difficulty in administering them. There may be some problems, however, in interpreting the results. For this reason, detail is given on how some of the tasks are to be interpreted. It has been our experience that preservice and in-service teachers and parents are very positive about giving tasks to children. If you are going to understand Piaget's theories and students better, you should have experience in providing activities and questioning individuals so that you can gain insights into the stages of cognitive development.

Each task to be administered outlines a basic structure for the interview. Feel free, however, to modify them so as to make hypotheses about the child's thinking during the interview. Certain specific suggestions for administering the tasks should be followed (see Chapter 4., pages 84–85 for specific suggestions).

Outlined on page 117 is an interview form to be used to note the task achievement of the student. It will probably be best for you to record the responses while you interview.

The interview form needs some clarification. In each session you should *plan on giving six or seven tasks*. The time for administering these will vary from twenty to forty minutes, depending on the age and cognitive level of the child.

Place a description of each task in the left-hand column. Check in the appropriate column whether the child achieved or did not achieve the task. In the column provided for the level of cognition, write the period the student demonstrated.

With many students you will not get a clear demarcation of stage. They might perform preoperationally on three tasks and concrete operationally on four. You probably would indicate the transitional stage on the basis of your limited interviewing measures.

Piagetian Interview Activities

Time and distance.   Tell the child two persons are walking the same speed and distance, except one is walking on a straight path and one is walking on a crooked path, as shown below. Ask, "Which one reaches his house first? Why?" Use two strings of equal length to represent the paths.

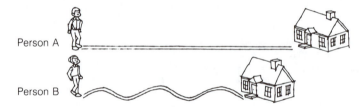

Discussion. Up to age nine, children usually have difficulty comparing the time taken and distance covered of two moving persons or objects. They believe going farther (in direction) takes more time. For this reason, pre-operational and early concrete operational children believe Person A will take more time.

Seriation.   Prepare ten cards of stickmen, dolls, flowers, or some animal so that they progressively increase in size. Place the first and last of the series on a table and tell the child to place the rest of them in order.

Discussion. During the concrete operational period, a child develops her ordering ability. This ability usually occurs during ages seven and eight. Many children, however, even in the third grade, cannot do the task. If they cannot do it, they probably also have difficulty with number because ordering is basic to understanding mathematics.

Ordering.   Show children, ages six through eight, stages of a developing moth, including the egg, larva, pupa, and adult. Discuss how the moth develops through these stages. Let the children look at the various stages of the organism and have them draw the stages in order of development.

Piagetian Interview Form: Concrete Operational Period

Name of Child _____ Interviewer's Name _____ Location _____

Age _____ Grade _____ Sex _____

Activity description (e.g., conservation of substance, class inclusion)	Achievement: + Task achieved − Not achieved	Indication of cognitive level (e.g., operation-al). Note: If child doesn't achieve level of task, it is assumed he is at a lower level.	Other comments about the stu-dent's behavior or statements	Justification (child's reason for responding as he did)
1.				
2.				
3.				
4.				
5.				
6.				
7.				
8.				
9.				
10.				

How many tasks were achieved?

How would you classify this student's level of development? Transitional? Concrete operational?

How would you justify this classification?

How could you confirm this level?

What are the educational implications of your interview?

Next, show them a picture of one of the stages and ask, "What would be the next stage? What was the stage before this? Why do you think so?"

Discussion. If the children can do this and give reasons for their placement of the stages, they probably are able to order. Many young children will not be able to do this. The activity is still valuable because it helps children grasp some concepts of development although they may not be able yet to inter-relate them. If they do not order correctly, they probably do not see the stages as a continuum of an organism slowly progressing to maturity. Children unable to do this probably reason by transduction.

Correspondence.   Obtain a tall, slender jar, a transparent glass bowl, and some beads, pennies, or marbles. Place one bead (or object selected) in the jar and then one in the bowl. Do this several times saying each time, "I am placing one bead in the jar, and now I am placing one bead in the bowl."

Ask, "Do I have the same, more, or fewer beads in the jar than I have in the bowl? Why do you think so?" If the child does not give the correct response, have her count the number of items in each container and then ask, "What do you think about the number in each now? Are there more, less, or the same?" If the child gives the correct answer and justification, you might repeat this activity, but this time place the beads in a jar and a corresponding number in a sack so that they are not visible.

Discussion. This task determines whether the child has developed the concrete operational ability of being able to do one-to-one correspondence. If she can do this, she must realize that for every bead you put in the jar, you also have placed one in the bowl. The number of beads in one container must, therefore, correspond to the number in the other. Using the sack in the second activity ensures that the child uses her mind and not just her perception to make conclusions.

Speed.   Obtain two toy cars of different colors. Draw on a piece of paper a line to indicate the end of a race. Place one of the cars behind the other at the start. Move both of these cars with each of your hands so that they come to the finish line at the same time. Ask, "Which of the cars was going faster, or did they both move the same? How do you know? How about the distance traveled? Did one cover a greater distance? When was one car ahead of the other? Why? Which one moved faster?"

Discussion. Young children believe if the cars finish the race together, they must be moving at the same speed. This is because they believe order, being in front or together, indicates speed. Usually at age nine or ten children take into consideration where an object started and stopped, distance traveled, and the time it took. If the child does not grasp this realization, he will have difficulty doing mathematical speed problems. This may occur even into the fifth and sixth grades. If a child cannot do such problems, use toy cars and other objects to help him discover the relationships of speed to time and distance so that he eventually will understand that speed = distance/time.

Conservation of substance.   Show a child a diagram of a kernel of popcorn and then draw a picture of it after it has popped. Ask, "Is there more corn after it is popped than before it is popped? Why has the volume changed?"

Discussion. Preoperational children, being perception bound, believe there is more corn to eat after it is popped. Concrete children know that altering the corn's state does not change its amount.

Reversibility.   Have children grow bean seeds or show them plants in various stages of development. After they have raised some plants, have them draw how they grew. The children should diagram something like below. Give the children a diagram of a young plant and ask them to draw how it would look in stages before and after this picture. Next, have the children draw several pictures showing the stages of development of plants in reverse order. Ask, "Why do you think your pictures are true?"

Discussion: If the children can reverse properly and give you reasons why they are drawing the plants in this order, they have probably achieved reversibility in their thinking. Checking for reversibility can be easily done whenever the children have prepared and learned something in one order and are then asked to reverse the order.

Reverse seriation.   Obtain twenty straws. The straws should be cut so that you have two series of ten straws each that progress in length. Set up one series from short to long and then ask the children to take the other set and place them in reverse order.

Discussion. This task identifies whether or not children can reverse the order of a series of objects. Children of seven can usually seriate, but many children ages eight through nine have difficulty in reversing the order.

Classification—Ascending and descending hierarchy.   Prepare a number of cards, some labeled *birds* with pictures of birds on them, some labeled *ducks* with pictures of ducks on them, and some labeled *animals* with pictures of various animals on them. Show these to a group of eight to ten-year-old children. Ask them to arrange the cards in groups according to each of the three labels. Next, place the "bird" pile on the "duck" pile and ask, "Is the bird label, now on top, still appropriate? Why?" Now place the "animal" pile on the others. Ask, "Is this appropriate? Why? Do all the cards belong in this pile? Are birds animals? Are ducks animals? If all the animals in the world died, would there be any ducks? Why or why not?"

Discussion. This activity determines whether a child understands class inclusion; that is, ducks are not only ducks but also birds (an ascending hierarchy). Ducks are a subgroup belonging to birds, a higher major group. Asking if ducks would remain if all the animals are killed determines whether the child can also descend a hierarchy (go from animals, a major group, to ducks, a subgroup).

Conservation of area.   Obtain eight cubes of sugar. Stack four together so that they appear as shown in diagram A below. Then, arrange the other four so they appear as in diagram B. Or prepare and show the child diagrams of the two situations. Ask, "Is the distance around (perimeter) A the same as that around B? Why?" Tell the child, "The other day a girl told me they were not the same perimeter, or distance around. What would you tell her? How would you prove it?"

Discussion. By this age, children will usually conserve area. But they think that if the area is the same, the perimeter must be the same too. If each square were two centimeters wide, the perimeter of A would be sixteen centimeters and of B, 20 centimeters. If the child does not come up with correct responses, have her count the sides of each of the diagrams and then ask, "What do you think about the perimeters?"

Conservation.   Rip a newspaper in half. Ask, "Do I have more, less, or the same amount of newspaper as I had before?" (conservation of substance) Ask, "Do the combined pieces of newspaper weigh more, less, or the same as the paper did before it was torn? Why?" (conservation of weight) Ask, "If I put these torn pieces of newspaper in a large tank of water, would they occupy more, less, or the same amount of space as when the paper was whole? Why?" (conservation of volume)

Discussion. Children do not develop conservation usually until after age six. In other words, they do not realize that physically altering one property of matter does not necessarily change its amount, weight, or the volume it will occupy. Conservation of substance and weight usually develop by age eight, while conservation of volume occurs later.

Number.   Obtain ten straws. If the child can count, have her count them one through ten. Point to a middle straw and ask, "If the last straw is ten, what is the number of this straw?" Place the straws together and have the child count them. Move the straws apart. Ask, "Do I have more, less, or the same number of straws now as before?"

Discussion. Preoperational children often can count but do not know number. To fully comprehend number children must understand the following:

  1. *Classification*—realize that the straws, although they may not look alike, are still straws.
  2. *Cardination*—realize that no matter how you arrange objects in a set, you still have the same number.
  3. *Ordination*—place the straws in order and realize that where the object is in the order determines its number.

Class Inclusion.   Show the children some fruit (e.g., ten raisins and two pears). Ask, "In what ways are these alike? What do you call them? Are there more raisins than fruit? If I took the fruit and you took the raisins, would I have more, or would you have more? How would you be able to prove who had more?"

Discussion. This activity tests again for class inclusion. Does the child realize that the subclass *raisins* is included in the major class *fruit*? Is the child overcome by the perception of a large number of raisins?

Going beyond the Tasks:
The Importance of Mental Structures

GUEST
EDITORIAL

Darrell G. Phillips
Science Education Center
University of Iowa

Much of the interest centered around Piaget has been devoted to the tasks, or individual interview problems, developed by Piaget and his colleagues. These tasks, especially the conservation tasks (e.g., number, amount, weight), have been used by authors of research studies as well as by classroom teachers. It is a tribute to Piaget's genius that these tasks, even though employing simple objects and terminology, typically reveal some surprising aspects of human thought; this fact possibly accounts for the continued interest shown by educators. But the real question, the educational question, of "Where do we go from here?" is not answered by these tasks. And it is this same question that has not been addressed by many of Piaget's followers in this country.

For example, consider the well-intentioned classroom teacher who learns and gives tasks to her students; then finds that many students fail the tasks. What next? What avenues are open? The teacher wants the students to pass the tasks, but often there is no recourse other than teaching (either overtly or covertly) the correct verbal responses to the students. "Well, what's wrong with that? Isn't that what we always do?" Quite so. If the child does not know the capital of Brazil, the teacher's job is to provide the answer. But to treat Piagetian tasks as no more than fact-recall test instruments excludes their richness of meaning and rejects their primary purpose: to test for the existence of mental structures.

Mental structures, as defined by Piaget, are systems of transformation. In other words, these structures are the mechanisms by which we interrelate, transform, and interpret data, information, or facts. For example, a given classification structure can be applied to *any* content, be it elephants, stars, events, or people. Mental structures, then, transcend or go beyond mere factual knowledge.

Piaget has outlined more than forty different mental structures for the concrete operational stage alone: eight structures for classification and relations, twenty-four structures for spatial relationships, and others concerned with time, movement, chance, number, conservation, and measurement. The major point is that these structures are interrelated within a given set as well as among different sets, thereby providing a powerful approach to the understanding of human learning.

As a brief example, consider the structures dealing with classification at the concrete operational level:

1. *Primary addition of classes*—Simple two or three-step hierarchies involving class inclusion (e.g., more cows or more animals).

2. *Secondary addition of classes*— complementary classes, singular classes, null class, and most importantly, "vicariance" (i.e., collies + all other dogs = chows + all other dogs).

3. *One-to-many multiplication of classes*—One class is related to several other classes. Requires the use of two or more criteria simultaneously.

4. *One-to-one multiplication of classes* — Several classes are related to several other classes. This generates classification matrices which employ two or more criteria simultaneously.

A teacher who has a working knowledge of these mental structures realizes a whole new spectrum of classroom applications. For example, awareness of the classification structures listed above leads to a number of important ideas: (1) that classification is *more* than sorting sets of objects into groups, and that such sorting gives rise to little more than "collections" which are not necessarily classes; (2) that memorizing a given classification scheme, or being told how to classify a set of objects, does not allow a student to learn how to classify; (3) that there is a definite *sequence* in learning how to classify, first two forms of additive, then two forms of multiplicative classification; (4) that such sequences can be used as a basis from which to design and plan appropriate classroom activities; (5) that these classification structures, once formed, can be used to classify any content, from observable objects to hypothetical entities; and (6) that students' progress in developing these structures can be assessed by using any number of appropriate tasks. And all of this is derived from just the four classification structures.

As one learns about these structures, the possibilities for classroom applications begin to multiply rapidly. The various sets contain internal relationships as well as relationships that carry across to yet other sets of structures. For example, the class inclusion characteristic of the first classification structure is found (in modified form) in the first structures for topological, projective, and Euclidean space, plus the first time structure. Such interrelatedness provides still more possibilities for classroom applications.

The learning of tasks and the presentation of tasks to human subjects is a necessary first step in understanding Piaget, but the tasks themselves are no more than diagnostic instruments for use in the determination of a person's intellectual level. Curricula cannot be developed from the tasks alone, nor do the tasks provide clues as to remedial activities or necessary prerequisites. The richness of the work of Piaget will not be realized until educators recognize the underlying patterns of intellectual development as outlined by the sets of mental structures.

BIBLIOGRAPHY

Bodin, Margaret A. *Jean Piaget*. New York: Penguin Books, 1980.
    The concrete operational period is given short treatment, but the book and chapter on "Logic in Action" is highly readable and recommended.
Brainerd, Charles J. *Piaget's Theory of Intelligence.* Englewood Cliffs, N.J.: Prentice-Hall, 1978.
    The chapter on concrete operations is very good. The presentation of replication studies is a real strength of this book.
Copeland, Richard W. *How Children Learn Mathematics* 2d ed. New York: Macmillan Publishing Co., 1974.
    If you teach children mathematics, this book is highly recommended.
Ginsburg, Herbert, and Opper, Sylvia. *Piaget's Theory of Intellectual Development.* 2d ed. Englewood Cliffs, N.J.: Prentice-Hall, 1979.
    Chapters 3 and 4 detail the concrete operational period.

Labinowicz, Ed. *The Piaget Primer*. Menlo Park, Calif.: Addison Wesley Publishing Co., 1980.
This book is designed for educators. The tasks are numerous and the graphics are excellent.

Piaget, Jean. *The Child's Conception of Number*. New York: Humanities Press, 1953.
This book is a presentation of Piaget's original work concerning the child's development of number concepts.

————. *Six Psychological Studies*. New York: Random House, 1967.
Educators will find this a good overview of the stages.

————. *The Child's Conception of Movement and Speed*. New York: Basic Books, 1970a.
This book reports a series of experiments on movement and speed.

————. *Genetic Epistemology*. New York: W.W. Norton & Co., 1970b.
In this book Piaget outlines the philosophical foundations of genetic epistemology. He does so clearly and with examples that educators will find understandable and applicable.

————. *The Child's Conception of Time*. New York: Ballantine Books, 1971.
Piaget's work with the child's conception of time is described.

Piaget, Jean, and Inhelder, Barbel. *The Psychology of the Child*. New York: Basic Books, 1969.
A very good general introduction to Piaget's theory.

————. *Memory and Intelligence*. London: Rutledge & Kegan Paul, 1973.

REFERENCES

Copeland, Richard W. "How Children Learn Mathematics," *Teaching Implications of Piaget's Research*. New York: Macmillan Publishing Co., 1970, p. 85.

Elkind, David. "Quantity Conceptions in Junior and Senior High School Students." *Child Development* 32 (1961): 551–60.

"Jean Piaget." *Saturday Review* (May 20, 1967): 38.

IV | EVALUATION
THE CONCRETE OPERATIONAL PERIOD

The evaluation for this chapter is divided into two parts. The first describes several different tasks for children. Explain how preoperational and concrete operational students would solve the same tasks. The second part of the evaluation is similar to those used in the previous chapters.

Some clay and two jars filled three-fourths full of water are presented to the student. The clay is divided into two equal parts in front of the child and shaped into round balls. The question is asked, "Are these two balls equal?" If the child does not agree, the balls are modified until she does think they are the same, and then one is flattened. The student is asked, "What do you think will happen to the water level of two equally filled jars of water if the round piece of clay is put in one and the flattened shaped is placed in the other?" Before placing the clay in the jars, the child marks on the sides of the jars how the water levels will change. The clay is placed in each of the jars. After the clay is submerged, the following questions are asked: "What happened? What does that tell you? Why?"

Describe how a preoperational student and a concrete operational student would respond to this task.

Students are presented with six pieces of paper. Three are large, medium, and small triangles and three are large, medium, and small circles. The students are asked to design a system for classifying the objects.

How would you expect preoperational children to classify the objects? Concrete operational students?

Listed below are some of the main topics covered in Chapter 5. Read each statement and rate it on the scale TWICE: once according to what you knew about the topic before starting this chapter and again according to what you've learned by completing the chapter. Circle the appropriate number and mark B for *before* and A for *after* next to the number as indicated below.

Topic	Personal Evaluation					
	Low		Moderate		High	
Example: Distinguish among important Piagetian mental operations	①B 2	3	4	5	⑥A	
1. Reversible thinking	1	2	3	4	5	6
2. Logical patterns of thought	1	2	3	4	5	6
3. Simple classification	1	2	3	4	5	6
4. Multiple classification	1	2	3	4	5	6
5. Class inclusion	1	2	3	4	5	6
6. Conservation	1	2	3	4	5	6
7. Transition of students	1	2	3	4	5	6
8. Simple ordering	1	2	3	4	5	6
9. Multiple seriation	1	2	3	4	5	6
10. Transitive inference	1	2	3	4	5	6
11. Number	1	2	3	4	5	6
12. Space and time	1	2	3	4	5	6

6 | The Formal Operational Period and the Reflective Student

Sometime during the secondary school years formal patterns of thought may emerge from the concrete foundations of the last period. According to Piaget, formal operational thought is the summit of cognitive development. Individuals demonstrating this level of thought reflect on their thinking, reason abstractly, and resolve problems through systematic consideration of possibilities. While formal patterns of thought emerge during the adolescent years, we certainly do not need to remind educators that most students do not clearly and consistently manifest this level of thinking. This observation has been confirmed by research (see "Guest Editorial" by Premo and Fahey, p. 141) as well as by everyday experience. The fact that most adolescents are capable of, but not performing, formal operations suggests that many of the patterns of thought described in this chapter are appropriate aims of instruction in middle schools, junior, and senior high schools.

I | EXPLORATION
THE FORMAL OPERATIONAL PERIOD

Probing the Period

For this chapter we probe the period through interviews. The interviews involve two individuals in Piagetian tasks that are designed to evaluate both concrete and formal patterns of thought. We start with Wendy, age fourteen and in the ninth grade at the time of the interview. Wendy is a good student with above average grades and a normal range of interests and activities for an adolescent. We then interview Laura, age twenty-two and a senior in college. She, too, is an above average student and has an average range of interests for a college student. The interviews deal with tasks that evaluate concrete levels of thought—conservation of matter and liquid—and two tasks that evaluate formal patterns of thought—proportional reasoning, and separation and control of variables.

Conservation of Matter

Interviewer. Do both clay balls have the same amount of material?
Wendy. There's a little more in this one.
Interviewer. Go ahead and take some clay off this ball, so that both balls are even.
Wendy. O. K., they're even (taking some clay off one of the balls).
Interviewer. Now, roll one of them out like a hot dog.
Wendy. That long?
Interviewer. O. K. That should be enough. Now, would you say that there is more or less or the same amount of clay in the hot dog as there is in the other sphere?
Wendy. About the same amount because I didn't take any clay from it before I started rolling it.
Interviewer. Is there any other reason that you could give to show that it is the same amount? You said that you didn't take anything from it so it should be about the same.
Wendy. I don't think there would be anything else that would. They're the same, because I didn't take anything, so I think they should be the same.
Interviewer. Would they be the same weight?
Wendy. Yes.
Interviewer. The same volume? If you put them into water, would they displace the same amount of the water?
Wendy. Yes.
Interviewer. The other day another student told me that there was more clay in the longer one. If that student told you that, what would you tell her?
Wendy. I'd ask her why she thought that, because I don't see how it could be more. If anything, it would be less because the clay would have rubbed off on the table.
Interviewer. What if she just told you, "I know that there is more clay there." What would you tell her?
Wendy. I would say she's crazy because I don't think there could be.

Did Wendy demonstrate logical patterns of thought?
Did she conserve substance?

Conservation of Liquid

Interviewer. Would you check and see if there is the same amount of water in these two glasses. Is the amount of water equal?
Wendy. Yes.
Interviewer. Why don't you pour the water from one of the glasses into the dish? Is there less or more or the same amount of water?

Wendy. The same.

Interviewer. How would you justify that answer? The same girl told me the other day that there is more when you pour the water into the dish.

Wendy. I still don't see how there could be more. I didn't add any more.

Interviewer. You didn't add any more, and you didn't take any out. So you think it's the same. How could you prove that? Is there some kind of test you could perform to convince me there is the same amount of water?

Wendy. No.

Interviewer. You didn't add any, and you didn't take any out. What if I told you the girl said there is more in the dish because it is wider.

Wendy. That wouldn't make a difference because it's not as deep as this other glass would be, so it wouldn't matter if it was wider.

Interviewer. So it's wider but it's not as deep and the glass is taller and that's narrower. O. K.?

Wendy. Yes.

What mental operations were demonstrated by Wendy's answers?
Did she demonstrate both inversion and compensation?
Which statements reveal the type(s) of mental operations?

Proportional Reasoning

Interviewer. O. K., Wendy, this test has you look at two stick figures. We'll call this one Mr. Tall and this one Mr. Short. Why don't you measure the height of the stick figures in big paper clips. How many paper clips high is the short figure?

Wendy. Four.

Interviewer. Now, how many paper clips high is the tall stick figure?

Wendy. Six.

Interviewer. How many paper clips high is the short one?

Wendy. Four.

Interviewer. Now, six and four, can you remember that? Put these big paper clips aside, and you don't get to look at them again. Here are some little paper clips. Measure the height of Mr. Tall in little paper clips.

Wendy. About eight.

Interviewer. We'll call it eight, O. K? This figure is eight paper clips high. How tall is Mr. Short in little paper clips? Can you figure out how tall this one would be with the information that you have?

Wendy. Six. Well, if Mr. Tall was six paper clips high and Mr. Short was four paper clips high with the big paper clips, and Mr. Tall was two more with the little ones, then Mr. Short would have to be two more with the little ones because they are two apart. The difference is two.

Interviewer. Do you want to check it?

Wendy. (Checks the height of the stick figures with the small paper clips.) This one is 5½, but this one is about 6½ or 8½. It's 5½.

Interviewer. Do you think that indicates that there is an error in how you figured it out or just that the paper clips were different sizes?

Wendy. Well, this one is about seven and one half and this is five and one half, so it's still a difference of two.

How would you describe Wendy's pattern of reasoning?
How did she resolve the proportional reasoning problem?
Would you say she demonstrated formal or concrete patterns of thought?

Separation and Control of Variables

Interviewer. Let's do one more. On this one you see these strings and weights are set up so each one is like a pendulum. But you see that there are different lengths of string and different weights. If you're trying to determine the period of a pendulum, which is the time of one swing, what do you think is the important variable? What is the important factor that determines how fast the pendulum goes back and forth? What I'm going to ask you to do is to show or somehow prove your answer to me.

Wendy. What matters is how long the string is and the weight of the weight.

Interviewer. So how can you check that?

Wendy. Well, hold all the pendulums at the same distance and then let them go like that and see which one goes farther.

Interviewer. Why don't you do that? Remember, there are three different weights and you can adjust the lengths however you would like.

Wendy. The longer the string and the heavier the weight, the farther out the pendulum will go.

Interviewer. What can you do to check that idea? If I said, O. K. I'll believe you if you prove it to me, how would you prove it?

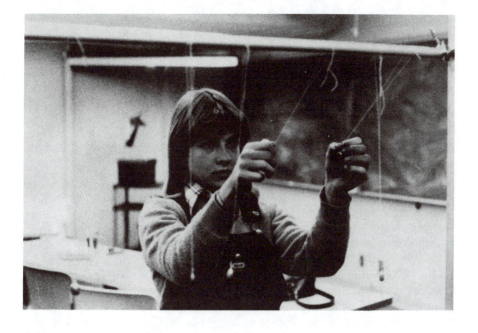

Wendy. These two are the same weight but different lengths. If you hold them out evenly and let them swing, this one goes out farther.

Interviewer. So, does it take the same time?

Wendy. This one goes back quicker. And then these two. It's the same thing; that one goes out quicker, but this one goes out farther.

Interviewer. What about the others?

Wendy. This one seems about the same.

Interviewer. What if you had the same lengths of string and two different weights?

Wendy. The heavier weight will go out farther, and the lighter weight would go out quicker.

Interviewer. Why don't you try that.

Wendy. O. K. This one goes out .... They are about the same.

Interviewer. What does that tell you about the length of string and the weight?

Wendy. The length matters the most because they both go out the same. So, it's really the length of the string that matters.

Interviewer. Can you check that? Can you do something else to prove that? With all of the other weights ... ?

Wendy. I thought these were the same.

Interviewer. No, they are different weights but the same length.

Wendy. The same thing.

Interviewer. It works?

Wendy. Yes, they're the same.

Did Wendy demonstrate a systematic separation and control of variables in this problem?

How would you characterize her reasoning?

Did she get the correct answer?

Is there a difference between the correct answer and patterns of reasoning?

Contrast often clarifies different patterns of reasoning. Here are the responses of Laura, a college student, on the same problems. As you read her responses, try to identify those passages that reveal reasoning patterns and mental operations.

Conservation of Matter

Interviewer. Would you say that both of those spheres have the same amount of clay?

Laura. Yes, they're equal.

Interviewer. You are sure they are equal?

Laura. Yes, positive. They look very equal at this point.

Interviewer. O. K. Why don't you roll one of them out into a snake. Now would you say the long piece of clay has more or less or the same amount of clay as the other sphere?

Laura. The same amount.

Interviewer. How do you know that? How could you demonstrate that to me?

Laura. Because we started with the same amount of clay to begin with. You could squish this back up into a ball, and it would look just like this one.

Interviewer. Is there anything else you could tell me about the clay that would demonstrate it was the same amount?

Laura. You could measure the volume, to see if you have the same volume in both pieces of clay.

Interviewer. Anything else?

Laura. You could weigh them.

Interviewer. They would have the same weight?

Laura. Yes. The same mass.

Interviewer. Is there anything else you could think of?

Laura. It seems like it is the volume and the mass that would demonstrate that both pieces of clay were the same amount.

What is your analysis of Laura's responses?
How do her responses on this task differ from Wendy's?

Conservation of Liquid

Interviewer. Is there the same amount of water in the two glasses?

Laura. Yes.

Interviewer. Pour the water from one of the glasses into the dish. Is there less or more or the same amount of water in the glass as there is in the dish?

Laura. The same amount.

Interviewer. Why? How would you explain that?

Laura. Well, you started out with the same amount in the glass. It doesn't change the water at all when you pour it into the dish. You didn't lose any in the process. We didn't gain any either.

Interviewer. Is there anything you could do to demonstrate that?

Laura. Well, you could pour the water back, or you could figure out the volumes of each of these containers and how much is filled with water.

Interviewer. What if I told you that the water in the dish looks like there is more because it is so wide?

Laura. But it's a lot thinner; I mean it's wider but it's thinner. The relationship between the width and the diameter is the same in the glass and in the dish.

Interviewer. Is there anything else you could do to demonstrate to me that there was the same amount of water in the dish?
Laura. Yes, pour it back into the glass the way it was before.

What factors of mental operations are demonstrated in Laura's answers? What differences can you detect between Laura's and Wendy's responses to this problem?

Proportional Reasoning

Interviewer. Here are two drawings of stick persons. I want you to measure both of them with big paper clips.
Laura. The big one is six paper clips tall, and the little one is four.
Interviewer. Now measure the tall one in small paper clips. How tall is it?
Laura. About eight small paper clips.
Interviewer. How many small paper clips would the small person be?
Laura. About 5⅓.
Interviewer. How did you figure that out.
Laura. I set up a ratio.
Interviewer. What was the ratio?
Laura. 4 over 6 is equal to x over 8. Figure that out. It works out that x equals 5⅓.
Interviewer. Do you want to check that to see if that's correct?
Laura. (Checks the height of the small person with paper clips.) It's pretty close. 5⅓.

How does Laura's response differ from Wendy's?

Separation and Control of Variables

Interviewer. Here are a number of different pendulums. There are different weights and lengths of string. What factor is most important concerning the period of the pendulum, which is the time of one swing? Demonstrate how you would solve this problem.
Laura. O. K. You take two weights that are the same, but they are on different length strings. Pull them back the same amount and let them go. It turns out that they have different periods.
Interviewer. Can you reach that conclusion based on just two comparisons?
Laura. You can assume the other ones would act the same. You could try it. Those two had the same weight. These two have the same lengths of string.
Interviewer. I am not clear what you've demonstrated.
Laura. Well, you keep all but one variable constant.
Interviewer. You've got the right answer, but I'm not sure you have the justification.
Laura. Well, when you set up an experiment where you have only one variable to check, only one thing that is different, then you have to test to see if that one variable is the thing that is causing the difference. Yet,

if you hold everything constant, then the test wouldn't show you any-thing; and if you have more than one variable at once, then you couldn't determine which variable it was that was determining the outcome.

Interviewer. O. K. If you were applying these ideas to this problem, what would you do?

Laura. Well, in this case, you have two weights that are the same, so that's constant; and you pull them back the same amount, so that's constant. And if you let them go with the same force, that's a constant, too. So, the only thing that is different about them is the length of the string.

Reasoning Strategies: Reversibility to Reflection

Piaget calls this stage *formal operational* because the types of reasoning man-ifested are systematic and involve logically complex processes. Operations no longer are restricted to use solely on concrete objects but can be per-formed on other operations as well. As a result of this development, the individual can now solve problems that can be resolved only through the use of reasoning strategies such as

1. Hypothetical-deductive thinking.
2. Using ratios and proportions.
3. Inductive reasoning.
4. Reflective abstraction.
5. Systematic isolation and control of variables.
6. Combinatorial logic.

Formal operational individuals differ considerably from those in the concrete operational stage. They no longer are limited to solving concrete types of problems but can think in terms of abstractions and multiple hypotheses. They understand and resolve relatively complex verbal prob-lems and perform complex logic. They symbolically represent thought processes and act or reflect on them (e.g., A may be greater than, less than, or the same as B, and it may be related in similar ways to C. Therefore, C may be related to A in the following ways.... Formal operational persons also stipulate what additional information is required to definitely know the relationship of A to B and C). Another example of formal thinking is solving ratio problems such as $A/B = X/Y$. The quantities for A, B, and Y may be given, and the student is to solve for X. In other words, formal operational students often function in an algebraic manner, letting symbols represent ideas and categories while simultaneously performing mental operations on them. Furthermore, the formal operational student utilizes several operations to resolve problems and to apply hypotheses to their solutions.

Performing higher levels of reasoning and abstract thought requires individuals to follow logical patterns and rules. Reflective students use their minds to a higher degree than students in earlier stages to check what is perceived. They are not overcome by perceptions as easily as individuals in the earlier stages. Because higher levels of thinking are structured and

Formal operational persons can think in terms of abstractions and can consider multiple hypotheses.

require that definite operational patterns and processes be followed, they are more formal in structure. Consequently, the formal operational individual's thinking is more likely to be internally rather than externally stimulated. That is, an external stimulus is not necessary to set off thinking. The formal operational individual, because of widened cognitive ability, relies more on the mind and, as a result, is characterized by planned behavior which increases his proficiency.

Another dimension can now be added to the development of logical thought.

Reflex Actions Sensorimotor Strategies Ages 0–2	Representation of Actions Intuitive Strategies Ages 2–7	Reversibility of Actions Practical Strategies Ages 8–11	Reflective Actions Formal Strategies Ages 12 onward

Students in Transition

Because of the significant advances in operational ability during this period, formal thinkers are capable of understanding, constructing, and applying abstract theories. Theoretical reasoning enables the individual to interact more effectively with the environment. However, adolescents vary considerably in their attempts at thinking. Many adolescents avoid thinking critically, as if to do so were to have dire consequences or demean their intellect and "self-concept." They appear to avoid cognitive challenge and tend to want to remain in the comparative comfort of the concrete stage. Others, presumably because of more success in school, maturity, and environmental differences, confront formal tasks with great tenacity. This is not to say that it is easy for them. It usually isn't. Present a problem requiring propositional or hypothetical-deductive thought and watch their "body language." Many of them fidget, grimace, or frown as they force their mind to perform the operations required. The result of such discomfort is a broadened intellect.

Most educators in upper elementary, middle, and junior and senior high schools will encounter students demonstrating patterns of reasoning that have *both* concrete and formal elements. As a matter of fact, educators can expect most students to demonstrate varied reasoning patterns. Understanding the difference between concrete and formal patterns is important for educators since this understanding provides direction as teachers attempt to help students achieve higher levels of thought.

There is another point worth mentioning. By early adolescence, behavior is multidimensional and multidetermined. Considering a student's response in class or answer to a task must include more than an analysis of the cognitive content. While Piaget perceives this period as the pinnacle of development, other theorists remind educators that the adolescent period is one of physical, social, and personal turmoil. The transition that occurs during adolescence is more than cognitive. Multiple factors should be reviewed in the evaluation of cognitive achievement. We can highlight these ideas with two examples. A student may not be motivated to answer questions thoughtfully and thoroughly; so while the student may be capable of formal thought, he does not make it evident. On the other hand, a student may have memorized an answer or procedure without understanding the problem. Here, then, is a case where the student would test as being at the formal operational level, but in fact is not at this level. These are only two instances from many that alert educators to the fact that a clear identification of formal thought may be difficult.

Many educators are confronted with the task of facilitating development from concrete to formal levels of thought. To do so requires educators to understand the major differences between the two stages. Since both concrete and formal periods are concerned with logical thought, what are some basic differences between the periods? There are two primary differences. First, in the formal operational period mental action no longer requires actual objects, events, or situations. For concrete students the realm of the real is possible. For formal students the realm of the possible is real. Inhelder and Piaget (1958) contrast the two periods:

> Concrete thought remains essentially attached to empirical reality. The system of concrete operations—the final equilibrium attained by pre-operational thought—can handle only a limited set of potential transformations. Therefore, it attains no more than a concept of "what is possible," which is a simple (and not very great) extension of the empirical situation. (p. 250)
>
> In formal thought there is a reversal of the direction of thinking between *reality* and *possibility* in the subject's method of approach. Possibility no longer appears merely as an extension of an empirical situation or of actions actually performed. Instead, it is *reality* that is now secondary to possibility. (p. 251)

The transition that occurs during adolescence is more than cognitive.

The second difference between the two periods is that in the formal operational period there is a more complete coordination of mental operations, particularly the reversibility of thought. The logical operations of inversion and reciprocity become coordinated into a single structure. The difference between the coordination of these operations at concrete and formal levels can be illustrated by referring to the conservation of matter task. When a ball of clay is transformed into a hot dog shape, concrete operational students will conserve matter across the changes. And they justify their answer by indicating the changes could be reversed. This is an example of inversion. The student may also indicate that the changes of one dimension (e.g., width) have compensated for changes in another dimension (e.g., height). This is an example of reciprocity. Concrete operational students can use either of these individually, but not in coordination. The formal operational student would use both inversion and reciprocity in justifying her response. Laura's responses to the concrete operational tasks were good examples of both inversion and reciprocity. You might go back to the "Probing the Period" section (pp. 125–133) and review her justifications. For comparison, you might also review Wendy's responses to the same tasks.

Coordination of the operations, inversion and reciprocity, occurs through a process termed *reciprocal assimilation*. This is simply the integration of diverse schemes. As cognitive development progresses, there is the construction of new patterns of thought through the modification and elaboration of existing patterns of thought. But, there is soon a need to consolidate and coordinate the developing systems. If this did not occur, there would be untold numbers of schemes, each serving its own purpose and requiring its own prerequisites. Instead, developing patterns of thought are coordinated in such a way that the two original patterns maintain their integrity and ability to operate separately. This is achieved through the process of reciprocal assimilation.

How can one tell if students are in transition? In general, the answer to this question is the most logical: students demonstrate concrete thought consistently and formal thought inconsistently. Figure 6.1 summarizes some differences between the two levels of thought.

FIGURE 6.1

A Comparison of Concrete and Formal Reasoning Patterns

Concrete	Formal
Students require objects, events, or actions for logical reasoning.	Students can reason abstractly without reference to concrete objects, events, or actions.
Conservation, class inclusion, ordering, and reversibility are characteristic reasoning patterns.	Theoretical, propositional, hypothetical, and combinatorial reasoning patterns are characteristic.
Students are unaware of inconsistencies and mistakes in reasoning.	Students are aware of inconsistencies and mistakes due to the use of mental checks and balances— reflective thought.
Students need clear, sequential directions for long and detailed projects.	Students can establish their own plans for long and detailed projects if given aims and goals.

Educators ask how the transition from concrete to formal thought occurs. Some would suggest that neurological maturation is responsible. This seems a reasonable explanation since physical development is quite pronounced during adolescence. But while important, maturation does not totally account for the transition. Some educators mention the influence of the family, church, and school as educational institutions. While important and contributory, social institutions alone do not account for the transition. Is it the accumulation experience? Well, yes, but not totally. Piaget suggests that all of these processes are coordinated by a fourth factor that he terms *equilibration*. Think of the transition process this way. While concrete patterns of thought are very good, they are still limited. As such, students will encounter problems they cannot resolve. As students attempt to resolve problems, they draw upon neurological factors, socially learned material, and physical experience. In the process they establish a new higher order, reorganization of intellectual structures. All the elements constituting old patterns of thought are coordinated and integrated into new patterns of thought. Equilibration is the focus of Chapter 8.

We will close this section by listing a few things educators can use to identify students in transition.

1. There is a rational but unsystematic approach to solving problems.

2. Reasonable observations are made of concrete problems, but abstract problems result in inadequate and inappropriate observations.

3. When confronted with an abstract problem, concrete procedures are applied.

4. There is inadequate planning and uncoordinated procedures in attempts to solve difficult problems.

5. A logical approach is used but checks and balances are not applied to assure accuracy and correctness of procedures or outcome.

6. Higher grades are achieved on concrete problems and lower grades are achieved on abstract problems.

II | EXPLANATION
THE FORMAL OPERATIONAL PERIOD

Educators are in a position to help facilitate formal reasoning by their students. With this in mind, you can view the explanations in this section as both a description of what a few students can do and what the majority should be encouraged to do.

The most complete discussion of formal operational thought is in *The Growth of Logical Thinking from Childhood to Adolescence* by Barbel Inhelder and Jean Piaget (1958). In addition to this source, Piaget devotes small portions of other books to the formal operational period. If you are interested, you might review *The Psychology of the Child* (Piaget and Inhelder, 1969), *Six Psychological Studies* (Piaget, 1967), and *The Child and Reality* (Piaget, 1973).

Formal Structures

When formal structures are developed, individuals exhibit thought that is comparable to propositional logic and elementary algebra. Piaget describes these patterns as the sixteen binary operations and the INRC group respectively.

The concrete structure of classification and seriation culminates in the formal structure of combinatorial, propositional logic. If given a problem involving two propositions, each of which may be true or false, an individual with formal intelligence can systematically generate all the logical combinations that may hold for the relationship between the propositions. Without getting lost in the terminology of propositional logic, we can tell you that there are sixteen possible outcomes when one combines two propositions, either one of which may be true or false. The individual systematically combines ideas into statements that are described by commonly used terms such as affirmation, implication, negation, conjunction, exclusion, equivalence, reciprocal implication, denial, and so on.

The second structure of formal thought is referred to as the INRC group. This structure is the culmination of the reversibility schemes that were first recognized as defining characteristics of concrete thought. Given a system in which transformations have occurred (e.g., a conservation task), the individual can follow the changes from one point to another and then mentally reverse the entire process and still maintain all the qualitative and quantitative properties of the material in the process. In order to do this the individual must understand the structural possibilities of Identity (I), Negation (N), Reciprocity (R), and Correlativity (C). Using the conservation of matter task as an example, the individual would realize that the material is still the same regardless of the shape (identity), that increased length is compensated for by decreased width (reciprocity), that thinness is related to length and fatness to height (correlativity), and that the entire process can be reversed to cancel the changes (negation).

Without very much effort it is easy to get lost in the formal terminology while examining logical contents. This is not our intention. We simply wish to identify some of Piaget's concepts relative to the formal period. We can certainly summarize this level of thought for educators by indicating that formal thought is generally identified with the cognitive capacities of mathematicians, logicians, scientists, and the like.

Formal Patterns of Reasoning

We really do not have to tell educators that adolescents do not reason like philosophers and scientists. But how widespread is formal thought among students in middle and secondary schools? Most evidence indicates that *at best* about a third of all students exhibit formal patterns of reasoning. The safest estimate is probably about 25 percent of students will display formal thinking during secondary school years. Remember that formal thinking does not come automatically with the biological changes of puberty. Cognitive development is a construction that includes biological maturation; yet it involves more: physical experience, social learning, and equilibration. We reiterate our position; as educators one of our tasks is to identify present patterns of thought and to facilitate development toward formal patterns of reasoning.

Cognitive development during adolescent years has recognizable elements of several basic patterns of thought; (1) the ability to reason without reference to concrete experience—reflective abstraction; (2) the ability to reason about the theoretical consequences of changes to objects and events—propositional thinking; (3) the ability to reason about the possible combinations of variables in a problem—combinatorial logic; (4) the ability to reason from particular to general conclusions—inductive reasoning; and

(5) the ability to reason from general premises to particular consequences—deductive reasoning. It is also clear that these patterns are related to one another and indeed are often seen in combination by educators.

Abstract reasoning. The thinking processes of adolescents begin to resemble those of adults because the individual can do relatively complex abstract reasoning. The formal individual is able, for example, to carry on a whole series of mental, logical processes using operations. She can hold a large body of information in her mind and perform several mental manipulations on it. It is precisely this *mental holding power* and the acting on and interrelating of what is held that demarcates formal students from those in the less cognitively developed stages, and explains why the student begins to comprehend legalistic, logical-mathematical thinking and complex literary criticism.

The formal operational student thinks of things not in her presence. For example, she can think of and describe an idealistic society. In addition, she can accept assumptions in solving problems. She can imagine an experiment not actually before her and describe its outcome, just as she can understand imaginary numbers.

The formal thinker also accepts assumptions for the sake of an argument, even if they are contrary to fact. A concrete operational student will not do this. For example, if you say to a concrete student, "If bridges were made of glass" or some other similar remark, she would indicate that she does not accept your statement. The concrete student is bound to the real world and, therefore, does not make conjectures. On the contrary, formal adolescents do perform abstract thinking.

During the latter part of the formal period, students begin to grasp double meanings in literature. For example, they are able to interpret *Gulliver's Travels* as more than just an adventure story. They also understand part-whole relationships better during this period. For example, they realize that reading a word, a line, or a sentence at a time may not result in comprehension of the author's message. The ideas have to be combined and considered as a whole.

Reflective thinking is one of the main processes characterizing a formal operational student. The student at this stage is able to do this type of reasoning because she can hold more information in her mind and perform mental operations on it. For example, the formal adolescent can solve the following problem by reflection:

Bob is fairer than John; John is fairer than Bruce.
Who is the darkest of these?

To do this, the adolescent must perform several operations such as:

(BOB)	is fairer than	(JOHN)
(JOHN)	is fairer than	(BRUCE)
Therefore, (BOB)	is fairer than	(BRUCE)

In order to resolve the problem, the child has to reflect over a series of propositions and identify their functions in the problem-solving process. In

Piaget Testing as a Change Agent

GUEST
EDITORIAL

Joe Premo
Consultant in Science
Minneapolis Public Schools

Patricia Fahey
Science Teacher
Minneapolis Public Schools

Information about Piaget and his developmental model of intelligence has been available to teachers for over fifteen years. It has been available in numerous books describing the stages of development and the specialized vocabulary that goes with the theory. Many science teachers have "heard the talk" but somehow it didn't become real to them. It was a formal presentation of a formal set of concepts. It was our desire to utilize Piaget's theory as a tool for curriculum change in our junior high school program in Minneapolis, Minnesota. We felt there was a mismatch between the mostly concrete students and the mostly formal concepts in the curriculum. We came upon a group-administered Piaget test developed by Anton Lawson at the Lawrence Hall of Science, University of California, Berkeley, California.[1] This instrument, Test of Formal Reasoning, had great appeal to us because it was a group test which could be administered to a whole class. This would allow us to gather data without the costly, and time-consuming individual interview. We felt the need for local, individual teacher verification of Piaget's findings. We felt that gathering data on their own students would bring home to teachers the need for curriculum revision to reflect the nature of their population.

The test consists of fifteen items and is administered as an incomplete demonstration for each item. Students observe the demonstration and answer a question by checking a multiple-choice response on their answer sheets. They are then required to write at least one sentence telling why they think their answers are correct. A correct score is obtained only when both the answer and the explanation are acceptable. Items test for conservation of mass, conservation of displaced volume, proportional reasoning, controlling variables, combinatorial reasoning, and probability.

Perhaps a note should be added here regarding this test. A paper-and-pencil, group-administered test definitely loses the sensitivity of the interview approach. When children are not allowed to manipulate their own materials, and merely watch demonstrations, something is lost. However, a group-administered test does have the definite advantage that it can be used by teachers with whole classes at once. This clearly increased the usefulness of the test in that it could be quickly used as a curriculum modification tool, where none existed before. One must be careful, though, not to generalize too far using only this tool.

The test was administered in science classes to nearly 1,100 students, in grades 7 through 9. The administration takes two full class periods on consecutive days, and all tests were given in science classes. Tests were administered at thirteen different schools. The test was administered by the consultant or resource teacher during the

---

1. Dr. Anton Lawson is presently a professor of science education, Department of Physics, Arizona State University, Tempe, Arizona.

first science class. The teachers observed and followed the protocol script so they could test each succeeding class. At the conclusion of the testing cycle, the consultant or resource teacher and the science teacher corrected the tests together. This interchange was extremely valuable since incorrect explanations reveal the thought processes being employed by the student. Our data indicated that approximately 65 percent of our seventh and eighth graders were concrete (0–5 tasks passed); approximately 30 percent were transitional (6–11 tasks passed) and 4 percent were formal (12–15 tasks passed). Ninth graders were approximately 43 percent concrete, 45 percent transitional, and 12 percent formal (see Table 6–1).

Table 6–1
Distribution of Scores by Grade Level

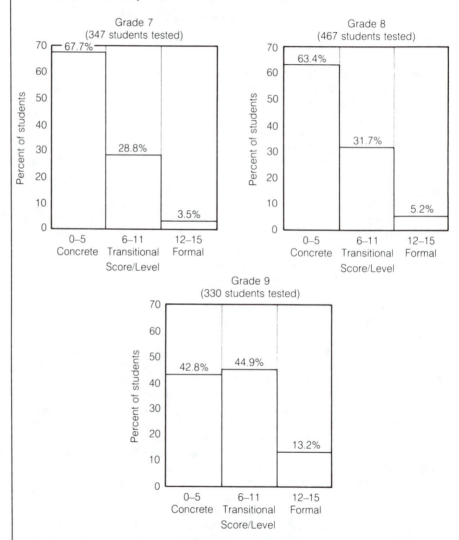

In contrast, you may note the differences when science students at grades 11 and 12 were tested using the same instrument. It is important to point out that the eleventh and twelfth grade students *selected* the science courses. So, one would expect higher percentages of formal operational reasoning among these students (see Table 6–2).

Table 6–2
Distribution of Scores by Grade Level

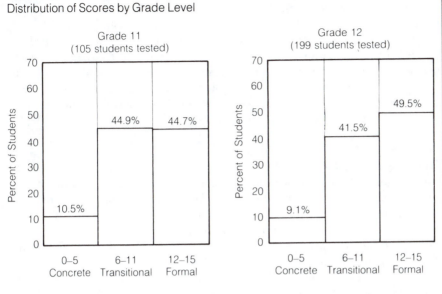

Outgrowths of Piagetian Testing in Minneapolis

Piaget's theory has relevance for Minneapolis, at the very least, as a curriculum change tool. Several spin-offs have already been implemented:

1. A series of in-service workshops were offered at a local college for credit or no credit, teaching current teachers some educational aspects of Piaget's theory.

2. Two units were written using the exploration, concept labeling, and concept application model of instruction. These two units were developed with two concepts commonly taught in junior high science. (An in-service workshop was held to explain these ideas to junior high science teachers, and to give them hands-on experience with this approach to teaching curriculum).

3. A series of science units have been written, as part of a federal project on Piaget. These units begin with concrete activities, expand to transitional activities, and finally include some formal activities all designed to teach the same concept.

4. An alternative form of the test was generated by the federal project and has been used as a posttest in some settings.

Generally, as a result of exposure to Piaget's theory, Minneapolis teachers have at least an awareness that students are constantly developing in ability, rather than being of fixed intelligence. In some teachers it has sparked a genuine interest in the nature of the child, and a concern for the direction in which their particular curriculum is leading these children.

other problem-solving situations a person does essentially the same thing as indicated below:

1. Notes the type of problem given
2. Determines what was known and what was unknown
3. Outlines the steps (operations) required to determine the unknown
4. Performs the operation mentally.

The formal student also performs reflectively after solving the problem by reviewing the operations performed, so that in the future, when presented with similar problems, she can easily determine their solution.

An example of abstract reasoning in science occurs when a student applies different patterns of reasoning to aspects of the experiment that are not directly observable. Students also reflect over an experiment in an effort to determine better ways to obtain more accurate data. Writers and artists perform similar functions when they critically evaluate their work in an effort to convey their ideas better.

Hypothetical-deductive thinking. Formal thinkers are characterized, furthermore, by hypothetical-deductive and propositional thinking. When confronted with a problem, they formulate hypotheses and then deduce conclusions from them. For example, an adolescent might think, "The way to get a car is to ask my folks for the money. No, they won't give it to me." (A hypothesis is constructed and then rejected.) "I will have to get the money myself." (Another hypothesis is proposed.) "It, therefore, follows that I shall have to get a job and save the money for it." (A deductive operational process is used.)

As you can see, hypothetical-deductive thinking is not limited by perception, memory, and possibility. Once an individual has established the premises (hypotheses), the conclusions can be deduced. All of this occurs at an abstract, symbolic level. This is why the term *formal* is used to describe the period and the word *reflective* is used to describe the student. Thinking transcends the realm of the concrete, the real, the practical and extends to the realm of the formal, the possible, the abstract.

The car example was used with a purpose in mind. It shows that formal patterns of reasoning may be evident as students think of matters beyond the classroom. For this reason educators are encouraged to pay attention to conversations and discussions by students that do not relate directly to academics. Such observations can reveal patterns of reasoning not shown in the classroom.

Syllogistic reasoning. The syllogism is a special case of hypothetical-deductive thinking. The syllogism takes the form of a major premise, a minor premise, and a conclusion. An example follows:

    a. All mammals nurse their young. (Major premise)
    b. This animal nurses its young. (Minor premise)
    c. Therefore, it is a mammal. (Conclusion)

Formal thinkers can also evaluate whether or not syllogisms are likely to be valid:

    a. All dogs bark.
    b. This animal barked.
    c. Therefore, it is a dog.

Formal thinkers realize that the premise "All dogs bark" may not be sufficient because other animals may also bark.

"It therefore follows that" is a key operation involved in hypothetical-deductive thinking and identifies an advancement over earlier periods of mental development. Because formal thinkers do evaluate their conclusions, their cognitive capacities and intellectual abilities expand tremendously. For individuals to have a concept of an object, they must act mentally on it or transform it. The ability to perform operations on operations, such as checking the validity of the premise above, enables formal thinkers to further broaden their conceptualizations and perceive problems from various vantage points enabling better resolution of them.

Propositional thinking.   Another variation on formal reasoning is propositional thinking. The adolescent may express a series of hypotheses in propositional form and reason as follows:

It is this or that.
It is both this and that.
It is this but not that.
It is neither this nor that.

Or she might perform logical propositions such as the following:

If A then B
e.g., If it is raining (A), then the sidewalks are wet (B).

If B then A
e.g., If the sidewalks are wet, then it is raining.

Not A then Not B
e.g., If it is not raining, then the sidewalks are not wet.

Not B then Not A
 e.g., If the sidewalks are not wet, then it is not raining.

If A then not B
e.g., If it is raining, then the sidewalks are not dry.

If not A then B
e.g., If it is not raining, then the sidewalks are dry.

The example could go on. If you think that these examples could be continued, and in fact you said to yourself, "What about *if B then not A*, or *if not B then not A*," you have probably started through the cognitive structure that is the basis for combinatorial logic. Remember that it is based on two propositions, either one of which may be true or false. For instance, it is raining or not raining, the sidewalks are wet or not wet.

The formal individual can relate any of the four propositions in his mind and, by reasoning, act on them to eliminate the nonappropriate ones. The individual may also hold one factor constant while varying the others. Doing this type of if-then thinking easily demarcates the formal student from those of other stages.

Combinatorial logic. Formal operational individuals are capable of performing combinatorial logic. This means they will use all possible combinations or factors related to a problem in solving it. For example, a student is presented with four jars containing colorless and odorless liquids. She is shown that a flask with some of these liquids plus a drop from another container labeled *g* will turn yellow. The student is then asked to attempt to duplicate the formation of the yellow solution and determine the role of each of the solutions. In order to solve the problem, the individual must first consider all conceivable combinations of liquids and then systematically go about combining various solutions and noting the effects of each. This problem is complicated since only one of the solutions plus *g* will turn yellow, and one of the other solutions will negate this reaction.

Proportional thinking. Formal operational individuals are able to understand and determine answers to proportion and ratio problems. For example, when given a lever problem, as indicated in the illustration, they are able to determine the answer. Chemistry problems often require proportional thought. For example: The burning of carbon (from wood or coal) is $C + O_2 = CO_2 \uparrow$. How much CO_2 will be produced if twenty grams of carbon is totally burned?

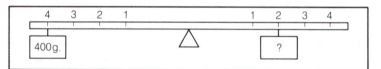

How much weight must be placed here to balance the beam?

Controlling variables. Formal thinkers realize that in solving a complex problem, they must be able to control all factors and change only one variable at a time in order to determine how it influences the reaction. An activity to determine whether children can perform this cognitive function involves presenting them with the pendulum problem such as we did at the beginning of the chapter. Various weights are given to them. They are asked to determine which variable affects the frequency (the number of round trip swings per minute) of the pendulum. They can vary the length of the string and weights. Concrete operational children usually vary both variables, length of the string and the weights, simultaneously, while formal thinkers isolate one variable at a time. They may keep the same weight on the string, swing it, and determine its frequency for a number of different lengths. In other words, they keep the weight constant while they vary the length.

Establishing a hierarchical classification system. As seen previously, students grow significantly in their classificational abilities in the pre-operational and concrete operational period. This continues further in the formal period when individuals are capable of establishing criteria for a hierarchical classification system. They are capable of building keys similar to those in botany, zoology, a library catalogue system, etc., in order to identify or locate a specific organism, object, or event.

The Reflective Student

By attaining formal thought, the student passes through the intellectual gateway to adulthood. In doing reflective, hypothetical-deductive, and propositional thinking, the formal adolescent is able to better use her mind to interact more effectively with both the physical and social environment.

The formal operational period begins around age twelve and continues into adulthood. The overriding characteristic of the period is the student's development of abstract reasoning. Accordingly, we describe the reflective student. There are several broad characteristics of adolescent thought patterns. Possibilities become real rather than reality determining what is possible. This is one way of expressing the fact that formal thought transcends the concrete situation. Another characteristic of the reflective student is the possibility to generate and consider all possible combinations for a given situation. Reflective students can reason inductively and deductively. They can start with a set of facts and provide a generalization, thus demonstrating inductive reasoning. They can also start with a major generalization and deduce a specific conclusion, thus demonstrating deductive reasoning.

The understanding of time and space increases significantly for the reflective student. The adolescent thinks of distant places and larger and larger units of space. She also thinks more of imagining long periods of time. The formal operational thinker also grasps the meaning of infinity, historical time, global geography, and interplanetary space. She can conceive of both present and future problems caused by changes in today's world.

Some thoughts on the reflective student's use of formal thought seem appropriate. Educators should realize that adolescents do not automatically employ formal patterns of thought. Most students in secondary schools are *capable* of formal thought, but most students do not *demonstrate* this level of thought. Any number of factors can influence adolescent performance; for instance, motivation, self-esteem, and peers. With this caution, educators are advised to view the formal period as optimum patterns of thought.

Educators should realize that adolescents (and many adults) use formal operations in situations where they have interest, concern, and expertise. This observation points to the importance of knowledge, the content of thought, as it relates to the level of mental functioning.

III | EXTENSION
THE FORMAL OPERATIONAL PERIOD

Analyzing an Interview

The following interview uses the same four tasks used in the "Probing the Period" section of this chapter. You should review Janet's responses to the

Figure 6.2
The Student's Developing Understanding of the World

Content	Sensorimotor Period — Beginning Characteristics	Preoperational Period — End/Beginning Characteristics	Concrete Operational Period — End/Beginning Characteristics	Formal Operational Period — End/Beginning Characteristics	Formal Operational Period — Continuing Characteristics
Action	Reflexive physical actions	Representational thought	Prelogical thought—Can reason in one direction	Logical-reversible thinking related to concrete experience	Combinatorial/propositional logic INRC group
Objects	Not permanent	Permanent objects	Conservation of identity	Conservation of quality, quantity classification, seriation, and number	Combinatorial logic, propositional logic
Space	No concept of space	Conceptualizes immediate space	Broadens concept of space	Understands relations within objects——elementary geometry	Understands relative space
Time	No concept of time	Conceptualizes short sequences and durations of time	Aware of past, present and future	Coordination of temporal order and duration	Understands relative time
Causality	No concept of cause/effect	Conceptualizes simple cause/effect relationships	Animistic	Understands cause/effect in concrete problems	Separation and control of variables in complex problems
Play	Repetition of reflexes	First symbolic play	Representative play	Practical play	Reflective abstraction and hypothetical thought
Imitation	Repetition of reflexes	First deferred imitation	Representative imitation	Practical imitation	Reflective abstraction and hypothetical thought
Self	No concept of self	First concept of self/not self	Egocentrism	Reduced egocentrism	Ideal self
Language	No language	First language	Egocentric language	Practical language	Abstract language

four tasks. This is an excellent opportunity to extend your understanding of both concrete and formal thinking to an actual case.

Conservation of Matter

Interviewer. Janet, examine the two pieces of clay. Would you say that there is the same amount of clay in the two spheres? If there isn't, take a little off of one and put it on the other.

Janet. They're even.

Interviewer. They're even. Why don't you roll one out into a snake or a hot dog shape. (She proceeds to roll out the clay.) Would you say that there is the same amount, more, or less clay in the snake than there is in the sphere?

Janet. The same.

Interviewer. The same? Why do you think they are the same?

Janet. Because the two spheres were even when we started, and I didn't add any clay and I didn't take any clay off.

Interviewer. Is there any other reason or demonstration you could give to show me that they are the same?

Janet. Sure, I could weigh the two, and they should be equal. I could displace water and test the volume, and they should be equal; I could roll it back up into a sphere, and it should be the same size as the other piece of clay. All of these things would show you that they are equal.

Conservation of Liquid

Interviewer. Janet, would you say that the water is the same or less or more now?

Janet. The same. Should I dump the glass of water into the dish?

Interviewer. Yes. Now that you have poured the water into the dish, is there less, the same, or more water in the dish?

Janet. It's got to be the same amount. Do you want to know why?

Interviewer. Yes.

Janet. Because if I poured the water back in there, it would come out equal, or if I measured it in a beaker or something, it would equal it. If I weighed it, it would also be the same.

Interviewer. The other day a student told me that she thought there was more water in the glass because it was higher.

Janet. Well, that may be, but the height of this glass is made up for by the diameter in the dish. It may be higher, but it is narrower. The dish is wider, but it is not as deep.

Provide an analysis of Janet's thinking.

Did she demonstrate concrete patterns of reasoning?
Identify the process that indicates the types of mental operations she used to justify her answers.
Would you say she is at the concrete operational level?

Proportional Reasoning

Interviewer. You have two stick persons. I want you to first measure the height of each one with the big paper clips.
Janet. This guy is six paper clips high. This guy is four paper clips high.
Interviewer. Measure the big stick man in small paper clips.

Janet. It is about 8 paper clips.
Interviewer. Now, how tall is the short stick man in small paper clips? Tell me how you are going to figure this out.
Janet. You want me to think out loud? Can I change him to being eight?
Interviewer. The answer to both questions is yes; think out loud and you may use eight.
Janet. Let's see, 6 over 8 is to 4 over something.
Interviewer. You get this puzzled look. Do you want a piece of paper?
Janet. Sure. The answer is 5⅓.
Interviewer. How did you get that answer?
Janet. Set up the ratios, 6 over 8 equals 4 over x. To solve for x I cross-multiplied 32 equals $6x$, then divided 32 by 6. This gave me 5⅓. So the small one is about 5⅓ paper clips high.
Interviewer. Why don't you check that.
Janet. It came out right.

Separation and Control of Variables

Interviewer. What you have to do is determine the factors that influence the period of swing of the pendulum. What are the identifiable factors that one should consider?
Janet. Well, there's the weight of the sinker, the length of the string, how

far back you pull it. I think that's about it. Now do you want me to figure out which one is the most crucial factor?

Interviewer. Yes. How would you go about finding the variable which is most important?

Janet. Well, I'll start with two that are the same weight but are different lengths. Everything else is the same. I'll pull them back the same distance and let them go. O. K., one is getting ahead of the other, so I know that the length must make a difference.

Interviewer. How do you know that?

Janet. Well, because that's the only variable that I didn't change or control. Just to double check it, I'll put two of these the same length. Now I have to check that variable.

Interviewer. O. K. Now what are you showing us? What are you doing now?

Janet. I'm going to show you that if I control for everything, they should have the same period.

Interviewer. Could this principle also hold then even if you used the smallest weight?

Janet. Sure.

Interviewer. Why don't you demonstrate that same principle with the smaller weights. Would that confirm your idea?

Janet. You would probably have to do it a couple of times. If these are both the length, they are not going to move. (At this point in the interview, Janet became very confused.) These two will move together at the same length, but this one and this one will not move together at the same length.

Interviewer. Then, why won't the weight? So, the weight's the variable, not the length of the string?

Janet. Well, if I change the length of this, I can get it to move the same as the one with a different weight.

Interviewer. Why don't you test that.

Janet. Well, it changes depending on what you're looking at. O. K., if you have them both the same length.

Interviewer. If it's not the weight that's the crucial variable and it's the length of string, then they should swing together. Do you see?

Janet. O. K.

Interviewer. Why don't you test it?

Janet. Well, they're not going to.

Interviewer. Do it very carefully and see what happens.

Janet. They're not going together.

Interviewer. So what's your conclusion?

Janet. Well, if you wanted them to go together, you could change the length and then your length could be the crucial variable, but if you want them to be the same length, to go together, then you have to change the weight. It depends upon what you want to concentrate on.

Interviewer. We want to concentrate on the period of swing. What is the important factor that determines the period of swing?

Janet. You want the same period? Then you have to change the length of one of the pendulums. Or else change the weight; make them even.

Interviewer. And how would you go about doing that? Changing the weight, showing me that that is correct? Changing the length? Holding the weights at different heights?

Janet. Showing you that if I add more weight it would make a difference?

Interviewer. Well, showing me that any of the things you said—the weight, the length, or the height—might make the difference.

Janet. That's what I showed you in these two. Equal weights and equal lengths and equal heights. They moved together.

Interviewer. So, which is the crucial variable?

Janet. The weight. If you shortened this string, it should swing the same, the period should be the same.

Interviewer. I don't understand that. If it's the weight that determines the period, then if you have two strings the same length, what you're telling me is that there is a different period? And you see that the two strings with the same length and different weights have the same period.

Janet. The length and the weight work together.

Interviewer. So it's both?

Janet. Right. But you wanted to know which one was most important. I told you that before; it changes depending on what you want to find out. If your pendulum can only be a certain length, then your weight is going to be more important. But if you only have a certain weight, then the length of your pendulum is going to be more important. So their importance changes. (She then tests strings that have different weights but the same length.) Oops, they were going the same right there. Exactly the same. They didn't do that before.

Provide an analysis of Janet's responses on these two problems.

Did she demonstrate formal patterns of reasoning?
Would you say she is formal operational? Concrete operational? Transitional?
What passages of the interview would you cite to justify your conclusion?

Interviewing Students: Tasks for the Formal Operational Period

Each of the tasks to be administered outlines a basic structure for the interview. Feel free, however, to modify them so as to make hypotheses about the child's thinking during the interview. Certain specific suggestions for giving the tasks should be followed. Please refer to Chapter 4 (pages 84–85) for suggestions.

Piagetian Interview Tasks: Formal Operational Period

Name _____   School _____

Class or Subject _____   Teacher _____

Sex _____   Level _____

Age _____ (yrs.) _____ (months)   General Demeanor _____

Date _____   Other _____

Proportional Reasoning

This task assesses the student's ability to apply the concept of ratio and proportion. The student is given an 8½ × 11-inch card. Stickmen are drawn on each side of the card, one being two-thirds the height of the other. The small and large stickmen should be constructed to measure four and six jumbo paper clips, respectively. Ask the student to measure the height of each of the stickmen with a set of eight connected jumbo paper clips. After the student has measured and recorded the heights of the two stickmen, the jumbo clips are replaced with a set of small paper clips. Ask the student to measure only the short stickman with the new set of clips. Remove the stickman. Then ask, "How tall is the large stickman in terms of the small paper clips?"

Six jumbo clips high

Four jumbo clips high

Task 1—Proportional reasoning responses

1. Predicted height of tall stickman: _____

2. Justification for prediction: _____

_____

3. Key statements indicating cognitive level: _____

_____

4. Classification of performance: _____

5. Suggestions for teaching: _____

Discussion The measurement of the tall stickman should be six jumbo clips and nine small clips in length, and the small stickman should measure four jumbo clips and six small clips. The criterion for success on this task is the ability of the student to accurately predict the height of the tall stickman in terms of small clips (i.e., nine clips). The student's justification must include a reference to direct ratio or proportion. The student may just guess and give you a number. If the child does, he is not demonstrating the use of formal thought. If, however, he tries to figure it on paper or reasons in a rational way, indicating that the situation is a simple proportion, he is demonstrating formal thought:

Small Stickman		Large Stickman
4 clips		6 clips
6 clips	=	x clips

Separation and Control of Variables

This task utilizes a simple pendulum consisting of a length of string about 80 cm. long and a set of varying weights. Ask the student to determine which variable or variables affect the frequency of oscillation of the pendulum (the number of swings per unit of time, e.g., second). (Note: Since the length of the string is the only relevant variable, the problem is to isolate it from the others. Only in this way can the student solve the problem and explain the frequency of oscillations.)

Task 2—Separation and control of variables responses
1. Question: Which variable or variables affect the frequency of oscillation of this pendulum?

Response: _____

_____

2. Question: Can you design an experiment to prove that your choice is correct?

Response: _____

_____

3. Key statements indicating cognitive level: _____

_____

4. Classification of cognitive level: _____

_____

5. Suggestions for teaching: _____

_____

Discussion. The criterion for success on this task is the student's ability to identify the one variable (length of string) that affects the oscillation of the pendulum. The student's justification must indicate that he *held all variables constant while manipulating only one variable* in reaching his conclusion. The student should initially indicate that variables involved in the problem could be weight, length of string, or height at which the pendulum is dropped. He may initially think a combination of these may affect the frequency. He may then describe a set of hypotheses and test these. However, before finishing he should *design an experiment controlling one variable at a time*, such as length of string, to find out whether his hypothesis is correct. In this way he should systematically eliminate the irrelevant variables. The ability to plan experiments to separate and control, or manipulate, *one variable at a time*, observe it accurately, and make proper conclusions characterizes formal thought.

Proportional Reasoning

The student is presented with a balanced scale consisting of a wooden rod with equally spaced numbered positions. Weights are attached as indicated in the diagram. Begin by using equal weights (ten grams) equidistant from the fulcrum (pivoting point). Remove one. Maintain equilibrium of the balance by holding the force arm. Ask, "Using any of the weights in front of you, how could you get the scale to balance?" After the student responds ask, "What other ways are there to balance the scale besides the one you chose?" Remove the weight from the scale. Place another weight nearer the fulcrum and maintain equilibrium by holding the force arm. Ask, "How may the scale be balanced by using the weights? How do you justify your responses?"

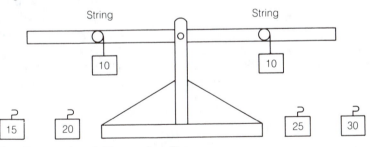

Task 3 — Proportional Reasoning Responses

1. Question: Using any of the weights presented here, how could you get the scale to balance?

Response: _____

_____

2. Question (Justification): How did you arrive at this answer?

Response: _____

_____

3. Key statements indicating cognitive level: _____

_____

4. Classification of cognitive level: _____

_____

5. Suggestions for teaching: _____

_____

Discussion. The criterion for success on this task is the student's ability to equate length times weight on one arm of the fulcrum with length times weight on the other arm or to figure out the problem by using proportions. In order for the student to balance the scale, he must apply the principle of levers.

Combinatorial Logic

Obtain five medicine droppers, baby food or other jars, and ten clear plastic cups. Prepare stock solutions of the following:

1. Dilute sulfuric acid (H_2SO_4) — 10 ml concentrated H_2SO_4 to 100 ml H_2O
2. Distilled H_2O
3. Hydrogen Peroxide — 3 parts of H_2O_2 added to 97 parts H_2O
4. Sodium Thiosulfate — 10 grams sodium thiosulfate to 1 liter of H_2O
5. Potassium Iodide — 5 g to 1 liter H_2O

Pour the stock solutions into the baby jars as follows: jar 1, dilute sulfuric acid; jar 2, water; jar 3, hydrogen peroxide; jar 4, sodium thiosulfate; and jar 5, potassium iodide, labeled *g*. The student is then given the four jars containing colorless, odorless liquids which are perceptually identical. Then present him with two glasses, one containing solutions 1 + 3, the other containing solution 2. The contents of the glasses are *not* revealed to the student. Several drops from jar *g* are poured into each of the two glasses. The student is asked to notice the reactions. (The container containing 1 + 3 turns yellow, the other remains unchanged.) The student is told that the two samples were prepared from the jars and that each contains *g*.

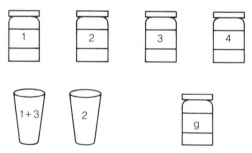

Ask, "Can you reproduce the color?" Ten plastic cups are made available, and the student is allowed to attempt to reproduce the color. Record the student's procedure. If the color is successfully reproduced, ask questions to determine if he can identify the functions of each liquid. (The child should indicate that jar 2 does not alter the reaction one way or the other and jar 4 eliminates the color.)

Task 4—Combinatorial Logical Responses
Record the procedure the student takes in solving the problem.

_____

_____

_____

_____

1. Analysis of procedure. Check which one(s) of the following the student was able to do.

   a. Made the color in one way. _____

   b. Made the color in two ways. _____

   c. Knew that all of 1, 3, and *g* were necessary. _____

   d. Knew that 2 had no effect, or did not help or produce the color. _____

   e. Knew that 4 removed or prevented the color. _____

2. Key statements indicating cognitive level: _____

   _____

3. Classification of cognitive level: _____

   _____

4. Suggestions for teaching: _____

   _____

Discussion. The main criterion for determining whether the student is a formal operational thinker is whether he establishes a *systematic procedure* for the role played by each of the solutions. Does he use, for example, a process of elimination? Does he realize that by combining 1, 3, and *g* the yellow solution occurs? If he cannot state these facts, but just goes about the activity by trial and error and does not indicate he understands the role of all the combinations, he is not a formal thinker.

Syllogism

Prepare several syllogisms to see whether the student can use deductive logic. For example:

All mailmen wear purple suits.   All persons are foolish.
John is a mailman.   Ms. Jones is a person.
(Then he wears _____?)   (Does it follow that Ms. Jones is foolish?)

Bob is taller than Bruce.
John is shorter than Bruce.
Therefore, Bob is what to John?

   Substitute symbols for words to see whether the student can use symbols well:

All B's = A's
C's = B's
Then all A's = _____

All X's < Y's
Z < Y
So Z > X

Task 5—Syllogism Responses
1. After reading the syllogisms to the students, have the students determine if their statements are valid or invalid.

2. Determine whether the students' justifications are logical.

3. Key statements indicating cognitive level: _____

_____

4. Classification of cognitive level: _____

_____

5. Suggestions for teaching: _____

_____

Discussion. The criterion for achieving on this task is the student's ability to successfully judge the validity of the arguments. In addition, the justification of each judgement must follow logical patterns of reasoning.

Hypothetical Reasoning

Show a student the following diagram of the top of a pool table. Ask him to trace how he would hit ball y so that it would collide with ball x, in each of the positions shown, to make x go into one of the corner pockets. After he has drawn several ways he could hit the y ball, ask him to describe any rule that could be used in the future. You might have to help the student construct a rule. Ask, "If you hit the ball straight on, how will it move? If you hit it on a 45° angle, how will it move?" (You have to diagram a 45° angle to ensure that he understands what you mean.) Ask, "Can you compare the reaction of a ball bouncing off a wall with $y's$ reaction to x?"

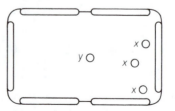

Task 6—Hypothetical Reasoning Response
1. Student's description of rule: _____

2. Justification for the rule: _____

3. Key statements indicating cognitive level: _____

_____

4. Classification of cognitive level: _____

_____

5. Suggestions for teaching: _____

_____

Discussion. The student should, in his own words, state that the angle of incidence equals the angle of reflection. If the student does state this rule, he should explain the meaning to be sure he has not memorized it. He need not use the above words, as long as he can explain the law or state some rule. For example, for a ball bouncing off a wall, the student might say that if the ball comes in on an angle at a point four inches from the wall and six inches along the wall from the point where it is going to hit, it will bounce four inches away from the wall when it is six inches along it from the point it hit.

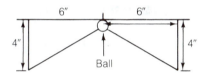

BIBLIOGRAPHY

Bodin, Margaret A. *Jean Piaget*. New York: Penguin Books, 1980.
The section on formal thought is helpful and simply written. The clarity of this book more than compensates for the brief attention given to the formal period.

Brainerd, Charles J. *Piaget's Theory of Intelligence*. Englewood Cliffs, N.J.: Prentice-Hall, 1978.
The chapter on the formal period is superb. It includes the general features of formal thought and research on various aspects of the period.

Cowan, Phillip A. *Piaget: With Feeling*. New York: Holt, Rinehart & Winston, 1978.
This book is a welcome addition to the references on Piaget. Chapter 10 on the cognitive aspects of formal development is excellent. But don't stop there. The special contribution of this book is to be found in the author's synthesis of both cognitive and affective aspects of development.

Flavell, John H. *The Developmental Psychology of Jean Piaget*. New York: Van Nostrand Reinhold Co., 1963.
A classic in the literature on Piaget's theory. Graduate level discussion. If you really want to understand the basis of formal thought, read Chapter 6.

Ginsburg, Herbert, and Opper, Sylvia. *Piaget's Theory of Intellectual Development* 2d ed. Englewood Cliffs, N.J.: Prentice-Hall, 1979.
Adolescence is covered thoroughly. This chapter is an especially good discussion of formal thought. Educators will benefit from the analysis.

Inhelder, Barbel and Piaget, Jean. *The Growth of Logical Thinking from Child-hood to Adolescence*. New York: Basic Books, 1958.
 The classic work on formal operational thought. The first sections give details of formal tasks. The last sections (mostly written by Piaget) provide theoretical explanations of the tasks.
Piaget, Jean. *Six Psychological Studies*. New York: Random House, 1967.
 While only a portion of this book is directly related to adolescence (pages 60–70), the majority of the book is readable and provides a good introduction to Piaget's theory.
————. *The Child and Reality*. New York: Grossman Publishers, 1973.
 As a book, reading is uneven. But, the educator will find many interesting topics: affective development, stages of development, perception, learning, and language.
Piaget, Jean, and Inhelder, Barbel. *The Psychology of the Child*. New York: Basic Books, 1969.
 A small section (pages 130–51) is devoted to the formal period. There is, however, some discussion of affective development during adolescence.

IV | EVALUATION
THE FORMAL OPERATIONAL PERIOD

Listed below are some of the main topics covered in Chapter 6. Read each statement and rate it on the scale TWICE: once according to what you knew about the topic before starting this chapter and again according to what you've learned after completing the chapter. Circle the appropriate number and mark B for *before* and A for *after* next to the number as indicated below.

Topic	Personal Evaluation					
	Low		Moderate		High	
Example: Distinguish formal from concrete operational thought	①B	2	3	4	5	⑥A
1. Abstract reasoning	1	2	3	4	5	6
2. Hypothetical-deductive reasoning	1	2	3	4	5	6
3. Syllogistic reasoning	1	2	3	4	5	6
4. Propositional thinking	1	2	3	4	5	6
5. Reflective thinking	1	2	3	4	5	6
6. Combinatorial logic	1	2	3	4	5	6
7. Proportional thinking	1	2	3	4	5	6
8. Separation and control of variables	1	2	3	4	5	6
9. Hierarchical classifications	1	2	3	4	5	6

7 Moral Development and the Ethical Student

Early in his career (circa 1930) Piaget spent some time investigating moral development. In the 1950s Lawrence Kohlberg extended and modified the original studies by Piaget. This chapter is an introduction to both Piaget's and Kohlberg's theories of moral development.

I | EXPLORATION
MORAL DEVELOPMENT

Probing the Period

The art teacher left the first grade room. James thought it would be fun to play with the paint. While playing with the paint, he spilled it and made a little spot on the floor. On the same day the art teacher asked John to get some supplies from the cabinet. As John opened one of the cabinet doors, he accidently knocked over fifteen cans of paint. The floor was a mess. After the second incident there was a lively discussion among the students. At one point the teacher asked if both students were equally guilty. The teacher also asked who was most disobedient, James or John.

Much to the teacher's surprise many students said that John was the more disobedient student. When asked why, the students said it was because he made a bigger mess.

What was your response to the teacher's questions? How would you explain the students' response that John was the more disobedient student? What were the bases of the students' justification? What were the grounds for your response and justification? We shall return to the discussion in Section II—"Explanations." Now, we want you to consider a moral dilemma:

The Cheating Student Dilemma

A student has been accused of cheating on an examination. The evidence is not clear as to the guilt or innocence of the student. The student has, however, recently been in trouble with school personnel, but not for cheating. One administrator has decided to expel the student for ten days. One teacher believes the student is innocent and thinks the administrator should not expel the student. When the teacher asks the administrator for the student's records to support the student's position, the administrator denies the teacher's request. The administrator tells the teacher that he is proceeding with the suspension on the grounds that (1) the student has been a discipline problem and probably cheated on the examination, (2) suspension from school may be a good experience for the student, and (3) whether this youth cheated or not doesn't make any difference; suspension would set a good example for any other students who might cheat. On the other hand, the teacher argues that (1) we do not know whether the student is innocent or guilty of cheating so we should assume innocence, (2) suspension may be bad for the student, not good, and (3) there are better ways to discourage cheating than to suspend this student. The teacher tried to persuade the administrator, but he would not change his position. Having tried everything, in desperation the teacher breaks into the administrator's office, steals the student's record, and takes his case to the teachers.

> Should the teacher have done this? Yes? No? Why? How would you justify your answer? Take a few minutes and write your answer and justification.

We shall return to a discussion of this particular dilemma later in the chapter.

II | EXPLANATION
MORAL DEVELOPMENT

Piaget's work on moral development is in *The Moral Judgement of the Child* (1965). Piaget's research on moral development was conducted in the early 1930s as a part of his study of egocentric thought. *The Psychology of the Child* (Piaget and Inhelder, 1969) also contains a section on "Moral Feelings and Judgements" that is a primary source for this section. Piaget studied the

moral reasoning of young children. The work of Lawrence Kohlberg extended Piaget's original work to adolescents and adults.

Piaget's Theory of Moral Development

Piaget's original work centered on children's practice of rules and consciousness of rules. He observed and questioned children about the rules of
playing a common game, marbles. The fundamental question of Piaget's
study was, What was the child's point of view concerning respect for rules?
He made naturalistic observations of the ways children of different ages
applied rules and of children's perceptions of rules.

Children below two years of age have no sense of rules; their play is
purely motor activity. If a child appears to be following rules, it is a physical
repetition of activity without consciousness of a rule.

From age two until about six rules are "followed" through imitation.
Children have a consciousness of rules, but the practice of following rules
is egocentric; that is, behavior is a simple imitation of what other children
have done. Children generally do not understand the social nature of
games. This is heteronomous obedience—rules come from others in authority. Children understand there are rules and they are obligatory, but
rules are not applied except through imitating or copying.

By ages seven to ten children recognize rules as important regulatory
mechanisms in social interactions. Children's awareness of rules is still heteronomous, though there is an emerging theme of autonomy.

Sometime around age eleven or twelve autonomy emerges over heteronomy in the child's understanding of rules. Cooperative play and cognitive
development both contribute to this realization. Rules are matters of mutual
consent; they are not immutable laws presented by authorities. Evidence for
this new realization of the autonomy of rules is seen in the preadolescent's
own legislating of rules for games and the cooperative agreement on different aspects of games.

In *The Moral Judgement of the Child*, Piaget states: "All morality consists in
a system of rules, and the essence of all morality is to be sought for in the
respect which the individual acquires for these rules" (Piaget, 1965, p. 13).
We have seen the development of the child's understanding of rules. First,
there is a heteronomous approach to rules. The word *heteronomous* is
derived from "hetero," meaning "from others." Thus, rules at this stage
come from others like parents or teachers, and the rules are perceived to
be unchangeable. The primary orientation of heteronomous morality is
constraint. In late childhood and early adolescence, autonomous morality
develops. *Autonomous* is derived from "auto," meaning self. Here the function of rules is independent of others. According to Piaget, an autonomous
understanding of rules develops through the cooperative interactions
among children. With time, children break their egocentric perceptions
and understand the position of others. Obligations, in the form of rules, are
reciprocal. Development of the idea of justice is similar to the child's consciousness and practice of rules.

For young children justice is obedience to authority. Justice is the rule. Obeying the rule, law, or command is the just action even if it is not fair, just, or equitable as perceived by adults. At this level there is a *moral realism* that results in objective responsibility when evaluating the degree to which a person is guilty/not guilty or, in the earlier example of John and James, obedient or disobedient. In the latter example, moral judgement is a result of quantity (e.g., the objective observation that John had spilled more paint, even though James had mischievous intentions). Later, there develops a moral *relativism* that results in the evaluation of intentions and situations in judging the actions of others.

There are important observations that should be made concerning the child's understanding and development of rules and justice. According to Piaget, cooperation among peers is a key to moral development.

> The sense of justice, though naturally capable of being reinforced by precepts and the practical example of the adult, is largely independent of these influences, and requires nothing more for its development than mutual respect and solidarity which holds among children themselves. (Piaget, 1965, p. 198)

Piaget's observation is important for educators. Cooperative interaction among students is fundamental to moral development. Though it is clear that educators should reinforce an idea such as justice by precept and practical example, Piaget has probably overstated his point. Mutual respect can and should be established between students and educators. Educators

Cooperation among peers is fundamental to moral development.

make allowances for different developmental levels of reading and mathematics. Recognizing different levels of moral development is also important for educators. Group projects and activities and cooperative development of classroom rules are but two examples of ways educators can encourage moral development.

Kohlberg's Theory of Moral Development

Lawrence Kohlberg's studies extended and clarified the original work of Jean Piaget. Importantly, Kohlberg used a greater age range of subjects, and he interviewed his subjects well beyond adolescence. In general Kohlberg's work has verified the earlier work of Piaget. This section is based on several papers by Kohlberg (1971, 1975a, 1975b). Though we shall not go into criticisms of his theory, you should know that others have done so (see Gilligan, 1977; Gibbs, 1977; Kurtines and Greif, 1974). And Kohlberg himself has recently indicated he is reconsidering various aspects of his theory (Munson, 1979).

Lawrence Kohlberg used Piaget's research on moral development as the foundation for advancing further investigation into this area. Kohlberg carried on numerous studies in the United States and other countries striving to better define moral development. One of his main works started in 1958 involved a longitudinal study of boys at ages ten and sixteen, and followed their value evolvement past the ages of twenty-four and thirty. Kohlberg has also made several cross-cultural investigations.

Kohlberg's research has further substantiated Piaget's belief that moral development is hierarchical in character. Kohlberg believes it consists of three levels, each containing stages. The three levels are (1) preconventional, or premoral, (2) conventional, or conforming, and (3) postconventional, or self-accepting, moral principles.

Preconventional Level

At this level the child is responsive to such rules and labels as good and bad, right and wrong. He interprets these labels in purely physical or hedonistic terms: if he is bad, he is punished; if he is good, he is rewarded. He also interprets labels in terms of the physical power of those who enunciate them. The level comprises the following two stages.

Stage One: Punishment avoidance and obedience orientation. The *physical consequences* of an action determine its goodness or badness regardless of the human meaning of value of these consequences. Avoidance of punishment and unquestioning deference to power are valued in their own right, not in terms of respect for an underlying moral order supported by punishment and authority. Briefly, moral decisions are based on the avoidance of aversive consequences. Behavior is simply obedience to authority. "I'll do what you say in order to avoid a spanking" characterizes moral judgements at this stage.

Stage Two: Seeking rewards.   In this stage the child agrees to rules or does things because they benefit her. Right action consists of that which instrumentally satisfies one's own needs and occasionally the needs of others. "Taking care of number one" is foremost in moral decisions. Human relations are viewed in terms similar to those of the marketplace. Elements of fairness, reciprocity, and equal sharing are present, but they are always interpreted in a pragmatic way. Reciprocity is a matter of "you scratch my back and I'll scratch yours," not of loyalty, gratitude, or justice. Successful ends can justify questionable means.

Conventional Level

Expectations of the individual's family, group, or nation are perceived as valuable in their own right, regardless of immediate and obvious consequences. The attitude is one not only of conformity to the social order but of loyalty to it; of actively maintaining, supporting, and justifying the order; and of identifying with the persons or group involved in it. The level comprises the following two stages.

Stage Three: Social approval orientation.   Good behavior is that which pleases others and is approved by them. There is conformity to stereotypical images of what is majority behavior. Behavior is frequently judged by intention. "He means well" becomes important. One earns approval by being nice. You don't do things because you might "lose face." Moral decisions and actions are based on what "pleases others." "Everyone was doing it" is a common justification for this stage.

Stage Four: "Law and order" orientation.   Authority, fixed rules, and the maintenance of the social order are valued. Right behavior consists of doing one's duty, showing respect for authority, and maintaining the social order for its own sake. Concern is for the larger community. A larger social orientation is the basis of deciding right from wrong. Social authorities (e.g., principals, presidents, and teachers) must be obeyed for the maintenance of social order. Rules and laws are viewed as static.

Postconventional Level

At this level there is a clear effort to teach to others a personal definition of moral values—to define principles that have validity and application apart from the authority of groups or persons and apart from the individual's own identification with these groups.[2]

Stage Five: Social-contract legalistic orientation.   This stage has utilitarian overtones. Right action tends to be defined in terms of individual

---

1. Kohlberg has recently indicated that due to difficulty in differentiating Stages Five and Six, they should be thought of as one stage (see Munson, 1979). We have decided to include discussions of Stage Six.

rights and the standards that have been agreed upon by the whole society. There is a clear awareness of the importance of personal values and opinions and a corresponding emphasis on procedural rules for resolving conflicts. Other than that which is constitutionally and democratically agreed upon, right is a matter of personal values and opinion. The result is an emphasis both upon the legal point of view and upon the possibility of making rational and socially desirable changes in the law through cooperative negotiation. Outside the legal realm, free agreement is the binding element of obligation. This is the official morality of the U.S. government and the Constitution.

Stage Six: Universal ethical-principle orientation.   Right is defined by the conscience in accord with self-chosen principles, which in turn are based on logical comprehensiveness, universality, and consistency. These principles are abstract and ethical, for example, the golden rule, Kant's categorical imperative (i.e., act only as you would have others act in the same situation). They are not concrete moral rules like the Ten Commandments. At heart, these are universal principles of justice, of the reciprocity and equality of human rights, and of respect for the dignity of human beings as individual persons. These six stages are summarized in Figure 7.1.

Figure 7.1
Kohlberg's Levels of Moral Development

	Stages	Motivation
Stage One:	Avoiding Punishment	Ethical decisions are made to avoid punishment. Self-gratification is important. Morality occurs mainly because of fear of punishment.
Stage Two:	Seeking Reward	Desire for personal reward and benefit. What is in it for me? What are the consequences?
Stage Three:	Social Approval	Anticipation of social disapproval or self-guilt. Has stereotypes of good and bad people.
Stage Four:	Law and Order	Anticipation of dishonor. Afraid of losing face or gaining dishonor. Follows social rules. Believes in rule maintaining. Exceptions cannot be made because everyone would start disobeying rules.
Stage Five:	Social Contract	Concern about self-respect or being irrational and inconsistent. Right actions are constitutional and democratically derived. Free agreement and contract binding between individuals. It is the way the American government operates.
Stage Six:	Universal Ethics	Concern about condemnation, about violating a person's principles, and about maintaining principles as a way of life. Sacredness of life; compassion for fellow humans, universal principle of justice.

Lawrence Kohlberg used moral dilemmas to evaluate individual levels of moral development. The essential part of understanding an individual's stage of moral development is not in the yes or no answer to the dilemma but in the justification for the answer. How do individuals justify their responses? "The Cheating Student Dilemma" to which you responded earlier can be used as an example of *pro* and *con* justifications at the different stages.

Stage One: Pro and Con Justifications

Pro. It wasn't bad to steal the student's file. There are other people more important than the administrator who knew it was a good thing to do. The consequences will not be great because the teacher tried to convince the administrator, but he would not listen. It wasn't a bad thing to do and not much damage was done.

Con. The teacher did not have the administrator's permission to get the file. This is stealing and that is bad. The administrator had decided what should be done in this case, and the teacher should obey the administrator or he will be punished.

Note that both justifications disregard the teacher's intentions. Rather, they focus on the goodness or badness of the act and the consequences. The *pro* position minimizes the act of stealing, while the con statement maximizes the position that stealing is bad. The *pro* position minimizes the administrator's role and appeals to other "more important" people (we might assume the superintendent, school board, or president of the teacher's union). Likewise, the consequences are minimized in the *pro* statement, while they are clearly a factor in the *con* position.

Stage Two: Pro and Con Justifications

Pro. It is clear that the teacher needed to defend the student, and if this required stealing, so be it. The student will no doubt repay the teacher for the favor. Stealing is probably O. K. in this case because it is only a small crime and the result will be really great. No real harm was done to the administrator or the school.

Con. The administration is acting on behalf of the teachers and students. They must each support one another if the school is to run smoothly. If the teachers support the administration, the administration will support the teachers; but one teacher cannot do what he wants. The teacher should have gone along with the administrator's decision.

The *pro* justification suggests that the teacher needed to steal the file for his own needs. And, the student will "no doubt" do the teacher a favor. This is the instrumental relativist; fairness is interpreted pragmatically and hedonistically. The *con* position is a simple and straightforward "you scratch my back and I'll scratch yours" orientation. Because Stage Two is strongly oriented toward physical power and obedience, the *pro* position was harder to write.

Stage Three: Pro and Con Justifications

Pro.   Stealing is generally not a good thing. However, this situation is extreme. The teacher isn't doing that much wrong when you consider how much he will help the student. Any professional teacher would have done the same thing. Besides, his peers will probably support him because they know that a good teacher tries to help students who need it.

Con.   The teacher really cannot be blamed if the student is suspended. It is inappropriate to condemn the teacher for not disobeying the rules. In other words, the teacher's duty is to support the rules of the school, and not stealing files is certainly a rule. Others will judge the administrator negatively if he is wrong. Now, others will rightfully not judge the teacher harshly because he did behave as teachers should.

   Both justifications appeal to interpersonal agreement among those associated with the problem. While rules are mentioned, the thrust of each justification is on acceptance and rejection of the teacher by his peers. This is the social approval orientation.

Stage Four: Pro and Con Justifications

Pro.   The administrator is wrong if he suspends a student for cheating and he doesn't even know if the student has cheated. You can't suspend someone for an example. In a sense the administrator broke the rules, so it was the teacher's duty to steal the file and try to defend the student. But, the teacher also broke the law and must be punished.

Con.   It is only natural for teachers to support students. What the teacher did was clearly against the law. All people, including teachers, must obey the law. How the teacher feels about the student, or the circumstances of the suspension, doesn't make any difference. You can see that the teacher should not have stolen the file by answering the question, "What if all teachers did what they thought best?" It is obvious there would be no order in schools.

   Both of these qualifications appeal to one's obligation to the law. The *pro* statement implies that the administrator will break the law, and that is wrong. At the same time, the statement ends by saying the teacher also broke the law and must suffer the consequences. The *con* position is clearly a law and order orientation. One does what the law says—no questions about it. The final two sentences indicate that anarchy would probably result if laws were not obeyed.

Stage Five: Pro and Con Justifications

Pro. It seems that the teacher and administrator should have been able to reach an agreement, but they couldn't. One must really consider all the circumstances before a judgement is passed as to the teacher being right or wrong in his actions. The laws would suggest that the teacher is wrong—he should not have stolen the file. On the other hand, there are situations which make the breaking of a law justified. This was one such situation. The administrator was not paying attention to basic tenets such as "a person is innocent until proven guilty." Violation of the student's basic rights is more serious than the act of stealing a file, especially since it was in support of the student, not for the teacher's personal gain.

Con. One can easily be tempted to side with the teacher since it is possible that good may come from the teacher's actions. But partial goods are often evident in wrongdoing. The same can be said about the administrator's actions. On balance, it is important to understand that the ends do not justify the means in either side of this problem. Though the decision is difficult, the teacher should not have stolen the file. The contract the teacher has with the social institution is stronger than the apparent violation of the student's individual rights.

The justifications at Stage Five become complex. Both responses weigh various aspects of the situation and consider the circumstances. There is a legalistic, constitutional tone to both statements. The general tone indicates neither the teacher nor the administrator acted appropriately, and it is difficult to condone or condemn either. Each statement hints that the best resolution would have been a cooperative agreement established through agreed upon procedures.

Stage Six: Pro and Con Justifications

Pro. If a choice must be made between following an administrative order and keeping another human from inappropriate and unjust actions, the higher principles of justice and human rights take precedence over the rule. It is ethically right for the teacher to do what he did.

Con. The ideal action for the teacher would be to follow his own conscience. He should have acted only as he would have others act in this situation. But in this case the teacher should not have acted as he did. Like most real situations, one must consider other factors and not solely one's conscience. A greater injustice was probably rendered the administrator and school personnel.

The higher moral principle of justice is the grounds for both *pro* and *con* positions. The *pro* justification seems a clearer application of justice in this situation. The grounds for the *con* position was the justification—Who would suffer the greater injustice? It is easy to imagine an equally powerful statement claiming the student would be rendered the greater injustice.

Determining a person's level of moral development depends on more than the decision the person makes. It also depends on more than your evaluation of the correctness of the decision. Remember, your evaluation of an answer's correctness is probably a result of your level of moral development. The justification is the crucial aspect of the evaluation. *The justification reveals the structure of the individual's moral reasoning.* The outcome of an athletic event does not define the sport. To understand basketball is not to know who won; it is to know the rules of basketball and to be able to differentiate it from football. As we tried to show in the *pro* and *con* discussions, it is not agreement that defines the stage. Educators must listen closely to the reasoning. The reasoning behind the justification will appeal to universal ethical principles such as the value of life, liberty, freedom, truth, or justice.

We can use justice as an example of the basis of moral reasoning. At Stage One justice is the power to punish. At Stage Two justice is respected for the usefulness it can have in bringing rewards to those who abide. At Stage Three justice is respected because others will respect the individual for doing so. At Stage Four justice is the law. At Stages Five and Six justice is a principle that comes into its own. Decisions are made in reference to the principle, not in reference to other things that may represent the principle (i.e., punishments, rewards, social esteem, and laws).

Kohlberg's Theory: The Foundations

According to Kohlberg, development through the stages is invariant. A student must develop reasoning skills at Stage Three before attaining Stage Four. Educators are cautioned against "teaching" higher stages since students will not be able to understand the reasoning.

Individuals can comprehend one stage higher than their present level of development. A student at Stage Two can comprehend a Stage Three argument. In fact, individuals are intrigued with the higher level of moral reasoning. They understand the positions and often find them better.

Individuals do not typically respond at one stage in all situations. About 50 percent of the time, they will respond at a certain level which is considered their developmental stage. It should also be pointed out that all individuals may violate school rules or policies at some time. However, those holding higher ethical principles are less likely to do so than their less principled peers.

Kohlberg (1971) has found that, although certain virtues and morals may vary from culture to culture, his moral stages are universal. Studies carried out with the Tayals (in Malaysia), Taiwanese, Mayas (in Mexico), Israelis, and Turks all confirmed this fact. There are, however, percentage differences among cultures as to the number found in each stage.

Kohlberg also found that middle class children tend to be at a more advanced level than those from the lower classes. Since the percentage of middle class individuals varies with the country, so does the number attaining these stages. Preliterate and semiliterate societies had an absence of people at Stages Five and Six. Comparisons of individuals from Catholic,

Protestant, Jewish, Buddhist, Moslem, and atheist backgrounds indicated no difference in the number reaching the higher ethical levels.

The development of ethical levels is dependent on the attainment of Piagetian stages because each new level of morality requires a set of logical operations not present in the prior stage. Evidence for this conclusion comes from Kohlberg's research (1971) in which he found that 93 percent of children age five through seven capable of thinking on the concrete operational level were able to do reversible operations at Stage Two of moral development, while those not able to think concretely were in Stage One of moral development. On the other hand, few children who were on moral Stages Three or Four failed to be able to perform inversion or reciprocity Piagetian tasks. Kohlberg found further that of all adolescents attaining Stages Five and Six of ethical development, about 16 percent of the population were also formal thinkers. This is not to say, however, that formal thinkers will necessarily be at the higher levels of ethics. The advantages of reasoning on one highest level may be evident to the individual, but the advantages of having high ethics may be less clear. It is easier to think formally when considering physical entities (e.g., the effects of gravitation) than it is to reason about moral issues. Research done by Kohlberg (1971) and others indicates, furthermore, that moral development correlates positively with IQ but not as well as ability to solve Piagetian tasks.

Kohlberg's Theory: Changing Stages

How do individuals develop to higher stages? Imagine a person at Stage Four having an argument with a person at Stage Five. In many respects the Stage Four argument will be inadequate. This situation can cause cognitive disequilibrium in the person at the lower stages. In attempting to regain cognitive equilibrium, the Stage Four person adapts his cognitive structure to the situation. Since arguments at the higher level are understood, some of these ideas are incorporated into the individual's patterns of reasoning.

The home environment contributes significantly to children's ethical development. Kohlberg found that children from higher socioeconomic levels are more ethically advanced than children from lower levels. This is essentially due to the difference in opportunities for children to assume roles of responsibility and in the difference of encouragement in participation in family discussions related to moral conflict situations. Children popular in school progress to higher levels of development significantly faster than those who are unchosen by their peers. Presumably, it is the experience of taking roles in the homes that makes it possible for some children (participants) to advance over others (nonparticipants).

The importance of the environment is further reflected in studies done in orphanages and reform schools (Kohlberg, 1971; Boryam and Kohlberg, 1971). Children raised in orphanages are mainly at the preconventional level, Stages One and Two, even up to age sixteen. Children in reform schools are at similarly low ethical stages, mainly Stage Two. However, research on the home, orphanages, and reform schools does not indicate that these environments necessarily have to include a warm and loving family for moral development to occur.

For value attainment to occur there must be a *just environment*. For example, when students are confronted in class with situations interfering with learning, they should be asked what might be done to rectify the problems instead of the teacher's using authority to correct them. *Students cannot be expected to learn to interact with others humanely or to resolve value conflicts unless they have opportunities to do so and are treated justly.*

The necessity for a just environment presents a dilemma to many of our institutions. Reform schools and prisons largely interact with their wards on Kohlberg's first levels—punishment and rewards. However, when individuals are returned to society, they must operate at higher levels. It is apparent, therefore, that part of the energy in reforming our social institutions should be devoted to encouraging progress to higher ethical levels. To do otherwise is to perpetuate their present inadequacies.

Kohlberg's Theory: A Just School

Kohlberg has become more interested in applying the idea of a just community to the school setting. He sees this approach as a means of facilitating moral development and nurturing a democratic citizenry. In 1974 he helped design a just community within a cluster school in Cambridge, Massachusetts. Half of each day students attend special English, social studies, and elective classes. Cluster school students and faculty determine procedures and policies through group consensus. Each person has one vote. Classes and meetings are democratic, that is, they are not dominated by those in authority. The objective of the just school is to give students an experience in democracy and thus develop their patterns of moral reasoning (Munson, 1979).

Research indicates that most students enter the program at Stage Two and progress to Stage Three or Four during their involvement. Critics have pointed out that the teachers must be extremely competent, well-trained, flexible, and open-minded. These qualities are in addition to traditional requirements of caring, organizing, and being able to use different teaching methods. So, it is possible. It isn't easy, but educators have known this simple truth for a long time.

The Ethical Student

Educators often tend to emphasize only the cognitive aspects of student development. Research by Jean Piaget and Lawrence Kohlberg has clarified ethical aspects of development. There are patterns of moral reasoning that identify the ethical student. Piaget has suggested that the ethical student is first a moral realist. Rules are derived from those in authority; they are rigid and static. Judgements are informed by the objective situation. Greater harm is determined by the amount of harm done; intentions of the actor are not considered. In early adolescence there is a passage from this heteronomous approach to rules to an autonomous approach. At this time the student is a moral relativist in that intentions and situations are evaluated in the process of making moral judgements.

Lawrence Kohlberg has described stages of ethical development. At the preconventional level the ethical student first has a punishment/obedience orientation (Stage One). He then becomes an instrumental relativist who makes moral decisions in terms of rewards (Stage Two). The conventional level is characterized first by social approval or being a good girl or boy (Stage Three) and then law and order (Stage Four). A few students develop patterns of moral reasoning that are postconventional. There is a social-contract (Stage Five) and a universal ethical (Stage Six) level of development.

Stage sequence does not vary. Individuals progress through the stages described by Piaget and Kohlberg. While educators can think of the ethical student even in the elementary school, higher levels of ethical reasoning take time. Educators can save themselves some frustration by not expecting students to reason at advanced levels of ethical development.

Students can understand ethical patterns of reasoning at one stage above their own. This idea is a good place to initiate the process of ethical development. In fact, students are intrigued with ethical arguments at the level above their own. There is "a moderate novelty" concerning arguments at higher stages. The ethical student somehow senses that higher level patterns of moral reasoning are more adequate.

The development of ethical reasoning patterns requires disequilibrium. Being engaged by the ideas and arguments of higher levels is the way development occurs naturally. As the student hears other ideas, he cannot quite understand the position. The result is a disequilibrium of cognitive structures. (This concept is the topic of the next chapter.) As the student resolves the cognitive disequilibrium, new, higher levels of reasoning patterns emerge. Educators can facilitate the process of ethical development by (1) helping students understand explanations by asking them what they do and do not understand; (2) providing information they understand; (3) encouraging them to try new patterns of ethical reasoning; (4) allowing time for new patterns of reasoning to emerge.

Ethical development results from interactions between individuals. Educators wishing to encourage ethical development should provide opportunities for both formal and informal interactions among students, and among students and teachers.

III | EXTENSION
MORAL DEVELOPMENT

Our understanding of the developmental process indicates that students do have ethical orientations from the earliest years and that their ethical patterns of reasoning can be developed through interactions with educators. How can educators extend their understanding of moral development to the teaching/learning process?

Be Aware of Moral Thinking

One of the first practical extensions for educators is to be aware of both your own and your students' general level of ethical thinking. How did you respond to "The Cheating Student Dilemma" presented in the first section and reviewed in the last section? Did you identify your pattern of reasoning among the stages outlined? The probability is that you, like most of us, are at the conventional level. Now that you are aware of your own level, try to listen to other ethical arguments of students, peers, and even arguments on television. See if you can identify different patterns of ethical reasoning.

Ethical Climate in the Classroom

It is possible to think of the ethical climate of your classroom and school. How do students perceive the school? Classroom? What are the classroom rules and policies? How are they enforced? On what grounds do you distribute rewards, punishments, responsibilities, rights, and privileges in your classroom? You can be certain that students are aware of the answers to these questions. Think for a moment about your classroom ethos. Is it primarily orientated toward avoiding punishment? Seeking rewards? Being good? Maintaining order? Honoring a social contract? Recognizing universal ethical principles? Obviously, each classroom has some of each, but it is possible to identify one dominating orientation. Why not try to establish a long-term ethical climate at the highest level understandable to your students?

The ethical climate of a classroom is reflected in its rules and policies.

You can start by reviewing the origin and nature of the rules of the classroom. Who establishes the rules? How are they enforced? What level of behavior is expected of students? How are rule violations resolved? Answering these questions will assist you in the process of identifying and clarifying the ethical climate of your classroom.

Cooperative Work for Students

We suggest that educators involve students in cooperative class projects, activities, problem-solving situations, and games. Teachers can provide the initial direction and then act as guides while students work together and help clarify any problems that arise. Many issues, problems, and conflicts will occur and be resolved naturally by the students. If teachers intervene, they can probe, listen, suggest, and clarify, but they should leave the final resolution to the students.

Natural Opportunities for Ethical Development

Educators interested in ethical development have numerous natural opportunities to facilitate moral reasoning within the school setting. Most of these opportunities occur in the normal course of teaching. Minor issues such as talking out of turn, doodling, daydreaming, writing notes, running in the halls, and bothering other students occur daily. School personnel must interact with students concerning these problems. The grounds for the educator's position and the justification presented by students both constitute an ethical position. In most cases these problems are violations of classroom or school rules. Educators can take a few minutes with the student, attempt to elicit the student's explanation of the problem and her reasoning as justification. Educators should then be able to present another (higher) point of view and reach a resolution that results in better classroom behavior and ethical development.

Group Discussions of Dilemmas

Educators can use group discussions of moral dilemmas as a means of fostering ethical development. There is certainly no shortage of local problems, school situations, classroom conflicts, issues on television or predicaments from subjects being studied that can provide the foundation for moral dilemmas. Dilemmas will vary with age, grade, and stage, but there are some common elements that you can use in designing dilemmas for your students.

Moral Development: From Theory to Practice

Charles R. Barman
Associate Professor of Education
Buena Vista College

In studies at two major American universities, students were asked to rank specific types of unethical behavior such as stealing or cheating on one's income taxes. Most of the students in this study perceived behavior involving dishonest actions toward individuals as being more unethical than acts of dishonesty toward an institution.[1] The social implications of this data are evident in our society today. Recent historical events, such as Watergate, exemplify the perceptions held by these students. It seems that some of our government officials may also have had difficulty perceiving their actions as unethical because they were not actions directed toward a specific person.

As educators, I believe that we share some of the blame for this apparent inconsistency in logic. Generally, education has divorced itself from moral issues in the curriculum. Instead, our educational system has advocated a very authoritarian policy and has thereby left little room for students to question and discuss moral issues.

Some educators, such as Lawrence Kohlberg, contend that this type of policy does not promote moral growth. According to Kohlberg, individuals develop moral reasoning through active involvement with moral issues. For example, individuals need to engage in a discussion or some type of interaction for moral growth to occur. Through this interaction, they may be confronted with some inconsistencies in their logic. If at this time they are mentally ready to perceive these inconsistencies, they might modify their reasoning and progress to a "higher level" of moral thought.

Kohlberg has studied the moral development of individuals in the United States and other parts of the world. From these studies he has constructed a model of how people develop moral reasoning patterns. His model consists of three main levels, each containing two subcategories or stages. Generally, his model states that an individual's moral reasoning develops progressively from a rather egocentric view to one of universal ideas.

Kohlberg's model can provide teachers with an idea of what reasoning patterns to expect from their students. For example, students that are at the preconventional level would tend to reason on a basis of self-centered needs. In contrast, conventional-level students would solve moral problems in a more traditional way, being influenced by their peers and the rules of society. Postconventional-level individuals would have the ability to base their moral decisions on values shared by other members of society, or they might act upon their own intellect, while respecting the values and attitudes of others.

1. A. Etzioni, "Should Schools Add Moral Education to Their Curricula?" *Minneapolis Tribune*, October 17, 1976.

To aid your students in moral development, it is imperative to carefully integrate experiences into your curriculum that allow them to consider moral issues. It is also important to be aware of the level of moral development of your students. According to Kohlberg, students should be confronted with moral problems one stage beyond their current reasoning abilities. In this way, they will have the opportunity to evaluate their present logic with each moral problem. They will see that some of their peers have different solutions to the problems. They may also discover that their logic is not totally consistent. It is through these discoveries that Kohlberg believes moral growth occurs.

My experiences in the last seven years and those of other colleagues demonstrate that it is possible to put Kohlberg's model into practice in classroom instruction. We have found four effective values education approaches: (1) the moral dilemma approach, (2) values clarification, (3) action learning, and (4) analysis.[2] These approaches are not methods of indoctrination. Instead, they allow students to examine values issues openly and freely, as well as formulate their own attitudes about them through the use of a variety of teaching strategies, such as case studies, dilemma situations, role playing, simulation exercises, and small-group discussions.

To incorporate these approaches in your classes, examine your present curriculum and identify areas where moral issues can be integrated. Then select the approach or combination of approaches that will most effectively deal with each specific issue. Keep in mind that when using them it is important to remain neutral with regard to each issue and to refrain from judging your students' responses.

If carefully constructed, with a knowledge of your students' current levels of moral development, these approaches can increase student interaction and may enhance moral growth. In addition, these techniques add personal meaning or relevance to your course and help develop decision-making skills.

---

2. For a detailed description and some examples of each approach, see C. R. Barman, J. J. Rusch, and T. M. Cooney, *Science & Societal Issues: A Guide for Science Teachers* (Ames, Iowa; Iowa State University Press, 1981) and D. P. Superka and P. L. Johnson, *Values Education: Approaches and Materials* (Boulder, Colo: Social Science Education Consortium, 1975.)

Designing Dilemmas for Classroom Use

1. Identify the conflict and theme for the dilemma (e.g., life, liberty, justice, truth, etc.).

2. Introduce the problem.

3. Clarify the conflict.

4. Be sure there is a dilemma (i.e., a choice between two equally unfavorable alternatives). Should the person steal or allow his wife to die? Should justice be done for the individual or the group, and so on.

5. Describe the situation and dilemma to the students in understandable terms.

6. Delineate the decision made by the main character in the dilemma.

7. Review the moral dilemma and describe what you perceive to be the pro/con positions for each stage (see earlier discussion of pro/con positions for "The Cheating Student Dilemma").

8. Ask for a definitive decision with reference to the dilemma (e.g., Should John have stolen the car? What should Mary do—stand up for her rights or allow the person to die?)

9. A good dilemma is simple, straightforward, and relevant to students.

10. Be sure to ask for a justification for the response.

After introducing the dilemma, the teacher should guide the discussion making sure the students stay on the topic. The teacher can point out inconsistencies in reasoning, and more adequate resolutions to the dilemma. Be sure to let the students answer the dilemma and justify their position.

Value Clarification in the Classroom

The purpose of value clarification is to aid students in developing processes to use in determining their own values. *Its purpose is not to indoctrinate.* An educator must be open and accepting of students' views, helping them clarify their values. The teacher, furthermore, must ensure that this attitude also prevails among the students for their classmates. In order to do this, instructors must have a clear definition of what a value is and how it differs from value indicators.

Raths, Harmin, and Simon, in their book *Values and Teaching* (1966) have defined a value as having the following characteristics: (1) cherished, (2) publicly affirmed, (3) freely chosen, (4) chosen from alternatives, (5) chosen knowing the consequences, (6) linked consistently with other values, and (7) acted upon. These authors consider the following not to be values but only value indicators: (1) beliefs, (2) attitudes, (3) opinions, (4) feelings, and (5) morals. These *value indicators* differ from values in that they are guides that have not met all the criteria listed for values.

In order for value clarification to be effective, teachers should evaluate the developmental level of each student and adjust instruction so that the child is confronted with moral problems one stage above his developmental attainment. By doing this, the instructor facilitates the student's involvement. The teacher should also confront students with their own illogic. In doing this, the teacher generally asks questions requiring students to search and identify certain concepts and principles they hold and their reasons for having them. The activities presented may provide structure or be unstructured, depending on the needs of the students and the type of investigation. When two ethical principles are in conflict, this is pointed out, and the students are asked to think of a higher ethic which would help solve the dilemma.

Sidney Simon and his colleagues (Simon, Howe, and Kirschenbaum, 1972) believe that morality cannot be taught directly but that the students, through active involvement, social interaction, and the use of their minds, must actively mediate moral principles. It is for these reasons that Simon and his colleagues have devoted considerable energy to translating ethical theories into action through value clarification activities.

The typical value clarification strategy starts with some area of conflict where students are confused or have not as yet attained all the criteria outlined for a person having values. These areas might include such topics as the following:

1. Sex
2. Politics
3. Contribution of technology
4. Pollution
5. Religion
6. Family relations
7. Individual tastes
8. Culture—what is pleasing in the arts, music, etc.
9. Style—clothing, hair, etc.
10. War and peace
11. Race and other biases
12. Death
13. Authority—how much is needed?
14. Rules—which are necessary and why?
15. Society and what it does to the aging

Typically, instructors using value clarification strategies present problems which require students to identify their own values or resolve situations where two values may be in conflict. Students may be involved in researching the topic, discussing the problem in small groups or class discussions, and then summarizing their own views. Through the value clarification procedures, students should learn to

1. Make choices when confronted with moral dilemmas.
2. Look at alternatives.
3. Consider the alternatives and their consequences.
4. Consider what they cherish most relative to the problem area.
5. Affirm their choices publicly.
6. Behave and live their choices.
7. Examine repeatedly patterns and behaviors in their lives.

Other general suggestions for establishing a value clarification environment in the class are as follows:

1. *Make the class student centered* rather than teacher centered. This can be done by dividing the class into groups consisting of four or five students and presenting a problem to discuss and resolve. Piaget and Kohlberg both stress peer group participation because of the greater possibilities for devel-

opment inherent in the socialization process. Social interaction requires the individual to perceive situations with different perspectives. In the process of playing different social roles in arguments and resolving them, the individuals arrive at what is just.

2. *Involve students in role playing.* Encourage them to play various roles related to moral activities. They should be asked to try to make decisions anyone can live with; in other words, to learn the meaning of justice.

3. *Have students consider some situation where there are moral breakdowns,* as in mob rule. They should evaluate the situation and discuss how such a thing can be prevented.

4. *Invite students to discuss their behavior* in class, school, and community.

5. *Give responsibility* to students as much as feasible.

6. *Expose students to real as well as verbal conflicts.* For example, ask, "In what ways can we treat each other in this class so as to make everyone feel comfortable, welcome, and wanted?"

7. *Present conflict situations requiring students to interpret and use ethical principles* one level higher than their own.

8. *Guard against imposing one's ethical principles on students.*

9. *Bestow trust on students.* The more this is done, the more students feel obligated to fulfill this trust.

An example of one value clarification strategy is called "Are you someone who . . . ?" In this strategy, questions such as the following are answered with a yes, no, or maybe. "Are you someone who

1. likes to break the curve on an exam?"
2. likes to stay up all night when friends visit?"
3. will stop the car to look at a sunset?"
4. will publicly show affection for another person?"
5. will do it yourself when you feel something needs to be done?"
6. could accept your own sexual impotence?"
7. could be satisfied without a college degree?"
8. could be part of a mercy killing?"
9. is afraid alone in the dark in a strange place?"
10. is apt to judge someone by his appearance?"
11. watches television soap operas?"
12. could kill in self-defense?"

This strategy allows a person to consider more thoughtfully what he values, what he wants of life, and what type of person he is.

The search for self as a conscious act is a continual ongoing process. As a person works and plays, this self-adventure becomes a touchstone for living. From knowing one's self (behaviors, patterns, etc.), a new confidence, an internal security, a sense of potency emerges which is life-giving. Too often in our lives we search outside ourselves for meaning and become preoccupied with assigning blame and trying to change others. A life of meaning lies within each of us by discovering and cultivating what we are right now. Know what you prize and cherish and act on it as you live fully each day of your life. (Massey, 1972).

BIBLIOGRAPHY

Boryam, M., and Kohlberg, L. "Development of Moral Judgement in the Kibbutz." In *Recent Research in Moral Development*, edited by L. Kohlberg and E. Turiel. New York: Holt, Rinehart & Winston, 1971.

Gibbs, John C. "Kohlberg's Stages of Moral Judgement: A Constructive Critique." *Harvard Educational Review* 47 (February 1977): 43–61.
Gibbs reviews the hierarchy of stages and finds support for the first four stages but not the higher stages.

Gilligan, Carol. "In a Different Voice: Women's Conceptions of Self and Morality." *Harvard Educational Review*, 47 (November 1977): 481–517.
An important criticism of Kohlberg's theory from the concerns and experiences of women. Gilligan presents critiques of Kohlberg's stages and then offers an alternative based on her research.

Hersh, Richard; Reimer, Joseph; and Paoletto, Diana Pritchard. *Promoting Moral Growth*, New York: Longman, 1979.
An excellent introduction for educators. Highly recommended for both theoretical and practical reasons.

Kohlberg, Lawrence. "From Is to Ought: How to Commit the Naturalistic Fallacy and Get Away with It in the Study of Moral Development." In *Cognitive Development and Epistemology*, edited by T. Mishel. New York: Academic Press, 1971.
An extensive overview of moral education and Kohlberg's theory of moral development.

————. "Moral Education for a Society in Moral Transition." *Educational Leadership* (October, 1975a): 46–54.
A good introduction to the topic of moral development.

————. "The Cognitive-Developmental Approach to Moral Education." *Phi Delta Kappan* (June 1977b): 670–77.

Kurtines, William, and Greif, Esther. "The Development of Moral Thought. A Review and Evaluation of Kohlberg's Approach." *Psychological Bulletin* 81 (August 1974): 453–70.
A comprehensive and insightful review of Kohlberg's theory.

Massey, Sara. "Value Activities." Unpublished paper. Portland, Maine: University of Maine, 1972.

Munson, Howard. "Moral Thinking—Can It Be Taught?" *Psychology Today* (February 1979): 48–68, 92.
This article is less technical than many critics. However, it is a comprehensive review and criticism of Kohlberg's theory. Attention is directed to Kohlberg's recent work with schools. While not answering the questions of the title, it is still an important article for educators.

Piaget, Jean. *The Moral Judgement of the Child*. New York: The Free Press, 1965.
This is Piaget's original work on moral development. Though long (406 pages), it is interesting reading. Topics include rules, adult constraint, lying, and justice.

Piaget, Jean, and Inhelder, Barbel. *The Psychology of the Child*. New York: Basic Books, 1969.
There is a short section on "Moral Feelings and Judgements." The brief

summary really does not do justice to Piaget's original work on moral development.

Raths, Louis; Harmin, Merrill, and Simon, Sidney. *Values and Teaching*. Columbus, Oh. Charles E. Merrill Publishing Co., 1966.

Simon, Sidney; Howe, Leland W.; and Kirschenbaum, Howard. *Values Clarification: A Handbook of Practical Strategies for Teachers and Students*. New York: Hart Publishing Co., 1972.

IV | EVALUATION
MORAL DEVELOPMENT

Listed below are some of the main topics reviewed in this chapter. Read each statement and rate it on the scale TWICE: once according to what you knew about the topic before starting this chapter and a second time according to what you have learned as a result of reading this chapter. Circle the appropriate number and mark B for *before* and A for *after*, as indicated below.

Topic	Student Evaluation					
	Low		Moderate		High	
Example: Important Piagetian levels of moral development	①B	2	3	4	⑤A	6
1. Piaget's concept of heteronomous obedience to rules	1	2	3	4	5	6
2. Piaget's concept of autonomous understanding of rules	1	2	3	4	5	6
3. Piaget's stage of moral realism	1	2	3	4	5	6
4. Piaget's stage of moral relativity	1	2	3	4	5	6
5. Characteristics of "preconventional" moral reasoning	1	2	3	4	5	6
6. Characteristics of "conventional" moral reasoning	1	2	3	4	5	6
7. Characteristics of "postconventional" moral reasoning	1	2	3	4	5	6
8. Characteristics of Kohlberg's Stage One—avoidance of punishment	1	2	3	4	5	6
9. Characteristics of Kohlberg's Stage Two—seeking rewards	1	2	3	4	5	6
10. Characteristics of Kohlberg's Stage Three—social approval	1	2	3	4	5	6
11. Characteristics of Kohlberg's Stage Four—law and order	1	2	3	4	5	6

12. Characteristics of Kohlberg's Stage
Five—social contract   1   2   3   4   5   6

13. Characteristics of Kohlberg's Stage
Six—universal ethics   1   2   3   4   5   6

14. Pro and con orientation to dilemma
justifications for each stage   1   2   3   4   5   6

15. The foundations of Kohlberg's
theory   1   2   3   4   5   6

16. The role of disequilibrium in the
development of ethical patterns
of reasoning   1   2   3   4   5   6

17. Designing dilemmas for class-
room use   1   2   3   4   5   6

18. Using value clarification in
the classroom   1   2   3   4   5   6

8 Equilibration and the Student's Construction of Knowledge

Having been introduced to the major periods of development, educators usually ask the logical question, "What can be done to facilitate development?" This question has several variations: "How can I accelerate development?" "How can I help students who are below expected developmental levels?" "What can teachers do to ensure appropriate development?" Generally, we do not think teachers should *accelerate* development. On the other hand, there is often the need to help individuals attain appropriate developmental levels, and there is certainly the need to assure continued cognitive development. Questions such as these move our attention from the observed *products* of development—the stages— to the *process* of development.

While the process by which individuals construct knowledge is essential, it is also a fairly complicated set of concepts. Even so, the ideas should be included because they do, after all, answer the question essential to education, "How do students learn?" We will now turn to themes that have been mentioned but not discussed in detail; namely, the organization and adaptation of intelligence, the process of cognitive equilibration, and the related concepts of assimilation and accommodation.

I | EXPLORATION
THE PROCESS OF EQUILIBRATION

Probing the Process

Look at the following problem:

$$O\ T\ T\ F\ F\ S\ S\ E\ N\ T\ E\ T\ T\ F\ F\ S\ S\ E\ N\ T\ \underline{\ ?\ }$$

What letter goes in the blank space? Take one minute and see if you can answer the question. After one minute continue to the next problem.

$$F\ M\ A\ M\ J\ J\ A\ S\ O\ N\ D\ \underline{\ ?\ }$$

What letter goes in the blank space? Take one minute and see if you can answer the question. Continue to the next question after one minute.

$$M\ T\ \underline{\ ?\ }\ T\ F\ S\ \underline{\ ?\ }$$

What letters go in the blank spaces? Stop and think about this problem for fifteen seconds. The letters *W* and *S* go in the blanks. If you did not solve the first two problems, the third should help. Go back and see if you can solve them now. Take a minute to do this. Did you get the answer? Now we will continue the discussion.

Stop reading and take a few minutes to analyze your own thought processes. Do this if you have a solution and can justify your answer, or if you still do not have an answer. Stop and think about your thinking.

What did you do first after seeing the problems? How would you describe your mental functioning? Would you use any of the following words: searching, surveying, probing, analyzing, testing, hypothesizing, checking? How would you describe your mental response: reasoning, contemplation, deliberation, pondering? How would you describe your mental state: absorbed, engrossed, reflective, focused?

Depending on the level of involvement, several of these words may describe your mental processes. This is the process of equilibration as you experienced it in this problem. As you will see, there is a range of responses depending on your understanding of the problem. Probably your response was one of several. You immediately knew the answers and could justify them with certainty. You thought through the problem, examining patterns of letters and aligning these with other patterns already known, and finally arrived at an answer that you could justify, but you were not certain of the answer. You engaged in some of the processes just described and still could not answer the first two problems. But, you solved the third rather easily, and then with an insight, returned to solve the first two problems and now feel certain about your answers and justifications. Finally, you may have thought about the problem and were unable to arrive at an answer. We can help you if you are in this group. *T* is the answer to the first problem and *J* is the answer to the second. Now that you have all the answers, can you provide an explanation for why these are the correct answers?

Reasoning Strategies: The Possible, Impossible, and Probable

Suppose fourth grade students were presented calculus. You can imagine how they would respond. They would listen for a few minutes and then become restless and perhaps even disruptive. If learning calculus was the goal, was achieving the goal possible, impossible, or probable? Clearly, the answer is *impossible*.

Now imagine a presentation to a college level introductory calculus class. The presentation is a review of addition, subtraction, multiplication, and division. How do you think college students would respond? If you said they would be bored, you are correct. Was the goal of understanding basic arithmetic possible, impossible, or probable? Certainly it was *possible*.

The third situation is the most important for our discussion; it is also the most difficult to describe. Using the variable already described, suppose there was to be a presentation of addition and subtraction to fourth grade students, or an introductory discussion of calculus to the calculus class. When the question about achieving goals is asked, the most accurate answer now seems to be *probable*. The abilities of the students would be such that they would probably be able to understand the discussions. Why probable? We use the term *probable* to identify the gray area between total understanding and total lack of understanding. While the concepts may not be immediately understandable to the student, they are within a range that should reasonably be understandable. The position being discussed is shown schematically along a continuum from possible to impossible.

POSSIBLE ⟶ PROBABLE ⟶ IMPOSSIBLE
(Concepts are al-   (Concepts are   (Concepts are
ready understood.)   challenging but   beyond
                        achievable.)   understanding.)

Students in Transition

Discussions of transitions in earlier chapters were concerned with progress from one stage to the next. The transition from a less to a more adequate understanding of reality is the central focus of this chapter. We want to emphasize, however, that the same processes apply at several different levels. One way of discussing "students in transition" for the equilibration process is to describe the creative/problem-solving process.

1. *Recognition of the problem.* Problems can be very complex and involved, so much so that some individuals may not recognize them as problems. You can think of this as a "readiness" for problem solving. For example, students need to know simple mathematics before they can recognize or solve calculus problems.

2. *Motivation to solve the problem.* Presenting a problem in class may or may not result in the student's being motivated to solve the problem. If the problem has meaning for the student because it is of interest and/or because materials related to the problem are physically present, motivation is enhanced. The problem should present a challenge, but one that is within the student's abilities. It should be neither too simple nor too complex. Students should work in an atmosphere which is conducive to exploration of problems. When these criteria are met, the student's behavior usually indicates a motivation to solve the problem. Students will be eager, interested, and engaged in the problem.

3. *Time to solve the problem.* Once you have engaged learners in a problem, they should have time to work on the solution. This is important to the entire transition. At first they will put forth a concentrated effort to resolve the problem using old ideas, habits, and bits of knowledge. This is the logical and analytical phase. However, for many problems this approach fails to produce results. You can tell when students are near the end of this phase because they show frustration, tension, and discomfort. They are at the end when they give up in apparent failure. But this is when the next phase begins. During this intuitive, nonrational, creative phase, new perceptions and new orientations emerge. Students may suddenly "see" the solution. The end of this phase is signaled by the excitement and exhilaration of this insight.

4. *Modification and elaboration of the solution.* When students reach a tentative solution, you should encourage them to test their ideas. Does the solution work? How does it stand up to the test of reality? With this step there can be some modification and then elaboration of the solution.

5. *Communication of the solution.* Without communication, solutions may have personal value but lack social import. The students should try to describe their solution. In many cases they will *need* to talk about their solution to the problem. They should be able to present their solution clearly and logically, both orally and in writing. In the process of presenting a solution, they should be encouraged to justify or explain the solution.

Problem solving and the process of equilibration bring together many aspects of psychology. For teachers they show the importance of both logical and creative thinking. Problem solving integrates the unique functions of both right and left hemispheres of the brain. We are now recognizing the importance of creativity in the problem-solving process and its place in the classroom. Teaching techniques, methods, and materials that actively involve students, the use of counterintuitive problems, and thought-provoking questions are all direct applications of Piaget's theory of equilibration.

Piagetian Theory and the Development of Creative Thinking

Alan J. McCormack
Science and Mathematics Teaching Center
University of Wyoming

Piaget's revolutionary studies of children's cognitive development have focused mainly on development of logic. Logical operations such as seriation, conservation, and multiple classification are based on an accepted set of rules and involve mainly convergent thinking. If you survey, as I have, the indexes of most of the books written by Piaget or about Piaget's ideas, you will very rarely find "creativity," "creative thinking," or "imagination" included.

But, children (as well as adults) have two ways of dealing with reality: one logical; the other creative. Both have their unique contributions to make to effective human functioning.

Since the days when Piaget was active in his studies of children's thinking, dramatic physiological discoveries have revealed new insights about the functioning of the human brain. Many researchers now believe that the left cerebral hemisphere is predominantly involved with logical, analytical, linear, and sequential thought. Thus, the left half of the brain is the controlling site of reason and so of most of the mental operations Piaget has so expertly described.

The brain's right hemisphere engages itself in visual or spatial relationships, some artistic talents and sensitivities, imagery, initial synthesis of new ideas, intuition, and other nonlinear mind functions. The left hemisphere is the practical logician; the right is the dreamer, the inventor, the artist.

In Western society, it seems that the left brain dominates the right. The work of the left hemisphere is easier to describe and is generally more valued—probably because left hemispheric products have more obvious practical benefits to society. After all, being able to read or see flaws in the logic of an argument is undeniably a useful thing to be able to do. To many people logic and analytical thinking seem "legitimate" skills, while fantasy and oddball inventiveness are kept closeted in the mind's attic.

When the above point of view is applied literally to the organization of a school curriculum, the result is a learning program that is virtually "half-brained." And, of course, a curriculum mainly oriented toward right hemispheric thinking would be equally ludicrous. The highest achievements of humankind have been brought about by the complementary workings of our two thought modes.

To be fair to Piaget, I must admit that some attention to creative brain processes is intimately entwined in his theories of cognitive development. Piaget has stated many times that logical operations are not something that can be transmitted ready-made to children. These operations are *constructed* by the child's mind based on his actions on real-world objects. Piaget terms the process of construction *equilibration*.

So all learning, to Piaget, is a process of creativity rather than receptivity. But this process seems to have an overall convergent orientation, culminating with the development of formal operational abilities during adolescence. Development of logic is the paramount thrust of Piaget's developmental scheme.

Some of Piaget's disciples have gone so far as to postulate that creativity is not possible at all before a person has mastered formal operational thinking. This is a viewpoint I reject and consider educationally destructive. I have seen many creative inventions, works of art, and insightful gems of word play originated in the minds of young children providing ample evidence of their creative abilities. In fact, rigorous attempts to force development of logical thinking can force creativity underground or even stifle the ability permanently.

We shouldn't be too intent on teaching children about our adult world of logic without paying due attention to their unique worlds of dreams and imagination. Learning to conserve and classify will develop naturally in most children. Let's not thwart development of their right-brain abilities by a diet of logic and reason that is too severe or administered too early.

II | EXPLANATION
THE PROCESS OF EQUILIBRATION

Instruction should be based on an understanding of the developmental process. For teachers this is both a psychological and practical problem. It is also a problem that is neither clearly understood nor adequately applied. Attention has almost always been directed toward the stages of cognitive development. While understanding the defining characteristics of each stage is certainly a step toward better instruction, there is another step. Most discussions of Piaget's theory omit the process of equilibration. The reasons for the omission are fairly simple; equilibration is a complex concept and Piaget himself was never very clear in his discussions of it. While difficult, the concept is understandable and absolutely essential to applying the theory in classrooms.

The Development of Thought (Piaget, 1975) is Piaget's major statement on the process of equilibration. This is a difficult book to read. Significant portions of *Six Psychological Studies* (Piaget, 1967), *Piaget and Inhelder on Equilibration* (Nodine, Gallagher and Humphreys, 1972) and *The Psychology of the Child* (Piaget and Inhelder, 1969) are devoted to equilibration. There is one other book written by the Geneva School on the topic of learning, *Learning and the Development of Cognition* (Inhelder, Sinclair, and Bovet, 1974). Before presenting the concepts aligned with equilibration, we shall review different perspectives of education in an attempt to provide a context for Piaget's theory.

Historically, development of concepts has been explained by one of three broad categories. For simplification and clarity we have chosen to use the words *transmission, maturation*, and *construction* for the following discussion. It should also be noted that there are parallels in biology, philosophy, and psychology concerning the ways and means of intellectual development. Understandably there have also been educational interpretations of these discussions.

Development Through Transmission

In this model, forces and pressures in the external environment impress themselves on the child's mind. The "bits" of knowledge are transmitted to the child as direct copies of reality and are stored in the mind for later recall and use. Behavior is the output of these accumulated inputs. For this system, the accumulation of writing on a blank slate is an appropriate metaphor. Psychological theory underlying this position is that of the associationist, behaviorist, stimulus-response advocate, or environmentalist. The most famous proponent of this position is probably B.F. Skinner.

The educational theories that are based on this system of philosophy and psychology are primarily concerned with the transmission of knowledge, rules, values, and morals collected over history. The important task is transmitting knowledge; the goal or objective is behavior that clearly indicates the individual has successfully accumulated the appropriate knowledge. The means to this end vary; behavior modification, programmed texts, and teaching machines are contemporary examples.

The process of equilibration is not part of the transmission view of development. Adherents to this psychology maintain that behavior can be explained without invoking an internal "mentalistic" model. Psychological growth is an accumulation of behaviors, and learning is a change of behavior. There is little recognition for discontinuous growth (i.e., stages of development).

Teaching through the transmission of knowledge is the dominant model used by educators. If we return to the question—"How does a student's understanding of the world improve?"—the answer is through the knowledge transmitted from the teacher to the student.

Development Through Maturation

The maturationists emphasize the growth and development of internal structures. The metaphor for this model is organic growth such as an acorn becoming an oak tree. The role of the environment is that of nourishment. Development proceeds in a preestablished pattern, the potential of which is latent but has to be made actual.

Different psychological theorists espouse this model. In this position both cognitive and emotional structures unfold in preestablished hereditary stages. Theorists such as Gesell, Ames, and Ilg have developed their ideas of growth within this tradition. The following briefly describes a variation on this position espoused by the child psychologists, Frances Ilg and Louis Ames:

> Behavior grows! Behavior has pattern and shape just as does physical structure.... Gone are the days when psychologists likened the child's body to a lump of clay which you...mold in any direction you choose.... Though the child's behavior can be strongly influenced by the kind of home and other surroundings in which he grows up, many of the changes which will take place in his behavior are determined from within. (Ilg and Ames, 1955, p. 1)

Another variation on this position is generally associated with the "romantic" educators. The best contemporary educational example is A.S. Neill's book, *Summerhill* (1960). The school environment is one of enough permissiveness to allow the inner "natural" structures to grow, flourish, and develop. This position emphasizes the real self of the child that is to be developed; thus, education centers on the child's emotional and intellectual growth, and not the transmission of the physical environment and culture.

In Freudian theory equilibration is primarily used to maintain health as the organism encounters personal crisis and/or intrapsychic conflicts between the id, ego, and superego. The stages of development (oral, anal, phallic, and genital) progress upon the restoration of an inner psychic balance via equilibration. The primary determinant of growth is not equilibration; localization of libidinal energy in bodily zones determines progressive development. Equilibration ensures this development is healthy. Recognition of both naturally occurring internal factors and transmission of concepts from the environment leads to the position held by Piaget.

Development Through Construction

The construction model utilizes a metaphor of chemical reaction or fusion. Core ideas are redefined, reorganized, elaborated, changed and, in short, constructed through the continuous interaction of the individual and the environment.

> One can conceive of intelligence as the development of an assimilatory activity whose functional laws are laid down as early as organic life and whose successive structures serving it as organs are elaborated by interaction between itself and the external environment. (Piaget, 1963, p. 359)

Piaget's position differs from the first, transmission, in that it does not exclusively accentuate experience from the environment; there is also recognition of the student's mental activity in the construction of knowledge. It is distinguished from the maturation position by the fact that it does not consider intellectual structures ready-made and innate. Piaget's emphasis is on the development of structures without invoking preformed or innate structures. He does, however, theorize that intellectual functions, the process of equilibration, is innate.

To summarize, development of the intellect is neither direct learning from the environment nor maturation; it is reorganization and construction of psychological structures as a result of interactions between the individual and the environment. Figure 8.1 summarizes the positions outlined in this section.

Development and Learning

Some problems concerning the educational application of Piaget's theory have resulted from a confusion between his conceptions of development

Figure 8.1
Developmental Perspectives and Education

Position	View of Student	Knowledge	Approach to Teaching
Transmission	Empty—must be filled with information	Copy of reality	External to internal
Maturation	Full—but structure must be allowed to mature	Emergence of structure	Internal to external
Construction	Empty—process of development is active	Constructed through interaction	Interaction between internal and external

and learning. Development is spontaneous and concerned with the totality of the cognitive structure. When, for example, we say a student is at the concrete operational level, we are referring to a total constellation of cognitive structures functioning at a certain level. Learning is directed and concerned with a specific external situation or problem. Learning thus concerns only single or selected cognitive structures. A child's first encounter with a ball and the problem of rolling the ball is a specific problem that will require applying the scheme of grasping the ball and coordinating a push of the ball in a certain direction. Through the coordinated action of grasping, looking, and pushing, the child has modified his structure of knowledge. Notice that the already developed structures are used to explain the action of rolling the ball. For Piaget, development explains learning, though for the prevailing psychology in education the reverse is true. That is, numerous small learnings accumulate and result in development (Piaget, 1964).

Intellectual Structures

A brief discussion of structure as Piaget uses the term will aid in a further understanding of his theory of development and the process of equilibration.

According to Piaget,

> A structure is a system of transformations. Inasmuch as it is a system and not a mere collection of elements and their properties, these transformations involve laws: the structure is preserved or enriched by the interplay of its transformation laws, which never yield results external to the system nor employ elements that are external to it. In short, the notion of structure is composed of three key ideas: the idea of wholeness, the idea of transformation, and the idea of self-regulation. (Piaget, 1970, p. 5)

The structure of intelligence is an internally organized whole that is continually being constructed as the individual cognitively adapts to the environment. Construction occurs through the process of self-regulation. The construction process results in a more integrated mental structure of a higher order. This process can be thought of as an interaction between the internal structure of knowledge and external stimuli. The result of the interaction is a new intellectual structure. The cognitive structure, then, refers to the way a student will adapt and organize incoming information. The incoming information is sometimes altered because of the student's cognitive organization, or the student alters the cognitive organization to fit the new information.

What about the *origin* of intellectual structures? Piaget's response is included in his book, *Structuralism* (1970).

> Human structures do not arise out of nothing.... We called these initial structures behind which we cannot go "general coordinations of actions," meaning to refer to the connections that are common to all sensori-motor connections. (p. 62-63)

The origin of intellectual structures is biological in the reflexive mechanisms: the coordinated actions of sucking, prehension, movement of appendages, and vision. Here, then, is an embryogenetic origin for the structure of knowledge that will undergo continual transformations as intelligence evolves.

Piaget elaborates on the difference between intellectual functioning and intellectual structures:

> If there truly in fact exists a functional nucleus of the intellectual organization which comes from the biological organization in its most general aspect, it is apparent that this invariant will orient the whole of the successive structures which the mind will then work out in its contact with reality. It will thus play the role that philosophers assigned to the *a priori*; that is to say, it will impose on the structures certain necessary and irreducible conditions. Only the mistake has sometimes been made of regarding the *a priori* as consisting in structures existing ready-made from the beginning of development, whereas if the functional invariant of thought is at work in the most primitive stages, it is only little by little that it impresses itself on consciousness due to the elaboration of structures which are increasingly adapted to the function itself. This *a priori* only appears in the form of essential structures at the end of the evolution of concepts and not at their beginning: although it is hereditary, this *a priori* is thus the very opposite of what were formerly called "innate ideas." (Piaget, 1963, p. 3)

Intellectual structures in relative stability describes the concept of developmental stage (e.g., sensorimotor, preoperational, concrete operational, and formal operational). For educators it is important to ask, What factors can explain a change of the intellectual structure? There are four factors contributing to development: first, physical growth and maturation; second, physical experience or the natural effects of environmental factors; third, social transmission which includes education; fourth, equilibration or the self-regulation of the cognitive structure. The process of equilibration balances the other three factors contributing to individual development.

Disequilibrium and Equilibration

Intellectual development is an adaptation in response to a discrepancy between the existing cognitive structure and a cognitive referent in the environment. The discrepancy results in a disequilibrium which produces a reconstruction that brings the system back to equilibrium. The factors of maturation, experience, and social transmission all contribute to intellectual development. According to Piaget, it is the more fundamental factor of equilibration that mediates the influence of the other three factors. That is, the three factors are equilibrated.

The concept of equilibrium is characterized by stability, compensation, and activity. The process of equilibration implies both mobility and stability. The intellectual structure, for example, is a system of actions and a continuous series of operations and adaptations. The system remains stable in the sense that basic structures remain; they may be elaborated but are not eliminated. Equilibrium also includes the mental compensations that result from the actions of the individual in mental response to discrepancies between mental structures and the environment. Activity is also synonymous with equilibrium. An individual must be sufficiently active to counter the external intrusions with compensations of the intellectual structure (Piaget, 1963, pp. 150–152).

The process of equilibration refers to three important levels of intellectual functioning. At the most dramatic level, it refers to the individual's developmental stage. At one period, such as the preoperational stage, there is a total set of intellectual structures in relative equilibrium. Then the combined factors of maturation, experience, and education bring about a major disequilibrium. The ensuing process of equilibration results in a new, higher order stage of intellectual functioning; in this case, the concrete operational period. The second level at which equilibration occurs is within specific subsystems such as conservation, classification, numeration, and so on. For example, there is the continuous construction of conservation concepts, each construction being identifiable and the total construction representing a higher, more integrated, functioning. There is a conservation sequence that follows a pattern of substance, length, weight, and volume. The third level of equilibration is the specific learning situation. Earlier examples of grasping a ball, conserving clay, or solving specific problems define this level of equilibration. Teachers are primarily concerned with this level in the daily interactions with students.

Educators can relate the three levels of equilibration to short, middle, and long-term components of instruction. The most immediate aspect concerning equilibration is the specific teaching situation and the methods and materials that may engage (bring about equilibration in) the learner. These lessons should be based on the student's developmental level and extend some aspect of the intellectual structure. Lessons should contribute to more complete development in areas such as classification, conservation, numeration, and so on. Finally, in the long term, there is a transition from one major period to the next.

Underlying the discussion of equilibration is the assumption that the individual has encountered a situation producing disequilibrium. The degree of disequilibrium can be thought of as the difference between the existing cognitive structure and a cognitive referent in the environment. Equilibration represents the process of reconstructing the intellectual structure in order to incorporate the cognitive referent into the individual's organization of knowledge. It seems, then, that a concept of optimum disequilibrium, or optimum mismatch, is important for learning and the classroom teacher because it is through the process of equilibration that learning and development advance. Jonas Langer has emphasized the concept of disequilibrium as it relates to change:

> To date, however, organismic theorists have looked on equilibration as an internal process of achieving the most balanced intellectual organization possible. They have tended to neglect the opposite side of the coin, namely, that the internal organization must be in disequilibrium for the child to perform an adaptive mental action and, therefore, for change to take place. (Langer, 1964, p. 36)

He further points out "when cognitive theorists have looked at disequilibrium, as in cognitive conflict studies, it has been defined as an external perturbation imposed on the child" (Langer, p. 36). According to Piaget, disequilibrium, and thus equilibration, takes place within the individual intellectual structure and is caused by the "external perturbation." There is also the added dimension of internal perturbation to which educators have given little recognition.

What can the teacher look for that might indicate disequilibrium? There are indications such as fluctuation in answers, understanding part of a problem, increasing logical organization in responses, looking puzzled, being engrossed in activity, and transferring knowledge to new situations. Most of these are common observations for the classroom teacher. The interpretation of the behavior and understanding that it is indicative of intellectual change are important applications of Piaget's theory.

After being introduced to Piaget's theory, with the usual emphasis on stages, teachers often ask what they can do to help students' intellectual development. Certainly recognition of stage differences among students is important. However, the stage as seen at any time in any individual is a product of the student's development up to that time. The process of equilibration has been the fundamental factor contributing to that development. The answer to the educational questions concerning Piaget's theory should give more emphasis to the process of equilibration, for it is the process which brings about development. In educational perspective, moderate disequilibrium is necessary for the resulting process of intellectual adaptation and thus a higher level of organization. The process of equilibration must explain two factors: the maintenance of the intellectual structure and the change in the intellectual structure. The concepts of organization and adaptation are used to explain the specific functioning of equilibration.

The Role of Organization and Adaptation

From a biological point of view, it is generally agreed that there are four basic tendencies of life. These tendencies are as follows: (1) the satisfaction of basic needs, (2) the maintenance of internal order, (3) adaptation to the environment, and (4) productivity or expansion as evidenced in growth and reproduction. Piaget assumes that there are psychological correlates of these biological concepts. The particular concern of this section is for the principles of organization and adaptation as applied to the cognitive structure. However, it should be understood that Piaget does give recognition to the other tendencies of need satisfaction and productivity. In final analysis all four tendencies must be integrated at either the biological or psychological level, or the individual becomes physically or psychologically ill.

Organization and adaptation are principal functions of the individual's psychological system. These two principles can be viewed as complementary aspects of a single process. Organization constitutes an internal aspect while adaptation is an aspect of the intellectual functioning that refers to an interaction between internal and external factors. Organization and adaptation are inherited; they are not, however, the intellectual structure. They constitute the functioning process that results in the development of intellectual structures. An integration and balance of organization and adaptation results in the maintenance as well as development of the individual's intellectual structure. The functions of organization and adaptation transform experience into a larger intellectual structure that the individual can then use in new situations.

Organization of the intellectual structure.   Organization is the maintenance of an internal order of the intellectual structure through the inherent tendency to systematize and integrate intellectual structures into coherent systems of a higher order. This tendency results in an apparently spontaneous transition to higher orders of intellectual complexity. A simple example may help clarify this process. Imagine a young child with two intellectual schemes that, as yet, are unrelated. The schemes are looking and grasping. Now imagine the child encounters a ball and spontaneously combines the two separate schemes into the more complex scheme of picking up the ball. The child has spontaneously organized the two separate schemes into a higher order structure. The behavior that is seen at any stage of development is a result of the individual's organizing process. The taking in and digesting of food is done within the total organism; the systems function without awareness of the organizing process. The same is true of the cognitive structure; organization proceeds without the specific awareness of the individual. The child in the example would not be aware of the specific schemes that were combined in the activity with the ball.

From an educational perspective, the organizing process will continue as a result of the student's interaction with things in the environment and with provision for thought and reflection. This points out two types of interaction that can result in higher levels of organization: (1) the interaction between the intellectual structure and the environment and (2) the interaction between different patterns within the intellectual structure. Concerning these two functions Piaget has said:

> The accord of "thought with things" and the accord of "thought with itself" express this dual functional invariant of adaptation and organization. These two aspects of thought are indissociable: It is by adapting to things that thought organizes itself and it is by organizing itself that it structures things. (1963, p. 8)

Examples of the interaction between "thought and things" are numerous and have been given throughout this book. An example of development through the interaction of "thought with thought" is Piaget and Inhelder's research on memory and their findings that indicated children remember a pattern of sticks arranged in a serial order better several months after exposure than they did a day after viewing the arrangement (Piaget and Inhelder, 1973).

The important thing for the teacher to understand is that there may be a disparity between the adult patterns of organization and the student's. The mind does not copy reality—it organizes it into existing patterns and often transforms the patterns in the process. Students' behavior and responses to problems reveal their patterns of organization. Experience and activity by the student can help development progress in its normal course. The greatest understanding a teacher can have is that a student's organization of knowledge is not that of an adult; a student's reality is organized differently from an adult's. It is not wrong—it is different.

Adaptation of the intellectual structure.   Adaptation is the process of changing the intellectual structure through interaction with the environment. The modification results in a development of the cognitive structure that will enhance further interchanges with the environment.

Intellectual adaptation consists of two processes that are simultaneous and complementary; these processes are *accommodation* and *assimilation*. An introduction to the principles of intellectual adaptation can be illustrated by the example cited earlier of a child encountering a ball for the first time. The child reaches for and tries to pick up the ball; in so doing she will adapt by accommodating to the object. She will have to squeeze hard enough to hold the ball, and she will have to alter her grasp to the size of the ball. At the same time, she may assimilate the ball into other schemes, perhaps one of the objects to be picked up, or thrown, or even chewed. For a moment let us imagine that this is the first ball the child has encountered, so she may think of all balls as having the properties of this ball; for example, small and blue. Encounters with other balls of various sizes and colors will slowly change her thinking because she will be required to adapt to the discrepancies between this pattern of organization of the ball and the reality of large red balls and medium size white balls. This adaptation will be accomplished through the continued processes of assimilation and accommodation.

Two biological examples of the adaptive process may be helpful in understanding the later discussion of the adaptive process as it applies to the development of cognitive structures. The use of biological analogies is quite appropriate. Recall that Piaget was a biologist and this background had an important influence on his conceptualization of the developmental process.

The first example is that of digestion. Food is taken into the system and transformed into forms that can be incorporated into the entire system. The changes occur through regulatory processes within the digestive system. These regulatory processes accommodate the different types of foods, fats, carbohydrates, proteins. The accommodation occurs at certain locations (e.g. mouth, stomach, intestine) and by certain digestive enzymes (e.g., amylases, proteinases, and lipases). The result of the adaptive process

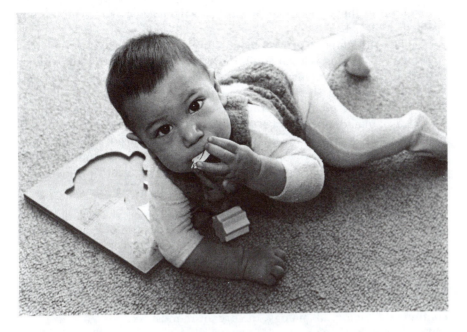

Through the continued processes of assimilation and adaptation the child's patterns of thinking will change.

is a change of the food and a distribution of the ingredients through the entire system. Assimilation is the process of changing; the foodstuffs become part of the structure of the organism.

Another biological example that emphasizes the process of adaptation, and in particular accommodation, is from immunology. Imagine a bacteria has entered the body. If you are immune to this bacteria, your body accommodates to the particular bacteria by producing antibodies which allow for assimilation by the lymph system with only minor disequilibrium of the biological system. Now suppose a second foreign body has entered the body, one to which you are not immune. There is a tremendous disequilibrium of the biological system. The process of equilibration includes a transformation and new structuring of antibodies in order to accommodate the structure of the new foreign body. There has been an adjustment in the immunologic structure that remains a part of that structure. So, reinfection will be met by immediate accommodation and assimilation. One can say the biological system has "learned" about the foreign body and "knows" how to react.

In the digestive example the simultaneous and complementary adaptive processes of assimilating and accommodating are in balance and functioning together to regulate the biological mechanisms that will transform the food until it is finally part of the whole system. The second example is slightly different. While both the adaptive processes are at work, there was an internal change of a basic structure (i.e., an antibody) in order to assimilate the foreign body. The biological system "learned" about the new antigen. This example was used because accommodation is largely not given recognition in the educational process. Mostly, teachers stress the assimilation of material.

To place the adaptive process in an educational perspective, assume that cognitive functioning is at an equilibrium when there is encounter with an object in the environment or the teacher asks a question, or assume you confront a puzzling situation such as those at the first of the chapter. Assimilation is the taking in of this experience and transforming it until it loses its original identity and becomes part of the existing cognitive structure. This is analogous to the taking in of food and incorporating it into the organism's structure or the assimilation of an antigen by an antibody. The act of assimilation is contingent upon the elements in the environment and existing intellectual structure. Piaget states:

> Intelligence is assimilation to the extent that it incorporates all the given data of experience within its framework...intellectual adaptation involves an element of assimilation, that is to say, of structuring through incorporation of external reality into forms due to the subject's activity. (Piaget, 1963, p. 6)

Simultaneous with assimilation of the environmental encounter is accommodation. The intellectual structure is readjusted to the external reality. To continue the biological analogy, the organism must accommodate its physical and chemical process to the properties of the object ingested before digestion occurs. Concerning accommodation Piaget states:

> There can be no doubt either that mental life is also *accommodation* to the environment. Assimilation can never be pure because by incorporating new elements into its earlier schemata the intelligence constantly modified the latter (schemata) in order to adjust them to new elements. (Piaget, 1963, p. 7)

Adaptation is a single event within which two simultaneous processes occur: accommodation and assimilation. There is an assimilation of external reality to the cognitive structure and an accommodation of the cognitive structure to external reality. In this view both the structure of knowledge and the external reality are modified in the process of adaptation. Because of the linear quality of writing they have been presented sequentially; in reality the processes are concurrent and in concert with one another. If an individual is at cognitive disequilibrium, the return to equilibrium is through adaptation. Here is a summary of the adaptive factors:

> If this fundamental interaction between internal and external factors is taken into account, all behavior is an *assimilation* of reality to prior schemata (schemata which, to some degree, are due to heredity) and all behavior is at the same time an *accommodation* of these schemata to the actual situation. The result is that developmental theory necessarily calls upon the concept of equilibrium since all behavior tends toward assuring the equilibrium between internal and external factors, or speaking more generally, between assimilation and accommodation. (Piaget, 1967, p. 103)

The Student's Construction of Knowledge

Psychological research on the process of concept development has made progress in recent years. Still, however, there are three different views of this process and they are all applied to classroom instruction. In the first view there are forces and pressures in the external environment that impress themselves on the student's mind. Knowledge has an exterior origin. Learning is a copy of reality. The second view emphasizes the growth and development of internal structures. Knowledge has an innate origin. Learning is an unfolding of these structures. The third view is that the development of concepts is a construction of knowledge which results from an interaction between the intellectual structure (but they are not innate) and the environment. Knowledge is a continuous and spontaneous construction. Learning is an adaptation and organization of experience. Equilibration is the process that explains the simultaneous maintenance and change of the intellectual structure. Maintenance and change occur through organization and adaptation respectively.

For Piaget, the aim of education is the facilitation of development. The application of this aim to the classroom is very different from the other two approaches that in their extreme forms are indoctrination and abdication by teachers. In the developmental approach the teacher is concerned with a change in the general cognitive structure and not a situation-specific change or a change that occurs due to maturation.

Applying the developmental approach to the classroom requires the teacher to understand the student's level of development. Then, the teacher can expose the student to problem situations that are slightly beyond this level. In doing so, the student will experience conflict and dissonance while applying the current level of cognitive structures to problematic situations at a higher level; thus, disequilibrium and equilibration. It has been said earlier, but it is important enough that it may need emphasis again. The student's construction of knowledge is a result of psychological *and* physical activity on the external environment. This is a process of equilibration between the cognitive structure and the environment. Historically, classroom instruction has emphasized, changed, and reorganized curriculum and materials more than focusing on the internal processes of the student. Piaget comments on this problem in education:

> In some cases, what is transmitted by instruction is well assimilated by the child because it represents in fact an extension of some spontaneous constructions of his own. In such cases, his development is accelerated. But in other cases, the gifts of instruction are presented too soon or too late, or in a manner that precludes assimilation because it does not fit in with the child's spontaneous constructions. (Piaget, 1962, p. 11)

As Piaget pointed out, educators have given little recognition to the accommodation part of adaptation. To do so requires two things: (1) an instructional style that emphasizes the student's level of development and (2) an understanding that the student's construction of knowledge occurs when the intellectual structure is modified through confronting problems and conflicting situations. It is important to remember that development explains learning; that is, the student has a cognitive structure that will be applied and modified in the learning situation. So, educators contemplating teaching with a recognition of Piaget's theory of equilibration should provide challenging situations that are within the students' parameters of intellectual adaptation. The challenges may be described by terms such as appropriate discrepancy, optimal discord, moderate novelty, tolerable mismatch, or reasonably problematic.

Teaching with Piaget's theory of equilibration in mind means presenting students with problems that are challenging but achievable.

The students' construction of knowledge can be assisted by using sequences of lessons designed to facilitate the process of development. This chapter, for example, was designed in just such a manner. In the exploration section you were presented with several problems that were puzzling, interesting, and motivating. You became involved in the problems. Your involvement set the stage for an explanation. The explanation was much more detailed and didactic. It was, however, related to experience you had early in the chapter. In the next section you have further opportunities to extend and apply concepts you gained in the first two sections. The students' construction of knowledge can be facilitated in the same manner.

III | EXTENSION
THE PROCESS OF EQUILIBRATION

The following are some educational strategies based on discussions in this and earlier chapters.

1. It is first of all important for the teacher to have an idea of the student's level of cognitive organization and patterns of reasoning. This might be accumulated through discussions and observations of the student's work.

2. Make an effort to present problems or ask questions that are slightly above the student's level. The pursuit of genuine problems, situations not quite understood or the resolution of conflicts, counterintuitive events, paradoxes, and puzzles will all produce a disequilibrium and subsequently equilibration.

3. The problems should be within the limits of adaptation; they should be challenging, but achievable, or to use Piaget's terms "moderately novel" as perceived by the student. Decision about the level of problems must be made through observing the student's behavior and listening to responses; the teacher simply cannot depend on the level of curriculum materials and assume they will engage the learner.

4. In solving problems, have the students explain their reasoning and justify their responses.

5. When there are inconsistencies or inadequacies in the students' reasoning patterns, help them first by accepting their answers; second, by suggesting other ideas or activities that may help resolve the inconsistencies; and third, by allowing them time to find the answers themselves.

BIBLIOGRAPHY

Cowan, Philip A. *Piaget: With Feeling*. New York: Holt, Rinehart & Winston, 1978.
    The entire book is recommended for educators. Equilibration is discussed in the second chapter.
Inhelder, Barbel; Sinclair, Hermine; and Bovet, Magali. *Learning and the Development of Cognition*. Cambridge: Harvard University Press, 1974.
    Probably the best discussion of *learning* in the context of Piaget's developmental psychology. Most of the book is devoted to descriptions of tasks and research results typical of the Genevian approach.
Labinowicz, Ed. *The Piaget Primer: Thinking, Learning, Teaching*. Menlo Park, Calif.: Addison Wesley, 1980.
    The author has devised an excellent means of presenting the concept of equilibration. See the section on "Piaget's Ideas on the Development of Thinking."
Gallagher, Jeanette McCarthy, and Reid, D. Kim. *The Learning Theory of Piaget and Inhelder*. Montery, Calif.: Brooks Cole Publishing Co, 1981.
    A truly appropriate book for educators. A major theme of the book is the process of equilibration as it applies to learning.
Nodine, C.F.; Gallagher, J.M.; and Humphreys, R.D., ed. *Piaget and Inhelder on Equilibration*. Philadelphia: The Jean Piaget Society (Temple University), 1972.
Piaget, Jean. "Cognitive Development in Children: Development and Learning." *Journal of Research in Science Teaching* 2 (1964): 176–86.

Very little of this article is directed toward equilibration, but it is a fine discussion of learning and development and Piaget's theory.

————. "Comments on Vygolsky's Critical Remarks" concerning *The Language and Thought of the Child* and *Judgement and Reasoning in the Child*. Cambridge: Massachusetts Institute of Technology, 1962.

————. *The Origins of Intelligence in Children*. New York: W.W. Norton & Co., 1963.

Piaget describes the origin and development of intelligence. The theme of intelligence as adaptation is clear and described in contrast to other theories of intelligence. The book is on the sensorimotor period and the six stages of that period.

————. *Six Psychological Studies*. New York: Random House, 1967.

Chapter 4, "The Role of the Concept of Equilibrium in Psychological Explanation," is a very good introduction to Piaget's use of the concept.

————. *Structuralism*. New York: Basic Books, 1970.

Chapter 4 on psychological structures contains an extended discussion of the adaptive process. The book is a good introduction to structuralism, a prominent orientation of Piagetian psychology.

————. *The Development of Thought: Equilibration of Cognitive Structures*. New York: The Viking Press, 1975.

Piaget's most complete statement on equilibration. However, it is very difficult reading.

Piaget, Jean, and Inhelder, Barbel. *The Psychology of the Child*. New York: Basic Books, 1969.

Piaget and Inhelder have integrated their discussion of the equlibration process throughout this book.

————. *Memory and Intelligence*. London: Routledge & Kegan Paul, 1973.

The book details a number of experiments conducted to evaluate the role of memory in the development of intelligence. Piaget and Inhelder found that memory interacts with intelligence, and this accounts for progressive improvement (versus forgetting) in some instances. The authors develop the concept of reconstructive memory.

Reid, D. Kim. "Equilibration and Learning." *Journal of Education* 161 (Winter 1969): 51–71.

Excellent summary of Piaget's concept. Educators should read this article. But, read it slowly and read it twice.

Wadsworth, Barry J. *Piaget for the Classroom Teacher*. New York: Longman, 1978.

Equilibration is discussed in several places.

References

Ilg, Frances, and Ames, Louis. *Child Behavior*. New York: Dell Publishing Co., 1955.

Langer, Jonas. "Implications of Piaget's Talk for Curriculum." *Journal of Research in Science Teaching* 2 (1964): 208–13.

Neil, A.S. *Summerhill*. New York: Hart Publishing Co., 1960.

IV | EVALUATION
THE PROCESS OF EQUILIBRATION

Listed below are some of the main topics covered in Chapter 8. Read each statement and rate it on the scale TWICE: once according to what you knew about the topic before starting the chapter and again according to what you learned by completing the chapter. Circle the appropriate number and mark B for *before* and A for *after* next to the numbers as shown.

	Personal Evaluation		
Topic	Low	Moderate	High
Example: The distinction between assimi- lation and accommodation	①B 2	3 ④A 5	6
1. Different models of teaching/learning	1 2	3 4 5	6
2. The difference between learning and development	1 2	3 4 5	6
3. The structuring and functioning of intelligence	1 2	3 4 5	6
4. The concept of equilibration	1 2	3 4 5	6
5. The role of disequilibrium in development	1 2	3 4 5	6
6. The process of organization	1 2	3 4 5	6
7. The process of adaptation	1 2	3 4 5	6
8. The concept of assimilation	1 2	3 4 5	6
9. The concept of accommodation	1 2	3 4 5	6
10. The application of the equilibration model to teaching	1 2	3 4 5	6

Extending Piaget's Theory: Applications, Recommendations, and Implications

The following pages are specific suggestions for instruction based on Piaget's theory. These suggestions are by no means exhaustive but should act as springboards to assist individuals in translating the theory into practice. As you become more aware of Piaget's work and how to apply it, many other ideas will undoubtedly manifest themselves and stimulate your utilization of the cognitive-developmental viewpoint.

I | APPLICATION
A TEACHING/LEARNING CYCLE

The preface and note to the reader both mentioned that this book has a design that is carried out within Chapters 2-8 and among all the chapters. The design is based on the learning cycle as originally developed by Myron Atkin and Robert Karplus (1962) and later by Karplus and his colleagues for the Science Curriculum Improvement Study and for Development of Reasoning workshops (Karplus et al. 1977; see Science Curriculum Improvement Study, 1977). The original learning cycle has been modified for the specific medium of a book length presentation of Piaget's theory. By now you should be aware of the design. Chapters 2-8 used an organizational scheme of *exploration, explanation, extension,* and *evaluation*. And, to a large extent the chapters can be organized into the same scheme; that is, Chapters 1 and 2 are explorations, Chapters 3, 4, 5, 6, 7, and 8 are explanations, Chapters 9, 10, and 11 are extensions of Piaget's theory, and Chapter 12 is an evaluation.

One of the most immediate applications of Piaget's ideas for educators is the use of a teaching/learning cycle. By now you should be able to judge the effectiveness of the approach. If you completed the exploratory activities, read the explanations, and then tried to extend the theory through interviews, problems, and further reading, you should be able to determine the effectiveness of the teaching/learning cycle—at least for this book.

Exploration

Exploration activities are specifically designed so students will have experiences basic to later conceptual understanding. Teaching during this phase is facilitative; that is, the teacher sets up situations, activities, and demonstrations that will allow students to learn through their own physical and mental activity. Concrete materials are essential for students who have not yet developed formal reasoning patterns; ideas are central for formal students. The teacher provides opportunities for student exploration with minimal direction by the teacher.

In this book, just as in teaching, different types of activities were used as explorations. There were problems with multiple-choice type answers, general overviews, interviews, descriptions of classrooms, thought puzzles, and guest editorials. In all cases, the explorations were designed to engage you in some aspect of Piaget's theory. You may have also noted that minimal direction was given. We simply directed you toward the experience and then had you explain the activity as best you could at that time. This is the essence of the exploration phase of the teaching/learning cycle. Different types of activities can be, and were, used for explorations. This is also the case for the classroom application of the teaching/learning cycle. Discussions, films, demonstrations, show and tell, and numerous other teaching methods can be used as exploratory activities. However, how the teacher uses the activity is crucial.

Using Piagetian terminology, the purpose of exploration is to bring about a natural disequilibrium within the student. A variety of techniques can be used, but it is very important that the activity be teacher facilitated and student centered. If the student shows a spark of puzzlement, the motivation of interest, and the need to solve the problem, you have been successful in designing an exploratory activity. If the student is bored or anxious, you have missed the target by either providing an activity with no challenge or too much challenge.

Has the activity provided the student with questions and/or situations that bring about disequilibrium? Have you engaged the learner or just presented the material? Have you provided an opportunity for the student to search for explanations? If you can answer yes to these questions, then you are well on your way to understanding the exploration phase of the teaching/learning cycle.

Explanation

The explanation phase is one most teachers can immediately identify. This is teaching as it is usually practiced. Within the teaching/learning cycle, explanation is the introduction of a way of ordering the exploratory experiences. Concepts or principles are introduced that will help clarify the student's problem. The explanation phase is teacher directed. The teacher directs the educational environment with the goal of clearly and precisely introducing appropriate concepts. Naturally, we recommend that educators use effective instructional methods.

In this book we have attempted to use a straightforward, simple presentation of concepts in the sections entitled "Explanations." Diagrams, charts, pictures, guest editorials, and summaries were all used as means to explain Piagetian concepts.

Teachers have many different techniques at their disposal; probably the one used most often is telling, or oral explanation. Our recommendation is to use this along with other techniques such as films, activities, the overhead projector, filmstrips, and so on. The point of this phase is to initiate the ordering process within the student. Provide words and concepts that the student can use to explain his experiences.

If the exploratory phase was designed to place the student in disequilibrium, the explanation phase is designed to reduce disequilibrium and initiate the adaptation and organization of mental structures. In the end, the student should be able to explain exploratory experiences in terms of concepts. For example, you should be able to explain a child's responses to tasks in terms of Piaget's ideas. Students will not immediately come to a state of equilibrium. Equilibration takes time. To continue the example just cited, you probably knew more about a certain stage of development after completing the exploration and explanation sections of the chapter, but you did not feel certain in your understanding. You needed more time and experience with the concepts. This is why the next phase, extension, is so important.

Extension

Once concepts have been explained, it is important to involve students in further extensions of the concept. In some cases the students may not fully understand the concept, or they may understand the concept only in terms of the exploration. Extension activities provide further time and experience. With time and experience students can resolve unanswerable questions and come to a new level of equilibrium. Extension activities also provide opportunities for slower students to comprehend basic ideas and advanced students to try their talents on new problems beyond the concrete explorations.

Extension activities are often quite similar to exploratory activities. In this book there have been interviews for analysis, guest editorials, bibliographies, and tasks to administer to students. All of these activities should have assisted further understanding of concepts within the chapter.

By implementing the teaching/learning cycle in your classroom, the probability of concepts being learned is markedly increased. Built into the cycle is time and experience for students of varying levels, ideas based on developmental and learning theories, and a lot of common sense and good judgement about educating students.

Evaluation

At some point in the teaching/learning cycle it is important to provide feedback to students concerning their understanding of concepts. Some informal evaluation may occur as early as the exploration phase, but we suggest that formal evaluation be completed after extension activities. Results of the evaluation should provide the student and the teacher with information about the student's understanding, and it should provide the teacher with information to better guide instruction.

Self-evaluation quizzes were provided in this book. This is only one of many means of evaluation. You may already be familiar with the many means of formal and informal evaluation. Formal evaluation is the use of tests, quizzes, and so on to determine the student's level of understanding. Educators also evaluate student understanding in informal ways such as asking questions, listening to discussions, and observing behaviors during class periods. We strongly suggest that formal evaluations be applied late in the teaching/learning cycle. And even more strongly we recommend that educators adjust their instruction in light of evaluation results. Evaluation is not grading. In the context of this instructional model, evaluation is to be used as feedback concerning the individual's understanding and application of concepts. If an individual has not achieved an understanding of concepts, appropriate parts of the teaching/learning cycle can be repeated. (See Figures 9–1 and 9–2.)

II | RECOMMENDATIONS
AN OUTLINE OF IDEAS BASED ON PIAGET'S THEORY

In a sense the last section was an exploration of one model of teaching implied by Piaget's theory. There was a general discussion without much attention paid to particulars. In this section we explain some of the particulars. We use the direct and succinct format of an outline to present the ideas.

I.   When you work with children, remember the concepts of cognitive development.

    1. All children pass through four main stages of cognitive development.

Figure 9.1
The Teaching/Learning Cycle

Concept Exploration

Students learn through their own activities.
Learning is "directed" by the objects, events, or situations.
Teacher guidance is minimal.
Activities should leave students with unanswered questions.

Concept Explanation

A concept or principle is presented.
The concept should be related to the exploration activity.
Different instructional materials and approaches can be used.
Instruction is teacher directed.
Instruction should help students answer their questions.

Concept Extension

Students are given different activities in which they must apply new concepts and
    reasoning patterns.
Additional time and experiences are used to extend student understanding.
Different instructional approaches can be used during this phase.

Concept Evaluation

Student learning is evaluated in a variety of ways.
Feedback is used by the teacher to recycle student through appropriate teaching/
learning phases.

---

2. Children of the same chronological age may vary considerably in
   their level of cognitive development. Different levels of cognitive
   development are evident in students' patterns of reasoning.
3. Because a child may perform one task that is at a specific level
   does not necessarily indicate that the child is at that level. Several
   tasks must be given to an individual in order to determine his
   cognitive level.
4. The development of a person's cognitive ability is of real relevance to that individual.
5. There are two main types of experiences: (1) physical (learning
   information) and (2) logical-mathematical (learning to perform
   mental operations). Physical experience occurs when children
   physically act on objects in the environment. They begin to realize that action is complex; for example, they find that objects
   may be ordered from short to long or vice versa. From physical
   experiences, the child becomes initiated into logical-
   mathematical experiences. Eventually the child develops mental
   structures which she will use to grasp abstract concepts.
6. A student develops patterns of reasoning only by having experiences that allow or stimulate thinking.

Figure 9.2
Applying the Teaching/Learning Cycle: Steps for Designing Lessons

Concept Exploration

1. Identify interesting objects, events, or situations that students can observe. This experience can occur in the classroom, laboratory, field, or through media presentations.
2. Allow the students time in which they can explore the objects, events, or situations. During this experience the students may establish relationships, observe patterns, identify variables, question events as a result of their exploration. In this phase the unexpected can be used to your advantage. Students may have questions or experiences that motivate them to understand what they have observed.

Concept Explanation

3. In this phase direct student attention to specific aspects of the exploration experience. Introduce concepts in a direct and formal manner. Initially, the lesson should be clearly based on student explorations. In this phase the key is to present the concepts in a simple, clear, and direct manner.

Concept Extension

4. Identify several activities in which students apply the concepts in new and different situations. Use of different activities will facilitate generalization of the concept by the students. Encourage the students to identify patterns, discover relationships among variables, and reason through new problems. During discussions and individual and group questions be sure to point out the central concepts that are being applied in the different contexts.

Concept Evaluation

5. Evaluate student understanding of the concept. If the student has not learned the material, decide which phase of the learning cycle would be most appropriate to facilitate learning. Provide further exploration, explanation, or extension activities for the student.

---

7. Cognitive development results from an interaction between the student and the environment (including the teacher).
8. Students are *active* participants in their development.
9. Development occurs through the process of equilibration (i.e., an imbalance between mental structures and experiences).
10. The process of equilibration can be initiated by educators through activities that engage the learner.

II.   Design a curriculum that facilitates development.

1. Stress intellectual development. It is not enough to teach just for facts; you must help students reach their human potential. Piaget's efforts have made intellectual development an important facet of a curriculum.
2. Follow Piaget's sequence of development in your curriculum. Since children pass through a sequence of stages, the curriculum

must be designed to accommodate appropriately the student's developmental progress.

3. Adapt curriculum materials to where the child is developmentally. Construct the curriculum to deal with the child's needs; do not wait until the child has met your criteria for entrance to the curriculum. Applying the teaching/learning cycle meets this need.

4. Utilize the "moderately novel" or "optimal mismatch" principle. Piaget believes that presenting children with moderately novel problems only slightly above their cognitive level assists them in advancing to higher degrees of operational ability. Let students choose their own problem-oriented tasks; they will usually choose things that are challenging. Exploration activities fulfill this implication.

5. Use Piaget's theory in any culture. Since Piagetian levels are universal, they provide a predictive base for constructing curriculum materials for any culture and country. Recall, however, that foreign, minority, and lower socioeconomic groups may vary in the rate they progress through growth stages.

6. Stress learning through action and discovery-oriented activities. Students learn only when they act mentally on what is being investigated. Curriculum materials should be oriented toward

Students learn only when they act mentally on what is being investigated.

discovery, inquiry, and creativity to help students develop. Provide activities for the student to make decisions and verify and deduce conclusions. Laboratory and field experiences should require students to use thinking processes such as hypothesizing, inferring, designing experiments, and formulating models. All of these processes can be applied through the teaching/learning cycle.

7. Involve students physically and mentally in acting on what is being learned. That is, use exploration and extension activities. Rather than having them always listen, have them read or create something and then share in small groups their views about the project's important qualities, creative value, and possible further activities. The groups then should decide what conclusions they wish to report to the class for discussion and evaluation.

8. Create more interaction; allow small groups to work on problems. Students resolving a problem in small groups of three to five facilitates more learning than do class discussions. This is due to greater student involvement and the advantage of a mix of individuals at different cognitive levels.

9. Involve students in role playing. Have them play roles in resolving problems. For example, students may take the part of famous scientists or public officials. This activity provides opportunities to perceive different viewpoints (thus reducing egocentricity) and involves active participation in the studied subject.

10. Use conflict strategies. Cognitive conflict activities within small groups give students opportunities to develop their cognitive

Small-group problem solving facilitates more learning than does class discussion.

processes. The students must resolve conflicts within the group by perceiving viewpoints other than their own.

11. Move from the concrete to the abstract. Educational materials and class activities should preferably start with the concrete and progress to an abstract level rather than the reverse.

12. Do not always use the direct approach. The direct way of attacking a problem, such as language development, may not always be the best way. Use other approaches to complement the direct approach. We have suggested using exploration and extension as complements to the traditional direct approach of explanation.

III. Teach for the facilitation of development.

1. Ask more questions than you give answers, especially divergent questions. Students should get involved in finding out and analyzing the meaning of what is being learned. Questions allowing for divergent answers stimulate creative and critical thinking. Convergent questions answered by *yes* or *no* should be avoided. When children make contradictions, say, "But you said a little while ago that ..." or "Which do you mean?"

2. Talk less and listen more, stressing nonverbal instruction. Sense when to be quiet. After asking a question, wait at least five seconds for children to answer. Remember, children need time to assimilate and accommodate information before they can respond intelligently.

3. Allow freedom of choice. Encourage and give students freedom to choose some of their learning activities so that they may use their minds to evaluate what should be studied. In this manner, they learn to develop commitment toward their studies.

4. Do not correct pupils' errors in reasoning. Rather, ask questions and provide experiences so that students correct their own mistakes.

5. Determine cognitive levels by giving students conservation or formal reasoning tasks and by asking questions to determine how they think. For example, you might have the student describe her mental steps toward resolving a problem.

6. Accept the fact that students may develop at different rates. Individuals who are behind their peers now may be equally capable in adulthood. Be aware also that most classes will have students at more than one level, and many in transitional stages.

7. As students evolve cognitively, they also progress to higher stages of ethical development; however, it is only with education that this parallel development occurs.

8. Children decrease in egocentricity through active social interaction because they are confronted with different views. They begin to find that the way they understand life is not the only viewpoint. Interaction involving argument and critical analysis is the basis for developing higher cognitive abilities.

9. Students must have the abilities gained at the one level before they may deal successfully with the required task of higher levels.

10. Pseudolearning occurs when students neither assimilate nor accommodate information. In such a case, children are required to memorize without understanding.

IV. Follow these specific recommendations for teaching in the beginning.

1. Begin the year with an assessment of your students' developmental levels. Pencil and paper tests are good for screening large groups. For individual students, tasks such as those listed at the ends of Chapters 3-7 are recommended.
2. Use exploration activities to begin a unit. As a general rule the explorations should use concrete objects.
3. Begin individual classes or lessons with a demonstration or activity designed to engage the students. Discrepant events, puzzles, novel experiences, surprising activities, uncertain problems, and curious adventures are all effective ways to initiate mental operations by students.

V. Follow these specific recommendations for the explanation phase of teaching.

1. Present concepts clearly.
2. Provide time for students to assimilate and accommodate experiences.
3. As students show signs of puzzlement (disequilibrium), help them "put the pieces together."
4. Make connections to concrete experiences in the students' lives.
5. Clarify students' reasoning patterns for them.
6. Have the students justify their answers regardless of the answer's correctness or incorrectness. Ask students questions such as the following: "How could you demonstrate that?" "Why do you think that is true?" "What is your evidence?"
7. Be a model of the reasoning patterns you wish to foster in your students. Reason out loud; tell about your hypotheses, justifications, and alternative explanations.
8. Give your students time and opportunity to think.
9. Provide opportunities for students to extend their understanding through activities based on similar concepts in different contexts.

VI. Follow these specific suggestions for the evaluation phase of teaching.

1. Be sure you test for reasoning, as well as content.
2. Ask students to justify their answers.
3. Make a conscious effort to help students who are reasoning at levels lower than that of their peers.

VII. When giving assignments, follow these recommendations.

1. Review texts to see the level at which most concepts are presented. If levels are too high, provide concrete experiences and/or examples that will help students.

2. Give the students problems requiring analysis and argument. Have them justify their positions.
3. Provide special puzzles, tasks, and activities that will initiate the process of equilibration.

VIII. When working with children at the sensorimotor level, (birth to two years), follow these recommendations.

1. Provide objects for play.
2. Let the child experience her world as much as possible.
3. Stimulate the child's sensory and motor behaviors.
4. Let the infant/toddler develop naturally through a rich and stimulating environment.

IX. When working with children at the preoperational level (two to seven years), follow these recommendations.

1. Make sure that children manipulate and group objects.
2. Involve preschool children in activities requiring social interaction.
3. Encourage children to play games such as "house" and "store," so they can act out various roles.
4. Ask children to make comparisons. Create activities where children need to know "which is," for example, which is taller, bigger, wider, heavier, or longer.
5. Encourage children to line up in rows from tall to short and vice versa so that they may become more involved in ordering operations. Give children tasks where they have opportunities to order objects.
6. Have pupils weigh objects. Let them play with balances and teeter-totter-like toys.
7. Bring in various examples of life cycles of animals and plants such as several pictures of butterfly development or the sprouting of bean and corn seeds. Examples of natural stages help children develop ordering ability.
8. Have children draw scenes with perspective. Encourage them to draw objects in approximately the same location as they are viewed; for example, if they see a cow in the far end of a field, they should place the cow similarly on the paper. They should also try to copy geometrical figures, some open and unconnected (like a half circle), others connected (like a square). Give them some outlines within which they would have to include objects or exclude objects; for example, they can be instructed to draw a square with a circle inside it, an ellipse with an arrow drawn tangent to it, or a few triangles with small circles inside and outside.
9. Have children tilt a closed container with colored liquid and draw how the water inside appears with the container slanted, upright, or lying flat. This activity may be repeated using several different types of plastic or glass containers such as those emptied of pop or milk.

10. Construct an inclined plane or hill. Place together different size marbles on top of it and let the children roll these down the hill and compare how they finish. This should help children eventually gain a concept of speed.

11. Ask children to justify their answers when making logical-mathematical types of conclusions. For example, when they say that a liquid poured from a tall glass into several glasses will still contain the same volume of liquid, ask, "Why do you think so?" "How would you prove that to another student?"

X. When working with students at the concrete operational level (seven to eleven years), follow these recommendations.

1. Continue any preoperational activities you believe are relevant for children in this age group.

2. Encourage children to discover concepts and principles. Although you should refrain from telling them outright, you may formulate questions relevant to what is being studied in order to help them focus on some aspect of their learning. Remember, it is necessary for children to assimilate and accommodate on their own, and the processes take time.

3. Involve children in operational tasks such as adding, subtracting, multiplying, dividing, ordering, seriating, and reversing, preferably in concrete ways where they utilize objects.

4. Plan activities where students must grasp the idea of an ascending and descending classification hierarchy.

5. Design many activities having children order and reverse order. Many third graders have problems in reversing order, such as going from tall to short rather than from short to tall, or listing the cities they would pass through in taking a trip to a large metropolitan center and then reversing their order in coming home.

6. Involve students in using horizontal and vertical coordinates. Achieve this task by asking them to locate places on city and state maps.

7. Present problems requiring students to isolate variables. Usually you will need to help students because they will not suggest all the possible variables.

8. Have students who are in the advanced part of this stage construct theoretical models tied to concrete examples; for example, they may explain molecular theory through the use of concrete models of atoms rather than by symbols.

9. Include activities which require conservation of area, understanding of continuous quantity, weight, and displacement of volume.

10. Have children define and state problems.

11. Involve students in testing all possibilities toward resolving problems. Help them discover what strategies they use to solve problems.

12. Particularly continue to ask students to justify their answers to logical-mathematical problems and situations encountered in

conservation tasks. Help students check the validity and accuracy of their conclusions.

XI. When working with students at the formal operational level (eleven years onward), follow these recommendations.

1. Encourage students to engage in problems requiring hypothetical-deductive reasoning, propositional thinking, theoretical reasoning, reflexive thinking, separation and control of variables, combinatorial logic, and other forms of abstract thinking.

2. Engage the students in questions and problems such as the following: "What was your hypothesis?" "How could you demonstrate that idea?" "How did you solve that problem?" "What other problems can be investigated?"

3. Be aware that the majority of students are probably at the concrete level or in transition to the formal level. This finding suggests that the teaching/learning cycle outlined earlier would be a good approach, for it could begin at the concrete and progress toward the abstract.

4. Provide time for maturation and activities with physical experience. Allow social interaction, and when you teach concepts, model formal patterns of reasoning.

5. Have the students establish classification systems.

6. Give students some freedom within limits, so they have time and opportunity for creating, inquiring, and problem solving.

7. Engage adolescents in discussions requiring synthesis, evaluation, and criticism of ideas, theories, and personal positions.

8. Challenge the adolescents' position by pointing out counter-examples, discrepant facts, and unanswered questions in their position.

9. Encourage students to argue using formal patterns of reasoning in areas where they are familiar with the content and where they have strong attitudes.

III | IMPLICATIONS
AN EXTENSION OF PIAGET'S THEORY TO EDUCATION

Few educators will argue against the desirability of an individual's developing his cognitive abilities, and Piaget's work gives us guidance here. Through his research, we are given new perceptions of the educational environment. By evaluating and utilizing Piaget's investigations, we should be better able to translate their implications effectively to our ends.

Educators are increasingly being called upon to justify what is being done in the schools. Many individuals are questioning the relevance of the present curricula for today's world. The knowledge explosion demands that educators survey information to determine its worth. Or, as Herbert Spencer put the question, "What knowledge is of most worth?" Regardless of the specific subject matter selected from the banks of knowledge, the development of reasoning remains one of the most important tasks for schools. Relevancy certainly must include having students learn how to use their minds in rational ways. Many school systems have already accepted this viewpoint as one of their major goals and are implementing programs to stimulate the development of cognitive ability. The work of Piaget and other cognitive psychologists has been instrumental in making educators more aware of this need. As Piaget's research becomes more widely known and understood by school personnel, the likelihood of greater efforts to provide for cognitive development undoubtedly will have more of an impact on the world's educational institutions.

In this section some implications of Piaget's theory are outlined. As you become more versed in Piaget's theory, other implications will undoubtedly come to mind.

Reasoning Is Not Memorizing

When parents and teachers become aware of Piaget's theory and administer some of his tasks to children, they are usually shocked to find that a child's reasoning is not the same as an adult's. Subsequently, they better comprehend that children do not perceive or think as adults, and they soon grasp that reasoning slowly evolves through a definite sequence. The typical adult often interacts with children as though they were capable of performing sophisticated mental operations. Adults familiar with Piaget's theory do not make such assumptions. They know children's thinking processes are not similar to theirs and, as a consequence, do not require children to perform mental tasks beyond their capabilities.

If educators force a child to perform operations beyond his capability, they may cause detrimental effects. For example, a concrete operational child required to give a formal operational response will be unable to reason an answer. The child, as a result, will fall back on his memory and learn to distrust his thinking ability. Children like this may soon learn that it is better not to think and, in fact, may often refuse to reason out answers. When confronted with a new type of problem, they guess at its answer, state they do not know how to work the problem, or demonstrate symptoms of anxiety. They expend little effort in trying to reason. For example, they do not ask themselves, What is the nature of the problem? What is known or unknown about it? As students, they memorize formulas without understanding them. If asked what will happen to a portion of a formula if a number is increased in one part of it, they do not know until they actually work out the problem. If they are asked to explain the relations between the parts of the formula, they are at a loss. Unfortunately, too many students have learned that the right answer is more important than reasoning. This problem exists in every classroom from the early elementary to the university level.

Teachers in the past have greatly influenced the development of memorizers instead of sophisticated, reasoning individuals. The emphasis on memorization at the expense of thinking may actually impede the development of reasoning. Children's habituation to relying on recognitional and evocational memory often has occurred because educators have not understood cognitive development or the role of reconstructive memory. In the light of Piaget's research, recognitional and evocational emphasis at the expense of operational, reconstructional abilities certainly is open to serious questioning. It is important, therefore, that educators comprehend the various memory abilities and the stages of mental development so that they can interact appropriately with children to enhance, not hinder, their reasoning abilities.

Learning Through Equilibration

Piaget underscores the fact that children think they must adapt to the immediate experience and reorganize modes of thought in light of the experience. The result is a new, more inclusive, mode of thought. Or, the child learns.

As children interact with the environment, they will naturally encounter situations and objects with which they are unfamiliar. These situations cause some puzzlement or query by the child. Piaget has termed this puzzlement *cognitive disequilibrium*. In order to resolve the pending situation, the child must change her way of thinking through the process of equilibration.

This one idea, equilibration, has extraordinary implications for educators. This is the process by which children learn through an adaptation of mental structures. Adaptation is divided into assimilation and accommodation. Assimilation is the taking in of environmental experiences and incorporating them into existing ways of thinking. Play is an example of almost complete assimilation. Accommodation is the modification of existing ways of thinking so that new experience can be incorporated into the cognitive structure. Imitation is an example of accommodation.

The processes of assimilation and accommodation usually occur together. Think of a young child who first throws a ball. The child has undoubtedly thrown other objects prior to the ball. There exists the concept (and behavior) of throwing, but throwing the ball is new and must be assimilated. It is also the case that the child must accommodate to the size and hardness of the ball if it is to be thrown. As the child is confronted with this new "throwing the ball" problem, he must adapt to the present situation. The new and somewhat elaborated ways of thinking about both throwing and balls are then integrated and coordinated, *organized*, into the child's cognitive structure. For this example, the child has learned about throwing a ball.

Learning through equilibration (adaptation and organization) requires activity by the student. This is certainly support for active involvement by students in the classroom. There is the added dimension of problem solving, providing some situations that will engage the learner. Then, the next steps will be easy since the child will try and solve the problem. Implications of these ideas include the following:

1. *Use methods that actively involve students*. Laboratory hands-on activities and field trips are all situations that provide active involvement by the students.

2. *Use counterintuitive problems*. This is a sure way to engage the student in a problem-solving situation.

3. *Use questions*. Questioning is one of the most common ways teachers try to engage the learner and establish disequilibrium. Carefully selected and thoughtful questions are essential to effective learning.

The process of equilibration explains how development occurs. Educators can influence this process by taking seriously a phrase that has been used repeatedly in this book—*engaging the learner*. Numerous examples have been given to illustrate this idea—discrepant events, puzzles, inquiries, questions, problems, and counterintuitive demonstrations. Once you have engaged the learner, give her time to establish a new equilibrium. As an educator you are in a position to facilitate this process, but give the individual time to come to a new equilibrium.

Education vs. Acceleration

Piaget believed children should be actively involved in the educational process. They should be confronted with novel and interesting situations. He has reiterated on several occasions, "There is no learning without experience." By this he means there is only as much meaning behind a word or thing as a child has had experience. Young children, therefore, need to encounter their environment through activity. These encounters should be with things and people during the sensorimotor, preoperational, and early concrete operational levels. This is not to say that active involvement is not also desirable in the formal stage, but the use of pictorial and symbolic language may play a greater educational role at this level.

Piaget's work implies that education should be student centered rather than teacher centered. This viewpoint arises from an understanding of the assimilation and accommodation process. A teacher may provide information, but, once children have this information, they should be required to act upon it to ensure that they internalize it and that it becomes a part of their mental structure. For example, an eighth grade science teacher may have students developing a conceptual understanding about a cold air front moving in over an area and then ask the children to construct a metaphor or analogy to describe what happens.

For Piaget, development explains learning. Some psychologists argue with this view. They hold the position that learning explains development. They think mental development will follow if a child learns a series of items in sequence. Once she has mastered these, she will achieve the desired level of mental ability. In other words, mental development can be accelerated providing the right competencies are identified for the child to learn in the right order. The sequencing of learning activity without taking into account the child's stage of mental development may be disputed because psychologists have not yet done sufficient research in the area, particularly with young children.

Piaget argues that there is a generalized system operating within the mind involved in assimilating and accommodating information. This system increasingly becomes more sophisticated as a child develops. Piaget agrees that you might accelerate the learning of a concept (e.g., of conservation) but questions whether or not you should attempt to achieve what he considers the American wish for accelerating mental development. Americans are usually trying to do something faster, more efficiently, and effectively; and American educators are no exception. Since it is the entire mental system that seems to progress through development, the training of children on one small part of that system will have little lasting or valuable effect. He says in this respect:

> Acceleration is certainly possible, but first we must find out whether it is desirable or harmful. Take the concept of object permanency—the realization that a ball, a rattle, or a person continues to exist when it no longer can be seen. A kitten develops this concept at four months, a human baby at nine months; but the kitten stops right there while the baby goes on to learn more advanced concepts. Perhaps a certain slowness is useful in developing the capacity to assimilate new concepts. (Hall, 1970, p. 31)

Rather than trying to accelerate learning, teachers should provide children with rich educational experiences at their stage of development and just beyond so the process of equilibration is activated. This means an educator should endeavor to determine a child's stage of development and adjust learning activities for his ability.

Intelligence or Cognitive Adaptation

Intelligence generally is measured by IQ tests. Traditionally, IQ tests have been designed along pragmatic lines. The psychologist constructed a series of questions and gave these questions to children. If the majority of children managed to get them right at a certain age, these items were thought to indicate the mental age. IQ is defined as the mental age divided by the chronological age. However, the problem with the traditional IQ test is that it has no theoretical basis except trial and error. Hardi Fischer in reviewing intelligence tests says:

> Most of the well-known intelligence tests are too verbal, also containing numerical tasks, or they depend on scholastic performance. Piaget's experiments, when used clinically, present a broader situation than these tests. In tests you have mostly a sort of performance to judge, but you don't know the underlying reasoning processes. Piaget's experiments give this information and they also permit an evaluation of educability. (1964, p. 438)

Piaget views intelligence as the continued process of adaptation and organization of inputs by the child's mind as he interacts with the environment. An indication of the sophistication of the child's reasoning is his ability to perform certain operational tasks. Piaget does not consider intelligence as being a fixed potential as is assumed by traditional IQ tests. He prefers to think of intelligence as being a progressive process of cognitive adaptation. For example, one child might perform concrete operational tasks before another, only to be surpassed by the slower child at a later time in development. Piaget, as well as other researchers, has shown that the rate of learning varies with development. The younger child takes much longer to learn even a simple task than do children in more advanced stages. Therefore, the nature of the task and the ease of performance give insights into the child's capabilities. Piaget-oriented tests, unlike traditional IQ tests, have diagnostic value and do not carry with them the "value" component of traditional IQ tests. The use of traditional IQ tests occasionally has crippling effects on students who are told that their IQ scores are below average.

Piagetian types of tests assess the cognitive ability of the child. Piaget believes there is a hierarchy of intelligence. Each level of intelligence is followed by another, more sophisticated, one. Decaré found in her research evidence to substantiate this view. In constructing an *object permanence task* evaluational instrument, she found that sensorimotor children never passed an advanced stage above the one they failed. She also found in studying ninety children that the conclusions Piaget reached after studying his three children were supported by her investigations (Decaré, 1965).

Efforts have been made to construct other types of Piagetian tests. Barbel Inhelder and Vinh-Bang at the Geneva Institute began work on some evaluational instruments in the 1950s. Object permanence tasks tests were devised for the sensorimotor period and conservation tasks tests were constructed for the elementary years. Each item on these tests attempts to determine the presence or absence of some cognitive ability. Unlike traditional IQ tests, a wrong answer gives as much information as a correct response. For example, if a child fails to do reversible thinking, he is not concrete operational.

Paul Ankney and Lyle Joyce (1974) developed a concrete operational paper-and-pencil test. Tisher and Dale (1975) and Gilbert Burney (1974) have prepared a test for the formal operational level. Anton Lawson (1977) of Arizona State University has also developed a valid and reliable classroom test of formal operations.

Although some Piagetian assessment measures have been developed, David Elkind (1971) cautions that too much hope should not be attributed to their contribution. He argues that traditional IQ tests give a broader measure of the individuals' abilities, have better predictive value in school curricula, and are more easily used by counselors and clinicians because of their philosophical and educational backgrounds than Piagetian tests. Tuddenham (1971), however, disagrees with Elkind in that he believes Piagetian tests can be particularly helpful in assessing certain curriculum renovations.

Curriculum Materials and Cognitive Development

Traditionally, curricula have been constructed by adults using different philosophical bases for their organization. One approach has been to emphasize *subject matter topics* and to arrange these to follow a logical sequence.

For example, in science, a sound lesson might be followed by one on light because both sound and light are wave phenomena and are, therefore, cognitively related.

Another approach has been to form a curriculum around major topics or generalizations of a discipline; this is the *conceptual scheme* approach. For example, in mathematics, the schemes might include properties and applications of probabilities or, in science, "matter exists in the form of units which can be classified into hierarchies of organizational levels."

A more recent approach has been to use the development of *cognitive competencies* as the main skeletal structure of the curriculum. In this design, learning of such abilities as measuring, observing, predicting, and so on is the basic concern. Subject matter is involved in the curriculum, but its importance is secondary to the child's learning to manifest certain of these cognitive processes. In this type of curriculum, subject matter becomes the vehicle for developing children's strategies of thought.

Recently, many science, mathematics, social studies, and language arts curricula have been designed using the discovery or inquiry approaches. These titles mean different things to different people, but essentially there is agreement among educators that, with this approach, the child is not told the answers to problems. The learning environment is structured to enable the child to discover through his own mental actions concepts and principles. The purpose of these approaches is to have children mediate and internalize concepts. Educators have used Piaget's theory as support for this type of curriculum. The role of the teacher is to set up the learning environment and act as a facilitator in helping children make discoveries. It is argued by the proponents of discovery that this approach has the advantages of increasing intellectual potency, shifting from extrinsic to intrinsic rewards, helping to learn how to discover, and aiding in memory processing.

In an inquiry approach, the role of the teacher is to act as a facilitator.

Experience with the Burney Logical Reasoning Test

GUEST
EDITORIAL

William D. Popejoy
Department of Mathematics
University of Northern Colorado

Rex R. Schweers, Jr.
Department of Mathematics
University of Northern Colorado

Teachers of grades six and seven may have students who are in transition to the formal operational period. Teachers of grades eight and nine may have students who are already at the formal operational period. We happen to believe that subject matter content has "cognitive loading"; that is, certain content may be learned by using only concrete operations, while other content requires the use of formal operational thought. For this reason, it is important to know to what extent a learner is formal when teaching courses that require formal operational thought. Since giving the formal tasks is difficult and time-consuming, few teachers bother to interview their students.

The Burney Test (see Burney, 1974), we believe, gives a reliable, though conservative, estimate of degree of formal reasoning. Of the twenty-one questions, seven assess the use of propositional logic, five assess proportional reasoning, three assess syllogistic reasoning, and six assess analogical reasoning.

What might one expect in the way of results when using the test? Burney found, when developing the test, that 27 percent of ninth graders, 49 percent of eleventh graders, and 78 percent of thirteenth graders were formal. In research completed at the University of Northern Colorado, the following results were obtained: In research at the University of Northern Colorado the test was given to 194 ninth graders; 16 percent were found to be formal and 41 percent to be transitional to formal. In another test of 1,414 eighth and ninth graders, 11 percent were found to be formal, while 40 percent were transitional to formal. Popejoy, Schweers, and Pavlik tested 52 sixth graders who had scored high on the concrete test and found that 8 percent were formal and 21 percent were transitional to formal. They found 7 percent of the eighth graders were formal and 42 percent were transitional to formal. When the test was given to about 600 college students, 55 percent were found to be formal and 37 percent to be transitional to formal—8 percent were found to be preformal.

In the United States, students in grades six through nine seem to be developing formal operational thought, but to greatly varying degrees. It appears that over 50 percent of students at these grade levels will possess little, if any, ability to use formal operational thought. Teachers at these grade levels should consider to what extent the content being taught, or the teaching style being used, requires the use of formal operations.

Jerome Bruner (1961) believes discovery learning increases intellectual potency because it forces the individual to use cognitive abilities in generating meaning. Realizing how her mind is capable of functioning, the student receives self-satisfaction—intrinsic rewards. Bruner believes that in order for individuals to want to use their minds and to continue to explore and become knowledgeable, they must have had success in doing this many times. Schools traditionally have emphasized the giving of extrinsic rewards in the form of grades, letters, etc. These are valuable, but Bruner argues that what is really needed is to have students become aware of using their minds. Bruner argues the only way a person learns to discover is to be involved in discovering. It is, therefore, extremely important for children to have multiple opportunities to make discoveries so that they develop their cognitive capacities.

David Elkind (1971), however, questions the interpretation of Piaget's ideas to support discovery teaching as a means of stimulating intrinsic motivation. He argues that the discovery emphasis now prevalent in education is misconceived since it assumes that intrinsic motivation can be built within the materials and methods used by the instructor. He points out that Piaget insists that motivation lies within the child. The child should choose the materials appropriate to him.

Although Elkind questions the possibility of building intrinsic motivation in materials and procedures, there is considerable evidence that the modern discovery or inquiry-oriented curricula have been educationally successful. Shulman, as a result of a conference on learning by discovery, summarizes the research in discovery as follows: "In the published studies, guided discovery treatments generally have done well both at the level of immediate learning and later transfer" (1968, p. 90).

In respect to cognitive development, Lovell (1971) found in a review of studies on the formal level that exposure to formal patterns of reasoning was effective in aiding a student to develop formal operations after age thirteen. He also noted that knowledge of the subject and a positive attitude toward it enhanced formal thought.

Harry Beilin (1970), editor of the *Journal of Experimental Child Psychology*, made an extensive review of research related to the effects of training in logical operations. He concludes: "The data from these diverse studies show that training makes possible an improvement in performance in practically every type of logical or infralogical operation" (p. 81).

Psychologists have known for years that the greater the involvement of the individual in the learning process, the more he comes to know. This involvement, however, usually has been taken to mean that the child mainly learns knowledge. Piaget's work has contributed to a shift in this viewpoint. Involvement now means to many educators the active participation of the child in performing operations. By the child's making such an investment, there is greater opportunity for cognitive development and concomitantly better learning and memory retention.

Piaget's work suggests that curriculum planners should consider the following:

1. Emphasize active involvement by children and intrinsic motivation.

2. Realize experience not only includes learning about phenomena but also cognitive adaptation and organization.

3. Develop a curriculum so that it moves from the concrete to the abstract. This is particularly important for the elementary level.

4. Design curriculum materials so that they take into consideration the stages of cognitive development.

5. Diagnose children's mental capabilities and modify the curriculum so as to help them develop their cognitive abilities. Adjust the curriculum to the child; not the child to the curriculum.

6. Assess the outcomes in performing mental operations, subject matter knowledge, and patterns of reasoning.

7. Include activities designed to "engage the learner."

8. Provide opportunities for exploration, explanation, extension, and evaluation.

Obviously there are many ways to organize curriculum materials and incorporate Piaget's ideas. Although the suggestions made above may aid curriculum planners, many problems still remain unresolved. Educators need to know far more about how children learn concepts and pass from one stage of development to another. Before curriculum experts can enhance the movement of children from stage to stage, much more information is needed. Piaget's work does, however, give the curriculum developer some assistance by indicating how learning activities should be sequenced, and his work has revealed the importance of sequencing. Furthermore, the clinical techniques Piaget has utilized for gaining insights into the child's cognitive operations and concept formation can be used by curriculum organizers to investigate other curricular problems.

Cognitive Development of Students in Schools

Although one would get the impression from reading Piaget's works that all children eventually achieve the operational abilities he outlines, research indicates that a sizeable number of students do not. Research, furthermore, shows that many students do not achieve certain tasks until several years after the time stated by Piaget. David Elkind (1961) for example, evaluated 469 junior and senior high school students in Norton High School, Norton, Massachusetts. He found large numbers of students ages 12.6 to 17.7 did not have good conceptions of quantity, and many seniors who should be well into the formal period of cognitive development still experienced difficulty in attaining abstract conceptions of volume.

John W. Renner and his colleagues did a study involving 588 students grades seven through twelve, sampled from the secondary schools in Oklahoma and found only 58 of them were definitely at the formal level on the tasks he administered. The majority of the students were concrete operational. The results of his study, based on conservation of a solid, conservation of weight, conservation of volume, the elimination of contradiction, and exclusion of irrelevant variables tasks are shown in Table 9.1. He suggests that what is being done to facilitate cognitive development in kindergarten through twelfth grade is open to serious questioning (Renner et al., 1971).

Ball and Sayre (1972) studied 419 seventh through twelfth grade science students, assessing their abilities in achieving five formal operational level tasks: stickman ratio, pendulum controlling variables, balance proportion, combining chemicals, and combinational logic and syllogisms. Their work corroborated the findings of Renner. The number achieving formal operational ability on each task is indicated in Table 9.2.

See also the guest editorial by Joe Premo and Patricia Fahey in Chapter 6. Their study also assessed the cognitive development of students in grades seven through twelve.

Ball and Sayre further discovered that there was a significant correlation between the number of tasks performed successfully and the scholastic grades received by the students. Those who were formal obtained generally higher scholastic grades. In grades 7 through 10, 94 percent of the formal students received grades of A or B, and in grades 11 through 12, 74 percent. Five formal students out of the sample did receive grades below C. However, the predictive value of these tasks did not have as much significance for grade 12 physics since there already is a higher percentage of formal students in these classes. The study further determined there was a positive correlation between the number of Piagetian tasks performed by the student and IQ.

Table 9.1

Tasks Completed	Developmental Level	No. of Students N=588
0–5	Preoperational	20
6–11	Concrete Operational	423
12–13	Postconcrete Operational	87
14–16	Formal Operational	58

Table 9.2

	% Success on Each Task				419 Students
Task	1	2	3	4	5 (SYL)
Grade	No. of Students				
7	70	6	13	24	33	39
8	70	7	16	41	49	60
9	74	12	11	40	51	70
10	81	26	28	60	64	77
11	67	72	51	85	88	93
12	57	81	69	93	88	95
Percent:		32%	29%	55%	61%	71%

Facilitating Cognitive Development

Daniel Ball
Department of Science Education
Ball State University

My convictions about the implications of Piaget's theory for educators have grown out of the results of some of my work and the work of a friend and colleague, Dr. Steve Sayre. Steve and I administered five formal operational tasks to 419 public school science students ranging in age from twelve to eighteen (seventh through twelfth grades) in an attempt to find how well these students perform formal thought (see Table 9.2). Formal thought requirements permeate many of the current texts and curriculum materials used by secondary students throughout the country, and indeed, the world. It would, therefore, seem logical that students should be able to perform at the level(s) required by the "printed word." From the results presented in Tables 9.3 and 9.4, it is apparent that the majority of junior high and senior high students do *not* do abstract (formal) thinking very well. Further, and perhaps more importantly, students are being penalized by teachers if they are not formal thinkers (see Table 9.3). Remember, the ability to perform at the formal operational level is a developmental phenomenon over which students have little or no control. It is much like physical development; students have minimal control over how tall they will be, or whether they can or cannot grow a mustache at a given age.

What are some implications of all this? What should a teacher be doing in a classroom of young adolescents to capitalize on findings of Piaget and others? Permit me to suggest a few things that could be done.

During activity periods such as laboratory work, *ask questions* of your students. Are the students attempting to perform the activity without understanding the what and why of the activity? Are they just performing a rote exercise? From our research, we found students below grade eight may have considerable difficulty in performing experiments that require control of variables. Ask students to justify their answers given in activity or lab sessions. Have students explain sources of errors in their work. Their answers will give you clues to how logical their thought patterns are. Ask students the following questions: How did you get your answer? What do you think went wrong with the experiment? How can you improve the experiment next time?

Listen to what your students tell you. By careful listening a teacher can often detect how children think (i.e., if they are operating on a concrete or formal level). This diagnostic tool of listening will allow you to prescribe subsequent learning activities for your students.

By far the most important implication of Piaget's work lies in this diagnostic/prescriptive approach to instruction. Elsewhere in this text, information is given on how to administer Piagetian tasks to your students. Beyond these, however, should exist a continual diagnostic/prescriptive attitude on the part of the teacher. Think and act this way. Ask questions. Listen to answers. Prescribe instruction based on how students think. You will find that learning is not always a result of prescriptions,

Table 9.3

Comparison of Junior High School Students' Grades with
Their Overall Performance on the Piagetian Task Instrument

Scholastic Grade	No. of Students Receiving	Formal Performance	Nonformal Performance	Percent Formal	Percent Nonformal
A	19	8	11	42.1	57.4
B	74	13	61	17.6	82.4
C	78	1	77	1.3	98.7
D–F	43	1	42	2.3	97.7

Table 9.4

Comparison of Senior High School Students' Grades with
Their Overall Performance on the Piagetian Task Instrument

Scholastic Grade	No. of Students Receiving	Formal Performance	Nonformal Performance	Percent Formal	Percent Nonformal
A	51	45	6	88.2	11.8
B	78	49	29	62.8	37.2
C	55	20	35	36.4	63.6
C–F	21	4	17	19.0	81.0

but rather a proper prescription based on proper diagnosis. Piaget has stated, "There is no learning without experience." Our job as teachers is to provide meaningful experiences for the students at their levels of thinking. And the possibility exists that there may be several levels of thinking in any given classroom. I believe that if a teacher knows these levels exist, she will do a much better job in helping facilitate cognitive development.

Achievement of cognitive tasks on the elementary level further indicated considerable variation as to what students were able to do. Millie Almy evaluated 629 second grade children to determine the number that were clearly concrete operational on seven different tasks. She found a relatively low number of these children were able to achieve most of the tasks as indicated by Table 9.5 (Almy, 1971).

As indicated by the work of Almy, Ball, Sayre, Elkind, and Renner, several studies have been done assessing students' cognitive development in schools. All of these studies have shown there are students with various developmental levels in every class. In no classroom did all students perform well on all tasks administered to them, and the evidence indicates many students were at different Piagetian levels of development. To teach students as though they were all the same in large group instruction is certainly of questionable value.

Teachers should evaluate students' cognitive abilities. If they cannot perform certain mental operations, they should be involved in activities contributing to the development of these abilities. Although activities to

Table 9.5
Developmental Levels of Second Grade Students

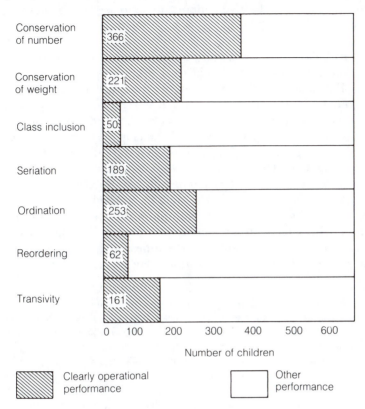

Number of children

Clearly operational performance   Other performance

achieve this end have met with varied success, it seems reasonable that involving children in performing reasoning tasks approximating their ability level will better ensure their attainment. With time and further research, it may well be possible to devise a series of activities to facilitate progressional achievement and even to help in making the transition from one stage to another. Clearly, Piaget's work and the research of other investigators indicate greater attention needs to be given to instruction to ensure better cognitive development of students in schools.

Developmental Delays and Students with Retarded Mental Development

The basis of intellect is action. It is important for the child to have opportunities to act upon objects. Through such actions, children develop perceptual ability providing the basis for cognitive development. Research indicates children may have nonphysiological perceptual problems causing learning disabilities. Some psychologists believe this may be due to a lack of physical experience during the sensorimotor period. Newell Kephart

(1960) has come to this conclusion. He has devised diagnostic remedial techniques for children suffering from these perceptual disabilities. He suggests these children be given opportunities to use their bodies in sensori-motor ways. In a sense, he strives to have them reenact the sensorimotor period of their lives.

Kephart believes that first learning is essentially derived from sensori-motor experience and that this in turn influences later cognitive development. If a child has deficient or faulty experiences during this period of development, his mental ability is affected as a consequence. To rectify such inadequacies, Kephart initially involves children in performing various types of motor patterns (e.g., crawling, balancing the body, throwing, catching, manipulating and grasping objects, etc.) until they become proficient in performing them. He then attempts to transfer this motor skill to perceptual ability so that they develop what he calls *perceptual-motor match*. This, he explains, is the process whereby the child increasingly uses his mind in the perceptual process to interact through muscular responses (motor reaction) with the environment. Motor explorations are the final arbitrators of all sensory information. Later in Kephart's approach, he tries to develop what he calls *form perception* and *space structure*. He says:

> Normally, the child develops through these various stages during the pre-school years and by the age of six or seven has achieved a space structure. In many children, however, the developmental process has broken down; at one of the earlier stages, the child either failed to develop further or developed in an atypical or distorted manner. Such breakdowns in the developmental sequence may be the result of environmental deprivations, injuries or defects in the organism, or emotional pressures with which the child has been unable to cope. Many of these breakdowns reveal themselves in the early elementary grades through difficulties in learning and low academic achievement. (Kephart, 1960, p. 120)

A teacher may be alerted to children's perceptual problems by observing whether they have difficulty in identifying certain letters or words. The instructor might test this further by having a child copy certain figures or letters. If the student is unable to do this well, he should be given many experiences with physical objects; for example, working with blocks placing them in boxes so that they just fit, drawing various shapes, forming things with his hands from clay. The child also may be given several figures and letters to trace until he does them with ease. Drawing circles, such as most of us did in learning how to write, may be particularly helpful to children having these problems.

After the child accomplishes these tasks with ease, he should be returned to reading and writing. If he still has trouble, his problem may be due to some other difficulty and he may be in need of specialized professional assistance. The clinical evidence supporting Kephart's theory is significant. The implications of Piaget's theory for educators are many and diverse. We have suggested only a few. We hope that the teaching/learning cycle model, the specific recommendations, and general implications have all helped you extend Piaget's theory to the practical world of educators.

GUEST
EDITORIAL

Piaget's Effect on the Field of Mental Retardation

Oliver P. Kolstoe
School of Special Education and Rehabilitation
University of Northern Colorado

It probably would be hard for Piaget to believe that his work would have had such a dramatic impact on the field of mental retardation. Ever since IQ tests became common tools for identifying mental retardation, there has been a continuing disagreement about whether the condition represents a quantitative or a qualitative intellectual departure from normalcy. Although Piaget did not work much with retarded individuals, others were quick to see the potential inherent in validating cognitive theory on a population whose major characteristic is cognitive weakness. Examining the relationship of Piaget's developmental levels to conditions of mental retardation provided a whole new approach to the qualitative-quantitative issue.

The earliest studies examined the ability of mentally retarded youngsters to demonstrate the same cognitive skills as their nonretarded peers. Results from many sources confirmed that the developmental levels were exhibited by the retarded. However, the stages were significantly delayed, and some were never reached.

A reasonable conclusion was that the mentally retarded were developmentally arrested. Further studies showed that the level of intellectual development essentially defined the condition. Mildly mentally retarded persons demonstrated concrete operational thinking, but investigators found no evidence of formal thought. The moderate and severe did not exceed intuitive thought while the profoundly retarded remained at the sensorimotor level.

The finding that degrees of retardation were restricted to specific kinds of thought processes lent credence to the belief that each of the developmental levels identified by Piaget was characterized by thought processes that were qualitatively different than the preceding levels. Mental retardation was indicated when the individual could not demonstrate the thought processes equal to those of his age peers. These findings led to another discovery; namely, that the developmental levels were more closely related to the mental ages of the retarded youngsters, than to their chronological ages, but that they seldom achieved academically at even their mental ages.

Robert Sund and William Sweeter verified the findings on mental age in science teaching. Using magnets, they found that mentally retarded youngsters were able to understand the physical properties up to approximately the level of their mental ages. This and other studies sparked an interest in teaching science concepts to the retarded—a venture that had previously been avoided because of the presumed inability of the youngsters to grasp the relationships involved.

One of the most extensive projects was really three curricular programs developed by the Biological Sciences Curriculum Study group at Boulder, Colorado. The first series "Me Now" began in 1969 and was designed for eleven to thirteen-year-old mentally retarded youngsters. Their mental ages ranged from about seven to nine or ten years. The series was directed toward an understanding of the self. The second program, "Me and My Environment," guided the fourteen to seventeen-year-old students through an exploration of their relationship to the environment. It was completed in 1976. The third program, "Me in the Future," completed in 1979, was a career oriented science exploration program for fourteen to seventeen-year-old mentally retarded students. All are compatible with the developmental levels of Piaget correlated with mental ages.

Extensive evaluations of the three programs by Richard Tolman, James Robinson, and their colleagues attest to the effectiveness of the format and the appropriateness of gearing the science tasks approximately to mental age levels (Biological Sciences Curriculum Study). Of even more interest was the finding that in using the criterion of successful performance on the science curricular tasks, the use of Piagetian cognitive levels was a better method of grouping the students for instruction than the use of IQ, age, and ethnic background combined. The IQ itself as a predictor of successful science learning was found to account for only about 20 percent of the variance in performance. This intensified the already serious concern of professionals as to the use of IQ tests in identifying mental retardation in the first place.

J. Pascaul-Leone in Geneva has developed a new theoretical basis for describing the strategies or schemes children use to solve problems (see Case, 1974). It is referred to as a neo-Piagetian approach and deals with not only the number of schemes children of different developmental levels have developed, but also their skill in selecting the proper ones needed to solve the problems. Studies by Ellis and Norman, Herman Spitz, and others (1979) determined that a major difficulty among retarded youngsters was their inability to apply various strategies to learning problems. This is consistent with the work of Robert Sternberg, Joseph Campione, Ann Brown, and Garnett Smith (1981) who report that mentally retarded youngsters are deficient in their abilities to determine which schemes to apply to problem solving even when they know how to solve the problems.

The long simmering controversy over whether mental retardation is a quantitative or qualitative intellectual deficiency may someday yield to the research approach of analyzing the components of the developmental levels described by Piaget. Definitive answers are yet to be discovered. The search so far has focused on the components of thought: scanning, encoding, mapping, inference, and transfer as they relate to reasoning problems. It has not been applied to the thought processes attributed by Piaget to various developmental levels.

It is an exciting thought that this might become the new frontier for research in mental retardation. In the meantime, while definitive answers are being sought, as teachers, we can feel quite secure that instruction should be geared to the developmental levels of Piaget but with retarded youngsters their mental rather than their chronological ages should be the guide for grouping them and for setting up programs of instruction.

References

Almy, Millie. "Longitudinal Studies Related to the Classroom." In *Piagetian Cognitive-Development Research and Mathematical Education*, edited by Myron F. Rosskopf et al. Washington, D.C.: National Council of Teachers of Mathematics, 1971.

Ankney, Paul, and Joyce, Lyle. "The Development of a Piagetian Paper and Pencil Test for Assessing Concrete Operational Reasoning." Ph.D. dissertation, University of Northern Colorado, 1974.

Atkin, J.M., and Karplus, Robert. "Discovery or Invention?" *The Science Teacher* 29 (1962): 45–51.

Ball, Dan, and Sayre, Steve. "Relationships between Student Piagetian Cognitive Development and Achievement in Science." Ph.D. dissertation, University of Northern Colorado, 1972.

Beilin, Harry. "Piagetian and Cognitive Development Research and Mathematical Education." In proceedings of an NCTM conference conducted at Columbia University, October 1970.

Biological Sciences Curriculum Study. "Formative Evaluation Series Reports: Me and My Environment." Boulder, Colo.: BSCS, 1973 to February 1976.

Burney, Gilbert M. "The Construction and Validation of an Objective Formal Reasoning Instrument." Ph.D. dissertation, University of Northern Colorado, 1974.

Case, Robbie. "Mental Strategies, Mental Capacity, and Instruction: A Neo-Piagetian Investigation." *Journal of Experimental Child Psychology* 18 (1974): 382–97.

Decaré, T.G. *Intelligence and Affectivity in Early Childhood,* New York: International Press, 1965.

Elkind, David. "Quantity Conceptions in Junior and Senior High School Students." *Child Development* 32 (1961): 551–60.

———. "Two Approaches to Intelligence." In *Measurement and Piaget,* edited by D. Green, M. Ford, and G. Flamer. New York: McGraw-Hill, 1971.

Ellis, C.F., and Norman, R., eds. *Handbook of Mental Deficiency, Psychological Theory and Research.* 2d ed. Hillsdale, N.J., Lawrence Erlbaum Associates, 1979.

Fischer, Hardi. "The Psychology of Piaget and Its Educational Applications." *International Review of Education* 10 (1964): 438.

Hall, Elizabeth. "A Conversation with Jean Piaget and Barbel Inhelder." *Psychology Today* (May 1970): 31.

Karplus, Robert; Lawson, A.; Wollmen, W.; Appel, M.; Bernoff, R.; Howe, A.; Rusch, J.; and Sullivan, F. *Science Teaching and the Development of Reasoning.* Berkeley: University of California, 1977.

Kephart, Newell C. *The Slow Learner in the Classroom.* Columbus, Ohio: Charles E. Merrill Publishing Co., 1960.

Lawson, Anton. "The Development and Validation of a Classroom Test of Formal Reasoning." Paper presented at the National Association for Research in Science Teaching, Cincinnati, 1977.

Lovell, Kenneth. "Some Problems Associated with Formal Thought and Its Assessment." In *Measurement and Piaget*, edited by Donald R. Green, Margerite P. Ford, and George B. Flamer. New York: McGraw-Hill, 1971.

Renner, John W.; Stafford, Donald G.; and Ragan, William B. "Research in Formal Operations." Mimeographed. Normal, Okla.; University of Oklahoma, 1971.

Science Curriculum Improvement Study. *Organisms*. Chicago: Rand McNally, 1977.

Shulman, Lee S. "Psychological Controversies in the Teaching of Science and Mathematics." *The Science Teacher* 35 (September 1968): 90.

Smith, Garnett J. "Encoding Componential Skills of Mentally Retarded Youngsters." Ph.D. dissertation, University of Northern Colorado, 1981.

Tisher, R.P., and Dale, L.G. Hawthorn, Victoria, Australia: Australian Council for Educational Research, 1975.

Tuddenham, Read. "Comments on Elkind's Paper." In *Measurement and Piaget*, edited by Donald R. Green, Margerite P. Ford, and George B. Flamer. New York: McGraw-Hill, 1971.

10 | Extending Piaget's Theory: The Disciplines

In this chapter we will discuss the implications of Piaget's theory for the basic academic areas of reading, science, and mathematics. By no means do we intend to imply Piaget's theory cannot or should not be extended to other disciplines such as social science, language arts, physical education, and fine arts. Rather, with limited space we had to confine our discussion to basic subjects, so we selected reading, science, and mathematics.

PIAGET'S THEORY AND READING

Introduction

> We suspect that the teacher who has mastered Piaget's techniques will become more diagnostic in his views of all areas of instruction. Accordingly, he may become much more skillful in pacing instruction in reading and writing skills to the individual child's apparent maturity and rate of learning. (Almy, Chittenden, and Miller, 1966)

Reading is a complex human ability. In order to read, children have to reach a certain level of neurological development, must be able to perceive well defined distinctions in shapes of letters, and have an experiential background in order for the words they use to have meaning. Children can decode certain symbols and mouth words without meaning, but this certainly shouldn't be confused with reading.

Reading involves deriving meaning from symbols. To do this children have to learn that sounds represent things. Next they must develop the

238

realization that a symbol can represent something. For example, a red light can represent stop. Later when a child draws a deer and the teacher writes *deer* below it, the teacher helps the child make association of the animal with the word symbol. By so doing, the child slowly comes to realize that words can represent things. The child must also learn different letters can represent the same sound and that some words may have different representations or meanings. Representing objects and ideas with symbols requires an abstraction process that must be developed. Unfortunately, children can learn to use symbols without understanding what they mean. To do so is one example of what Piaget calls false learning. To learn to use symbols without understanding must be highly confusing to children. Once they grasp the idea that symbols can substitute for things, they must further develop the realization that different shapes on pieces of paper can stand for different kinds of sound. This undoubtedly requires a tremendous mental leap for the child to internalize because it is based on building abstractions on abstractions.

Children may also become confused in other ways as to what is required in the reading process. For example, a procedure used by some teachers is to have children learn several words where the first letter changes like *pop*, *hop*, *mop*. This is a poor practice because a child might generalize from such an activity that the first letter is the cue to what words mean. This certainly isn't the case. In trying to interpret what reading is, children often construct such incorrect rules. For example, some children believe that the number of letters in a word is important and that their position has nothing to do with the word meaning (Sinclair, 1977, pp. 75-76). In writing words, they may get the number and kinds of letters correct but the sequence incorrect. Other children believe that any small difference in the way words are written must indicate a small difference in meaning. This in fact is true for Chinese but not English. Problems in reading as outlined above should have sensitized you to the developmental nature of reading.

Basic Operations Involved in Reading

Children can mouth sounds. This appears to be reading without having developed mental operations. But if there is to be true reading with comprehension of what is going on in the process, then the attainment of certain mental operations is required. Murray and Pikulski (1975) point out that students who simply decode words are like those who count but fail to conserve. Piagetian scholars have concluded that several operations are associated with reading. These operations include the following:

seriation
one-to-one correspondence
ordering
spatial relations
temporal relations
classification
conservation
transitivity
number

Reading Ability Correlates with Piagetian Achievement

Cindy Polk and David Goldstein (1979) found that early readers achieve significantly higher on Piagetian tasks. They also found that the early readers did particularly well on conservation of weight, mass, and length tasks. The authors state: "A followup test of reading achievement at the end of the first grade showed that Piagetian scores for all subjects were significantly correlated with reading achievement while intelligence was not" (Polk and Goldstein, 1979, p. 8).

Some level of thinking is required in all reading. This means certain operations are performed whenever students read. This should be obvious when one looks at sentence structure. There are variations in word order operating within the sentence structure. If the word order changes, the meaning changes. Children, in order to interpret and manipulate language, must then know the ordering operation. They must be able to order not only to understand sentences but words themselves. Each word has an ordered sequence of letters. The ordering operation is fundamental to children reading with comprehension. Words also may represent a class and each of these in turn may be included in other classes. Therefore, an understanding of class inclusion is essential; for example, knives, forks, and spoons are classes that may be included in the major class, silverware. Conservation may also be involved in understanding sentences since words may represent ideas that must be conserved if the intent of a passage is to be understood. Words and sentences may also require temporal comprehension. They may indicate the present, past, or future, short or long periods of duration, geological time, light years, or infinity. Comprehension of sentences may also require the student to use one-to-one correspondence. Concepts may be stated that correspond with other concepts requiring students to perform one-to-one correspondence operations (e.g., when it rains, plants grow better). Then, too, the mere act of reading requires seriation. The child has to understand the need to go from left to right and top to bottom of the page and interpret seriational concepts, such as "greater than this" but "less than that." Transitivity also may be involved whenever the child has to interrelate a series of concepts. Spatial relational operations are required for a child to discriminate differences in letters (e.g., p from q), letter size and shapes, use of large and small letters in print and script, etc. Conceptualization of number and its conservation for various entities within a sentence are needed for comprehension in sentences where objects are in some way being enumerated. Reading then may demand a number of operations that a child must utilize if he is going to read effectively with comprehension. Murray and Pikulski (1975) summarize the operational nature of reading by saying, "Reading can be conceived as the mental construction of classes, relations, systems, transformations and implication products for print" (p. 56).

Which Operations Are Facilitative of Reading?

Which of the above operations are perhaps most facilitative of enhancing reading? At the present state of Piagetian research, the answer is not clear.

There is some evidence that the ability to conserve and class inclusion are good predictors of reading readiness and may be facilitative of reading.

Millie Almy and her colleagues state, "the findings of our studies of a rather substantial correlation between performance in conservation tasks and progress in beginning reading suggests that, to some extent, similar abilities are involved. A program designed to nurture logical thinking should contribute positively to reading readiness" (Almy, Chittenden, and Miller, 1966, pp. 139–40).

Murray and Pikulski (1975) also believe in the importance of conservation in the reading process. They say in this respect: "It makes as much sense to speak of conservation of letter as conservation of number" (p. 57). Educators can see that class inclusion is also required to understand relationships of parts of a word to the whole.

When Should Reading Be Taught?

If the ability of performing operations is facilitative to reading, and the evidence suggests it is, then it would seem reasonable that reading should be taught when children have either developed or are in the process of developing the prerequisite operations. Yet, if you look at reading programs, many schools actually have a significant part of their student populations involved in reading who are not able to perform many of these operations. Recall the operations once again associated with reading. Millie Almy (1971) evaluated the developmental level of 629 second graders. Relatively few of the children were able to complete the mental operations required in reading. (See Table 9.5 in Chapter 9, p. 231.)

Recall what Almy said about those who don't conserve. They are more likely to be students who do not read and who will experience failure in reading. These children are usually identified as having reading difficulty by the third grade. Benjamin Bloom (1976, p. 151) found that continued reading failure with these preoperational children significantly affects their self-concepts and contributes to negative feelings toward school continuing through to the twelfth grade. It is for these reasons that several Piagetian scholars have criticized the early emphasis on reading for all children and have suggested either a more flexible or a delayed approach. Hans Furth believes that focusing on reading in the primary school years is detrimental to the development of intelligence for many children. He says:

> Let me be quite blunt. Reading and writing should have no more emphasis or focus in a child's life in early school grades than toilet training has in an infant's first years.... Seriously, while the written word is the means par excellence for expanding a mature intelligence, the early pressure on reading must be exposed not merely as contributing little or nothing to intellectual development, but in many cases, as seriously interfering with it. (Furth, 1970, pp. vii–ix)

Furth suggests elsewhere that reading readiness is extremely variable. Some children may begin the reading process as early as age 4½ while others may still have difficulty at 8½. It is for these reasons that he believes it is far more important to focus on the development of what he considers to be more relevant and basic, and that is thinking—the development of operational abilities (Murray and Pikulski, 1975, p. 54).

David Elkind believes that with present reading practices it is highly advisable to delay reading instruction until children are eight years old. He further believes that reading emphasis as it is presently found in the primary schools contributes significantly to children's poor self-concepts. He states: "By grade two it is hard to distinguish emotional problems from reading problems, which came first?" (Elkind, 1975).

Raymond Hock questions the value of early reading emphasis from research having to do with the development of the different hemispheres of the brain. He suggests that too much emphasis on early reading may contribute to excessive development of the left brain at the expense of the right brain. This may be detrimental to the development within the child of such human attributes as intuition, the ability to be metaphorical, and creative thought. Hock further states: "There is absolutely no practical reason to teach the child to read at such an early age. They do not need it for anything they do, and there is some evidence that damage results from initiating reading too early" (Hock, 1977, p. 48).

The International Association for the Evaluation of Educational Achievement in Stockholm, Sweden, has compared reading achievement in fourteen different languages with approximately a quarter million students in 9,000 schools with 50,000 teachers. Different national school systems vary as to when they begin formal education. In some countries students begin school a year or more earlier than those in other countries. In spite of these differences, their study found that the number of years of schooling was not strongly related to achievement in reading. Their study indicated that when assessment was determined at ages 10–11 and 14–14.11 that those students who started school a year later achieved relatively as well on the reading test as those with an extra year. This seriously questions the effectiveness of early reading emphasis (Thorndike, 1973).

Focusing on Thinking Rather Than Memorization

To focus on memorization in the reading process is not to focus on the development of thinking operations that are basic to reading. Such a focus is undoubtedly inefficient and detrimental to learning to read. This teaches the child that learning equates with memorizing without meaning, which certainly is not a goal of most educators. Barry J. Wadsworth (1978) summarizes his and others' concerns about the emphasis of learning to read by memory. He writes, "The child who tries to assimilate an external structure (which many children try to do in an effort to do what is desired of them by adults) runs the risk of resorting to memorizing" (p. 132). Memorization can be inefficient and stifling. As early as 1898, John Dewey wrote: "No one can estimate the benumbing effect of continued drill in reading as mere form" (Wadsworth, 1978, p. 29).

Szent-Gyorgi, a Nobel Prize science laureate, also questions the advisability of overemphasizing memorization. He says:

It is widely spread opinion that memorizing will not hurt, that knowledge does not harm. I am afraid it may. Dead knowledge dulls the spirit, fills the stomach without nourishing the body. The mind is not a bottomless pit, and if we put in one thing, we might have to leave another out. By a more live teaching we can fill the soul and reserve the mind for the really important things. We may even spare time we need for expanding subjects. (Szent-Gyorgi, 1964, pp. 1278–79)

Children Read at a Cognitive Level

All texts, questions, tests, and other evaluational measures require students to respond at some cognitive level. Unfortunately, in many instances, what these require cognitively is *not* appropriate for many students. The text, for example, may demand the child to equilibrate some formal abstract concept while the child is still at the concrete operational level. The child may learn, as a consequence, that learning in itself may be mysterious and meaningless.

Educators, therefore, must not only use traditional reading formulas to determine readability but should also look at the cognitive processes demanded for any reading material. They should endeavor to better identify concrete operational and formal operational words and phrases so that, in the interplay between themselves and their students, they are better able to adjust the instructional level to the student.

In considering the readability of materials, the teacher should look at the cognitive processes required for understanding the material.

For the concrete operational child it is essential that you become sensitized to the fact that these children's reading ability is highly dependent upon passages involving concrete actions. If abstract ideas are presented, several concrete examples should be given so that children can associate them to their own concepts. For example, in using the word *conservation*, concrete examples may be *explored* to demonstrate different ways people conserve things and then the word should be *explained*. After this, the student should be encouraged to *extend* her use of the word.

With the advent of formal thought, abstract interpretation slowly develops and certain logical processes evolve making it possible for children to comprehend passages that were obscure before. They can now read critically. It is with the development of formal reasoning that language begins to play a more significant role in involving and developing a child's reasoning abilities. Before this it is highly questionable as to how effective reading is in developing rational processes without active involvement of some kind.

Murray and Pikulski (1975) state: "When Piaget set out to observe the intellectual development of young children below age 12, he quickly came to the conclusion that high-level thinking is centered on action and in no way on language" (p. 47).

Why are certain English courses considered to be appropriate for the senior high school? It should be apparent that much of the reading and class assignments of these courses require formal interpretations in order for the student to read them with comprehension. Similar reading demands are made in other courses as well, such as in physics, mathematics, history, and those involving the interpretation of the United States Constitution or parliamentary and common law. The advent of formal reasoning makes it possible for students to be successful in interpreting their reading because their thinking can be hypothetical, logically self-consistent, and controlled. They can ensure that this occurs because they can reflect on the quality of relatedness of their thoughts. They are also capable of looking for hidden meanings, abstracting concepts and principles, and eventually understanding allegory. Because students can do abstract and reflexive reasoning, they are able to identify the main thought in a passage. Obviously, these operational abilities have a great effect on the level of reading comprehension. Any reading program assessing comprehension where reasoning is required must, at least to some degree, discriminate against those who are cognitively less advanced and favor those who are more developmentally advanced. Literature courses can be facilitative in developing formal reasoning provided instructors use these courses for this purpose. Instructors, however, must look upon their courses as means to accomplish cognitive development and not just focus on content goals.

Focusing on Operational Thinking

Reading teachers generally believe that the most effective way to improve reading is to have children read. There is, however, considerable evidence suggesting other kinds of involvement may be equally, if not more, facilitative for the development of reading. For example, the British found that children involved in body movement exercises in their schools learned to read significantly better than those who did not (Department of Education and Science, 1967).

There are several studies that have found children involved in learning science through discovery approaches also improve in their reading ability. This is so even though they may have had actually less reading instruction

Cognitive Development and Reading

Delbert L. Barber
Director of Reading Academy
Laramie County Community College

Research Shows

The results of my recent research, conducted in two western high schools with an enrollment of 3,000, demonstrated that only 41 percent of the randomly selected population (N = 200) was formal operational as measured by the Ankney-Joyce and the Burney paper and pencil tests. Further, it was discovered that concrete operational students understood concrete concepts and generated exclusively concrete expressive language. These findings, combined with my classroom experiences and the research of others, have contributed to my conclusion that educators should become knowledgeable about appropriate techniques to identify student cognitive level of functioning and the use of this information to plan appropriate teaching strategies that accommodate student learning through reading.

Insights for Educators

When establishing the purposes for reading an assignment, whether it is a narrative chapter or a science laboratory activity, educators must be aware of the prerequisite cognitive operations required for students to complete that assignment successfully. For example, the prerequisite cognitive operations required to combine specific facts and draw the main idea from a narrative reading selection most often would include three concrete operations: seriation, class inclusion, and conservation. On the other hand, the operations required to complete a laboratory activity in which the student was to make oxygen would include all five concrete operations: seriation, transitivity, class inclusion, conservation, and one-to-one correspondence.

A Challenge for Writers

Authors and publishers must become aware of the significance of cognitive development, the research supporting it, and its application when creating textbooks and other educational materials. In light of the fact that 80 percent of the concepts in existing biology textbooks are formal, there is a tremendous gap created between where 59 percent of the students are functioning cognitively and where they are expected to function cognitively. This gap can only be bridged if professionals apply their knowledge of cognitive development to manipulate linguistic variables in order to maximize comprehension of the concepts being presented. For example, a formal concept requiring formal cognitive development is as follows: Two strands of DNA are joined by their bases in forming the double helix; adenine joins thymine and guanine joins cytosine. A student cannot concretely experience the DNA molecule because its existence is hypothetical and not observable. The cognitive operations necessary to understand DNA are as follows: propositional thinking, separation of variables, and combinatorial operations. In preparing the lexicon to enhance the understanding of this formal concept, writers must begin with concrete models and concrete language and apply the operations of one-to-one correspondence, class inclusion, seriation, transitivity, and conservation before expecting the student to grasp the more formal operations inherent in that formal concept.

Professional Cooperation for Logical Progression

If as educators, authors, and publishers we expect formal operational thinking and formal expressive language from students we must present materials in a logical progression from concrete operations to formal operations. Only this will enhance the students' natural succession to formal level functioning.

---

because of the time they were involved in learning science. Donald H. Kellogg (1976) found that first graders using the Material Object Unit of the Science Curriculum Improvement Study (SCIS) for two hours each day for several weeks improved significantly compared to the control group in reading as determined by the Metropolitan Reading Readiness Test. The Materials Object Unit involves children in identifying properties of objects, sorting or classifying, conserving, plus several other cognitive processes. The control group in this study was involved in a commercially prepared reading readiness program. The Metropolitan Reading Readiness Test (1962) is divided into six subtests. They are Word Meaning, Listening, Matching, Alphabet, Numbers, and Copying. Kellogg's experimental group numerically outgained in all of these subtests except copying. The gains in matching numbers and meaning were the most significant.

Mary Budd Rowe (1969) found similar results when working with elementary children in New York City. She involved children in process-oriented science instruction. Although many of the students actually had less reading time because of this science instruction, they, nonetheless, significantly increased in their reading scores compared to control classes.

Ayers and Mason (1975), using the discovery-oriented *Science, A Process Approach* (SAPA) curriculum with kindergarten children, also found that they scored significantly higher on several of the subparts of the Metropolitan Readiness tests compared to the control groups. Mary and Jerry Ayers (1973) in working with children in Appalachia also concluded that SAPA helped to develop these children's logical thinking required in other parts of the school curriculum, such as reading.

Mary Budd Rowe (1975) in summarizing research related to science teaching states: "Children who come from environments which fail to supply consistent experiences that encourage mental growth of the kind required in schools, seem to be especially helped to recover through science programs" (pp. 23–25). Rowe also states in her summary that it was found that reading teachers of second and fourth graders who were trained to use SCIS (*Science Curriculum Improvement Study*) were more likely to require thinking and encouraged students to think more frequently.

Other studies have shown that the cognitive processes related to reading can be raised. Joachim Wohlwill (1967), for example, found that conservation could be improved by instruction. No studies, as yet, have been done to include the development of several cognitive processes simultaneously (e.g., conservation, ordering, class inclusion, etc.) to determine their effects in facilitating reading ability. Nor have there been any studies to indicate which of the cognitive operations are the most facilitative of the reading process. Although, Almy et al. (1966) and Wohlwill (1967) believe conservation is very important.

Enhancing Reading Skills

One way to further reading abilities is to try to develop the cognitive processes that are fundamental to comprehension. This should be done, as with all Piagetian learning, through the use of teaching methods where the child is *actively* involved in the process; the topics being studied should be of interest and, if possible, generated by the child. For example, the child might ask, "What do snakes look like?" The teacher may then introduce a book on snakes and the child learns and writes about snakes.

Piaget has pointed out that real learning must have *adaptive value* if it is to be equilibrated. The relevance of this idea for reading is that for information to be learned by the children through reading, they must be interested in it and be able to equilibrate it into their own mental structures. Reading goals should not be entirely imposed by adults. Children must see some reason to read and value reading and discovering things in the process.

Wadsworth (1978) in reviewing reading programs has suggested that Sylvia Ashton-Warner's approach in integrating spelling, writing, and reading is an appropriate application of Piaget's active method to reading instruction. What Warner suggests is that the teacher ask every child each day what word or words he would like to write. She would then write in large letters the word or words on cards. The cards would then be given to the child. The child is encouraged to trace over the words with his fingers and later copy them. Later in the day the teacher would go over the words in each child's deck of cards. The words that the child recognizes are retained in the deck and those that he did not retain are eliminated. After several weeks, the child slowly builds up a deck of recognizable words. The children eventually have enough words in their decks so that they can write simple stories using these words. By so doing they move from individual words to constructing words into phrases and eventually sentences and paragraphs. This approach appears to be consistent with Piaget's concept of active learning in that the activity starts with the child's experience and moves from it into language skills. Any child-experience-based method has the advantage of ensuring that children are more likely to have referents for the words they want to see written. For example, if the student asks about the word *lightning,* she probably has experiences of seeing lightning. She can then better associate the experience with the word. Imagine a child trying to learn a word in which she has no referents. This is like teaching color to the congenitally blind. Students developing an experience based written vocabulary soon realize that the symbols for everyday words are meaningful and important. This is no small step for a child to make and one too frequently assumed to exist in children by adults.

The following are some suggestions for enhancing reading skills that are consistent with Piagetian theory.

1. Begin at the child's level of cognitive development. Do not assume some exterior reading goal of where a child is supposed to be.

2. Consider the advantages of reading groups with children of different reading levels.

3. Children will read and learn to read at different rates. They have different rhythms and rates of equilibration, and these should be considered when working with them in reading.

4. Good listeners are more likely to be good readers. Read to children and invite them to act on what they have heard. For example, read them a poem or story and then perform some body movements to demonstrate what they interpreted. Have children in class discussions listen to what has been read and to each other. They should respond to each other's remarks rather than just to the teacher.

5. Do not assume children have to learn letters before words. Children often can recognize several words from their experience. For example, they may be able to read the name of their favorite hamburger drive-in before knowing the letters.

6. In getting children to read and understand symbols, begin with some signs that they know (e.g., street and road signs; arrows for directions; railroad signs; symbols for banks, fast-food places, food products, money, etc.).

7. Have students choose and develop how they are going to organize the material they have read rather than prescribing closely how this should be done and the method of presenting it.

8. Remember the need for the socialization process. Have students discuss what they read or write with one another, in small groups, or in circles.

9. Have students read each other's work. It is a rich resource for causing cognitive disequilibrium.

10. Have students edit each other's work, newspapers, magazine material, etc.

11. Have them paraphrase and contrast treatments in different studies, writing, etc.

12. Invite several students to combine their papers into one. For example, if they have studied a topic together, they could write a paper on it and read and change it to make it more coherent.

13. Invite students to read and make evaluations of some problem and how they would set about to solve it.

14. Have formal operational students reflect over what they have read. Ask them, "If you were going to change or write it again, what would you do?"

15. Remember students sometimes will respond only concretely to written passages even if they are formal thinkers. Endeavor to get them to also give formal responses.

16. Constantly remind yourself that many individuals were once thought to be incompetent in language, or at a minimum, to have a reading dis-

A Proposal for Bonding Language and Concept Development

Robert A. Pavlik
Department of Reading
Cardinal Stritch College

Rex R. Schweers, Jr.
Department of Mathematics
University of Northern Colorado

William D. Popejoy
Department of Mathematics
University of Northern Colorado

Let's advance beyond the use of traditional readability formulas in describing the ease or difficulty of printed material. Instead, let's consider a total readability process. The ideal readability process would begin by identifying and considering significant readability factors:

1. Conceptual ease or difficulty.
2. Linguistic ease or difficulty.

In essence, where might readers find their bases for assimilation—in the concept being conveyed, in the language being read, or in a combination thereof? The ideal readability process would yield specific implications for teaching and studying.

Identifying Conceptual Ease or Difficulty

A concrete concept involves logical operations with actual objects within one's experiences—such operations as performing mathematical operations or classifying. *A formal concept* involves sophisticated, intellectual operations within or beyond one's experiences—such operations as controlling variables in an experiment or formulating theories. In other words, such physical and mental operations are synonyms for concepts. Printed materials, in essence, contain static levels of physical and mental operations about given topics.

We suggest that teachers raise these questions when previewing material requiring reading:

1. What physical and mental operations will be required of the reader?
2. What proportion of the intended readers have operational facility with such physical and mental operations?

Answers to these questions will help teachers shape the entire learning experience when reading is involved in studying a topic.

Identifying Linguistic Ease or Difficulty

The labels of concrete and formal might also be applied to the language students read. *Concrete language* might involve such surface structure characteristics as graphic aids, simple sentence structures, and sensory vocabulary. Such surface structure characteristics would yield concrete language when their deep structure attempts to control action. *Formal language* might involve such surface structure characteristics as the use of symbols, complex sentence structures, and abstract vocabulary. Such surface structure characteristics would yield formal language when their deep structure either promotes abstract thinking or orders thinking.

Ultimately, the labels of concrete and formal are hypothetical and theoretical. However, we believe that teachers need intuitively to consider how surface structure and deep structure interact.

We suggest that teachers raise these questions when previewing material requiring reading:

1. To what extent does the language require translation?
2. To what extent does the sentence structure facilitate/inhibit assimilation?
3. To what extent does the language attempt to promote abstract thinking, order thinking, or control action?

Answers to these questions will help teachers either to identify specific teaching or studying strategies or to select other materials.

Facilitating Accommodation and Equilibration

Sensitivity to conceptual and linguistic factors yields a matrix of four modules: Cc—Concrete concept shaped within concrete language, Cf—Concrete concept shaped within formal language, Fc—Formal concept shaped within concrete language, and Ff—Formal concept shaped within formal language. We propose that such sensitivities will help facilitate learner assimilation, but not necessarily accommodation or equilibration.

More specifically, teachers and textbooks use instructional verbs which yield vague parameters and assumed steps for completing assignments and taking tests. For example, what are students to do when they *review* a play—summarize its setting and episodes, or criticize character development and theme? Approximately seventy other common instructional verbs like *compare*, *evaluate*, *prove*, and *weigh* demand our precise definitions in order to facilitate accommodation and equilibration.

In conclusion, this proposed readability process provides teachers with a means for bonding the language and concept development of their students. Assimilation requires sensitivity to the nature of the concepts and language being read. Accommodation and equilibration require precise and appropriate definitions for common instructional verbs.

---

ability. They overcame the problem through the persistence and help of persons who cared about their reading.

17. Recall that performance improves not so much because of drill or exercises in language analysis, but rather by experience in which students receive feedback from a positive reinforcing educator.

18. Apply the learning cycle approach to reading. Children can first have *explorations* of concrete objects, then have *explanations* where words, sentences, and paragraphs are introduced. Then, children can *extend* their abilities through use of their reading skills. Finally, their achievement can be *evaluated* (see Chapter 9.)

SCIENCE AND MATHEMATICS IN THE DEVELOPMENT OF REASONING

Piaget's theory is involved with the development of logical-mathematical reasoning characteristic of the kind of thinking required in resolving scientific and mathematical problems. Many modern science and mathematical curriculums try to develop reasoning processes and use a structural approach as suggested by Piaget. It should be expected, therefore, that these curriculums would have considerable similarity in how they incorporate Piaget's active method and in the kinds of operational thinking they try to develop.

Both these disciplines develop the cognitive abilities of the child. Mathematics, to a large degree, is the language of the sciences. Through its use in activities, children gain better insights about scientific concepts and principles. Scientific activity contributes to the enhancement of logical-mathematical reasoning. Science and mathematics reinforcing each other in the learning environment facilitate better cognitive development.

Scientific activity contributes to the development of logical-mathematical reasoning.

Interrelationship of Science and Mathematics in Schools

Because science and mathematics are so integrally involved, much of the science activity on the elementary and secondary school level has mathematical implications and many mathematical problems have scientific ramifications. The National Science Teachers Association (NSTA) in their

publication, *Theory into Action in Science Curriculum Development*, emphasized the following:

> One cannot speak realistically of a sound science curriculum without considering
> the important role played by mathematics.
>
> Mathematics is the language by which one describes the order in nature and
> which in turn leads to a clearer understanding of that order. (1964, p. 3)

The relevance of mathematics to science is apparent since scientists collect data. The data they collect can be of two types, dichotomous or metrical.
The word *dichotomy* comes from the Greek word *dichotomia* which means to
divide into two parts. The word *metre* comes from the Greek word *metron*
which means to measure. If a scientist looks at an experimental situation in
a dichotomous way, she looks at it in an all or none way.

For example, if a scientist wants to determine whether light is necessary
for seeds to sprout, she may perform an all-or-none type of experiment.
She establishes two groups. One group of seeds receives light; the other
group, the control, receives no light. From the experiment, she will be able
to determine whether light is necessary for the seeds she is using to sprout.

In setting up an experiment to determine how much light is necessary,
the scientist would have to design it so that she could obtain metrical, or
measurable, data. She would have to establish an experimental situation to
determine how intense the light would have to be over varied periods of
time to get seeds to sprout. Obviously this metrical experimental situation
would be far more sophisticated than the simple dichotomous experiment,
and mathematics would be required in determining the intensity of light
and the periods of time.

Because mathematics aids in delving more deeply into understanding
natural phenomena, the metrical aspects should be encouraged as much as
possible in science activities. Dichotomous types of experiments may be
done in the primary grades or as an introductory experiment but should be
followed by open-ended questions leading to metrical experimental situations, especially in the higher grades.

Science and Mathematics Develop Reasoning

Piagetian operations are required in order for children to achieve well in
the basics. This is especially so in science and mathematics. Some of the
operations basic to sciences and mathematics are

Conservation of substance
Causality
One-to-one correspondence
Ordering
Seriating
Classification
Number

Students who do not do these well, and this includes many children ages
seven to eight, have trouble reading and solving mathematical and scientific

problems. This is so because they are still preoperational, not able to reason logically. Science and mathematics curricula involving children in performing the above operational tasks help students overcome such inadequacies.

If you look at science and mathematics curricula, particularly in the primary grades, you will discover some duplication. This is not unnecessary duplication because students on the preoperational level need many similar experiences in areas such as conservation, in order to develop their cognitive abilities. Several curricula, therefore, include Piagetian types of activities in developing operational competencies. And, these competencies are not only fundamental to these disciplines but all subjects requiring thinking. For example, Stafford and Renner (1976) have found that the Science Curriculum Improvement Study (SCIS) significantly caused gains in conservation of length, number, and other conservation abilities in first graders. Kellogg (1976) found that the Materials Objects Unit was the main contributor to this increase in operational ability. This unit contains many experiences found in primary mathematics programs.

As reported earlier, Ayers and Mason (1969) found that kindergarten children using *Science, A Process Approach* (SAPA) curriculum materials did significantly better on the Metropolitan Readiness Test on Number as well as other abilities. Mary and Jerry Ayers (1973) in a similar study done with kindergarten children in Appalachia concluded that SAPA significantly helped children develop their thinking, or operational abilities.

Because of this research and other studies as well, Mary Budd Rowe (1975) has come to the conclusion that science is especially important not only because it helps children develop mental operations but also helps develop in children a greater willingness to solve problems. The willingness to solve problems is critical for children learning science and mathematics. She, furthermore, believes this is especially important for disadvantaged children. She says:

> Without science experiences, disadvantaged children tend to be frightened and frustrated by simple problems. Their problem-coping skills simply do not develop satisfactorily. With it, they usually learn strategies for attacking problems. (p. 25)

Piaget (1973) believes the primary task of the school should be the development of reasoning. If this is so, how should the school facilitate such development? Piaget states that science and mathematics can be instrumental in achieving this objective providing teachers use the *active method* in teaching. He argues that the traditional methods of teaching mathematics are counterproductive for many students. Remember that Bloom has shown that by the third grade a sizeable number of students can already be classified as mathematics failures. This should not be the case. Piaget has said that every normal student is capable of learning mathematics providing that the instruction is experiential and moves from where the student is structurally rather than imposing an existing structure. Piaget says, "In mathematics, many failures in school are due to the excessive rapid passage from qualitative (logical) to the quantitative (numerical)" (p. 15). Students beginning to learn mathematics must first interact with objects and qualitatively develop concepts, such as more than or less than, and operations such as conservation.

Children learn most basic mathematical operations by interacting with objects in the environment prior to learning them through the use of mathematical symbols. For example, apples (a class) and oranges (another class) are fruit (a third class) is similar to saying one group plus another group equals a third group. If students are not able to group or classify in this manner, it is futile to involve them in additive mathematical symbolization.

Piaget believes that children must develop basic operations such as classification, class inclusion, and conservation before they can understand mathematical signs and symbols. To force students to use mathematical notation before they have developed the necessary fundamental operations affects their attitudes detrimentally. He says:

> Above all, they remain convinced of their inadequacy and give up beforehand, inwardly considering themselves defeated. Students who are thus reputedly poor in mathematics show an entirely different attitude when the problem comes from a concrete situation and is related to other interests. (Piaget, 1973, p. 98)

The focus of mathematics should, as much as possible, evolve from the interests of the student and the spontaneous activity of the class activities. This is typified by the British in the use of their "integrated day" or with the teaching/learning cycle approach we have suggested in Chapter 9.

Mathematics should not be taught as though it were only a question of truths available mainly through the use of abstract mathematical language. Mathematics is first of all *actions on things and the operations that are coordinated relative to them.*

Mathematical Abilities and Cognitive Stages

Children begin to become logical when they pass into the concrete operational stage. Mathematics is a logical system requiring at its very minimum logical consistency. Many adults assume because children can count that they understand the meaning of number; often children can count years before they understand the meaning of number. Piaget states that for children to know number they must be able to coordinate several operations including class inclusion and serial ordering. Of course, these operations in themselves are related to other operations as well. For example, a child must realize that things that can be classified also are conserved—that spreading them out or grouping them close together doesn't change their number or class. When counting fingers, the child has to discover that the third finger is three because it is the third in the order and follows the second and is before the fourth finger. She must also understand that three includes three objects and this number can be obtained by combining different arrangements of objects. In some way or other, all of the above operations are involved in a child's conceptualizing the meaning of number. Yet, if you refer to Table 9.5 in the preceding chapter done by Millie Almy (1971, p. 233), you will see how few second graders can do these operations.

Table 9.5 indicates that the majority of second graders have serious inadequacies with many of these operations. Information of this type seriously questions what is being done in primary school mathematics and suggests that operational insufficiency is a primary cause of many children failing to learn mathematics. This, in turn, leads to the development of a poor self-concept that may affect children's achievement in the subject the rest of their school years (Bloom, 1976).

Many teachers, however, are oblivious to this information. They have children adding and subtracting before they even know the meaning of number. What these teachers are doing is teaching children to think that mathematics is a mysterious subject; to distrust their own reasoning processes; to diminish their self-concepts; and to set the stage for math anxiety.

Piaget's theory helps the mathematics teacher to become a better diagnostician of cognitive abilities. For example, if a child can't add, a Piagetian-oriented teacher looks for the cause within patterns of reasoning or cognitive stage. She will not give the student more addition so that the student can fail or learn just by rote memory. She will search for the apparent operational insufficiencies that the student might have. For example, she might discover that the child can't order; she now understands why the child is experiencing difficulty in using number. Now she can select several options to help the child develop the ordering operation before involving him in further mathematical activities requiring addition. At the very least, her awareness of why the child is experiencing mathematical difficulties should help her perceive the student in a more positive manner.

What has just been said about primary children is likewise true for upper grades. All mathematical performance requires a certain cognitive ability level. For example, algebra, geometry, and calculus require a high degree of formal reasoning. Students studying these subjects must perform certain formal operations in the problems they resolve. When a student cannot do a problem, the Piagetian-oriented instructor attempts to diagnose whether or not this is due to a lack of cognitive development and to adjust the instruction accordingly. To do this does not make the role of the teacher easier. It does, however, help the educator become more understanding of her students.

If a student is not able to do the operations necessary to perform mathematical tasks, the teacher has two options. She can delay giving the tasks to the students until they are cognitively ready to do them, and/or she can involve students in concrete activities that are interesting to them and provide opportunities for them to perform the operations. Research indicates that to do so does help students become more operationally proficient. The teacher, however, must expect students to be involved in several experiences providing the same mental operation, such as ordering, before they become able to perform the operation. Also, she should not limit the activities to one operation but include others involving closely related operations; for example, class inclusion and conservation. Once the students achieve basic proficiency, the teacher can then involve them in activities having to do with number, addition, and subtraction with confidence that they will learn to comprehend mathematics better. The students will then experience more success causing their feelings toward mathematics to be affected positively.

Mathematics Reveals Relationships

Mathematics, in addition to its measurement uses in scientific investigation, is also used to reveal relationships. Mathematics is often used by the scientist to organize data so that meaning may be evolved from it. Look at Newton's formula for the law of gravity:

$$F = \frac{GM_1M_2}{d^2}$$

where F = force
M_1 = mass of one object
M_2 = mass of another object
d^2 = distance between the two masses (objects), squared
G = a constant, its value is 6.67×10^{-11}

What relationships can you see among the force, the mass of the objects, and the distance between objects? What will happen if the distance (d) is increased between the two objects? Substitute some simple number for d in the formula and you will see. What will happen if the mass of one of the objects is increased? Substitute simple numbers for the masses in the formula. The formula enables you to see the relationships of gravitational force to the masses of any two objects and the distance between them. Newton's formula for the law of gravity is a fantastic intellectual tool which enables you to determine the gravitational relationships of any object to any other object in the entire universe.

A student who uses her mind to devise and use formulas in this manner demonstrates a great cognitive advance over a student who just plugs things into a formula without operationally becoming involved. The mathematics or science instructor who endeavors to have students discover the interrelations of the formula as outlined above provides experiences whereby the student has opportunities to develop her reasoning abilities.

Using Mathematics in Elementary School Science Curricula

The elementary science study. Although the Elementary Science Study (ESS) has been mainly concerned with science, many of the units produced actually deal with the development of mathematical operations as well. Some of the units are Mirror Cards (Grades 1–7), Light and Shadows (Grades K–3), Attributive Games and Problems (Grades K–8), Peas and Particles (Grades 4–6), Primary Balancing (no grades listed), Changes (Grades 1–4), Optics (Grades 6–8), Pattern Blocks (Grades K–5), Balloons and Gases (Grades 6–8), Tangram (Grades K–8), Mapping (Grades 6–7), Musical Sound (Grade 6), Matrix Blocks (Grades K–8), Measuring (Grades K–3), Counting the Slide Rule (Grades 7–8). Many of these units are especially suited for exploratory activities. In this sense, the ESS program reflects a Piagetian orientation.

Science curriculum improvement study. SCIS has utilized Piagetian operations in its curriculum. Its Teacher's Handbook outlines and explains how these operations are developed in the lessons. Since the operations are basically logical and mathematical in character, they contribute to the learning of mathematical concepts. Examples of some of the selected activities from the various levels of the curriculum are outlined below:

Grades K–3—Material Objects
1. Sorting objects according to some property
2. Reversibility, mentally reversing actions
3. Serial ordering

Grades 3–6—Populations
1. Representing data by means of histograms
2. Sorting liquids according to some property
3. Graphing

Grade 4—Relative Position and Motion
1. Describing object location from various viewpoints
2. Forming correspondences between properties and variables
3. Describing locations of objects mathematically by coordinating two distances

Grade 4—Environments
1. Averaging data

Grade 5—Energy Sources
1. Graphing
2. Measuring and conserving liquids
3. Isolating variables and keeping one constant

Grade 5—Communities
1. Averaging data
2. Using proportional reasoning

Grade 6—Ecosystems

Using data relative to the cyclic movement of materials

Science—A process approach.   SAPA integrates mathematics with science particularly in three areas: *measuring, using number, and using space-time relationships.* Examples of some of the types of activities included under these sections from the primary level are listed below. It is suggested that you consult the SAPA materials for the grade you are going to teach, especially since they can be easily integrated into any science program. This is particularly true of their mathematically oriented activities since they require very simple and very few materials.

The following examples are not quoted directly from SAPA but are modified slightly to give you a more concise impression and relate them to Piaget's work.

PRIMARY LEVEL

I. Using Space-Time Relationships
   A. Recognizing and using shapes.
      1. Making triangles, circles, ellipses.

2. Making people out of triangles, circles, rectangles (the materials used can be pieces of paper or blocks of wood).
3. Identifying, when given several squares, the largest and smallest square.
4. Playing games with shapes.
5. Turning a triangle many ways and having children describe how it looks.
6. Tracing shapes on a chalkboard and naming them.

B. Using correspondence and establishing coordinate orientation.
1. Teacher making a triangle on the floor and one on the chalkboard.

C. Using number (one-to-one correspondence).
1. Matching a row of either real, plastic, or paper drawings of saucers and cups.
2. Pairing children.
3. Asking children if they can think of things that can be paired.
4. Placing several blocks and toy cars on a table and asking the children how they would find out whether there are more cars than blocks.

D. Ordering
1. Placing three shoe boxes filled with lollipops on a table and asking the children how they can tell which has the most and least in it.
2. Introducing several sets and asking the children to compare and order the sets from the least to the most.

Note that the above activities follow Piaget's ideas relative to the cognitive ability of children. They are designed for individuals in transition to or in the lower levels of concrete operational ability. They strive to facilitate the development of cognitive operations which are mathematical in character. You are strongly urged to look at other activities for the grade level you will teach and determine the cognitive processes involved.

Secondary School Science

Research indicates secondary school science courses can cause a significant increase in formal operational reasoning providing they are inquiry oriented (Lawson and Renner, 1975). Unfortunately, recent research indicates that many secondary science teachers do not understand the nature of inquiry and they do not apply what they do understand. They focus on content rather than inquiry or reasoning processes and thereby defeat the purpose of the curriculum. These teachers are really teaching the history of science rather than the nature of science (DeRose, Lockard, and Paldy, 1979).

Some secondary science courses are more facilitative of formal reasoning than others. This is, in part, due to the nature of the cognitive level of the concepts they teach. Some courses may have far more concrete operational level concepts compared with others. For example, general science and green version BSCS (Biological Science Curriculum Study) are more concrete than blue version BSCS biology is (Lawson and Nordland, 1977).[1]

---

1. Green version BSCS is an ecological approach to biology, while blue version BSCS is a biochemical approach.

Richard Moyer and R. Lloyd Brown (1978) found that success in meteorology and geology in high school was a function of "formal operational thought development."

John Renner and Rosalie M. Grant (1978) analyzed six physics textbooks: *Investigations in Physics,* Lyons and Carnahan, *Modern Physics,* Holt, Rinehart & Winston, *Physics*, Physical Science Study Committee, D. C. Heath and Co., *Physics*, Silver Burdett, *Project Physics*, Holt, Rinehart & Winston, *The World of Physics*, Addison Wesley Publishing Co., for their operational level.

They found that the content in these texts could be divided into major and minor concepts. Generally each chapter of the texts focused on some major concept and the minor ones were used to develop an understanding of these. The texts contained 130 major concepts all of which were formal, and many, but not all, of the minor concepts were also formal. Obviously a student who is not formal or in transition to being formal would experience considerable difficulty using these texts and related curriculum materials. Physics courses that endeavor to facilitate cognitive development of non-formal students by using concrete experiences have significantly increased their enrollments.

Mathematics Teaching and the Active Method

Mathematics instruction should be done through the use of the *active* method. Of course, how students are involved in the method may vary considerably from preschool to college. It is essential for young children to be involved in performing actions on physical objects. This is not as necessary with formal operational individuals who have had extensive experiences with objects. They need to be involved in reflexive thinking where they reflect on what they have done in resolving problems. They also need "counterexamples" that make them reconsider their solutions. Clearly the emphases, as pointed out by Polya (1963), should be in having them work at the nature of the operations they need to resolve a problem; for example, identifying the nature of a problem, its knowns and unknowns and then the kinds of operations needed to determine from the known what the unknown is. The emphases for students in transition to formal and those who are formal should be involvement in the utilization of formal reasoning processes and awareness of how they are using them. Piaget urges that teachers cease being lecturers. They should be guides in stimulating student initiative in doing what for them would be mathematical research (Piaget, 1973).

Many mathematics texts and curriculum programs have used Piaget's work, to some degree, as a base for constructing their materials. Examples of activities that have been developed at the elementary level for activity-centered instruction are as follows:

Multibase arithmetic blocks
Cuisinaire rods
Tangrams
Geoboards

Many diverse mathematical games
Attribute games (these are used both in science and math)

Materials such as these must be used to involve students in performing operations facilitative of cognitive development. Piaget (1973) has particularly spoken out against instruction where cuisinaire rods have been used to learn the facts (figurative) instead of operational activity.

Mathematics Programs

The Zoltan P. Dienes Mathematical Approach.   Zoltan Dienes, professor of education at Branden University, Manitoba, Canada, has developed a multibase arithmetic blocks program that translates Piaget's ideas of how children learn mathematics. Dr. Dienes did not study under Piaget, but his preparation led him to similar conclusions. He received his Ph. D. in mathematics from the University of London in 1939. Later he enrolled at Harvard Center for Cognitive Studies where he worked under Jerome Bruner and received a B.S. in psychology in 1961. His interest in receiving a background in psychology was motivated by the question: "Why do most people find mathematics difficult?" He wondered whether the mathematics foundations young children receive might have something to do with it. As a result for more than twenty years he has studied the problem. He has devised several concrete learning materials including multibase blocks, logic blocks, trimath, quadrimath, and logic. He says of his approach:

> It appeared to me to follow that if a more constructive approach to children's training and thinking were adopted, we should have much greater success in mathematical achievement. I tried in a small way to reorganize mathematical work in some classrooms turning the classrooms into laboratories of discovery and construction using specially designed materials which later developed into the now well-known multi-base and algebraic materials. (Dienes, 1978, p. 4)

In 1962 Dienes founded the International Study Group for Mathematics Learning (ISGML) which has centers in Europe, South America, and the South Pacific all of which are doing research and developing programs related to this methodology. This group publishes the *Journal of Structural Learning* reporting on its research and activities.

Dienes has published numerous articles, books, and films related to his approach. Some of Diene's publications are: *Mathematics in the Primary School* (1964), *Approach to Modern Mathematics* (1967), *Introducing the Elements of Mathematics* (1969), *The Arithmetic and Algebra of Natural Numbers* (1965) (Manual of instructions for use with the multibase arithmetic blocks and the algebraical experience materials), and *Geometry Through Transformations* (1967), which was written with the collaboration of E. W. Golding.

The Dienes approach essentially translates what Piaget calls the active method and is similar in design to the teaching/learning cycle suggested in this text. Dienes believes, as does Piaget, that children must first learn mathematics through acting on objects. These objects may be placed in the learning environment by the instructor. As students interact with them, they slowly discover some of their properties and begin to discover regularities. For example, things can be ordered. By doing so, students construct abstract concepts; after constructing such concepts, they are more likely to be ready for reading and to use graphics and later symbols such as numbers to represent what they have discovered.

Dienes is presently working on an Italian reading series that is "full of mathematics, logic, even some moral problems, as well as language" (Dienes, 1979).

Copeland's Text for Teachers.   Professor Richard Copeland has written a text (1974a) for preparing elementary and middle school teachers to use Piagetian theory in the teaching of mathematics. The text gives specific suggestions of activities to use and how to sequence them relative to the cognitive level of the students. He covers such topics as classification, learning number, addition and subtraction, multiplication and division, fractions and proportions, time, moving from topology to Euclidean geometry; structuring space in terms of vertical and horizontal axes, measurement in two and three dimensions, and projective geometry, plus several others. In each section he spells out the developmental sequence of how concepts in the area occur. This is helpful because if a student is experiencing a problem the instructor can interact with the student and determine where he is experiencing operational difficulty.

Copeland's procedures and methods are a compilation of the work of Piaget that is found in several different publications. Copeland has brought them together so that they are easily accessible and helpful for teachers. He has also produced a companion booklet entitled *Diagnostic and Learning Activities in Mathematics for Children* (Copeland, 1974b).

The British Nuffield Mathematics and Science, 5/13 Projects.   A group of British mathematicians during the 1960s decided to revise mathematical instruction so that it more appropriately integrated what was known about how children develop and learn. The Nuffield Foundation funded them. They produced, as a result, the Nuffield Mathematics 5/13 Project. The 5/13 refers to the children's ages for which the program has been designed. Basically this program follows a Piagetian approach since children are first involved in concrete experiences before abstract concepts are developed. The general design of instruction follows to a high degree the "learning cycle" discovery format mentioned in this text. This program was followed by the Nuffield Science 5/13 Project which has similar Piagetian philosophy and organization but is for science students ages five to thirteen. In the primary and lower elementary grades there is considerable overlap between the math program and Science 5/13 since they both are attempting to develop similar Piagetian operations.

Summary

Reading is a complex human ability involving perception, the interpretation of signs and symbols, and mental structures. Several operations are involved in the reading process. These include seriation, one-to-one correspondence, ordering, spatial relations, temporal relations, classification, conservation, transitivity, and numbers. As these operations develop, reading ability likewise improves. Reading ability correlates with cognitive level. Certain operations, such as conservation and class inclusion, are thought to be more critical than others in facilitating reading.

Because many children do not develop the operations mentioned above early in the primary grades, many Piagetian scholars believe that emphasizing reading for these children should be delayed at least until age eight. Doing so will positively affect these students' feelings about reading, school, and their self-concept. The present reading emphasis before age eight tends to focus on rote memorization, which is detrimental to the development of reasoning and operational development.

Teachers need to evaluate reading materials for their operational level and determine whether they are appropriate for their students. Research indicates that when teachers focus their instruction on the development of operational abilities such as conservation, reading improves.

Reading should be taught through the use of the active method where students' spontaneous interests are used as the basis for language arts. An example of an application of Piagetian theory is to ask each child a word or words he would like to write. Some other suggestions for developing reading are as follows: (1) Have students express their reading goals; (2) group children of differing levels together to read the same thing; (3) develop listening abilities; (4) use socialization processes in reading by discussion and sharing; (5) have students read and edit each other's work; (6) invite students to combine their papers; (7) have students reflect on what they read; (8) apply the learning cycle to reading instruction.

Science and mathematics are closely related. Mathematics in many ways is the language of science, and science experiences contribute significantly to learning cognitive operations required in mathematics. This is so because most basic mathematics operations are learned by children through interacting with objects prior to their understanding of mathematical symbols. Piaget has stated that mathematics in essence really is the process of performing actions on things and the operations that are correlated relative to them. He further points out that students' mathematical conceptualizations are at first qualitative (e.g., this is greater than that). When students have an understanding on this level, they are then ready for metrical analyses.

Some of the basic operations that science develops for children in learning mathematics are conservation of length, number, substance, one-to-one correspondence, ordering, seriation, and classification.

All mathematics requires students to perform at a certain cognitive level. If children are unable to add, for example, this may be due to the fact that they can't order or perform one or more of the operations outlined above.

Mathematics and science both involve students in problem solving. This activity offers excellent opportunities for students to use and develop operations. Mathematics also is demanded for objectivity in science and helps students understand better the relationships of phenomena.

Several Piaget-oriented science and mathematics curricula and teacher training materials have been prepared to help facilitate the development of cognitive abilities of children. There is evidence that if these are used they can be effective in facilitating cognitive development. It is essential, in Piaget's view, however, that such curricula must involve the active method if they are to be effective in facilitating cognitive growth.

REFERENCES

Almy, Millie. "Longitudinal Studies Related to the Classroom." In *Piagetian Cognitive-Development Research and Mathematical Education*, edited by Myron F. Rosskipt et al. Washington, D. C.: National Council of Teachers of Mathematics, 1971.

Almy, Millie; Chittenden, Edward; and Miller, Paula. *Young Children's Thinking: Studies of Some Aspects of Piaget's Theory.* New York: Teachers College Press, Columbia University, 1966.

Ayers, Jerry, and Mason, George E. "Different Effects of Science—A Process Approach upon Change in Metropolitan Readiness Test Scores among Kindergarten Children." *The Reading Teacher* (February 1975): 23–25.

Ayers, Mary, and Ayers, Jerry B. "Influence of SAPA on Kindergarten Children's Use of Logic in Problem Solving." *School Science and Mathematics* 73 (December 1973): 768-71.

Bloom, Benjamin. *Human Characteristics and School Learning.* New York: McGraw-Hill, 1976.

Copeland, Richard W. *How Children Learn Mathematics.* New York: Macmillan, 1974*a*.

Copeland, Richard W. *Diagnostic and Learning Activities in Mathematics for Children.* New York: Macmillan, 1974*b*.

Department of Education and Science. "Children and Their Primary Schools." A report of the Central Advisory Council of Education (England), Vol. I, Her Majesty's Stationery Office, London, England, 1967, p. 197. (This is sometimes referred to as the Plowden Report after Lady Plowden who chaired the Council.)

DeRose, James V.; Lockard, J. David; and Paldy, Lester G. "The Teacher Is the Key: A Report on Three NSF Studies." *The Science Teacher* 46 (April 1979): 31–37.

Dienes, Zoltan P. *Mathematics in the Primary School.* New York: Macmillan, 1964.

————. *Approach to Modern Mathematics.* New York: McGraw-Hill, 1967.

————. *The Arithmetic and Algebra of Natural Numbers.* New York: Educational Supply Association, 1965.

————. *Biographical Notes, Historical and Professional Information.* Manitoba, Canada: International Study Group of Mathematics, Brandon University, 1978.

————. *Introducing the Elements of Mathematics.* New York: McGraw-Hill, 1969.

————. Personal correspondence dated May 13, 1979 to Robert B. Sund. This program for grades 1 and 2 may be obtained from Giunti,Via Vicenzo Gioberti 34, 50121 Firenze, Italy.

Dienes, Zoltan P., and Golding, E. W. *Geometry through Transformations.* New York: Educational Supply Association, 1967.

Elkind, David. "Piaget in Childhood Education, Applications for Teachers and Teaching." (Audio tape). Hollywood, Calif.: Listener Educational Enterprises, 1975.

Furth, Hans. *Piaget for Teachers.* Englewood Cliffs, N.J.: Prentice-Hall, 1970.

Hock, Raymond. "Does Early Teaching of Reading Unbalance Brain Hemispheres?" *Phi Delta Kappan* 8 (January 1977): 444.

Kellog, Donald. "Experience, Conservation Reasoning, and Reading Readiness." In *Research, Teaching and Learning with the Piaget Model*, edited by J. Renner et al. Norman: University of Oklahoma Press, 1976.

Lawson, Anton E., and Norland, Floyd H. "Conservation and Reasoning Ability and Performance on BSCS, Blue Version Examinations." *Journal of Research in Science Teaching* 14 (1977): 69–75.

Lawson, Anton E., and Renner, John W. "Piagetian Theory and Biology Teaching." *The American Biology Teacher* 37 (September 1975): 336–42.

The Metropolitan Reading Readiness Test. New York: Harcourt Brace Jovanovich, 1962.

Moyer, Richard H., and Brown, R. Lloyd. "A Study of Piagetian Concrete and Formal Reasoning and Success in High School Geology and Meteorology." *Colorado Journal of Educational Research* 18 (Fall 1978): 17–18.

Murray, Frank B., and Pikulski, John J. *The Acquisition of Reading, Cognitive Linquistic and Perceptual Prerequisites.* Baltimore, Md.: University Park Press, 1975.

National Science Teachers Association, Curriculum Committee. *Theory into Action in Science Curriculum Development.* Washington, D.C.: National Science Teachers Association, 1964.

Nuffield Mathematics 5/13 Material. New York: John Wiley & Sons,

Nuffield Science 5/13 Project. New York: John Wiley & Sons,

Piaget, Jean. *To Understand Is to Invent.* New York: Grossman Press, 1973.

Polk, Cindy L. Howes, and Goldstein, David. "Early Reading and Concrete Operations." *The Genetic Epistemologist* 8 (April 1979): 8.

Polya, Gregory, "On Learning, Teaching, and Learning Teaching." *Mathematical Monthly* (June–July 1963): 611.

Renner, John W., and Grant, Rosalie. "Can Students Grasp Physics Concepts? *The Science Teacher* (October 1978): 30–33.

Rowe, Mary Budd. "Science Silence and Sanctions." *Science and Children* 6 (March 1969): 11–13.

————. "Help Is Denied to Those in Need." *Science and Children* 12 (March 1975): 23–25.

Sinclair, Hermina de Zwart. "Intellectual Development, Research and Education: Excerpts from a Seminar." The Teachers Center Project, Southern Illinois University, Edwardsville, October 10–12, 1977.

Szent-Gyorgi, Albert. "Teaching and the Expanding Knowledge. *Science* 46 (December 4, 1964): 1278–79.

Stafford, Donald G., and Renner, John W. "Development of Conservation Reasoning through Experience." In *Research, Teaching, and Learning with the Piaget Model*, edited by J. Renner et al. Norman: University of Oklahoma Press, 1976.

Thorndike, R. L. *Reading Comprehension Education in Fifteen Countries: An Empirical Study.* New York: John Wiley & Sons, 1973.

Wadsworth, Barry J. *Piaget for the Classroom Teachers.* New York: Longman, 1978.

Wohlwill, Joachim F. "The Case of the Prelogical Child." *Psychology Today* (1967): 25.

11 Extending Piaget's Theory: Activities

As educators come to understand Piaget's theory, they naturally seek applications of the theory for classroom practice. This chapter contains activities that are designed for use by classroom teachers. The tasks are not designed as diagnostic tasks; these have been provided within earlier chapters. The activities are designed to involve students in learning activities that will facilitate development.

The activities are arranged within sections for preschool, primary, intermediate and middle/junior high levels. We suggest that you review the activities to see if they are appropriate for your classrooms. By now you should be aware of the fact that children's developmental levels are only *generally* aligned with ages and grade levels.

ACTIVITIES FOR PRESCHOOL

ACTIVITIES WITH SIMPLE OBJECTS AND MATERIALS

Spools

Materials   Spools of all sizes, balls of various sizes, strings, rubber bands of various thickness.

Opening Questions   "What kind of game could you play with these materials?"
"What other things could you do with the spools?"

Have a spool race by pushing small and large spools to see which will roll the farthest. Arrange the spools in different ways and roll balls against them to see how they scatter. See who can make the highest stack of spools before they fall. Make a spool necklace. Paint the spools different colors, tie string around them, and swing them. Drop the spools and see how they fly related to how they are released. Make a spool wall; that is, line the spools up. Drop them in an aquarium or gallon jar filled with water and see how deep they drop in the water.

Some Possible Activities

Balls

Balls of different sizes, including ping pong balls, golf balls, tennis balls, and larger ones; straws, boards to make inclined planes.

Materials

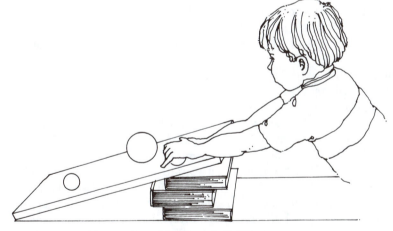

"What things could you do with these balls?"

Opening Questions

Find out which ball rolls the easiest across the floor. What happens to the balls when they are kicked? Which ones will roll down an inclined plane the farthest? Find out which balls balance best. Throw the balls against a wall at different angles and find out how they bounce off the wall (e.g., how should they throw the ball so it will come back to them?). Float the balls in water and find out which float and which do not. Also notice how deep they sink in the water. Line the balls up in a line and then roll a ball down an inclined plane so it hits the end of the line. Then roll two balls down the

Some Possible Activities

plane, so they hit the line one after another. Place all but one of the balls in a close group, roll the single ball into the group and see how the balls scatter. Play croquet with different balls. Play roll and hit the person with a ball. Construct a tetherball.

Marbles

Materials   Marbles of different sizes, inclined plane, two boards or two meter sticks.

Opening Question   "What can you do with these marbles?"

Some Possible Activities   The children can do any of the above activities suggested for balls. Place a board on top of the marbles and move them around. Transport something on the boards this way across a room. Place two boards parallel to each other. Leave enough distance for the marbles to move between them. Place marbles in the row between the two boards. Shoot other marbles so they hit one end of the row. Invite students to suggest some marble games.

Roller Skates

Materials   Board to put on top of a skate, boards to make inclined planes, oil can, newspaper, several objects of different weights.

Opening Question   "What can you find out about skates?"
"What kind of skate race could we have?"
"How many bricks or cans with rocks could you move with skates?"

Some Possible Activities   Invite the children to find out how far a skate will go when it is rolled down an inclined plane. Have a contest where they see how many cans or bricks they can move across the room without one falling off. Invite them to place a board on a skate and see how they can balance it so that the skate will be able to carry a lot of material. Have the children go outside and find out on what surface the skate moves the best and the worst. Have them play hit the skate, where one child pushes a skate out in a circle and the other children try to hit it with their skates. Invite students to turn their skates upside-down and slide boards and other objects over the wheels. They should also spin the wheels to find out how they move. Give the children a skate whose wheels do not move very well and ask them what they could do to get the skates to move better. Later give them a juice can and some paper and ask them what they could do with them.

Blocks

Materials   Blocks of different sizes.

Opening Question   "What can you build with these blocks?"

The children can build towers, bridges, or enclosures for animals. Sort blocks on the basis of shape or color.

Some
Possible
Activities

Wheels and Things That Roll

Small round wheels, buttons, toy cars, small round rocks, oranges, apples, thimbles, boards to make inclined planes, milk bottle caps, thumbtacks, and matchboxes.

Materials

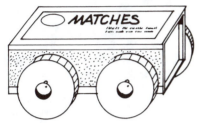
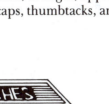

"What can you do with these things?"
"What kind of game could you play?"
"How could you make a toy car using the matchboxes and other things?"
"Which of the things that you see are wheels? Which are not wheels?"
"How are wheels different from the other things?"

**Opening
Questions**

The children could try seeing how far different things would roll on the floor or down an inclined plane. They can also make toy cars from the matchboxes, using the bottle caps or buttons tacked to the side for wheels. Children may also be invited to make toy cars out of a small square board; axles could be made from clothes hangers. The axles are nailed to the board and bent at the ends after the button or bottle cap wheels are attached.

**Some
Possible
Activities**

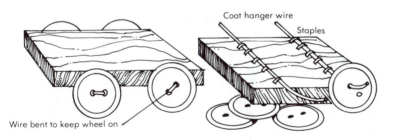

Coat hanger wire
Staples
Wire bent to keep wheel on

ACTIVITIES USING COLOR

Name the Color

Several different colored objects.

Materials

"What do you notice about these objects?"
"What colors are these objects?"

**Opening
Questions**

Give children several objects with different colors, and ask them to identify and learn the names of their colors. After they do this, have them find and name things in the room that are of the same colors.

**Some
Possible
Activities**

Group by Color

Materials   Several different colored objects.

Opening Questions "How could you group these things?"

Some Possible Activities Give children several objects and ask them to group them by color. Ask them to find other objects in the room that they could place in the same groups.

Group by Color and Shape

Materials   Several different colored objects of different sizes having different shapes. For example, red, yellow, green squares, circles, and rectangles.

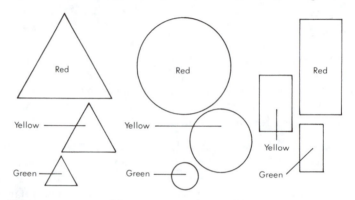

Opening Questions "What different ways could you group these objects?"

Some Possible Activities Give the children several different objects that vary in color and shape. Ask children to group together those that are of the same color and shape.

ACTIVITIES TO MAKE FOOD

Making different types of foods helps children see how things can be changed. This activity also develops in children a better understanding of how their *actions* can cause an effect.

The children should prepare and mix the ingredients as much as possible. Make a series of diagrams to illustrate the steps they need to follow in preparing the foods. For example, one for popcorn is shown below:

Make Popcorn

Materials   Popcorn, pan with a cover, cooking oil, and a heat source.

Opening Question   "How can we make popcorn?"

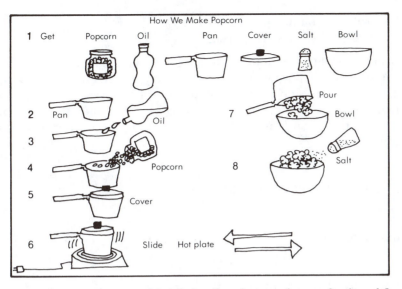

How We Make Popcorn

1 Get   Popcorn   Oil   Pan   Cover   Salt   Bowl

2 Pan   Oil   7   Pour
                                                                    Bowl

3   Oil

4   Popcorn   8   Salt

5   Cover

6   Slide   Hot plate

Place the popcorn in a pan with a little oil and move the pan back and forth over the heat source. Invite children to listen for evidence that the corn is popping. Ask them when they think the popcorn is done and ask them how the popcorn has changed. Have children draw how the popcorn changed. **Possible Activities**

Make Bread

Things needed to make bread. See a recipe book for directions. **Materials**

"How can we make bread?" **Opening Question**

Make bread. Cook some for different lengths of time. Invite children to compare the different effects. **Possible Activities**

Make Ice Cream

See a cookbook (e.g., *Better Homes and Gardens*) on how to do this. **Materials**

"What is your favorite food?"
"How many of you like ice cream?"
"How could we make ice cream?" **Opening Questions**

Invite the children to make different kinds of ice cream. They should mix the different ingredients together and note the different things they add. You might give them nuts, pieces of candy, coconut, dried fruit, chocolate, carmel, etc., that they could add as they wish. **Some Possible Activities**

Make Popsicles

Fruit juices, straws or popsicle sticks to stick in the ice trays. **Materials**

Opening Questions	"How many of you like popsicles?" "How could we make some popsicles?"
Some Possible Activities	Provide the children with the different juices and tell them they can make them any way they want. Invite them to try to make different possible shapes and colors, and to add small pieces of fruit (e.g., pineapple if they would like to try it). Let some of the popsicles melt and ask the children what they think will happen if the melted popsicles are put back in the freezer again.

ACTIVITIES FOR PRIMARY GRADES

Class Inclusion

Materials	Show several pictures of plants and animals.
Opening Questions	"How many plants are there?" "How many animals are there?" "Are there more animals than plants?" "Are there more living things than animals?"
Materials	Invite students to collect pictures of animals that move fast and slow. For example, a fly or rabbit and a turtle or a snail. Try to get more examples of fast animals than slow ones. Place the pictures of the fast and slow ones on the bulletin board.
Opening Questions	"What are all the pictures of?" "How many slow animals are there?" "Are there more fast animals than animals?"
Discussion	Class inclusion is a very important cognitive ability. It is a good indicator that a student is developing representational thought which is so essential in using symbols such as letters of the alphabet. A child who has difficulty with class inclusion probably will have problems with reading.

Draw the Hidden Object

Materials	A paper bag and several different shaped objects (e.g., a cube of sugar, a button, a matchbox, a triangular piece of cardboard).

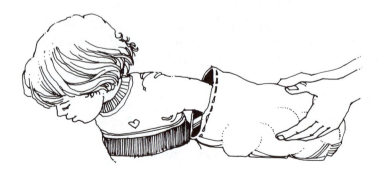

"How well can you tell what is in the bag without looking at it?"   Opening Question

Have students put their hands in a bag and feel the different objects. They should then say what they think the objects are and draw them. After they have done this, they should place their hand back in the bag to select and pull the objects out to see if they were right.   Some Possible Activities

Tying Knots

String, rope, and buckets filled with objects.   Materials

"What kind of knots can you make?"
"Who can draw a knot with string?"
"Who can draw a knot with rope?"
"Who can copy a picture of this knot?"   Opening Questions

Which of these would make a knot?"

"Which knot in this picture is a false knot?"

"Which knot is a tight knot?"
"Which knot is a loose one? Why do you think so?"
"How could you find out?"

Invite children to tie different kinds of single knots and to show you how they made them. Have them tie a rope to a bucket and lift things over a bar that serves as a beam, or use a single pulley. Ask them to draw pictures of the knots they made. Have them look for knots in their classroom and school. Students who have trouble making knots may also be invited to make tracings of single knots.   Some Possible Activities

Animals

The next three activities are designed to introduce children to differences among animals, plants, and the environment.

1. Draw animal faces
These pictures should show how animals look when they are mad, when they are happy, and when they are hungry.

2. Draw a Baby Giraffe
Have children draw a baby giraffe and then measure the neck and legs.

Have them look at a picture of a giraffe. Ask, "How well did you draw the legs?" "How well did you draw the neck?" "What do giraffes eat?"

3. Paste Pictures of Pets

Make a pet chart like the one below:

PETS

Cats	Dogs	Other Pets

Have children place different pictures of pets on the chart.

4. Invent Your Own Animal

Have the children invent their own animal and make a name that describes it.

5. Make an Animal Calendar

Have the children paste a picture and the name of an animal on a calendar for each day. The children should suggest the animal to be placed on it. Each child should have a chance to draw one for a day on the calendar.

6. Make a Bird Mobile

Invite the children to draw or make some paper birds and hang them from a mobile.

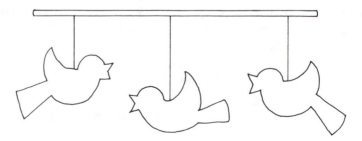

Plants

1. Feel a Tree

Have children hug a tree trunk, feel its surface, describe how it feels, smell the bark. Have the children draw and give a name for their favorite tree.

2. Press Plants

Invite children to collect parts of plants (e.g., leaves and flowers). Have them press them between newspapers. Place some books or something heavy on the newspapers. After several days, remove the weights and newspaper. Discuss how drying helps to preserve the plants and food.

Maps

1. Make a Map

Have the children make a map of their classroom, school, or community. Invite the students to identify important places on the map.

2. Make a Pollution Map

Have children draw on a map the places around their school or community where there is pollution. Use concrete examples (e.g., waste paper, garbage, places where there is a lot of people smoking, etc.).

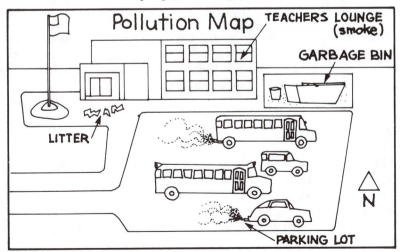

3. Make a Three-Dimensional Map
Invite children to make a three-dimensional map showing lakes, mountains, forests, fields, rivers, towns, etc.

4. Place Animals and Plants on a Map
Invite the children to take a walk around the school, community, or a zoo. Have them make a map and draw on it where they saw different animals and plants.

5. Make a Plant Map
Have children draw and learn the names of different plants that grow around the school.

One-to-One Correspondence

Materials   Obtain five bottle caps, five buttons, and five straws, or any other types of markers that you wish to use for example coins. Have the students line up the buttons in a row and then do the same thing with the bottle caps directly across the buttons.

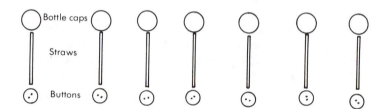

Opening Questions   "Are there more, less, or the same amount of buttons as bottle caps?" Then, move the buttons so that they are spread out but do not move the buttons. "Are there now more, less, or the same amount of buttons as bottle caps?" "Why?"

If the children think there are more buttons than bottle caps, *ask:* "Please count them. Now what do you think?"
If they still do not realize that each button corresponds with each bottle cap, have them connect each pair by placing a straw between them. Then *ask:* "Are there more, less or the same amount of buttons as bottle caps now?"

Discussion   If students still do not conceptualize one-to-one correspondence, just smile and have them place the materials in a box to be collected. Repeat this activity several times using different markers until children do conceptualize one-to-one correspondence.

Ordering

The students are to be able to place objects in order. Give ten cards with different size animals on them to children. Each drawing of the animal should increase in size over the previous one. Tell the children to place the animals in order, starting with the smallest. Tell them to number the animals in order. Have the children check their answers with each other. Note if they seem to order mainly by trial and error or have some organized procedure for doing this. If the students do this well, you may want to give them four more pictures that fit in between these pictures. Have them place the new pictures where they think they belong. If they do this well, they probably are able to order relatively well.

Associativity

The student is to realize that it doesn't matter how you arrange things. The number or area will remain the same.

1. Place ten counters, blocks, or buttons in a straight line and have students count them. Then move the counters to form a circle. **Materials**

"Are there more, less, or the same number of counters now as when they were in a straight line?" **Opening Questions**
"How would you prove you are right?"

Note this activity is also related to conservation of substance and number, but here you are trying to find out if students know that reorganizing the counters doesn't change their number. **Discussion**

2. Invite students to count counters in two directions (e.g., from left to right and then right to left) to see if they get the same number. Have them count two groups of objects (e.g., one group containing three and another group containing two) and then count all of them to see what number they get. Then have them count first the group of two objects and then the group of three objects to see what they get.

If they have associativity they will realize that three and two equals five and that two and three equals five objects. **Discussion**

Kites

Plastic such as that used by dry cleaners and paper to cover the kite, small pieces of wood to form the supports, string, transparent tape or glue, cloth for the tail. **Materials**

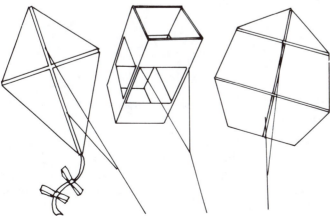

Opening Questions
"How can we make some kites?"
"What will we need?"
"How should they be constructed?"
"What shape should they be?"

Some Possible Activities
Encourage the children to plan in small groups how they are going to make their kites. Then they should construct them. After they have done this, you might bring in some books on kites. Discuss the role of the tail and how it helps to stabilize the kite. Have them experiment with how long the tail should be by flying their kites on windy and calm days. If there is a local kite store, invite the children to visit it. Discuss some of the dangers of flying kites near power lines. Point out that they should *never use thin wire instead of string to fly a kite because of the danger involved if it hits a power line.* Invite them to make several kinds of kites and find out how different cultures use them. For example, the Japanese use kites to celebrate certain holidays.

Who Can Lift the Most with a Tongue Depressor?

Materials
Tongue depressor, rice or other small seeds, small paper cups.

Opening Question
"Who can lift the most seeds with a tongue depressor?"

Some Possible Activities
Have the students compete in using their tongue depressors to see who can lift the most number of seeds and place them in containers. Later they might be invited to modify their depressors so as to lift more seeds.

Making Soap Bubbles

Materials
Water, wire, liquid soap, and a container. To make soapy water, use five to ten squirts of liquid soap in it.

Opening Question
"What does the shape of the loop on the wire, have to do with the kind of bubbles you make?"

Some Possible Activities
Encourage students to make all kinds of different shaped loops with the wire. Have them try to find what kind of loop makes the largest bubbles, the smallest. They should also determine the best mixture for making soapy bubbles. Try to see that they control the variable (e.g., the amount of soap used when experimenting).

Activities for Intermediate Grades

Conservation of Length

1. Draw the following pictures of the snakes.   **Materials**

"What do you notice about the lengths of the snakes on the left?"   **Opening**
"Comparing the two snakes on the right, is the coiled snake longer, shorter,   **Questions**
or the same length as the other snake?"

2. Take a rope and lay it out flat. Then curl it. Then lay it flat again.

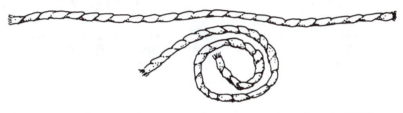

"Is the rope now longer, shorter, or the same as when I curled it?"   **Opening**
                                                                       Question

You might invite students to measure the rope's length. Even if they mea-   **Discussion**
sure it, they will not conserve length and will still think the curled rope
is shorter.

Conservation of Length

Show the students two strips of paper.   **Materials**

"Are these strips the same length?"   **Opening**
Cut one of the strips into two pieces and combine the pieces so as not to   **Questions**
make a straight line as indicated above. Tell the students that you have a
rabbit that is going to move along the two paper paths.
"Would the rabbit make just as many hops on each path or would it make
more or less hops on one of the paths?"
"Why do you think so?"

If the child thinks the uncut paper is longer, then he isn't conserving length
and will have difficulty understanding units and measurement.

Materials   **Conservation of Area**

Cut two pieces of paper into rectangles. Ask, "Do these two pieces of paper cover the same amount of table?" Cut one piece of paper diagonally as shown in B and arrange each resulting triangle as shown in C.

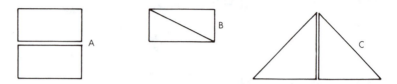

Opening   "Do the cut pieces of paper in C cover as much area as the paper in A?"
Questions   "Why do you think your answer is correct?"
"How could you prove your answer is right?"

Discussion If the students suggest that C covers as much area as A, this is an indication that they can conserve area. They should then suggest that if the two pieces of paper were combined together as in A, then C would be the same as A. This indicates that they are capable of *reversing* and establishing *logical necessity*. This means that they reason as follows: since nothing has been taken away, the paper covers as much. Reversibility and logical necessity are intrinsically involved in conservation tasks.

Ascending a Class Hierarchy

Materials   Prepare ten pictures of animals. Include some birds, fish, and mammals.

Opening   "Please group these any way you want."
Questions   "How did you group them? Why did you group them that way?"
"Which of these groups were fish?"
"Which of these groups were birds?"
"Which of these groups were mammals?"
"Is there some way we can place all of these in one group?"
"What would the group be? Why?"
"Are birds animals?"
"Are fish animals?"
"Are mammals animals?"

Discussion If children realize on their own that all these groups are animals, and that the subgroups of birds, fish, and mammals can be grouped under animals, they are able to ascend a classification hierarchy.

Make a Hot Air Balloon

Different sizes of plastic bags, small candle string, scissors, a small light **Materials**
paper or cardboard box to hold the candle in, and transparent tape.

Plastic bag

String

Candle

Box

"How can you make a hot air balloon from these materials?"   **Opening Question**

Suggest that students consider carefully how the weight of the box will **Some**
affect how the balloon works. When students make their own balloon out **Possible**
of plastic, they can wrap the ends of the plastic around a ring. **Activities**

Ring

Water Drops

Waxed paper, paper towel, napkins, typing paper, plastic wrap, eye drop- **Materials**
per, and food coloring.

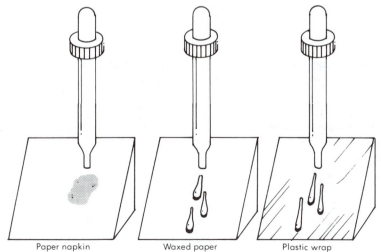

Paper napkin   Waxed paper   Plastic wrap

Opening Questions

"What will happen when you drop droplets of water on these different kinds of paper and plastic?"
"How would you find out?"
"What paper will hold the water the best?"
"What paper or plastic will water run off the easiest?"

Some Possible Activities

Have the students find which paper and plastic absorbs the water the best and the least. Have them play water droplet chase. Use red food coloring to make some drops red and blue coloring to make some blue drops. Drop the water into separate drops distant from each other on wax paper or plastic wrap. Place one red drop and several blue drops on the paper. Invite the students to capture all the blue drops, one at a time, with the red drops. Have the students make slides of the same lengths and inclination that the drops can go down. They can vary the material they use for the slide. Two students should compete with each other to see which slides the drops will move down the fastest.

Paper Airplanes

Materials

Different kinds of paper (e.g., typing, construction paper, poster board, plastic backed paper, etc.).

Opening Questions

"How can you make a paper airplane out of these materials?"
"Which kind of paper will make the best airplane?"
"What would an airplane have to do to be good?"

After the students have made their airplanes, *ask:*
"How do you feel about your airplanes?"
Suggest that they try to make an even better airplane.

"If someone is having trouble with their airplanes, would you please help them?"
Discuss some things they might try to make their airplanes fly farther. Later *ask:*
"What have you discovered about your plane? What seems to affect how the plane flies?"

Some Possible Activities

Invite students to set a distance goal and try to reach it by modifying their planes or making new ones until they reach it. Discuss how the size of the wings, shape of the nose, and the tail affect how the plane flies. Have them time how long their plane stays up and determine what they can do to increase the time.

Observe some birds or films of them and discuss how they differ—which ones soar the best and why.

Invite them to see how good their spatial relations are by having each student sail his plane, one at a time. Another student will see if he can hit it in midair with his plane. After this discuss what can be done to prevent air collisions.

Ask the following questions: "What can you learn from birds that might help you make better airplanes? What factors seem to affect how your airplane flies? How do you think your airplanes would fly with the wind or against the wind? Why? What could you do to find out? What could we do to make our planes more attractive? How could we display them?"

Invite students to make gliders and test how they fly.

Constructing a Set Containing a Single Element

Show six triangles. Let the triangles be all red or green, with one of them yellow. On the back of the yellow one, make an *x*. Show the children both sides of the triangles. Then place all the triangles color side up with no markings.

Materials

"Which one of these objects is entirely different than the others?"
"What makes it different?"
"How could we group all these objects?"

Opening Questions

If students identify the triangle with the *x* on the back as making it different, they are able to establish a set having a single element.

Discussion

Making All and Some Relationships

The student is to realize that some objects (those in the subset) are also included in the group referring to all of the objects (the set).

Cut triangular, circular, rectangular shapes out of colored paper.

Materials

"Are all of the squares red?"
"What color are all the circles?"
"What color are the triangles?"
"Are all the triangles red?"
Invite the students to group all the triangles together.
"Are all these triangles?"
"Are some of these triangles green?"
"Are they all green triangles?"

Opening Questions

Some children in this age group have difficulty differentiating between *some* and *all* because they do not have a concept of class inclusion. The advent of this ability indicates the children are beginning to develop the class inclusion operation. They still may not, however, understand that all dogs are also animals.

Discussion

Reordering

Cut ten straws so they vary in length from short to tall. Prepare ten pictures of trees ordered in a similar way.

Materials

Ask the children to order the straws from short to tall and place the trees in the opposite order (tall to short) next to them.

Opening Questions

Reordering means to be able to order in different ways; forward as well as backward. This activity requires children to do each as well as one-to-one correspondence. For every large tree, there is a small straw.

Discussion

Spatial Reasoning

Materials Show a tipped bottle and tell the students that the bottle is supposed to be half-filled with water.

Opening Questions "How you think the water would look in the jar." After they have finished their drawings, take a bottle and fill it half-way with water. Have them check their drawings with what they saw.

Discussion Children do not have a good concept of coordinates. Therefore, they will draw the water oriented to the sides or bottom of the jar rather than to the table on which it is sitting.

ACTIVITIES FOR MIDDLE/JUNIOR HIGH GRADES

Conservation of Displacement Volume

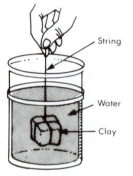

Materials Obtain a graduated cylinder or use a jar. Fill it three-fourths full of water.

Opening Questions Take a cube of clay and wrap a string around it so that it can be lowered into the water.
Instruct the students to place a rubber band around the cylinder to estimate where the water will be when the clay is lowered in it. Lower the clay very slowly. *Ask*, "How good was your estimate?" Now tell them to move the rubber band so that the top of it marks where the water is. Now take the clay out of the water. Cut it in half. Tie each half with string. Say to your students, "Estimate where you think the water level will be now when you lower these two halves into the water. Use a marking pencil to mark where you think the water level will be. Do not move your rubber band. Place your two pieces of clay in the water slowly. What did you discover? Can you give a rule for what you discovered?"

Discussion If the children explain that the volume of the two halves of clay is the same as the whole piece and these displace the same amount of water, they conserve displacement volume. It is the volume here and what it displaces that is important, and not the weight.

Law of Buoyancy

An object will float if the weight of its volume is less than an equal volume of water. The object will float above the water line when its weight displaces an equal amount of weight of water.

Tell students that 1 ml. of pure water weighs 1 gram. Have them make a small boat out of clay or a small milk carton. Have them weigh the boat. Tell the students you have a rectangular barge that weighs 500 grams and has a volume of 1000 ml.

Materials

How much water would it displace? How far would it sink into the water? Why?

Opening Questions

If the students suggest that it would sink about halfway in the water, they probably understand the concept of buoyancy. A further check would be to give them problems where odd numbers of weights and volumes are used for the barge.

Discussion

They should then estimate how many grams and milliliters of water their ship will displace. Have them obtain a large graduated cylinder or calibrated beaker and fill it three-fourths full with water. Determine the amount of water in the container and then place the boat in it. Ask, "How far does the ship sink in the water?" Add a 10 gram weight and determine how high the water moves. Ask, "How high would it move with a 20 gram weight? Why?"

Conservation of Internal Volume

Present the students with twenty-seven small cubes arranged to form a large cube. Tell the students that each cube represents a hollow room; the rooms have open doors between them. Inside the cube there is a butterfly that flies from room to room. These rooms can be arranged by the owner since they are modules.

Materials

One day the owner had to move the modules to a different lot. She had to arrange the modules in a different way as shown on the right.

Opening Questions   "Is there just as much, more, or less space inside now for the butterfly to fly? Why?"
"How would you prove it?"
"How could you use mathematics to prove it?"

Discussion   If the students indicate that since no rooms have been taken away or added, therefore there is the same amount of interior, they are using logic to justify their answer. A more sophisticated response, showing higher cognitive abilities, would be to demonstrate that the number of rooms is the same.

Spatial Relations

Materials   Show one surface of a cube.

Opening Questions   "How many *edges* can't you see?"

Discussion   Most students have difficulty perceiving the object from different viewpoints. Many adults have difficulty with the problem and suggest other numbers rather than eight. There are actually twelve *edges* on a cube. The view of one surface shows four of the twelve edges; so, the answer to the question is eight. You could repeat the activity, asking how many *corners* cannot be seen. How many *sides* cannot be seen? You may have to point out that a side is a flat surface, an edge is where two sides meet, and a corner is where three sides meet.

Continuous Divisibility

The concept of continuous divisibility is related to the concept of infinity.

Materials   Provide students with a paper circle, ruler and pencil. Ask them to divide the circle several times.

Opening Questions   If they keep at it for awhile, *ask*:
"How long could you keep on dividing the circle?"

Discussion   If they come up with the idea that this could go on and on and on, they have grasped the initial idea of infinity and realize that some things in nature can be continually divided (e.g., the measurement of temperature, time, motion, and change). If you suspect students understand the possibility of divisibility, ask, "How long could you go on dividing a rod or line?"

Reducing the Sound of a Radio

Materials   A small radio; several different size boxes, each of which can fit over one or more of the others and the radio; cloth; paper; insulating material; cotton balls.

Opening Question   "How can we reduce the sound of this radio using these materials?"

If possible, have two radios available with the same volume and invite two groups of students to have a deadening-the-sound race in a stipulated amount of time. Later discuss how sound can go through objects and what kinds of things deaden sound well.

Some Possible Activities

Have a Metric Broad Jump

Metric tapes or metric sticks.

Materials

"How far can you hop?"
"How far can you broad jump?"

Opening Questions

Have the students jump in groups of five and determine the average jump and/or hop of their groups metrically.

Some Possible Activities

Have a Balloon-Distance Race

Balloons, metric tape or meter stick.

Materials

"Which team can get their balloons to go the farthest?"

Opening Questions

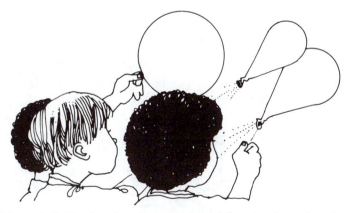

Go outside and divide the class into groups of five. Each student is to blow her balloons up as much as she dares. One student in each group releases her balloon. The second student then goes to where that balloon landed and releases his balloon. This continues until all members of the team have had a turn. The distance is then measured metrically to determine how far

Some Possible Activities

the balloons went from the starting point. The team whose balloons went the greatest distance wins.

What Will Happen to Ice Cubes Placed in Alcohol and Water?

Materials   Two 300 ml. beakers—one half-filled with water, the other with alcohol; and ice cubes.

Opening Questions   "What do you think will happen if an ice cube is placed in water?"
"What will happen if it is placed in alcohol?"

Some Possible Activities   Place the ice cubes in water and alcohol. Invite the students to weigh equal volumes of alcohol and water and to compare which has a greater density. They then might do an additional activity where they compare how a hard-boiled egg sinks in water but floats when salt is added to the water.

What Can You Find Out about Isopods?

Materials   Isopods, metric ruler, straw or stirring stick.

Opening Question   "What can you find out about isopods?"

Some Possible Activities   Invite students to measure the isopods and determine how they vary in size. Find out if the isopods prefer a dark or light place, a warm or cold place. Determine how they move and how they can smell or see. Have an isopod race.

Conservation of Weight

Materials   Obtain some clay. Have students prepare two round balls that weigh the same. They can check their weight by using a balance.

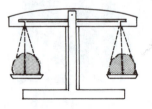

Opening Questions   "Please make one of your clay balls into a hamburger shape. Will your clay now weigh more, less, or the same amount as before? Why?"
"How could you tell?"
Have the students weigh their clay and find out.
Ask these questions:

"What did you find out?"

"Why do you think it weighs the same?"

"Is there some rule you can give about changing things and their weight?"

If the students state that spreading things out changes the thickness but also **Discussion** increases the area covered so that there is no loss in weight, they are giving a compensation type of justification. This means that the weight of the increased area compensates for the loss in weight in the thick area. If they state that if the ball was rolled up again it would weigh the same, they are demonstrating reversibility. This means they can reverse their thought processes. Both reversibility and compensatory reasoning characterize concrete operational thought.

Descending A Classification Hierarchy

Ensure that the students know the characteristics of mammals. Prepare ten **Materials** pictures of mammals, birds, and other animals. Include several dogs as well as other mammals, and ducks as well as other birds.

"Please group these animals in any way you would like. What groups did **Opening** you get?" **Questions**

"How many mammals did you get?"

"How many birds did you get?"

"Is there any way you can divide your mammal groups? Why?"

"Is there any way you can change your bird group?"

"What group of animals do dogs belong to?"

"What group of animals do ducks belong to?"

"What group do mammals belong to?"

"What groups do birds belong to?"

Ask the students to mix all the pictures again and make just a few groups. Then, take these groups and try to make more subgroups.

"How did you group your animals?"

"Why did you group them that way?"

If students can go from animals to mammals and birds and then to dogs and **Discussion** ducks, they indicate they can descend a classification hierarchy.

Classifying Objects

Cut twelve triangular, circular, and rectangular shapes from colored paper. **Materials** Draw and paste pictures of plants, animals, or houses on nine of these. Leave the other three papers blank.

Opening Question "Will you please group these any way you wish?"
The students should now place the shapes into just two groups. They should group them as blank and nonblank.

Discussion Children up to age eleven have difficulty realizing the existence of a null set. This may be attributed to their concrete thinking.

Interrelating Two Attributes or Classes

Materials *Prepare a work sheet such as the following:*

(red)   (yellow)   (blue)   (orange)   black)   (green)

△	△	△	△	△	△	
						(leaf green)
						(bush green)
						(grass green)
						(box)

All these items are green.

The shapes across the top of the chart are triangles of different colors. The items in the column far right are all green.

Opening Questions "How are all of the top row objects alike or different?"
"How are all the things in the squares that go up and down alike or different?"
"What do you think should be placed in the blank space?"

Discussion This activity should develop the classification skills of children who have. difficulty with this skill.

Ordering by Weight

Materials Try to obtain six or more metal containers of the same volume or use medicine vials of the same volume and fill them with different kinds of materials. For example, salt, sand, dirt, water, baking soda, rice, flour, etc. Tell the students to place these materials in order by weight. Later have them weigh the objects and order them.

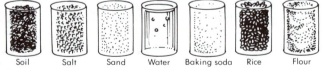

Soil   Salt   Sand   Water   Baking soda   Rice   Flour

Opening Questions "How good were your estimations?"
"How could you improve your estimations?"

Discussion Children usually have difficulty doing this up to two years after they can order by length or height.

Measuring a Large Area by Using a Single Unit

Cut a rectangle as shown in A. Then cut a triangle as shown with one side   **Materials**
2 cm. long.

"How would you use triangle B to determine the area in A?"   **Opening**
"Why do you think your response is correct?"   **Questions**

If students achieve the task, this shows that they can use units to determine   **Discussion**
area by superimposing. In this case they superimpose the small triangle on
the rectangle and then total the number of triangles used to state the area
in triangles. More advanced students may be able to determine the area
mathematically.

BIBLIOGRAPHY

Copeland, Richard. *Diagnostic and Learning Activities in Mathematics for Chil-
dren*. New York: Macmillan Publishing Co., 1974.
    An excellent set of mathematical activities. There are suggested activities
    for ages four through twelve. Activities are in the areas of space, number,
    logical classification, and measurement.
Furth, Hans G., *Piaget for Teachers*. Englewood Cliffs, N.J.: Prentice-
Hall, 1970.
    The second half of this book has suggested activities for symbol-
    picture logic, thinking games, creative thinking, social thinking, and
    musical thinking.
Furth, Hans G., and Wachs, Harry. *Thinking Goes to School*. New York:
Oxford University Press, 1975.
    There are 179 games for educators. Excellent in their applicability and
    appropriateness for educators.
Kamii, Constance, and DeVries, Rheta. *Physical Knowledge in Preschool
Education*. Englewood Cliffs, N.J.: Prentice-Hall, 1978.
    The first part of this book describes a rationale for physical (Piagetian)
    activities. The second section details seven activities. Finally, there is a
    very helpful section on designing activities and integrating activities in
    the classroom.
Labinowicz, Ed. *The Piaget Primer: Thinking, Learning, Teaching*. Menlo Park,
Calif.: Addison Wesley Publishing Co., 1980
    Activities and tasks are interspersed throughout the book. There are
    many helpful suggestions for educators.
Schippert, Frederick. *Reasoning Activities without Reading*. Troy, Mich.:
Midwest Publication, 1975.
    Very good activities for preschool, early childhood, and exceptional stu-
    dents. Symbols for large, small, dots, shapes, etc., are used to develop

concepts in the areas of relations, area, geometric shapes, classification, sets, proof, and congruence and similarity.

Sharp, Evelyn. *Thinking Is Child's Play*. New York: Avon Books, 1969.
A book of games for preschoolers. The activities should be very helpful for early childhood and primary level educators.

Wadsworth, Barry J. *Piaget for the Classroom Teacher*. New York: Longman, 1978.
The text includes twenty assessments for educators. Most are classical Piagetian interviews.

Piaget's Theory: An Evaluation for Educators

There is one question that directs the discussion of this chapter. Will Piaget's theoretical ideas be applied to educational practices? Piaget's theory has already had an influence on educational theory. This conclusion is based less on what Piaget said about education and more on what educators think he said about education. Hardly an educational meeting passes that reference to Piaget's theory is not made. This observation also clarifies the fact that educators generally know about Piaget. Still, the application of Piaget's ideas is a difficult question to assess, for the answer is a matter of degree. However, it is important to review the potential impact of Piaget's ideas as best we can. Our assessment should provide a supplement to those already done for psychology, philosophy, and education (See e.g., Murray, 1979).

This book, *Piaget for Educators*, implies that there are significant aspects of Piaget's theory that are applicable to education. Much of the discussion in earlier chapters has attempted to bridge the chasm between theory and practice. It is still the case that Piaget's theory cannot resolve many problems facing educators. So, we must narrow the discussion to a question that is central to this chapter—To what degree will Piaget's theory have an influence on educational practices?

Throughout the history of American education, various psychological theories have influenced educational practices. *Theories of Learning and Instruction* (Hilgard, 1964) contained a review of the history of psychology (1900–1950) that assessed the influence various psychological theories have had on American education. The review identified six factors that any psychological theory must have to gain a significant place in education. The six factors are (1) a scientific foundation; (2) an explanation of social problems; (3) an account of developmental phenomena; (4) a promise of practicality; (5) a concern for the individual; and (6) an emphasis on cognitive processes. These six categories do provide a comprehensive, though necessarily general, evaluation of Piaget's theory.

IS PIAGET'S THEORY SCIENTIFIC?

Criticism and Confirmations

Piaget's theory has been criticized for not being scientific. Usually these criticisms are based on a conception of science different from that of Piaget. Specifically, critics have pointed out the lack of controls, small samples, and absence of statistical analyses in Piaget's research. Educators should realize that many of these criticisms originate from empiricism and logical positivism, positions in science that are dominant in American psychology.

Piaget's own view of scientific psychology was that it is (1) a science of humans in general; (2) built on the interaction between subject and object; (3) a key to all sciences because it explains ideas and operations used in the development of science; (4) not possible to dissociate psychology from epistemology; and (5) basically a science of interdisciplinary cooperation (Piaget, 1977).

Piaget was a structuralist (Piaget, 1970c) and a biologist (Piaget, 1971). This is mentioned because his scientific orientation is quite different from the research tradition in American psychology. Piaget approached his work much as an ethologist might. There is indeed much value in this methodology. In fact, many important discoveries in psychology have been based on this approach. Piaget attempted to identify universal features of cognitive development by observing the behavior of children in certain situations. Piaget's position was that small samples and the clinical methods are adequate if the investigator does identify structures common to all individuals. Other researchers can evaluate the findings through subsequent research that verifies or refutes the original observations. The findings of cross-cultural Piagetian research provide an example of this second step. Nevertheless, it is reasonable to question the reliability of Piaget's observations, the generality of his results, and especially the many theoretical concepts derived from his original research. If indeed his theory is to have an influence on education and psychology, we must review it in the systematic tests and procedures of contemporary research. Please note, however, that this position is very different from initial criticisms that questioned Piaget's theory on methodological grounds.

Conversely, Piaget continued a lifelong dialectic with logical positivism, which Piaget admitted was his "whipping boy" (Bringuier, 1980). Evidence for this assertion is found throughout Piaget's writing (see, e.g., Piaget, 1971). A very clear discussion of Piaget's position among other important psychological systems is to be found in a chapter entitled, "The Multiplicity of Forms of Psychological Explanations," written by Piaget, Fraisse, and Reuchlin in the book, *Experimental Psychology: Its Scope and Method* (Fraisse and Piaget, 1968).

Piaget's theory is open to criticism. We can rightfully ask questions such as, Has Piaget's theory been confirmed by other researchers? Is his theory universally applicable? Are Piaget's experiments adequate to develop his theories? Has Piaget accounted for all cognitive processes?

The number of published research studies based on Piaget's theory is astronomical. To review these studies is far beyond the limits of this chapter. Educators interested in Piagetian research should consult the eight-volume series entitled *Piagetian Research* (Modgil and Modgil, 1977). Several journals also have published numerous research studies based on Piaget's theory, including *Child Development*, *Developmental Psychology*, *Journal of Experimental Child Psychology*, and *Journal of Research in Science Teaching*. In general, studies completed outside of Geneva have confirmed the basic tenets of Piaget's theory.

The question of universal applicability of Piaget's theory raises the issue of cross-cultural research. Piaget has discussed the need and significance for cross-cultural verification of his theory (Piaget, 1976b). Cross-cultural studies have investigated two of the central tenets of Piaget's theory: first, that progress through developmental stages is invariant; and second, that developmental stages have common cognitive content. Cross-cultural studies have generally confirmed the invariant sequence of stages, though the stage of formal operations is not attained in some cultures. And the ages at which stages are attained vary widely among cultures. It has been found that cognitive performance within stages varies. To clarify, Piaget asserts that any stage of development reflects a complete underlying structure. This structural wholeness should result in consistent responses on tasks designed to evaluate a level of thought (e.g., concrete operations). A number of studies report that, for example, conservation is dependent on the materials used (Dasen, 1977a, 1977b, Ashton, 1975). The varied results leave open the question of the universal applicability of Piaget's theory. Explanations of the variations of results vary depending upon the orientation of the researcher. Researchers have looked to differences in language, cultural experiences, and education as important factors underlying the research results.

Piaget's research is open to criticism from the standpoint of design. One criticism is that Piaget often did not design his experiments carefully enough to exclude alternative explanations (Boden, 1979). This problem is clearly exemplified by Novak's (1978) discussion of Piagetian research and Ausubelian theory. Novak was able to explain many Piagetian concepts and particularly children's responses to assessment tasks in terms of Ausubelian theory. A second criticism is that Piaget often theorized too much from too little evidence. At times, Piaget wrote extensive theoretical analyses based on few observations. For example, see Piaget's discussions in the last sections of *The Growth of Logical Thinking* (Inhelder and Piaget, 1958).

While Piaget's research contributions to our understanding of cognitive development are substantial, his work often focused exclusively on the use of logical patterns of reasoning and largely neglected other cognitive processes that are important (e.g., creativity, problem solving, and "right hemisphere processes"). Along this line of criticism, he also tended to overestimate the autonomy of logical development and underestimate the effects of other factors such as the social, motivational, and education influences (Boden, 1979). This criticism is one of emphasis and degree since Piaget did clearly include social experience, education, and motivation as important factors influencing cognitive development (see Piaget and Inhelder, 1969; Piaget, 1937).

As far as educators are concerned, Piaget provided few clear responses to their questions about cognitive functioning, in particular the cognitive processes by which individuals progress from one stage to the next. Piaget did address this problem in *The Development of Thought* (1975). But, the statement is abstract and more philosophically based than empirically based. In another work, *Learning and the Development of Cognition*, Inhelder, Sinclair, and Bovet (1974) have provided research evidence to support the role of equilibration in the process of cognitive development. Still, from an educational view, Piaget's work in this area is less than clear and applicable. We think that in many respects the research of others may be more fruitful for educators (see, e.g., Larkin, 1980 and Johnson et al., 1980). A few criticisms of Piaget's theory have been mentioned. There have been others (see, e.g., Siegal and Brainerd, 1977; Phillips and Kelly, 1975; Smedslund, 1977; Bruner, 1966; and Bruner, Oliver and Greenfield, 1966).

The Piagetian Paradigm

The title of this section is based on Thomas Kuhn's book, *The Structure of Scientific Revolutions* (1970). The question of this section, "Is Piaget's theory scientific?" can be reviewed by examining the degree to which Piaget's theory meets the essential criteria of a scientific paradigm. The position argued here is that Piaget's theory is indeed the basis for a major paradigm in psychology and education, and thus, on these grounds we have an affirmative answer to the question concerning the scientific character of Piaget's theory (see Lawson, 1979; Case, 1979; Kamii, 1979). According to Kuhn, a paradigm is a "universally recognized scientific achievement that for a time provides model problems and solutions to a community of practitioners" (Kuhn, 1970, p. viii). Piaget's theory has provided broad conceptual and methodological orientations that are based on shared examples from other researchers. The types of research questions, the metaphysical assumptions, and the acceptable (and unacceptable) results for researchers are implicitly defined by the paradigm.

There is also a social psychological dimension to the paradigm. Kuhn says that a paradigm stands for the entire constellation of beliefs, values, techniques, and so on shared by members of a given community (1970, p. 175). Discussions among Piagetian, Ausubelian, and Brunerian schools of cognitive development demonstrate the Kuhnian point of "shared commitment" by persons within competing paradigms.

During a period of "normal" science, research centers on important aspects of the paradigm, articulation of components, and verification of theoretical predictions. This is precisely the case for Piagetian theory. However, as research continues, anomalies within the paradigm are identified. In future sections, we shall see that this is now occurring. At first, these results are ignored or aspects of the theory are modified to account for the anomalous results. The fact that Piaget's published research and theory, even though criticized, fits the criteria of a major scientific paradigm supports the position that Piaget's theory is a scientific paradigm for psychologists and educators.

In summary, Piaget's theory is derived from actual observations that have been generally confirmed by researchers outside of Geneva. Piaget's methods were not aligned with those of the research tradition in American psychology. There have been criticisms beyond those of Piaget's methods. Criticisms have included the universal applicability of criteria within stages, and the role of language, education, and other cognitive processes. There is strong evidence supporting a Piagetian paradigm for psychological and educational researchers. In conclusion, the scientific character of Piaget's theory would have to be rated high.

Scientific Character of Piaget's Theory

```
       |_____x_____|
   High 10    9    8    7    6    5    4    3    2    1 Low
```

DOES PIAGET'S THEORY ADDRESS SOCIAL PROBLEMS?

Piaget's theory does not really adequately address any of the distinctly social problems confronting education. Piaget never intended that his theory should be applied to problems such as desegregation/integration, equal opportunity, budget cuts, reductions in staff, and the numerous other problems besetting educators. So, while one can rightfully say that Piaget never intended to address social problems and thus this criticism is inappropriate, as long as educators do look to psychological theories to help resolve social problems, one must rate Piaget's theory low on this criterion.

There is also the problem of social influences on cognitive development. Throughout his work, Piaget gave recognition to the influence of social factors (see Piaget, 1976b; Piaget and Inhelder, 1969; Piaget, 1965). It is justifiable to concentrate on one aspect of development (e.g., cognition) and not study other aspects of development (e.g., social, motivational). But at some point, especially when one has as comprehensive a theory as Piaget, a greater recognition must be given to other factors that may influence cognitive growth. Language, motivation, and social interactions among children are three examples of areas Piaget should have researched more thoroughly, especially from an educational point of view.

Two aspects of Piaget's theory do seem appropriate to the question of social problems: the development of social responsibility and the development of psychopathology.

Development of Social Responsibility

In the *Moral Judgement of the Child* (1965), Piaget reports his investigations on the development of social responsibility (see Chapter 7). According to Piaget, social responsibility develops through two periods, one of moral constraint and one of moral cooperation. Moral constraint is a period where social responsibility is imposed from without, by adults and teachers, and results in heteronomy and moral realism. Moral cooperation slowly emerges from this period. One of the primary factors influencing the emergence of the next period is social interaction. With moral cooperation social responsibility develops within, through the student's own understanding and mediating of rules, order, and so on. The result is autonomy and moral relativity.

Piaget did discuss educational implications of his findings. He first concluded that his theory did not support authoritarian and purely individualistic methods of teaching. Imposing on students a fully worked out system of discipline was not appropriate. Piaget's position was that the natural interaction among students and between students and teachers will ensure normal development of social responsibility. Teachers should be "collaborators," not masters. Piaget states that "group work," "self-government," and activities are the teaching methods implied by his findings (Piaget, 1965, p. 404).

Unfortunately, Piaget's discussions of social development did not include the period of adolescence. Also, he had little more to say after the work described above. We can surmise that the process of developing social responsibility is congruent with Piaget's interactionist and constructivist position. But, this really does not provide much direction for educators.

Lawrence Kohlberg (1976) extended Piaget's original work on moral judgement and social responsibility (see Chapter 7). According to Kohlberg, there are three periods of moral development: preconventional, conventional, and postconventional. Each period has two stages summarized here as (1) avoidance of punishment, (2) seeking rewards, (3) seeking social approval, (4) obeying the law and maintaining order, (5) social contracting, and (6) universal ethical principles.

In recent years Kohlberg's theory has been criticized. There have been general criticisms of his theory (see, e.g., Kurtines and Greif, 1974; Fraenkel, 1976). His theory has also been specifically criticized for not incorporating concerns and experiences of women (Gilligan, 1977), for not meeting stage criteria for Stages 5 and 6 (Gibbs, 1977) and for containing scientific and cultural bias (Simpson, 1974). The criticisms have caused Kohlberg to revise portions of his theory, in particular the postconventional levels (Munson, 1979).

Piaget's Theory and Psychopathology

Discussion of psychopathology and healthy development is a direct application of Piaget's theory to social aspects of education. The application has the potential of helping educators understand behavior problems and classroom discipline. As you may recall, Piaget had some experience with psychopathology early in his career (see Chapter 1). But, he conducted no research and wrote very little about psychopathology. In recent years Piaget's associate Barbel Inhelder and others in Geneva have completed research on mentally retarded, psychotic, and dyslexic children (Inhelder, 1976a, 1976b; Schmid-Kitsikis, 1976).

In addition to research conducted in Geneva, other authors have discussed psychopathology from a Piagetian perspective (see, e.g., Cowan, 1978; Gallagher and Reid, 1981; Reid and Hresko, 1981; Wolff, 1979). These reports are insightful in that they are discussions of Piagetian concepts, such as equilibration, in the context of various forms of psychopathology and developmental problems. And they represent important initial efforts to apply the Piagetian paradigm to psychopathology. Still, much more can be done concerning the application of Piaget's theory to developmental delays, learning disorders, and behavior problems.

The applicability of Piaget's theory to the social problems of educators is not very high. There are some issues that might be addressed in the future, but at present his theory does not provide educators with much direction concerning social processes and problems.

Applicability of Piaget's Theory to Social Problems

```
|_____x_____|
High 10    9    8    7    6    5    4    3    2    1 Low
```

DOES PIAGET'S THEORY ACCOUNT FOR DEVELOPMENT?

Among educators perhaps the best known of Piaget's theory is his stages of development. Anticipating our answer to the question of this section, we must respond "yes." To say the very least, Piaget's theory offers an account of development. Still, there is need for a review and discussion of various components of the general question of development.

Developmental Stages

According to Piaget, children develop through a series of stages: sensorimotor, preoperational, concrete operational, and formal operational (see Chapters 3, 4, 5, and 6). For the importance placed on the concept of stage, Piaget said very little about the stage concept during his life. According to Piaget (1973), there are five criteria for a stage: (1) the order (not age) of succession is constant; (2) structures from one stage are integrated into the next; (3) structures are represented as wholes (*structure d'ensemble*); (4) there is a level of preparation and one of completion; and finally, (5) there must be a distinction between the process of formation (disequilibrium) and the final equilibrium. A much more thorough set of criteria for stages has been suggested by Flavell (1972). Flavell's criteria provide meaningful criteria for evaluating stage theories of development, including Piaget's.

Our discussion will center on research based on each of the stages. Questions educators will find central to the discussion include the following: Do the stages in fact exist? Is development through the stages invariant? Are the defining characteristics of stages similar to those Piaget described?

The sensorimotor period is the first stage of cognitive development (see Chapter 3 for a discussion of this stage). Most research attempting to confirm the existence and cognitive content of the sensorimotor period has been supportive. Uzgiris and Hunt found that cognitive content developed in the sequence predicted by Piaget (Uzgiris, Hunt, and McVicker, 1974). Similar results were also obtained by Corman and Escalona (1969) and Kramer, Hill, and Cohen (1975).

One particular aspect of the sensorimotor period—the development of object permanence—has been extensively investigated by researchers outside of Geneva. Research has not yet revealed a clear picture of the development of object permanence. Important inconsistencies in acquisition of object permanence have been observed (Bower, 1974, and Harris, 1975). One should note that object permanence research has had methodological problems due to the age of children in the sensorimotor period. Still, the results are not conclusive; perhaps more definitive confirmation or refutation will be found in the future.

The second major stage of development is the preoperational period (see Chapter 4 for a discussion of this stage). Egocentrism, causality, language, and identity are the topics from the preoperational period that researchers have studied. Studies by Borke (1977), Chandler and Greenspan (1972), and Rubin and Maioni (1975) have all indicated that Piaget's original reports of children's egocentric orientation are certainly open to question, and probably incorrect. Researchers have found much higher frequencies of correct responses by younger children (three year olds) than predicted by Piaget. Piaget's interpretation of his results was that children were unaware of the existence of other viewpoints (egocentric) and that this capacity emerged through the preoperational period. Now, it seems much more likely that children are aware of other viewpoints as early as three years of age, but they lack the language and ability to communicate this awareness.

Piaget claimed that children's explanations of causality are highly animistic. Generally, this claim has been supported by research outside of Geneva (Dennis, 1938; Russell, 1940; Laurendeau and Pinaid, 1962). Young children give very animistic explanations of causes. With increasing age, there is decreasing appeal to animistic responses.

Language, according to Piaget, is highly egocentric during the preoperational period. Research on language has paralleled the findings cited on egocentric perspective (McCarthy, 1954; Flavell, Botkin, Fry, Wright, and Jarvis, 1968; Looft, 1972; Kohlberg, Yaeger and Hjertholm, 1968). Overall, the observed proportion of egocentric speech never exceeds 50 percent, even in the youngest children. So, egocentric language does not seem to dominate children's speech. This finding is very important for educators, for young children do have the aim of communicating with others much more than Piaget has suggested. On egocentric perspectives and language, we must conclude that Piaget's theory has questionable inconsistencies with other research.

Identity, the qualitative component of conservation, is the final area of review. Piaget theorized that qualitative attributes of materials would be conserved before quantitative attributes were conserved. Generally, research has been consistent with Piaget's idea that identity is achieved during the preoperational period (DeVries, 1969, and Brainerd, 1977a). But, these researchers question the emergence of identity as early as Piaget suggested.

The concrete operational period is the next developmental stage (see Chapter 5 for a discussion of this stage). The majority of research on Piaget's theory has been concerned with the concrete operational stage. A complete review of the research on the period is far beyond the scope of this chapter. We shall, therefore, select topics, provide summary statements concerning the research, and provide some examples of studies supporting the summary statements.

Conservation is the first topic. Piaget's predictions concerning the development of conservation have been very well substantiated by research outside of Geneva (Uzgiris, 1964). Research on relations (i.e., seriation, multiple seriation, and transitive inference) has not been as abundant as that on conservation. One line of research (Braine, 1959, 1962) has indicated that Piaget's placement of transitive inference in the concrete operational period was incorrect; it is probably a preoperational ability. Research on classification has had mixed results. Generally, children pass multiple classification tasks before class inclusion tasks; indeed, the latter may be a formal operational ability (Kohnstamm, 1967). The three-stage development of concepts related to number has been confirmed. However, the parallel development among number and other concrete operational abilities (e.g., classification, relations) has been seriously questioned (Brainerd, 1977b; Gelman, 1972; Zimiles, 1966). Piaget's ideas concerning the development of spatial relations have generally been supported (Laurendeau and Pinard, 1970). But there is some question about the age at which children pass tests dealing with Euclidean contents. It is probably much later than Piaget predicted (Smedslund, 1963; Thomas, Jamison, and Hummel, 1973).

The formal operational period is the final stage of cognitive development (see Chapter 6 for a discussion of this stage). Piaget's use of propositional logic has been questioned by logicians. In general the logicians argue that Piaget's propositional logic and the propositional logic of philosophers are not the same. Piaget's logic is redundant, includes items that are not philosophical propositions, and are interdependent; the latter not being a characteristic of logical propositions. This conceptual criticism of Piaget's theory has been best presented by Ennis (1975, 1976). Research results on propositional operations have been mixed. Concrete operational children have been found to solve *valid* forms of propositions, and both concrete and formal operational students have not solved *invalid* propositions. Concerning other formal operational schemes, research results have also been mixed (see, e.g., Bruner and Kenney, 1966; Chapman, 1975). Educators are directed to papers by Deanna Kuhn (1979), Driver and Easley (1978), Neimark (1975) and Keating (1979) for discussions of the formal period and education. Much more research is needed before definitive statements can be made concerning Piaget's predictions of formal operational characteristics.

The Age and Stage Problem

Educators have tacitly applied a maturation model to Piaget's developmental theory. This problem is seen in statements such as "If John is ten years old, he must be concrete operational." The underlying assumption is that age and stage are directly related. Piaget always maintained that the ages given for stages were only averages. Piaget states:

> However, if the order of succession of stages has shown itself to be constant—each stage is necessary to the construction of the following one—the average age at which children go through each stage can vary considerably from one social environment to another, or from one country or even region within a country to another. (Piaget, 1972, p. 7)

Stages should be thought of as helpful labels indicating general patterns of thought. Likewise, the ages associated with stages are average indications of the emergence of cognitive processes associated with that stage. Finally, it must be recalled that Piaget (1973) claims that there is a level of preparation and completion for each stage. Educators will thus find many students "in transition."

Piaget's theory has been shown to provide a substantial account of developmental phenomena. And, considering the breadth and depth of his theory, replication studies have shown his theory to be substantially accurate. Even though there are some aspects of his theory that have been found to be inaccurate, and he did not detail a comprehensive theory of development, still the rating on development must be high.

Ability of Piaget's Theory to Explain Development

High 10   9   8   7   6   5   4   3   2   1 Low

IS PIAGET'S THEORY PRACTICAL?

Most psychological theories, not to mention philosophical theories, are criticized by educators for not being practical. Basically, educators want theories that apply to everyday classroom problems with predictable and concrete results. The corpus of Piaget's writing provides little practical advice for educators. Probably the two most significant statements on education are *Science of Education and the Psychology of the Child* (Piaget, 1970b) and *To Understand Is to Invent* (Piaget, 1973b). Still, a comprehensive theory of cognitive development must have some practical value for educators. The practical value of Piaget's theory can be evaluated by the provision of aims, goals, and objectives and the provision of specific methods and programs to accomplish educational goals. Piaget provided aims but did little to suggest programs and methods. The evaluation here will be a balance of Piaget's original work and the work of others who have evaluated Piaget's theory for educators (see, e.g., Kuhn, D., 1979; Duckworth, 1972).

The Aim of Education

Facilitating the cognitive development of students has long been a goal of education. Certainly Piaget's theory provides educators with an aim of cognitive development. Kohlberg and Mayer (1972) have argued this position. Educators have tended to apply Piaget's theory to aims and objectives, usually seen in the form of advancing children to higher levels of reasoning and/or stages of development. This particular application of Piaget's theory has been criticized for its unquestioning acceptance of the theory and the application of incompletely defined stages to the aims and goals of education (Kuhn, D., 1979). Still, Piaget's theory provides educators with some practical aims of instruction.

The American Question

If educators assume an aim of development, it is reasonable to ask if development can be accelerated. This has been termed the American question by Piaget. Piaget has rather bluntly dismissed the question and stated that development results from a combination of maturation, experience, and equilibration. Educators have tended to emphasize social transmission as the means of accelerating development (see Chapter 8). Piaget was rightfully put off by an apparent need to teach everything earlier, faster, and more efficiently. So, what is the answer to the question, Can development be accelerated? The answer is yes—but only to a limited degree. In fact, the answer must be yes or else Piaget's theory of stage development would have little or no practical importance for educators. The point is that to *accelerate* is not very important, but educators should be able to *facilitate* development within the context of Piaget's theory.

Developmental delays often come to the attention of educators. When these problems are observed, there must be something that educators can do to assist the developmental process. Research in the area of training studies has demonstrated that students can learn Piagetian concepts (see, e.g., Brainerd, 1978; Linn, Chen, and Thier, 1977; Lawson and Wollman, 1976). On the matter of learning as it relates to Piaget's theory (in particular the process of equilibration), we suggest Piaget's (1975) work on equilibration and especially recommend *Learning and the Development of Cognition* (Inhelder, Sinclair and Bovet, 1974) and *Learning Theory of Piaget and Inhelder* (Gallagher and Reid, 1981). Shorter discussions of the learning process are to be found in Chapter 8 of this book. See also Reid (1979) and Bovet (1981).

Curriculum and Instruction

Piaget's theory has stimulated the development of several different curriculum programs (see, e.g., Furth and Wachs, 1974; Kamii and DeVries, 1978; Karplus, 1974; and Lavatelli, 1970). Curriculum programs based specifically on Piaget's theory have received mixed reviews with reference to cognitive development (Kuhn, 1979).

Instruction based on Piaget's ideas would use "active methods" (Piaget, 1970, 1973) that focus on an interaction between the student and materials (see Chapters 8 and 9). The aim is to engage the learner in an "optimal mismatch" between his present level of understanding and an existing problem. We have suggested that the learning cycle is a good application of this aspect of Piaget's theory (see also Karplus et al., 1977, and Karplus, 1979).

After considering the practicality of Piaget's theory and the work of others who have attempted to apply Piaget's theory, we evaluate this factor as follows.

Practicality of Piaget's Theory

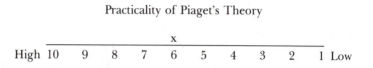

	x								
High 10	9	8	7	6	5	4	3	2	1 Low

DOES PIAGET'S THEORY ACCOUNT FOR INDIVIDUAL DIFFERENCES?

Understanding the cognitive development of individuals, and subsequent individual differences, was precisely the goal of sixty years of research by Piaget. Though he addressed social and affective differences (Piaget and Inhelder, 1969), the unconscious (Piaget, 1976a), and moral development (Piaget, 1965), Piaget has been criticized for not saying more on these topics.

Testing

Tests have been constructed and validated for teachers interested in evaluating students' levels of cognitive development. As educators use these instruments, their sensitivity to individual differences will be increased, and their ability to provide effective instruction will be enhanced.

Most Piagetian assessments have been individual interviews. For educators these are very time consuming. For this reason several pencil and paper tests have been constructed (see, e.g., Raven, 1973; Ankney and Joyce, 1974; Burney, 1974; Tisher and Dale, 1975; Lawson, Karplus and Adi, 1978; and Lawson, 1978). Tests such as these are helpful for educators wishing to identify and respond to individual differences in the classroom.

Brain Growth

Piaget consistently maintained that cognitive development was tied to the whole process of embryogenesis, especially as it concerned the development of the nervous system and mental functions (Piaget, 1964). Recent research by Herman Epstein has provided valuable insights into the maturation process, particularly brain growth (Epstein, 1974, 1977).

The brain increases significantly at certain times of life and hardly at all at other times. These increases occur as indicated in Table 12.1. Research indicates that approximately 85 percent of children fall within the growth spurts as indicated in Table 12.1 (Epstein, 1978a).

Table 12.1
Periods of Brain Mass Increase

1. 3–10 months
2. 2–4 years
3. 6–8 years
4. 10–12 years
5. 14–16+ years (earlier for girls)

What causes the brain to increase in mass during these periods? The increase correlates with the amount of protein found in the brain. This protein is not used to produce new brain cells, neurons, but rather is used by the neurons to send out many new projections. Some of these pick up stimuli and others send stimuli to other cells. By the addition of these projections, the brain cells are actually increasing the possibility of greater interchanges among themselves. Brain growth, then, results mainly in an increase of the total nerve network. This increase in nerve cell interconnections then makes it possible for the mind to perform new patterns of thought. These increases—except for the fifth one—correlate relatively well with the Piagetian stages. It should be noted that the major work of Piaget has not been involved with studying late adolescence. So, the discovery of a fifth stage would not be expected from Piaget's works. There is, however, some evidence for the existence of a fifth stage that correlates with Epstein's brain mass increase for this level. Arlan (1975) has identified a stage for ages fourteen through sixteen where the individual generates relatively sophisticated types of problems similar to those of a mature scientist.

Epstein believes that cognitive development can be enhanced considerably, if appropriately challenging experiences are provided during growth spurt periods. While children are in intermediate, low-growth periods, they should not be given intellectual challenges above their level. He argues that to do so may cause them to develop psychological rejection processes. If children are presented with material too far above their mental level, they will probably fail. The failure of several similar tasks results in a poor self-concept. The children then learn that it is not wise to become involved in such activity. In the future, when confronted with similar tasks they are cognitively able to do, they will not try.

Epstein argues that challenging new types of cognitive experiences need to be provided for students during brain growth spurt periods. He also thinks that only enrichment activities that reinforce and broaden a child's operational and conceptual understanding on her cognitive level should be used during the plateau periods. What does this mean for teaching? It means that when children are in transition from one brain growth and Piagetian stage to another, they must be involved in challenging, moderately novel or optimal mismatch types of activities. If they are not stimulated during these growth periods, their development may be detrimentally affected. In other words, for students to develop their neurological networks, their neurons must be stimulated and used if these new branches are to be retained (Epstein, 1978b).

In conclusion, Piaget's theory, complemented by the work of others (e.g., Epstein), provides a framework for understanding individual differences in the classroom. Work on group tests for Piagetian levels further provides the classroom teacher with a means of evaluating individual differences. Now, it seems the crucial problem is one of assisting the teacher interested in addressing individual differences in groups of thirty or more students. While Piaget's theory is of little practical account in this respect, the application of a learning cycle approach such as that advocated in this book is one way of meeting individual differences within groups of students.

Piaget's theory does account for individual differences and suggests a very real concern for individual development. The work of others has helped to clarify maturation and apply the theory through classroom testing. We must rate Piaget above average in this category.

Piaget's Theory and Individual Differences

			x							
High 10	9	8	7	6	5	4	3	2	1 Low

DOES PIAGET'S THEORY ADDRESS COGNITIVE PROCESSES?

Piaget's theory does address cognitive processes; in fact, this topic is central to his theory. There are several areas worth elaboration since cognitive processes are a great concern to educators.

Memory

There is one facet of Piaget's theory that has not been addressed; that is memory. Memory implies the grasping of past experiences and includes retention of information and structures of intelligence. In Piaget's theory there are several types of memory: recognitive, evocative, and reconstructive. Recognitive memory occurs when children use their minds to recognize something present that they experienced in the past. Evocative memory is manifest when a child recalls a situation, object, or idea that is presently absent but remembered. Reconstructive memory occurs when an individual brings to mind and relates actions, schemes, or operations that bear on a problem (Piaget and Inhelder, 1973). Educators will find Piaget and Inhelder's discussions of memory and intelligence very interesting, especially the role of reconstructive memory since it is a process through which one can apparently remember an event *better* after a period of time.

This finding by Piaget and Inhelder certainly provides a conception of memory different than that that most educators apply.

Equilibration

Equilibration has been mentioned throughout this chapter and book (see Chapter 8), so discussion here will be brief. Equilibration is central to cognitive processes within Piaget's theory. Yet, Piaget did not really give equilibration the clear and elaborate discussion it deserves. The book, *The Development of Thought* (Piaget, 1975) is not especially helpful for educators. We think this is a serious omission from the major work of Piaget. For educators the result has been an emphasis on stages of development and not on the *process* of development.

Logic, Problem Solving, and Creativity

Piaget's theory places almost exclusive emphasis on logical patterns of thought. He probably overemphasized logic at the expense of other cognitive processes such as creativity, problem solving, and brain lateralization (right/left hemispherical functioning). In fact, in some of his writing it seems he assumed there was a set of logical structures within individuals at a particular stage (e.g., formal operational period) and then tried to confirm their existence (see, e.g., Inhelder and Piaget, 1958).

Subject Matter

An area of concern for educators is subject matter. Does Piaget's theory provide direction for determining topics and subjects to be taught? Very broadly, yes. Topics such as causality, time, space, number, and conservation are all important subjects. However, Piaget's concerns were larger than specific subject matter, but his theory certainly focuses on cognitive content and thus supports the long-standing role of subject matter as a focus of education.

Our evaluation of the degree to which Piaget's theory addresses cognitive processes is low. At least, it is lower than one would have expected for a theory of cognitive development. While it is justifiable for Piaget not to address all aspects of cognitive processes, he could have addressed those he did with greater clarity and empirical evidence. Further, he did omit some cognitive processes that recent research indicates are central to cognition, learning, and development.

Piaget's Theory and Cognitive Processes

```
                         x
    |_____|
  High 10    9    8    7    6    5    4    3    2    1 Low
```

CONCLUSION

In this evaluation we have tried to point out some criticisms of Piaget's theory. On balance, his theory will no doubt have a lasting influence on education. This is neither to say that all aspects of the theory are correct nor that aspects confirmed by research will stand for all time. Piaget's theory is a major psychological paradigm that will continue to provide research problems and practical applications for decades.

Though Piaget said little about education, and he could rightfully be criticized for this, we can look on his lack of comment in another way. In a sense Piaget adhered to his own theory when it came to educational implications. As we have seen throughout this book, students must be actively involved in their own intellectual development. Or, to use a title from one of Piaget's books (1973b), in order to understand one has to invent. There is no reason to conclude that this simple idea does not apply to educators as well. In order to apply Piaget's theory effectively, educators must understand their students, their subjects, their pedagogy and then invent their unique educational practices. In the end, we conclude what the title of this book implies, Piagetian theory is for educators and it will have a lasting impact on education.

REFERENCES

Ankney, Paul, and Joyce, Lyle. *"The Development of a Piagetian Paper and Pencil Test for Assessing Concrete Operational Reasoning."* Unpublished doctoral dissertation, University of Northern Colorado, 1974.

Arlin, Patricia K. "Cognitive Development in Adulthood: A Fifth Stage?" *Developmental Psychology* 11 (1975): 602–6.

Ashton, Patricia Teague. "Cross Cultural Piagetian Research: An Experimental Perspective." *Harvard Educational Review* 45 (1975): 475–506.

Boden, Margaret. *Jean Piaget.* New York: Penguin Books, 1979.

Borke, Helene. "Piaget's View of Social Interaction and the Theoretical Construct of Empathy." In *Alternatives to Piaget: Critical Essays on the Theory*, edited by L. S. Siegel and C. Brainerd. New York: Academic Press, 1977.

Bovet, Magali. "Learning Research within Piagetian Lines." *Topics in Learning and Learning Disabilities* 1 (1981): 1–9.

Bower, T. G. R., *Development for Infancy.* San Francisco: W. H. Freeman, 1974.

Braine, M. D. S. "The Ontogeny of Certain Logical Operations: Piaget's Formulation Examined by Nonverbal Methods." *Psychological Monographs* 73, No. 5 (1959).

———. "Piaget on Reasoning: A Methodological Critique and Alternative Proposals. In *Thought in the Young Child*, edited by Kessen and Kuhlman Monographs of the Society for Research in Child Development, 27, No. 2 (1962).

Brainerd, C. "Feedback, Rule Knowledge, and Conservation Learning." *Child Development* 48 (1977a):

_____. *The Origins of the Number Concept.* New York: Praeger, 1977*b*.

_____. *Piaget's Theory of Intelligence.* Englewood Cliffs, N.J. Prentice-Hall, 1978.

Bringuier, Jean-Claude. *Conversations with Piaget.* Chicago: University of Chicago Press, 1980.

Bruner, Jerome, "The Course of Cognitive Development." *American Psychologist* 19 (1966): 1–16.

Bruner, Jerome, and Kenney, H. "On Relational Concepts." In *Studies in Cognitive Growth*, edited by J. Bruner, R. Oliver and P. Greenfield, New York: John Wiley & Sons, 1966.

Bruner, J.: Oliver, R.; and Greenfield, P., eds. *Studies in Cognitive Growth.* New York: John Wiley & Sons, 1966.

Burney, Gilbert. *The Construction and Validation of an Objective Formal Reasoning Instrument.* Unpublished doctoral dissertation, University of Northern Colorado, 1974.

Case, Robbie. "Intellectual Development and Instruction: A Neo Piagetian View." In *The Psychology of Teaching for Thinking and Creativity*, edited by A. Lawson. Columbus: ERIC, 1979.

Chandler, M.J., and Greenspan, S. "Ersatz Egocentrism: A Reply to H. Borke." *Developmental Psychology* 7 (1972): 104–6.

Chapman, R. "The Development of Children's Understanding of Proportions." *Child Development* 46 (1975): 141–48.

Corman, H.N., and Escalona, S.K. "Stages of Sensorimotor Development: A Replication Study." *Merrill Palmer Quarterly* 15 (1969): 351–61.

Cowan, Phillip A., *Piaget with Feeling.* New York: Holt, Rinehart & Winston, 1978.

Dasen, Pierre. "Are Cognitive Processes Universal? A Contribution to Cross-Cultural Piagetian Psychology. In *Studies in Cross-Cultural Psychology*, Vol. 1, edited by Neil Warren. New York: Academic Press, 1977*a*.

_____. *Piagetian Psychology: Cross Cultural Contributions.* New York: Gardner Press, 1977*b*.

Dennis, W. "Historical Notes on Animism." *Psychological Review* 45 (1938): 257–66.

DeVries, R. "Constancy of Generic Identity in the Years Three to Six." *Monographs of the Society for Research in Child Development* 34, No. 3 (1969).

Driver, Rosalind, and Easley, Jack. "Pupils and Paradigms: A Review of Literature Related to Concept Development in Adolescent Science Students." *Studies in Science Education* 5 (1978): 61–84.

Duckworth, Eleanor. "The Having of Wonderful Ideas." *Harvard Educational Review,* 42 (1972): 217–31.

Ennis, R. "Children's Ability to Handle Piaget's Propositional Logic: A Conceptual Critique." *Review of Educational Research* 45 (1975): 1–41.

Epstein, Herman. "Phrenoblysis: Special Brain and Mind Growth Periods: I: Human Brain and Skull Development." *Developmental Psychobiology* 7 (1974): 207–16.

_____. "A Neuroscience Framework for Restructuring Middle School Curricula." *Transescence: The Journal of Emerging Adolescent Education* 5 (1977): 6–11.

_____. "Growth Spurts During Brain Development: Implications for Educational Policy and Practice." In National Society for the Study of

Education Yearbook, Part II, Chapter X, pp. 343–70. Chicago: University of Chicago Press, 1978*a*.

————. "Test of a Neuroscience-Based Cognitive-Level Grouping Junior High School Curriculum." Unpublished paper, Brandeis University, Waltham, Massachusetts, 1978*b*.

Flavell, John H. "An Analysis of Cognitive-Developmental Sequences." *Genetic Psychology Monographs* 86 (1972): 279–350.

Flavell, J.: Botkin, P.; Fry, C.; Wright, J.; and Jarvis, P. *The Development of Role Taking and Communication Skills*. New York: John Wiley & Sons, 1968.

Fraenkel, Jack. "The Kohlberg Bandwagon: Some Reservations." *Social Education* 40 (1976): 216–22.

Fraisse, Paul, and Piaget, Jean. *Experimental Psychology: Its Scope and Method*. New York: Basic Books, 1968.

Furth, Hans, and Wachs, N. *Thinking Goes to School: Piaget's Theory in Practice*. New York: Oxford University Press, 1974.

Gallagher, Jeanette, and Reid, D. Kim. *The Learning Theory of Piaget and Inhelder*. Monterey, California: Brooks/Cole Publishing, 1981.

Gelman, R. "The Nature and Development of Early Number Concepts," In *Advances in Child Development and Behavior*, edited by H. Reese. New York: Academic Press, 1972.

Gibbs, John C. "Kohlberg's Stages of Moral Judgement: A Constructive Critique." *Harvard Educational Review* 47 (1977): 43–61.

Gilligan, Carol. "In A Different Voice: Women's Conceptions of Self and Morality." *Harvard Educational Review* 47 (1977): 481–517.

Harris, P. L. "Development of Search and Object Permanence During Infancy." *Psychological Bulletin* 82 (1975): 332–44.

Hilgard, Ernest, ed. *Theories of Learning and Instruction*. The Sixty-Third Yearbook of the National Society for the Study of Education. Chicago: The University of Chicago Press, 1964.

Inhelder, Barbel. "Some Pathologic Phenomena Analyzed in the Perspective of Developmental Psychology." In *Piaget and His School*, edited by B. Inhelder and Chipman. New York: Springer-Verlag, 1976*a*.

————. "Operatory Thought Processes in Psychotic Children." In *Piaget and His School*, edited by B. Inhelder and Chipman. New York: Springer-Verlag, 1976*b*.

Inhelder, Barbel and Piaget, Jean. *The Growth of Logical Thinking from Childhood to Adolescence*. New York: Basic Books, 1958.

Inhelder, Barbel; Sinclair, Hermine; and Bovet, Magali. *Learning and the Development of Cognition*. Cambridge: Harvard University Press, 1974.

Johnson, Paul; Ahlgren, Andrew; Blount, Joseph; and Petit, Noel. "Scientific Reasoning—Garden Paths or Blind Alleys." Paper presented at Biological Sciences Curriculum Study Conference on Research in Science Education, Boulder, Colorado, 1980.

Kamii, Constance. "Teaching for Thinking and Creativity: A Piagetian View." In *The Psychology of Teaching for Thinking and Creativity*, edited by A. Lawson. Columbus, ERIC, 1979.

Kamii, C., and DeVries, R. *Physical Knowledge in Preschool Education: Implications of Piaget's Theory*. Englewood Cliffs, N. J.: Prentice-Hall, 1978.

Karplus, Robert. *Science Curriculum Improvement Study: Teachers Handbook.* Berkeley, Calif.: University of California, Lawrence Hall of Science, 1974.

_____. "Teaching for the Development of Reasoning." In *The Psychology of Teaching for Thinking and Creativity,* edited by A. Lawson. Columbus, ERIC. 1979.

Karplus, Robert; Lawson, A.; Wollman, W.; Appel, M.; Bernoff, R.; Howe, A.; Rusch, J.; and Sullivan, F. *Science Teaching and the Development of Reasoning. General Science.* Berkeley, Calif.; University of California, Lawrence Hall of Science, 1977.

Kohlberg, Lawrence. "Moral Stages and Moralization: The Cognitive Developmental Approach." In *Moral Development and Behavior*, edited by Thomas Lickona. New York: Holt, Rinehart & Winston, 1976.

Kohlberg, Lawrence, and Mayer, Rochelle. "Development as the Aim of Education." *Harvard Educational Review* 42 (1972): 449–96.

Kohlberg, Lawrence; Yaeger, J.; and Hjertholm, E. "The Development of Private Speech: Four Studies and a Review of Theories." *Child Development* 39 (1968): 691–736.

Kohnstamm, G. "Piaget's Analysis of Class Inclusion: Right or Wrong?" The Hague: Mouton Press, 1967.

Kramer, J. A.; Hill, K.; and Cohen, L. "Infant's Development of Object Permanence: A Refined Methodology and New Evidence for Piaget's Hypothesized Ordinality." *Child Development* 49 (1975): 149–55.

Kuhn, Deanna. "The Application of Piaget's Theory of Cognitive Development to Education." *Harvard Educational Review* 49 (1979*a*): 340–60.

_____. "The Significance of Piaget's Formal Operational Stage in Education." *Journal of Education* 161 (1979*b*): 34–50.

Kuhn, Thomas. *The Structure of Scientific Revolutions.* Chicago: University of Chicago Press, 1970.

Kurtines, William, and Greif, Esther. "The Development of Moral Thought. A Review and Evaluation of Kohlberg's Approach." *Psychological Bulletin* 81 (1974): 453–70.

Larkin, Jill. "Understanding and Problem Solving in Physics." Paper presented at Biological Science Curriculum Study Conference on Research in Science Education, Boulder, Colorado, 1980.

Laurendeau, M, and Pinard, A. *Causal Thinking in the Child.* New York: International University Press, 1962.

_____. *The Development of the Concept of Space in the Child.* New York: International Universities Press, 1970.

Lavatelli, C. S. *Piaget's Theory Applied to an Early Childhood Curriculum.* Boston: American Science and Engineering, 1970.

Lawson, Anton. "The Development and Validation of a Classroom Test of Formal Reasoning." *Journal of Research in Science Teaching* 15 (1978): 11-24.

_____. "The Developmental Learning Paradigm." *Journal of Research in Science Teaching* 16 (1979): 501–5.

Lawson, Anton; Karplus, Robert; and Adi, Helen. "The Acquisition of Propositional Logic and Formal Operational Schemata During Secondary School Years." *Journal of Research in Science Teaching* 15 (1978): 465–78.

Lawson, Anton and Wollman, Warren. "Encouraging the Transition from Concrete to Formal Cognitive Functioning — An Experiment." *Journal of Research in Science Teaching* 13 (1976): 413–30.

Linn, M.; Chen, B.; and Their, H. "Teaching Children to Control Variables: An Investigation of a Free Choice Environment." *Journal of Research in Science Teaching* 14 (1977): 249–55.

Looft, W. R. "Egocentrism and Social Interaction across the Life Span." *Psychological Bulletin* 78 (1972): 73–92.

McCarthy, D. "Language Development in Children." In *Manual of Child Psychology, edited by L. Carmichael.* New York: John Wiley & Sons, 1954.

Modgil, Sohan, and Modgil, Celia. *Piagetian Research. Volumes 1-8.* New Jersey: Humanities Press, 1977.

Munson, Howard. "Moral Thinking: Can It Be Taught?" *Psychology Today* (1979) 48–68, 92.

Murray, Frank B. *The Impact of Piagetian Theory.* Baltimore: University Park Press, 1979.

Novak, Joseph D. "An Alternative to Piagetian Psychology for Science and Mathematics Education." *Studies in Science Education* 5 (1978): 1–30.

Phillips, D. C. and Kelly, Mavis. "Hierarchical Theories of Development in Education and Psychology." *Harvard Educational Review* 45 (1975): 351–75.

Piaget, Jean. "Principal Factors Determining Intellectual Evolution from Childhood to Adult Life." In *Factors Determining Human Behavior,* edited by Adrian et al. Cambridge: Harvard University Press, 1937.

————. "Cognitive Development in Children." *Journal of Research in Science Teaching* 2 (1964): 176–86.

————. *The Moral Judgement of the Child.* New York: Free Press, 1965.

————. *Psychology and Epistemology.* New York: The Viking Press, 1970a.

————. *Science of Education and the Psychology of the Child.* New York: Grossman Publishing, 1970b.

————. *Structuralism.* New York: Basic Books, 1970c.

————. *Biology and Knowledge.* Chicago: University of Chicago Press, 1971.

————. "Intellectual Evolution from Adolescence to Adulthood." *Human Development* 15 (1972): 1–12.

————. *The Child and Reality.* New York: Grossman Publishers, 1973a.

————. *To Understand Is to Invent.* New York: Grossman Publishers, 1973b.

————. *The Development of Thought: Equilibration of Cognitive Structures.* New York: The Viking Press, 1975.

————. "The Affective Unconscious and the Cognitive Unconscious." in *Piaget and His School,* edited by B. Inhelder and Chipman. New York: Springer-Verlag, 1976a.

————. "Need and Significance of Cross Cultural Studies in Genetic Psychology." In *Piaget and His School,* edited by B. Inhelder and Chipman. New York: Springer-Verlag, 1976b.

————. "What Is Psychology?" *American Psychologist* (July 1978): 648–52.

Piaget, Jean, and Inhelder, Bärbel. *The Psychology of the Child.* New York: Basic Books, 1969.

Raven, Ronald. "The Development of a Test of Piaget's Logical Operations." *Science Education* 57 (1973): 33–40.

Reid, D. Kim, "Equilibration and Learning." *Journal of Education* 161 (Winter 1979): 51–71.

Reid, D. Kim, and Hresko, Wayne. "Piaget Learning and Learning Disabilities." *Topics in Learning and Learning Disabilities* 1 (April 1981):

Rubin, K. H., and Maioni, T. L. "Play Preference and Its Relationship to Egocentrism, Popularity and Classification Skills in Preschoolers." *Merrill Palmer Quarterly* 21 (1975): 171–79.

Russell, R. W. "Studies in Animism: II, The Development of Animism." *Journal of Genetic Psychology* 56 (1940): 353–66.

Schmid-Kitsikis, Elsa. "The Cognitive Mechanisms underlying Problem Solving in Psychotic and Mentally Retarded Children." In *Piaget and His School,* edited by B. Inhelder and Chipman. New York: Springer-Verlag, 1976.

Siegel, L. S., and Brainerd, C., eds. *Alternatives to Piaget: Critical Essays on the Theory.* New York: Academic Press, 1977.

Simpson, Elizabeth Leone. "Moral Development Research: A Case Study of Scientific Cultural Bias." *Human Development* 17 (1974): 81–106.

Smedslund, Jan. "The Effects of Observation on Children's Representation of the Spatial Orientation of a Water Surface." *Journal of Genetic Psychology* 46 (1963): 195–201.

———. "Piaget's Psychology in Practice." *British Journal of Educational Psychology* 47 (1977): 1–6.

Thomas, H.; Jamison, W.; and Hummel, D. "Observation Is Insufficient for Discovering That the Surface of Still Water Is Invariably Horizontal." *Science* 181 (1973): 173–74.

Tisher, R., and Dale, L. *Understanding in Science Test.* Victoria: Australian Council for Educational Research, 1975.

Uzgiris, I. "Situational Generality of Conservation." *Child Development* 35 (1964): 831–44.

Uzgiris, I., and Hunt, J. McVicker. *Toward Orderial Scales of Psychological. Development in Infancy.* Urbana, Ill.: University of Illinois Press, 1974.

Wolff, Peter. "Piaget and Mental Health." In *The Impact of Piagetian Theory,* edited by Frank Murray. Baltimore: University Park Press, 1979.

Zimiles, H. "The Development of Conservation and Differentiation of Number." *Monographs of the Society for Research in Child Development* 31, No. 6 (1966).

Index